P9-CKO-546

S·A
Special A

TADASHI & AKIRA 9 YEARS OLD.

Volume 16

Story & Art by

Maki Minami

STORY

★At the tender age of 6, carpenter's daughter Hikari Hanazono suffered her first loss to the wealthy Kei Takishima in a wrestling match. Now the hardworking Hikari has followed Kei to the most elite school for the rich just to beat him! I call this story "Overthrow Takishima! Rise Above Perpetual Second Place!!" It's the story of Hikari's sweat, tears and passion, with a little bit of love thrown in! ★ Going into her second year, Hikari is tied at 2nd place with a transfer student named Iori Tokiwa. Hikari and Iori hit it off once they discover a common goal—first place! Hikari eventually realizes that Kei is jealous of their new bond, so she tries to back off and get some space from Iori.

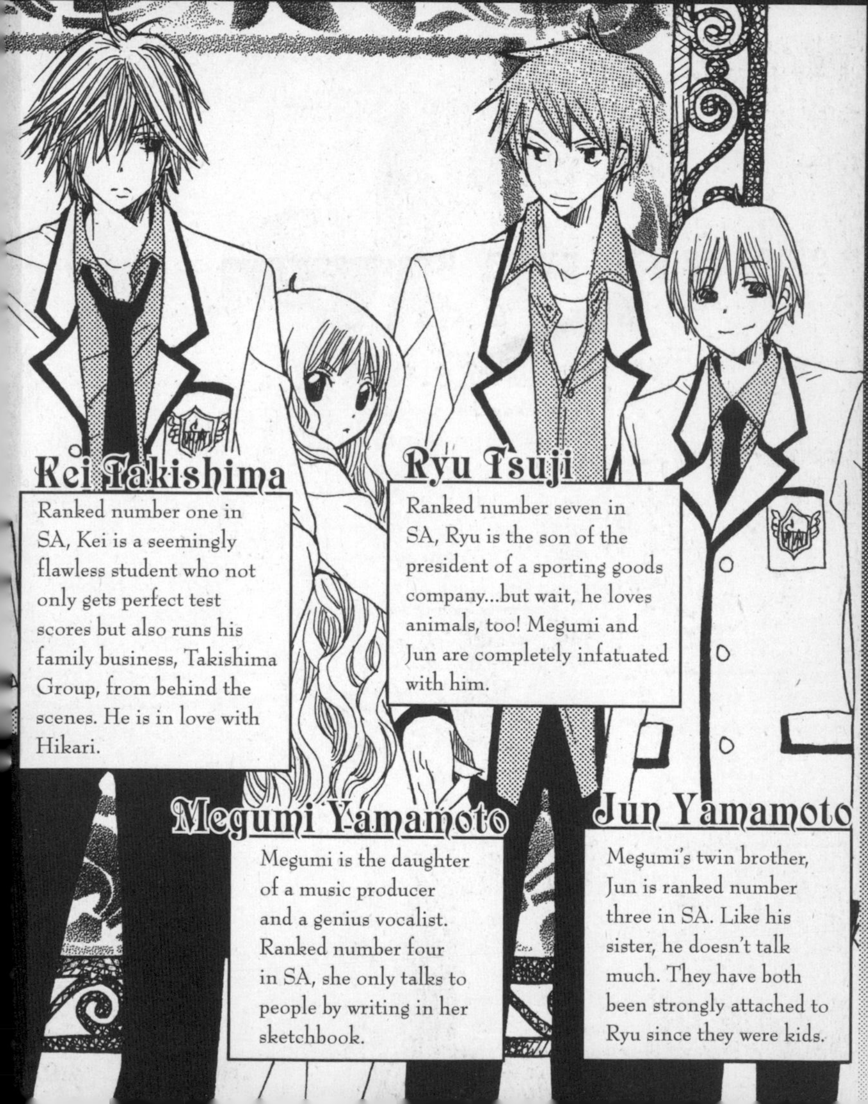

Kei Takishima

Ranked number one in SA, Kei is a seemingly flawless student who not only gets perfect test scores but also runs his family business, Takishima Group, from behind the scenes. He is in love with Hikari.

Ryu Tsuji

Ranked number seven in SA, Ryu is the son of the president of a sporting goods company...but wait, he loves animals, too! Megumi and Jun are completely infatuated with him.

Megumi Yamamoto

Megumi is the daughter of a music producer and a genius vocalist. Ranked number four in SA, she only talks to people by writing in her sketchbook.

Jun Yamamoto

Megumi's twin brother, Jun is ranked number three in SA. Like his sister, he doesn't talk much. They have both been strongly attached to Ryu since they were kids.

S·A CHARACTERS

What is "Special A"?

Hikari goes to an elite school called Hakusenkan High School. This school divides each grade level into groups A through F, according to the students' test scores. Group A includes only the top seven students in each class. Then the top seven students from all grades' A groups are put into a group called Special A, which is considered much higher than all others. Known as SA, they are "the elite among the elite."

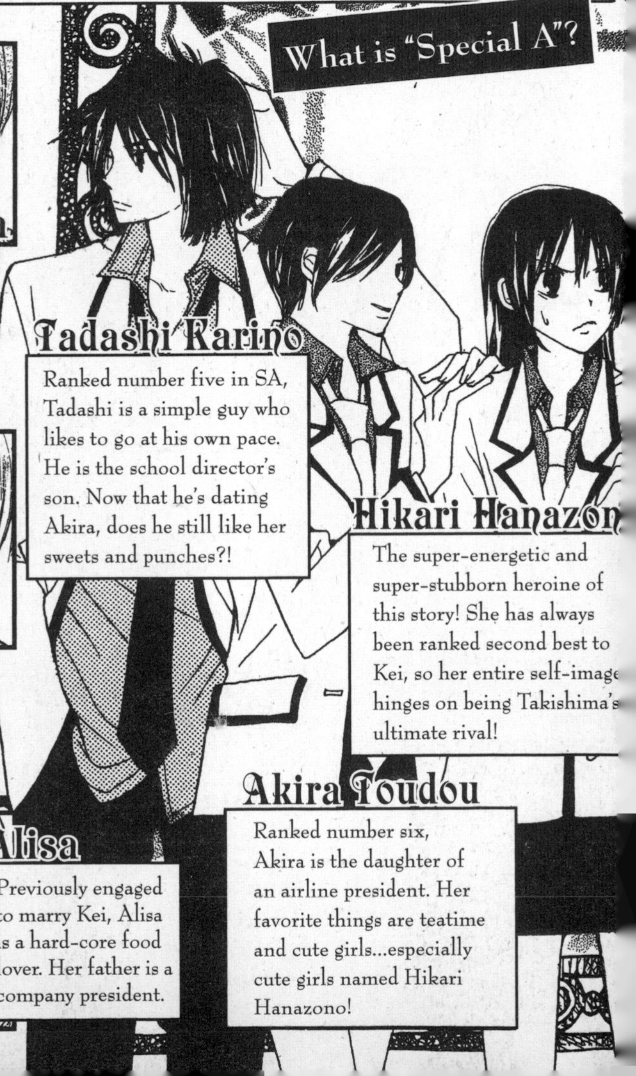

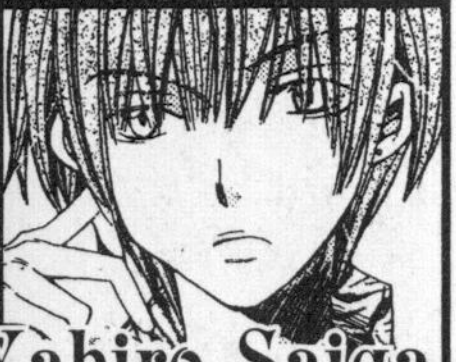

Hikari Hanazono

The super-energetic and super-stubborn heroine of this story! She has always been ranked second best to Kei, so her entire self-image hinges on being Takishima's ultimate rival!

Tadashi Karino

Ranked number five in SA, Tadashi is a simple guy who likes to go at his own pace. He is the school director's son. Now that he's dating Akira, does he still like her sweets and punches?!

Yahiro Saiga

A childhood friend of Kei and Akira. His family is richer than the Takishima Group.

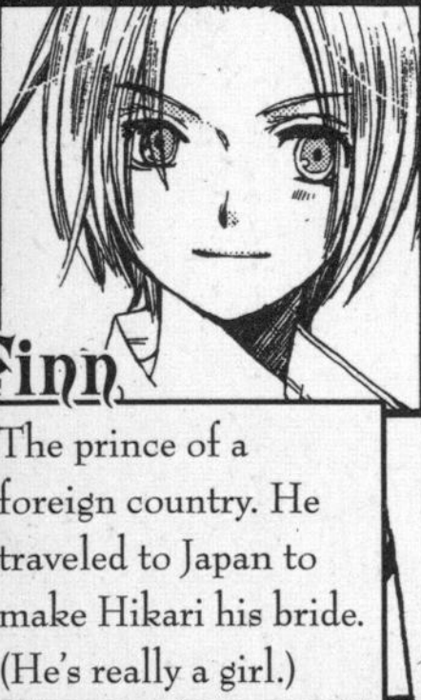

Akira Toudou

Ranked number six, Akira is the daughter of an airline president. Her favorite things are teatime and cute girls...especially cute girls named Hikari Hanazono!

Finn

The prince of a foreign country. He traveled to Japan to make Hikari his bride. (He's really a girl.)

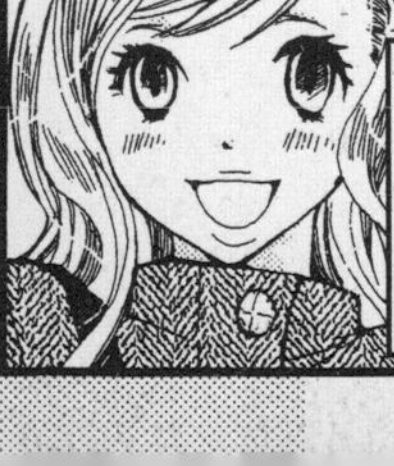

Alisa

Previously engaged to marry Kei, Alisa is a hard-core food lover. Her father is a company president.

Contents

KISS

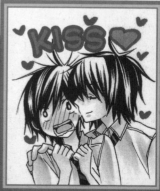

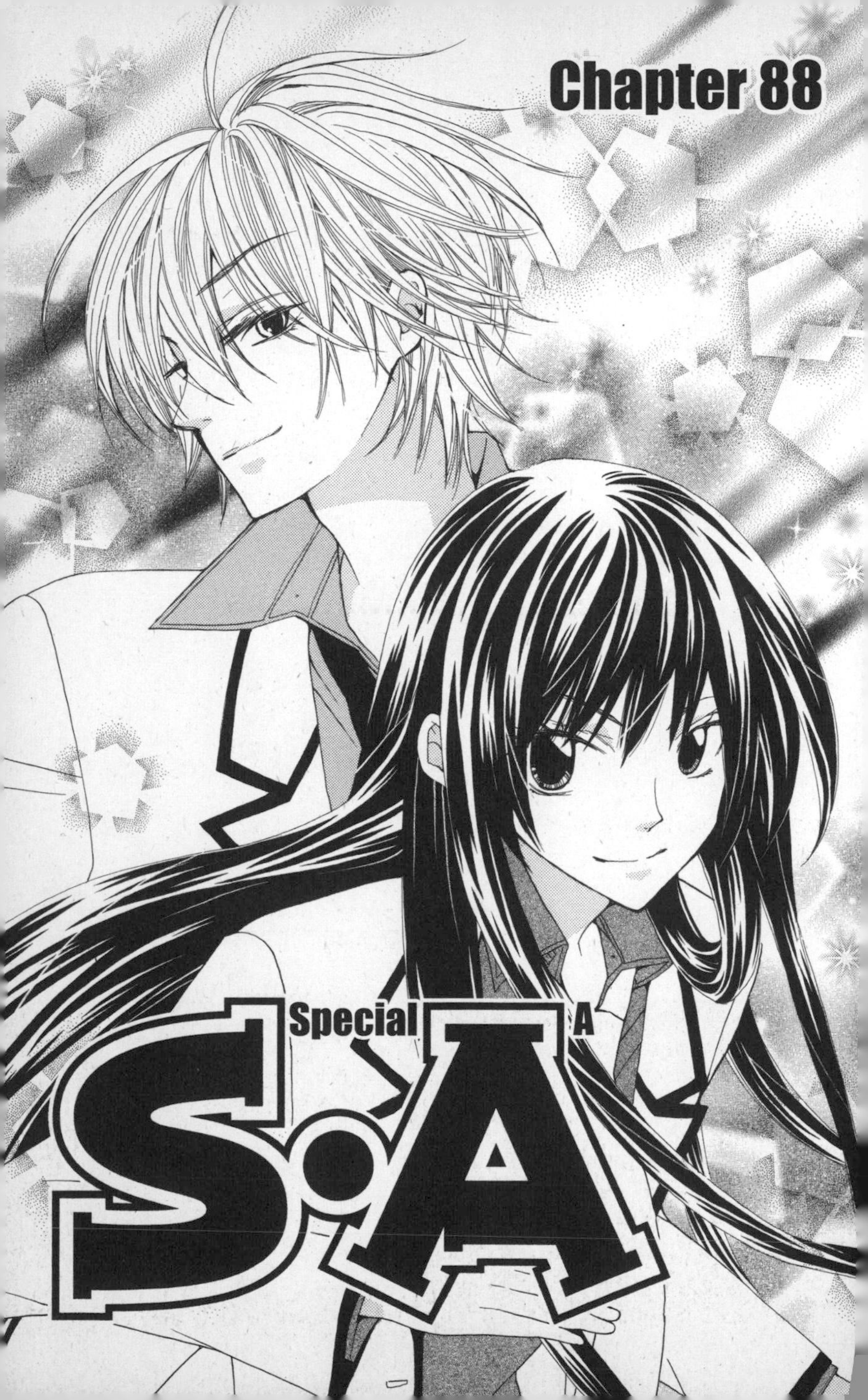
Chapter 88
Special
A
S.A

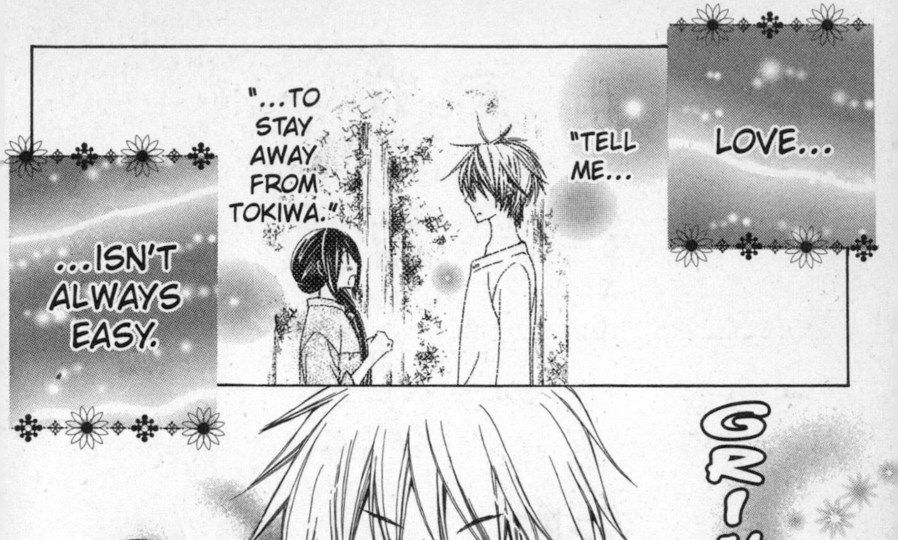
LOVE...
"TELL ME...
"...TO STAY AWAY FROM TOKIWA."
...ISN'T ALWAYS EASY.
GRIN
GRIN
HANAZONO ...

• COVER, ETC. •

• TADASHI AND AKIRA ARE ON THE COVER OF VOL. 16, JUST LIKE ON VOL. 2. AND THE TITLE PAGE SHOWS TADASHI AND AKIRA IN CHAPTER 55 OF VOL. 10. IT'S WHEN AKIRA WAS CRYING, RIGHT BEFORE HIKARI YELLED HER NAME. ♡ (RANDOM)

• I HAVEN'T COLORED IN A COMIC FOR MYSELF IN A LONG TIME. THAT WAS FUN!

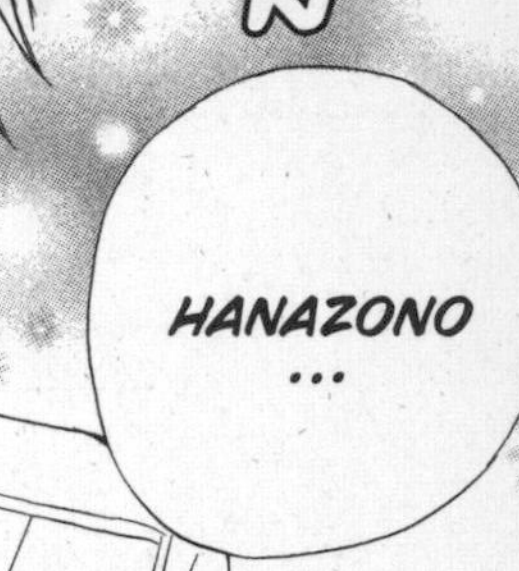

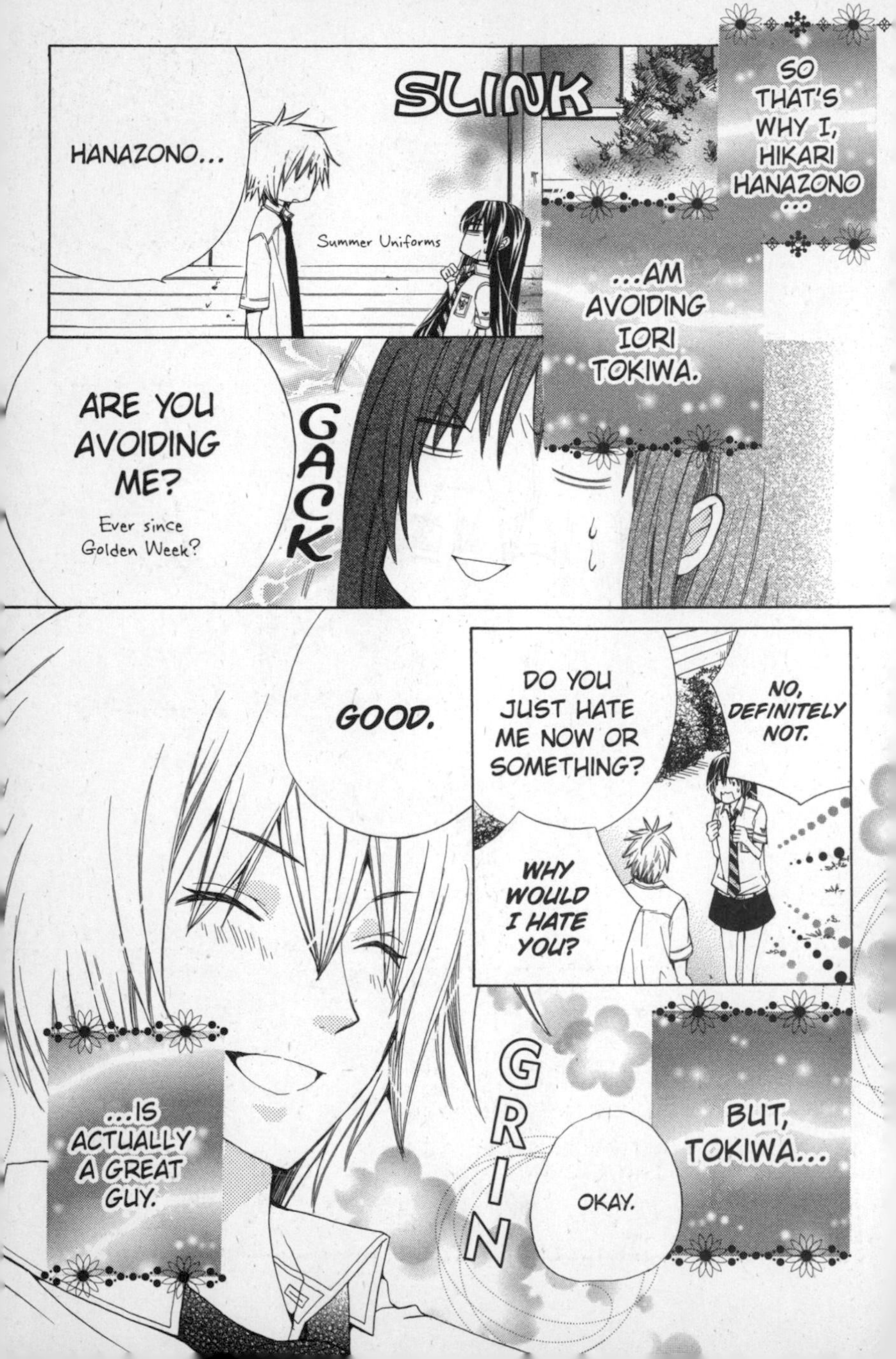
SO THAT'S WHY I, HIKARI HANAZONO...
...AM AVOIDING IORI TOKIWA.
SLINK
HANAZONO...
Summer Uniforms
GACK
ARE YOU AVOIDING ME?
Ever since Golden Week?
DO YOU JUST HATE ME NOW OR SOMETHING?
NO, DEFINITELY NOT.
WHY WOULD I HATE YOU?
GOOD.
BUT, TOKIWA...
OKAY.
GRIN
...IS ACTUALLY A GREAT GUY.

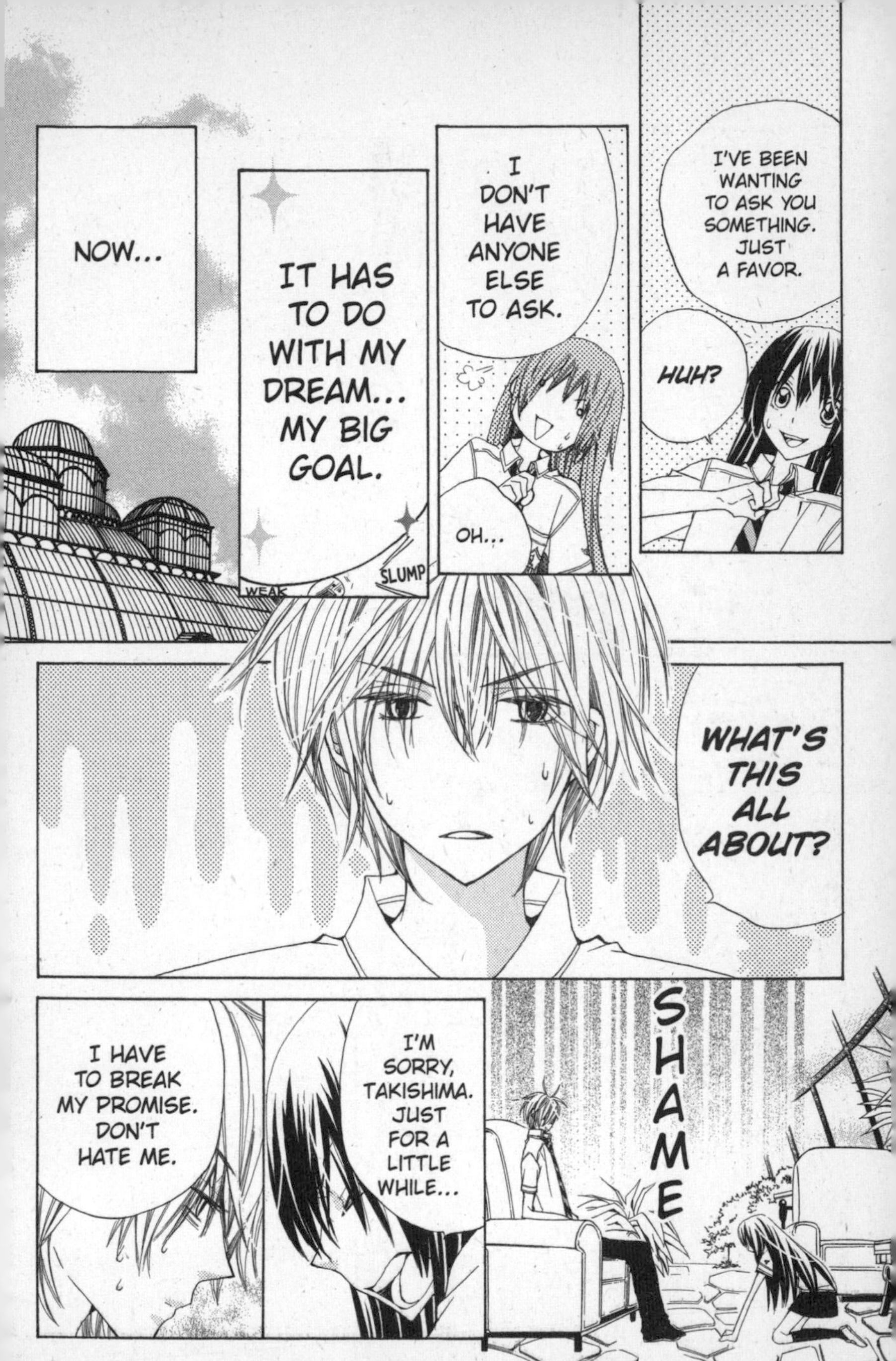
I'VE BEEN WANTING TO ASK YOU SOMETHING. JUST A FAVOR.
HUH?
I DON'T HAVE ANYONE ELSE TO ASK.
OH...
IT HAS TO DO WITH MY DREAM... MY BIG GOAL.
SLUMP
WEAK
NOW...
WHAT'S THIS ALL ABOUT?
SHAME
I'M SORRY, TAKISHIMA. JUST FOR A LITTLE WHILE...
I HAVE TO BREAK MY PROMISE. DON'T HATE ME.

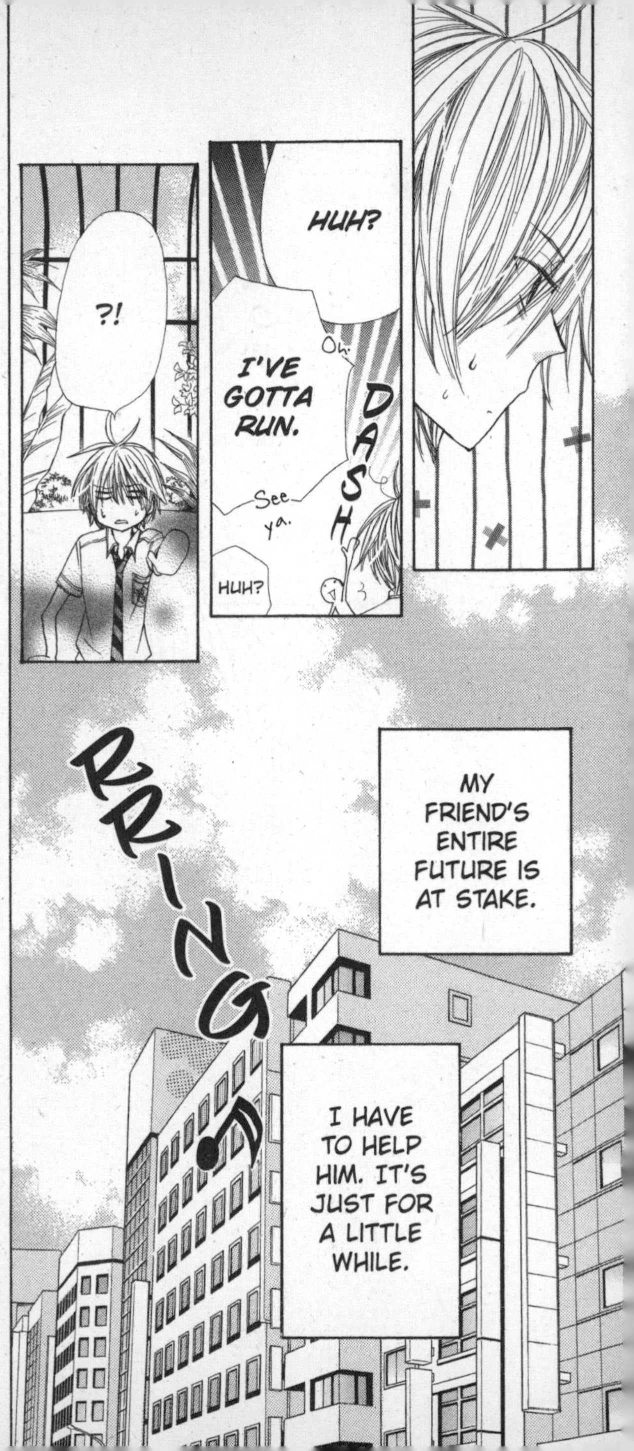
HUH?
Oh.
I'VE GOTTA RUN.
DASH
See ya.
HUH?
?!
MY FRIEND'S ENTIRE FUTURE IS AT STAKE.
RRING
I HAVE TO HELP HIM. IT'S JUST FOR A LITTLE WHILE.

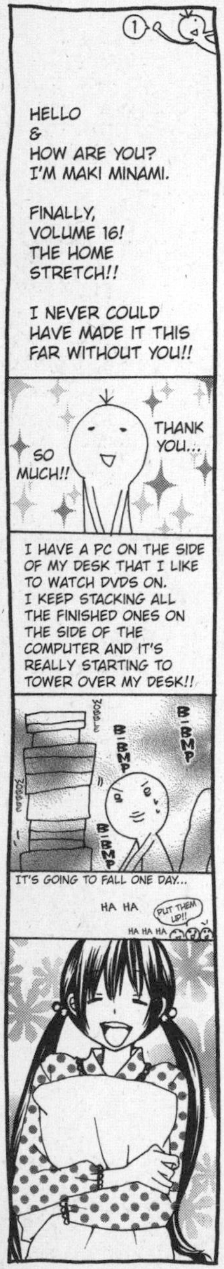
1
HELLO & HOW ARE YOU? I'M MAKI MINAMI.
FINALLY, VOLUME 16! THE HOME STRETCH!!
I NEVER COULD HAVE MADE IT THIS FAR WITHOUT YOU!!
THANK YOU...
SO MUCH!!
I HAVE A PC ON THE SIDE OF MY DESK THAT I LIKE TO WATCH DVDS ON. I KEEP STACKING ALL THE FINISHED ONES ON THE SIDE OF THE COMPUTER AND IT'S REALLY STARTING TO TOWER OVER MY DESK!!
WOBBLE
B-BMP
B-BMP
WOBBLE
B-BMP
IT'S GOING TO FALL ONE DAY...
HA HA
PUT THEM UP!!
HA HA HA

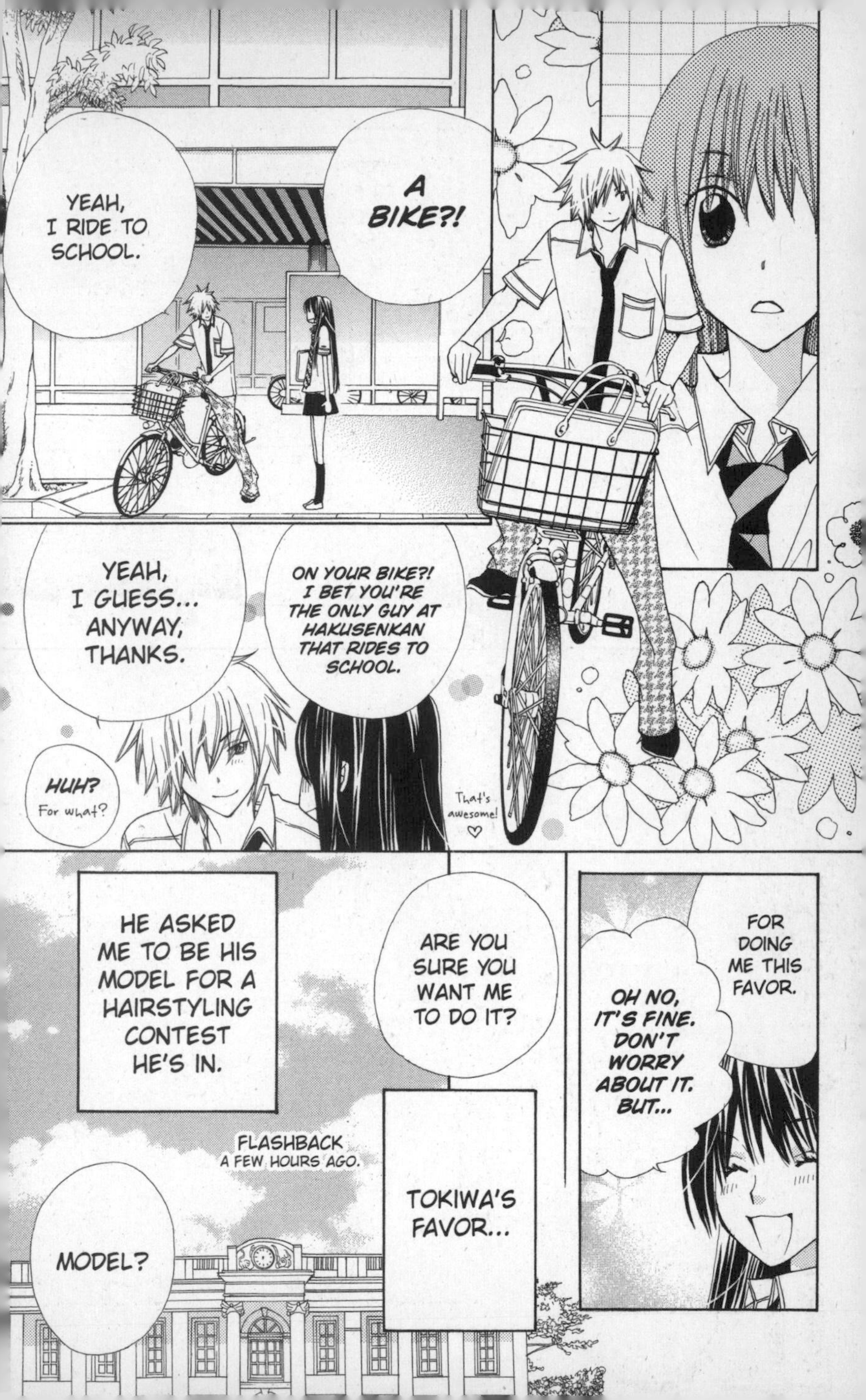
A BIKE?!
YEAH, I RIDE TO SCHOOL.
ON YOUR BIKE?! I BET YOU'RE THE ONLY GUY AT HAKUSENKAN THAT RIDES TO SCHOOL.
That's awesome! ♡
YEAH, I GUESS... ANYWAY, THANKS.
HUH? For what?
FOR DOING ME THIS FAVOR.
OH NO, IT'S FINE. DON'T WORRY ABOUT IT. BUT...
ARE YOU SURE YOU WANT ME TO DO IT?
TOKIWA'S FAVOR...
HE ASKED ME TO BE HIS MODEL FOR A HAIRSTYLING CONTEST HE'S IN.
FLASHBACK
A FEW HOURS AGO.
MODEL?

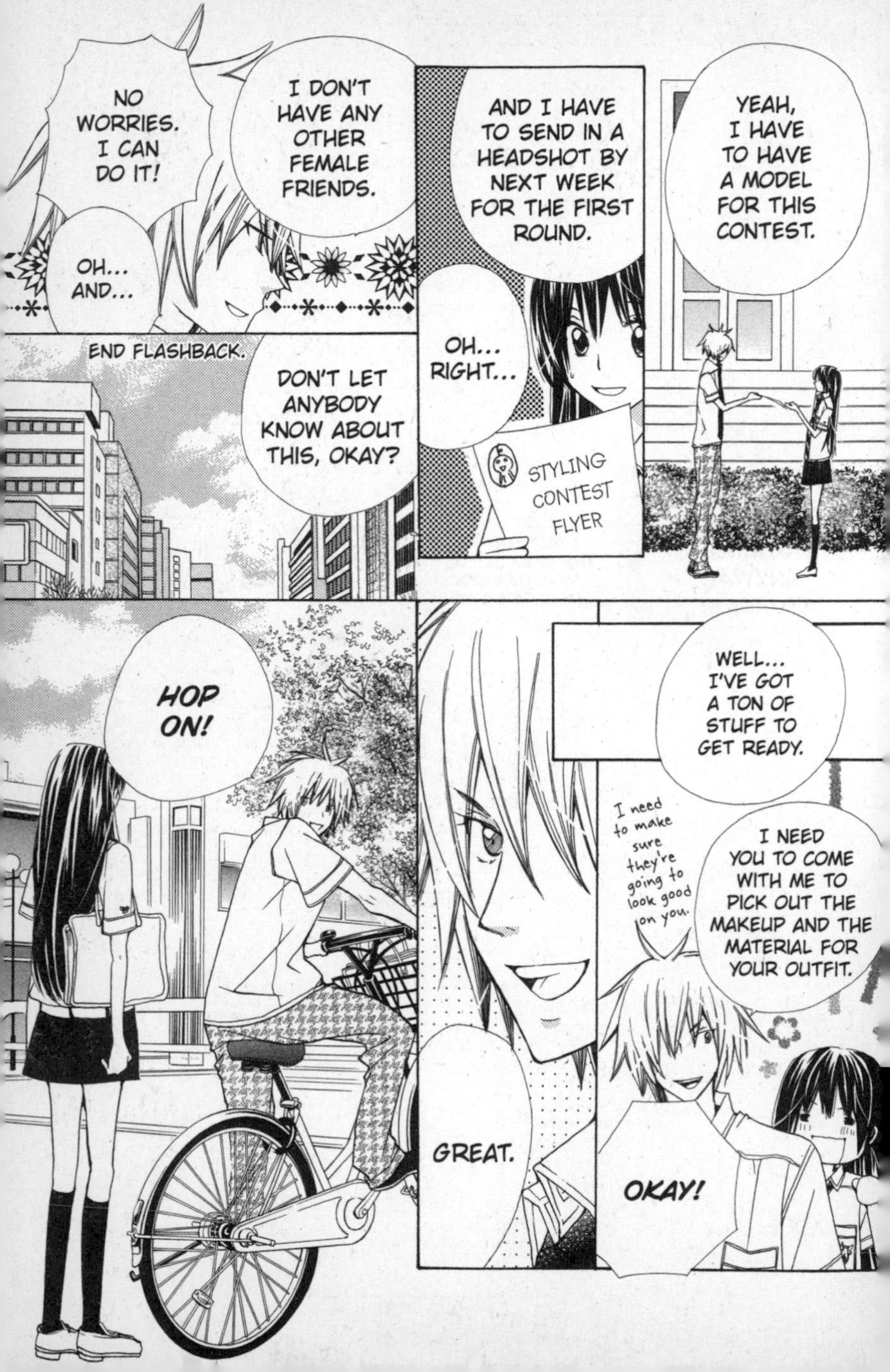
YEAH, I HAVE TO HAVE A MODEL FOR THIS CONTEST.
AND I HAVE TO SEND IN A HEADSHOT BY NEXT WEEK FOR THE FIRST ROUND.
OH... RIGHT...
STYLING CONTEST FLYER
I DON'T HAVE ANY OTHER FEMALE FRIENDS.
NO WORRIES. I CAN DO IT!
OH... AND...
DON'T LET ANYBODY KNOW ABOUT THIS, OKAY?
END FLASHBACK.
WELL... I'VE GOT A TON OF STUFF TO GET READY.
I NEED YOU TO COME WITH ME TO PICK OUT THE MAKEUP AND THE MATERIAL FOR YOUR OUTFIT.
I need to make sure they're going to look good on you.
OKAY!
GREAT.
HOP ON!

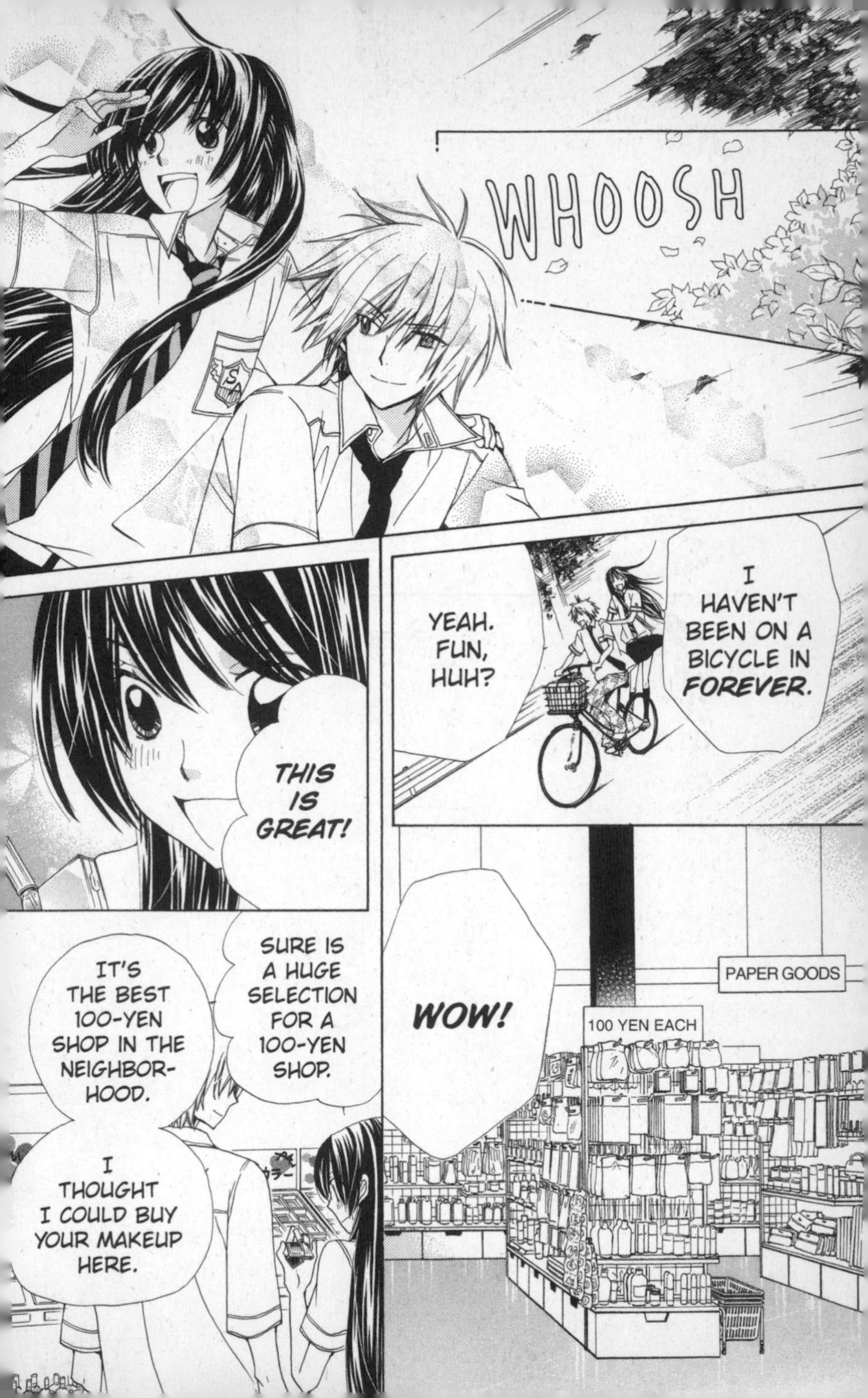
WHOOSH
I HAVEN'T BEEN ON A BICYCLE IN ***FOREVER.***
YEAH. FUN, HUH?
THIS IS GREAT!
WOW!
PAPER GOODS
100 YEN EACH
SURE IS A HUGE SELECTION FOR A 100-YEN SHOP.
IT'S THE BEST 100-YEN SHOP IN THE NEIGHBOR-HOOD.
I THOUGHT I COULD BUY YOUR MAKEUP HERE.

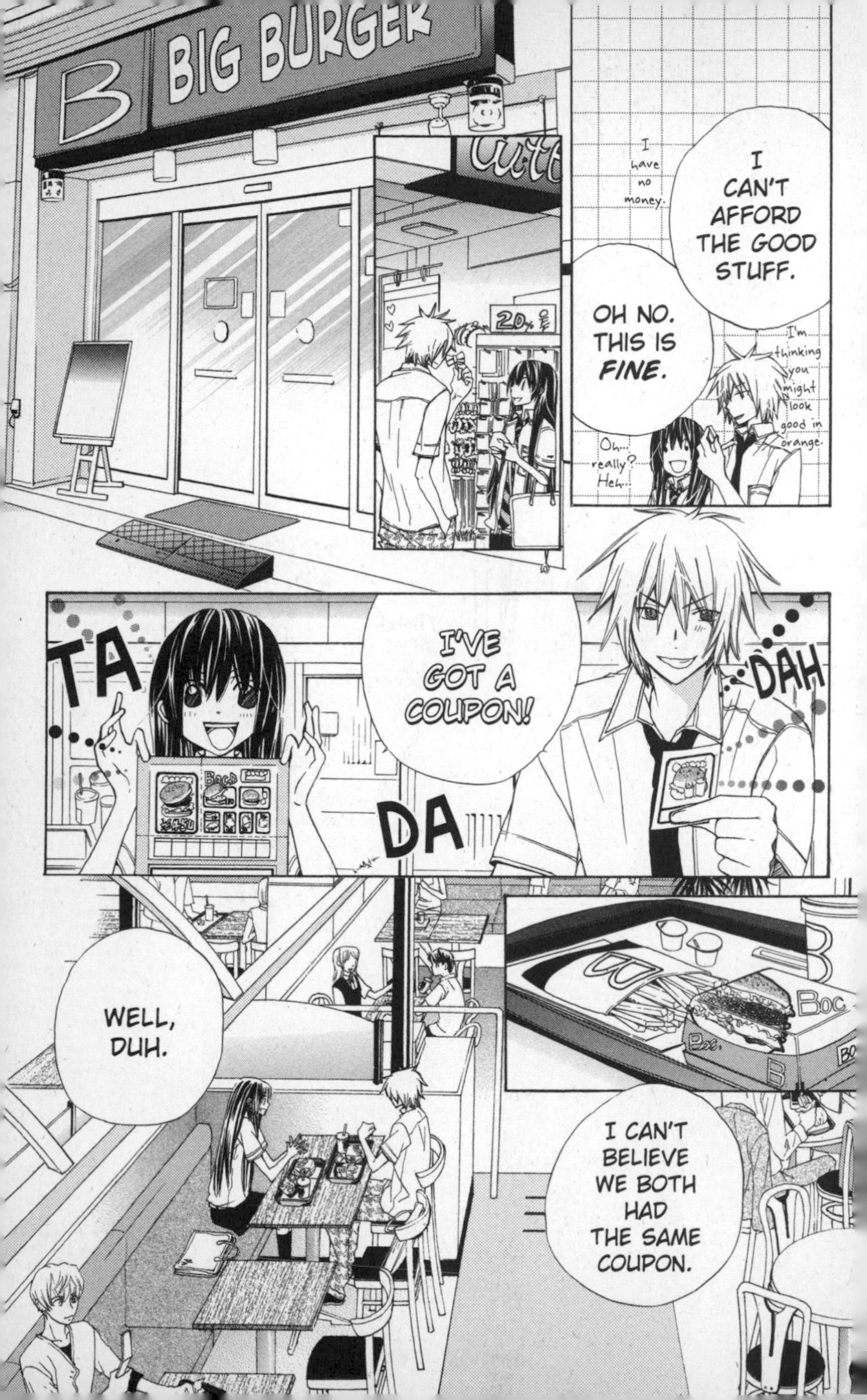
I have no money.
I CAN'T AFFORD THE GOOD STUFF.
OH NO. THIS IS FINE.
I'm thinking you might look good in orange.
Oh... really? Heh...
BIG BURGER
I'VE GOT A COUPON!
DAH
TA
DA
I CAN'T BELIEVE WE BOTH HAD THE SAME COUPON.
WELL, DUH.

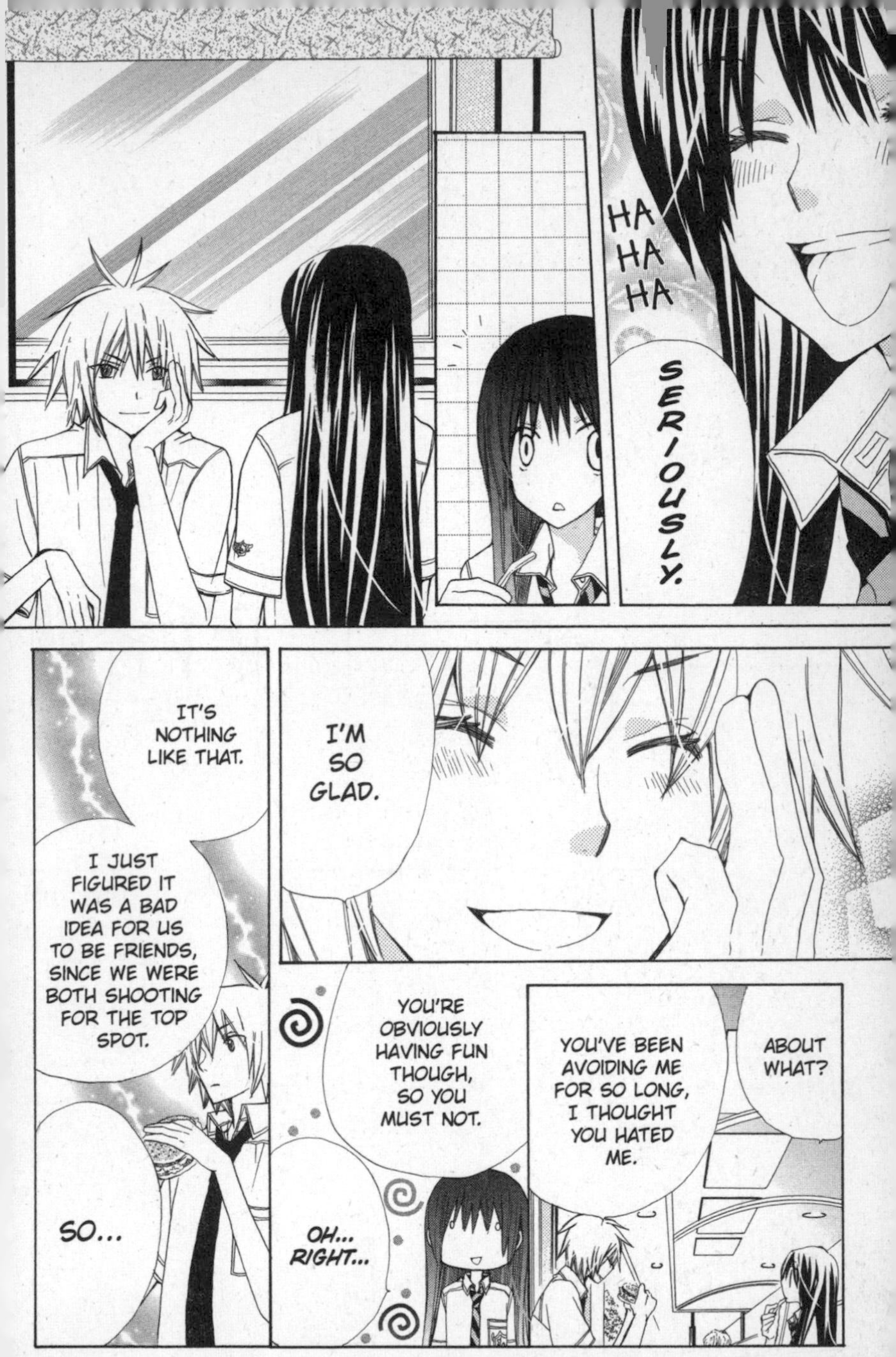
HA HA HA
SERIOUSLY.
I'M SO GLAD.
ABOUT WHAT?
YOU'VE BEEN AVOIDING ME FOR SO LONG, I THOUGHT YOU HATED ME.
YOU'RE OBVIOUSLY HAVING FUN THOUGH, SO YOU MUST NOT.
OH... RIGHT...
IT'S NOTHING LIKE THAT.
I JUST FIGURED IT WAS A BAD IDEA FOR US TO BE FRIENDS, SINCE WE WERE BOTH SHOOTING FOR THE TOP SPOT.
SO...

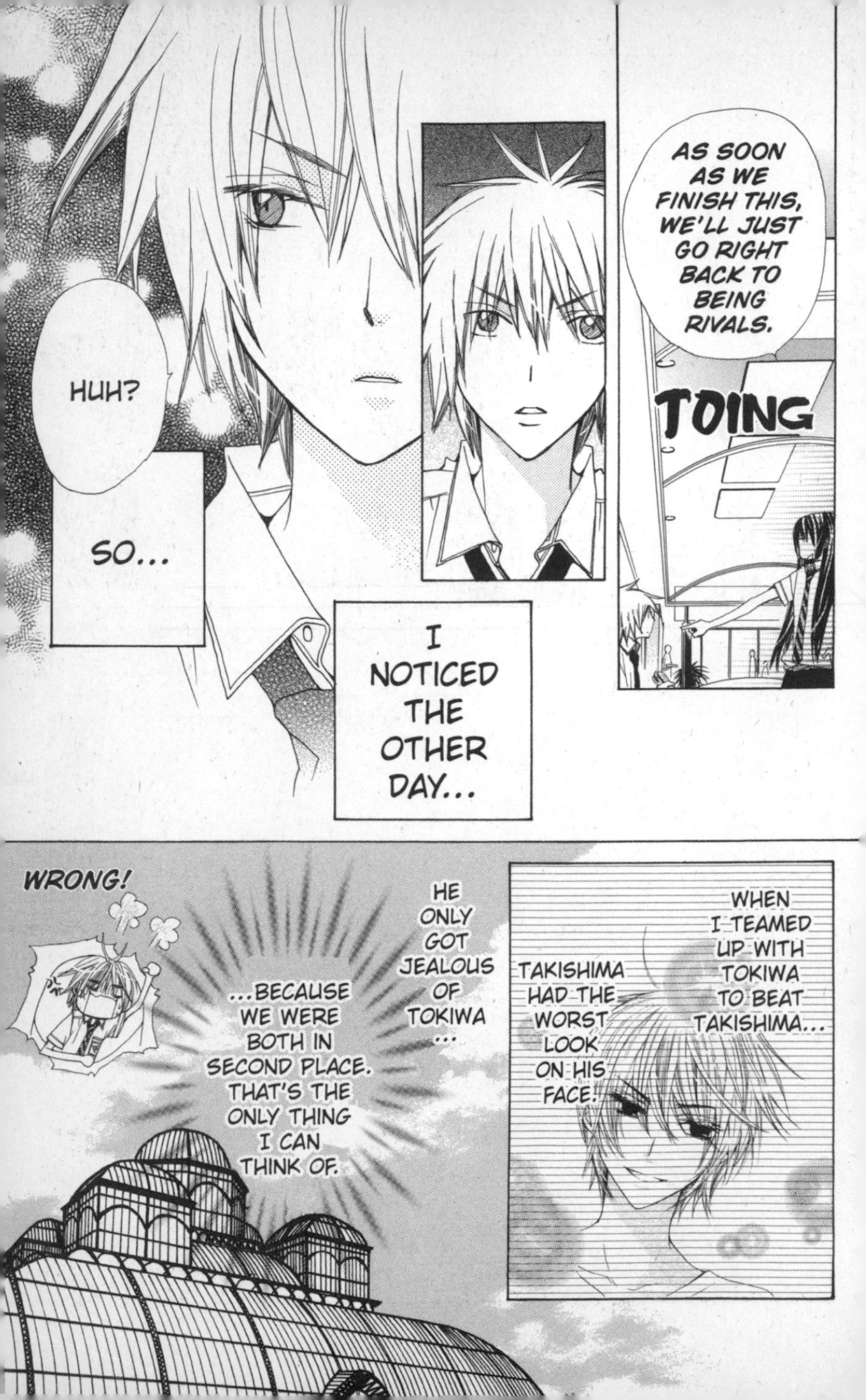
AS SOON AS WE FINISH THIS, WE'LL JUST GO RIGHT BACK TO BEING RIVALS.
TOING
HUH?
SO...
I NOTICED THE OTHER DAY...
WHEN I TEAMED UP WITH TOKIWA TO BEAT TAKISHIMA...
TAKISHIMA HAD THE WORST LOOK ON HIS FACE.
HE ONLY GOT JEALOUS OF TOKIWA...
...BECAUSE WE WERE BOTH IN SECOND PLACE. THAT'S THE ONLY THING I CAN THINK OF.
WRONG!

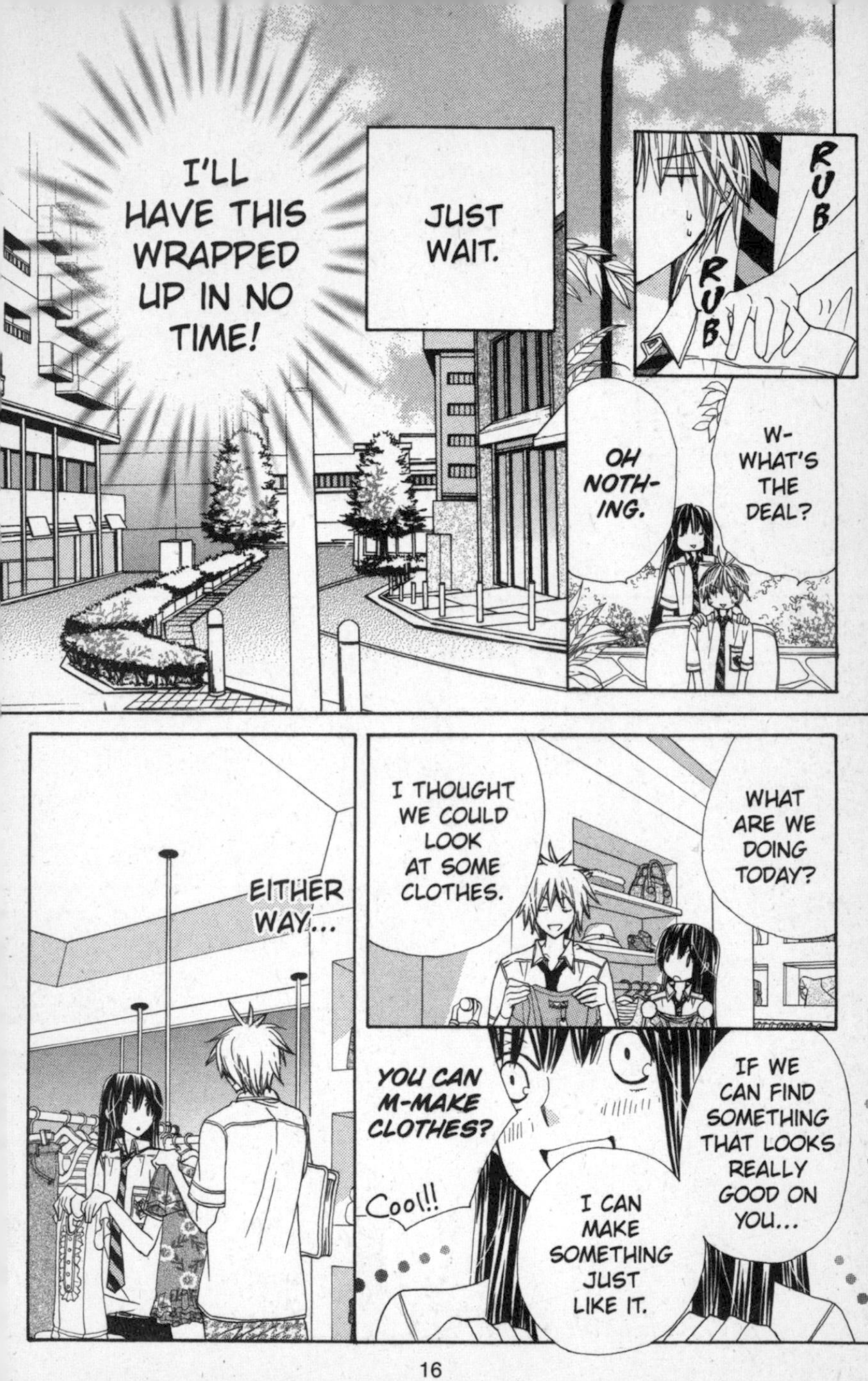
RUB
RUB
RUB
W- WHAT'S THE DEAL?
OH NOTHING.
JUST WAIT.
I'LL HAVE THIS WRAPPED UP IN NO TIME!
WHAT ARE WE DOING TODAY?
I THOUGHT WE COULD LOOK AT SOME CLOTHES.
IF WE CAN FIND SOMETHING THAT LOOKS REALLY GOOD ON YOU...
I CAN MAKE SOMETHING JUST LIKE IT.
YOU CAN M-MAKE CLOTHES?
Cool!!
EITHER WAY...

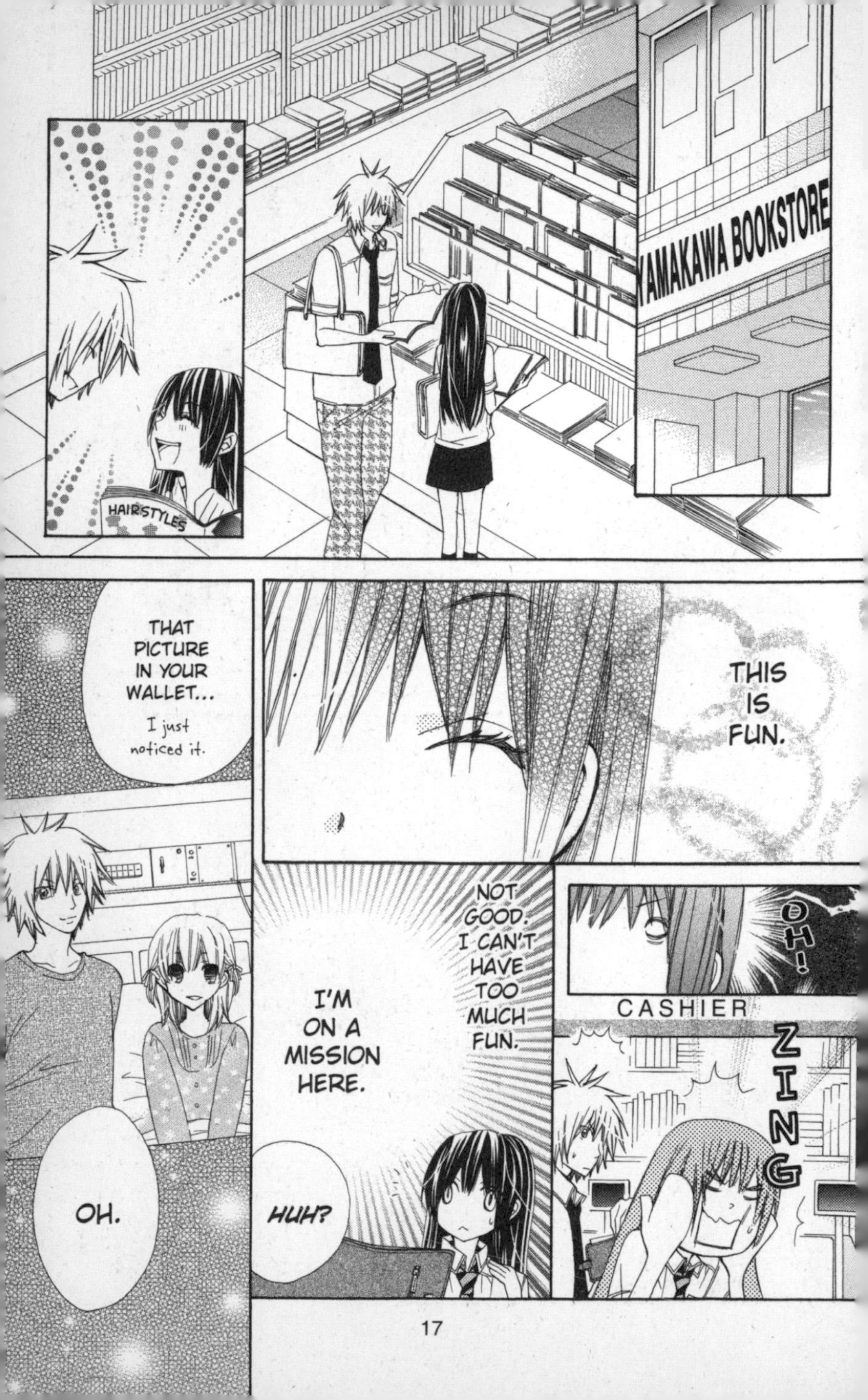
YAMAKAWA BOOKSTORE
HAIRSTYLES
THIS IS FUN.
OH!
CASHIER
ZING
NOT GOOD. I CAN'T HAVE TOO MUCH FUN.
I'M ON A MISSION HERE.
HUH?
THAT PICTURE IN YOUR WALLET...
I just noticed it.
OH.

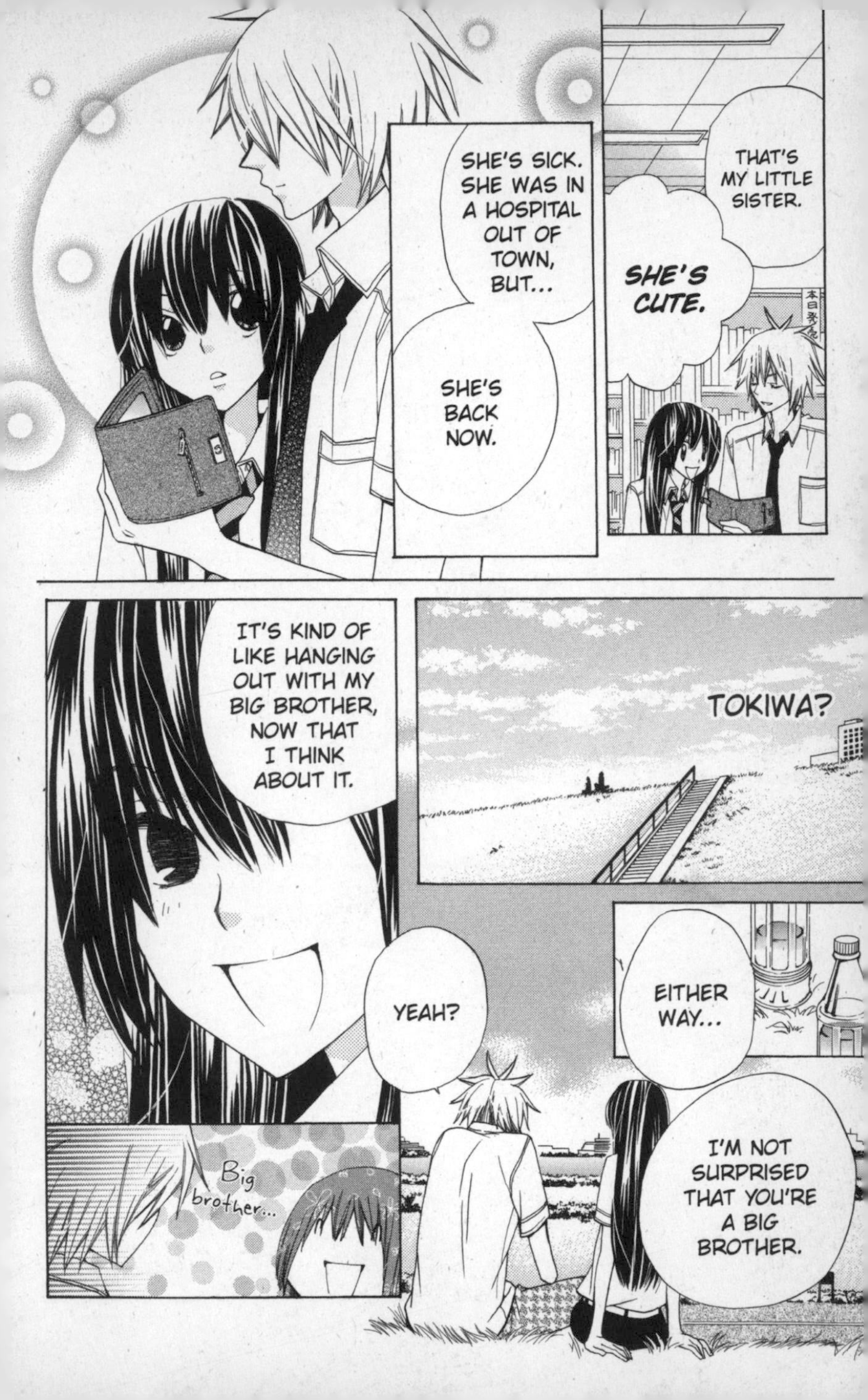
THAT'S MY LITTLE SISTER.
SHE'S CUTE.
SHE'S SICK. SHE WAS IN A HOSPITAL OUT OF TOWN, BUT...
SHE'S BACK NOW.
TOKIWA?
EITHER WAY...
I'M NOT SURPRISED THAT YOU'RE A BIG BROTHER.
YEAH?
IT'S KIND OF LIKE HANGING OUT WITH MY BIG BROTHER, NOW THAT I THINK ABOUT IT.
Big brother...

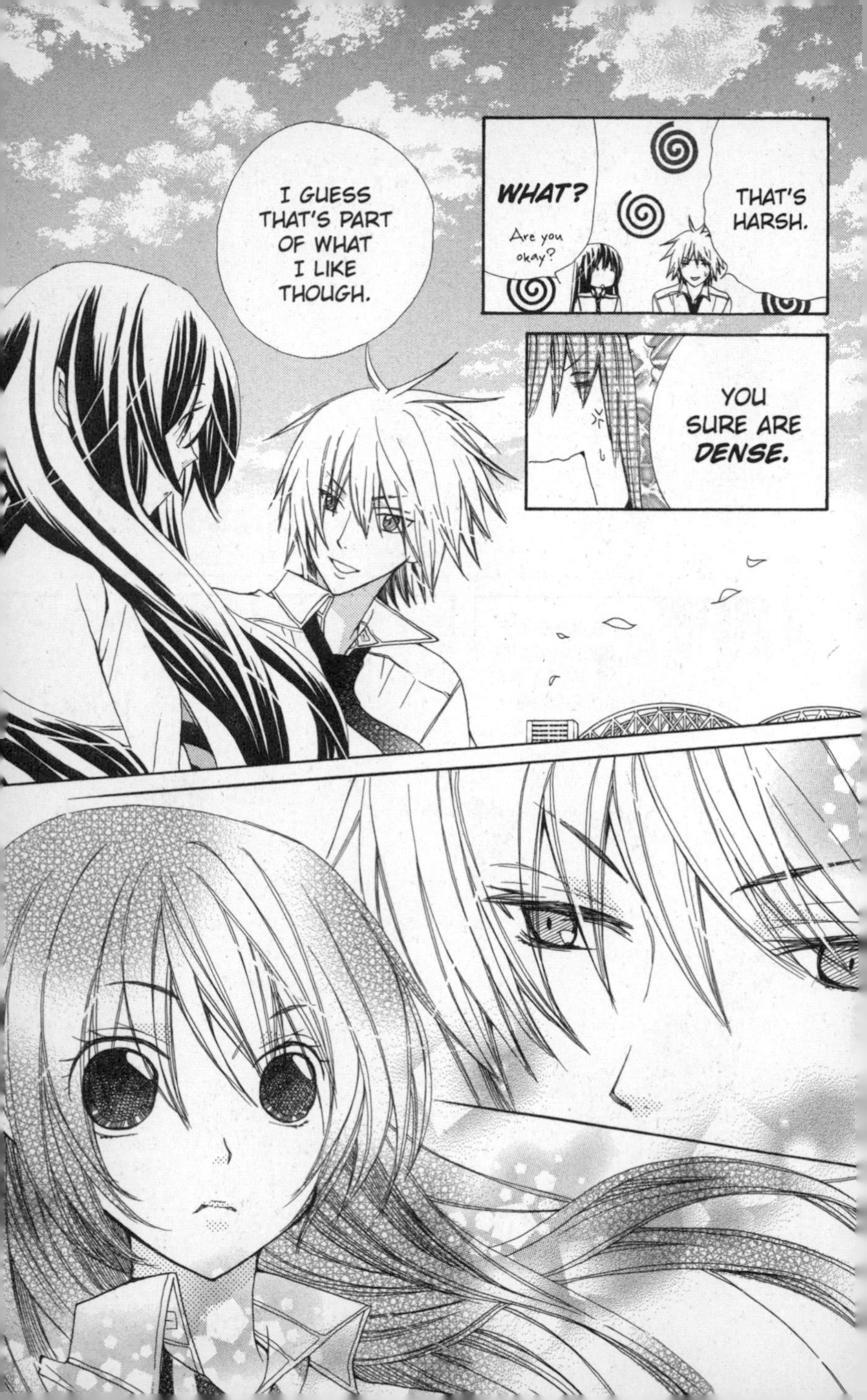
THAT'S HARSH.
WHAT?
Are you okay?
YOU SURE ARE DENSE.
I GUESS THAT'S PART OF WHAT I LIKE THOUGH.

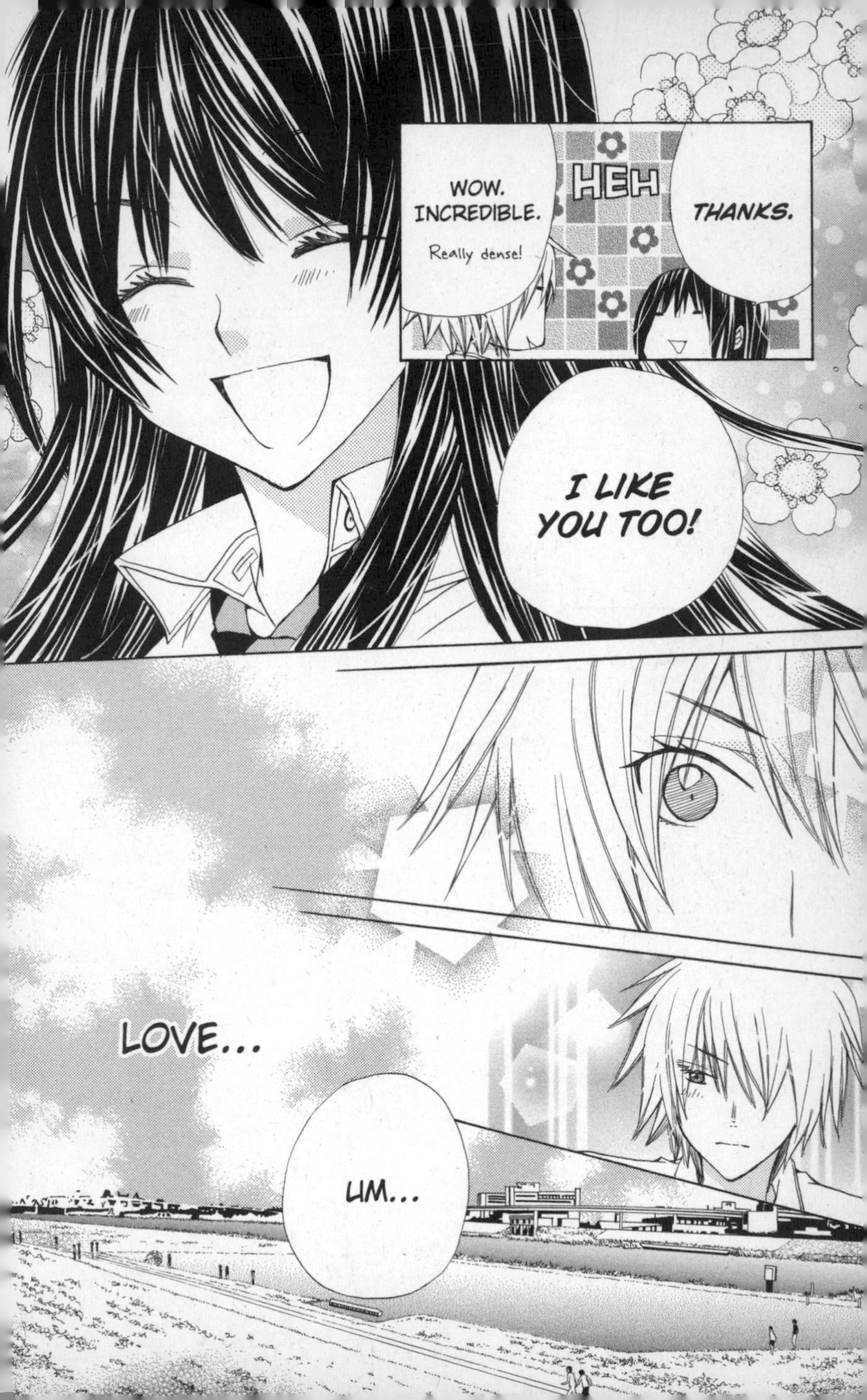
THANKS.
HEH
WOW. INCREDIBLE.
Really dense!
I LIKE YOU TOO!
LOVE...
UM...

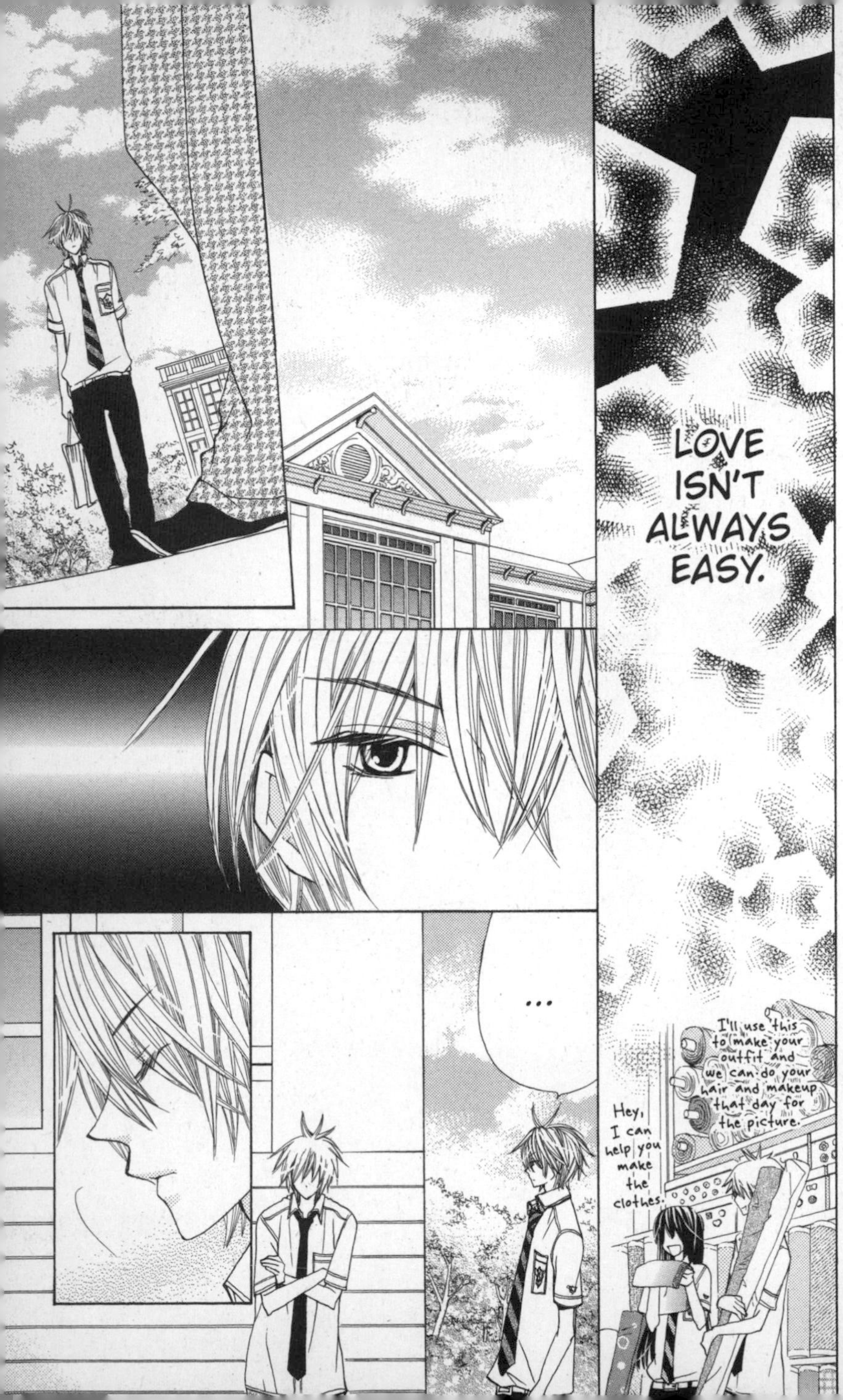
LOVE ISN'T ALWAYS EASY.
I'll use this to make your outfit and we can do your hair and makeup that day for the picture.
Hey, I can help you make the clothes.
...

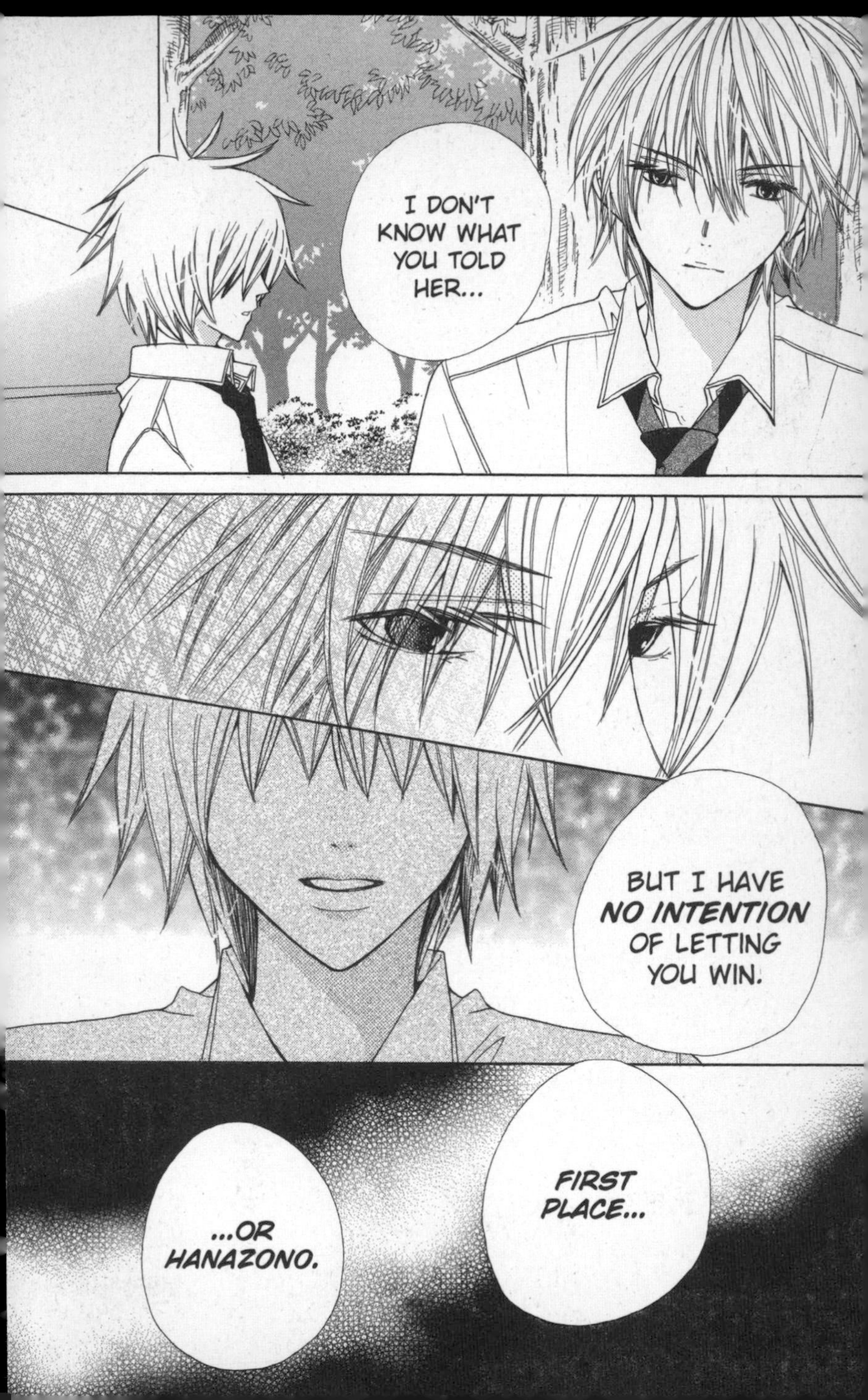
I DON'T KNOW WHAT YOU TOLD HER...
BUT I HAVE NO INTENTION OF LETTING YOU WIN.
FIRST PLACE...
...OR HANAZONO.

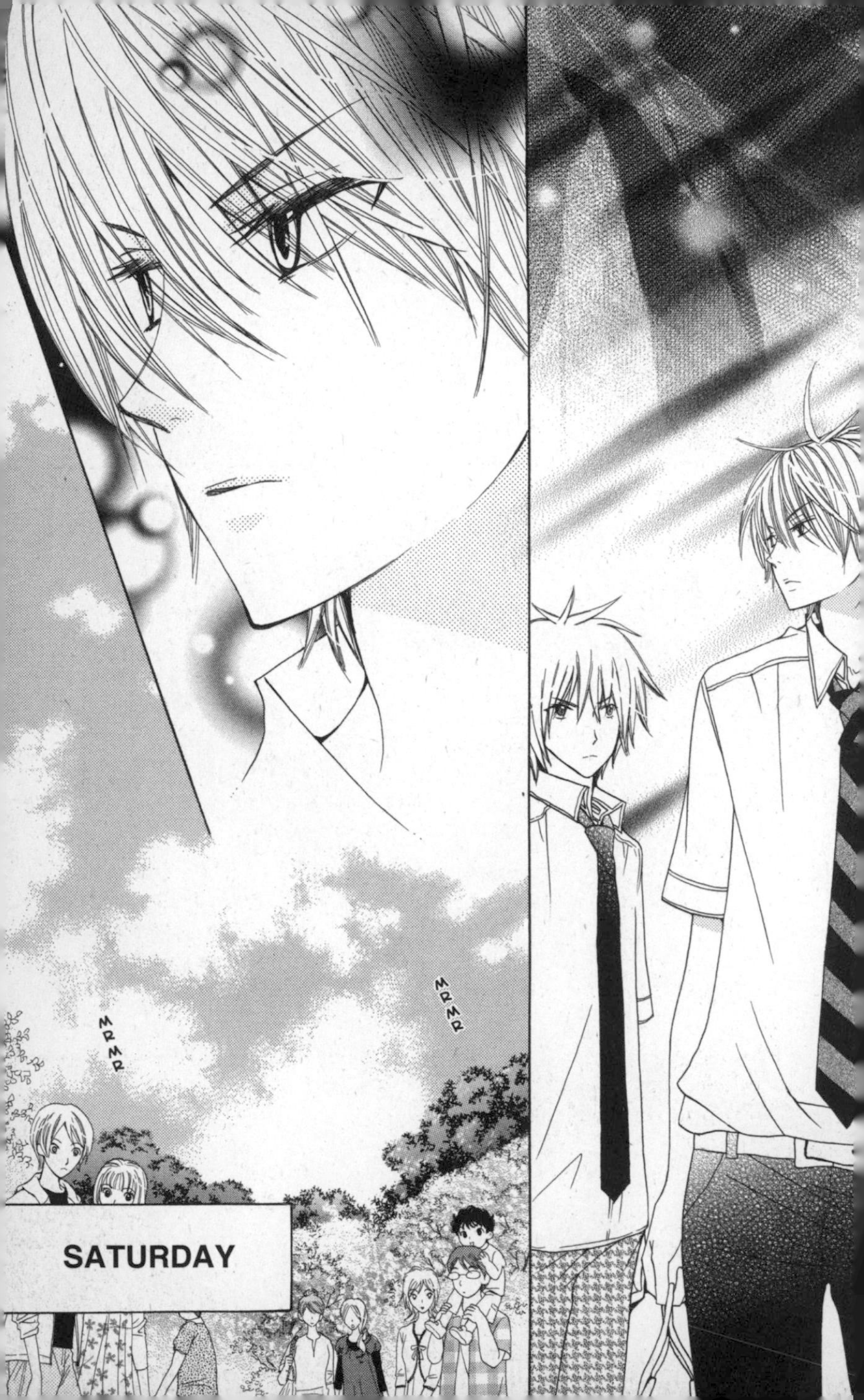
MRMR
MRMR
SATURDAY

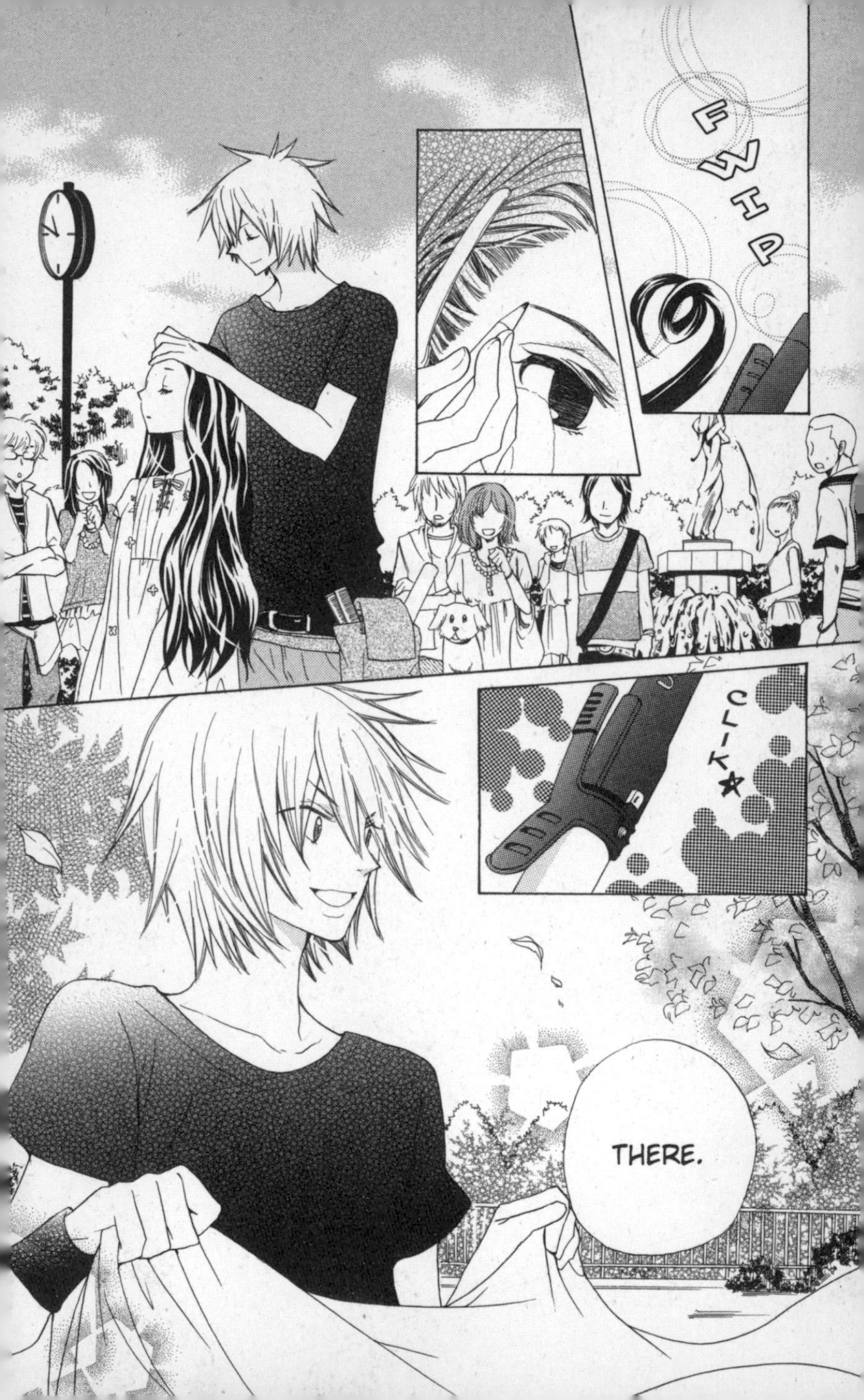
FWIP
CLIK☆
THERE.

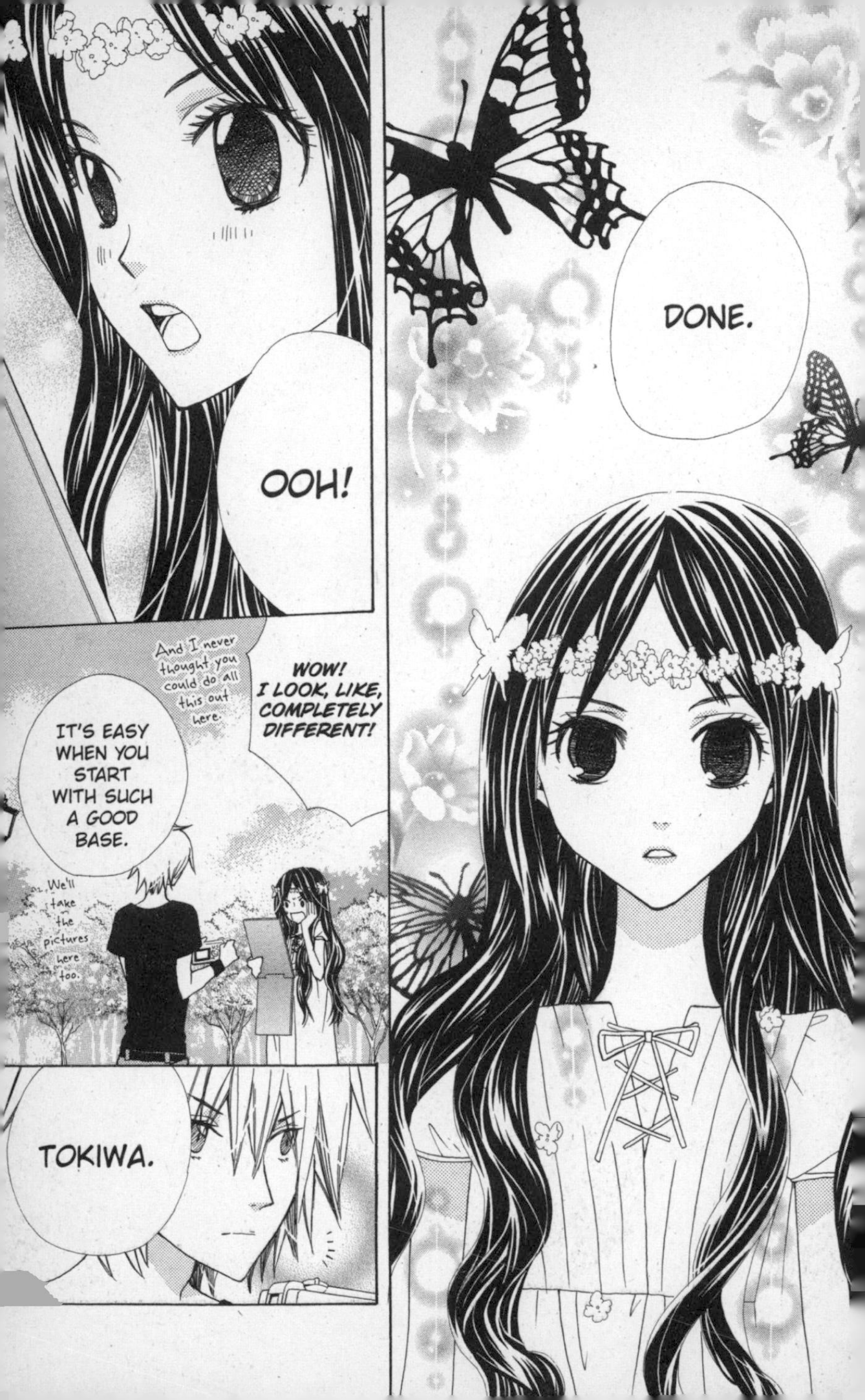
DONE.
OOH!
WOW! I LOOK, LIKE, COMPLETELY DIFFERENT!
And I never thought you could do all this out here.
IT'S EASY WHEN YOU START WITH SUCH A GOOD BASE.
We'll take the pictures here too.
TOKIWA.

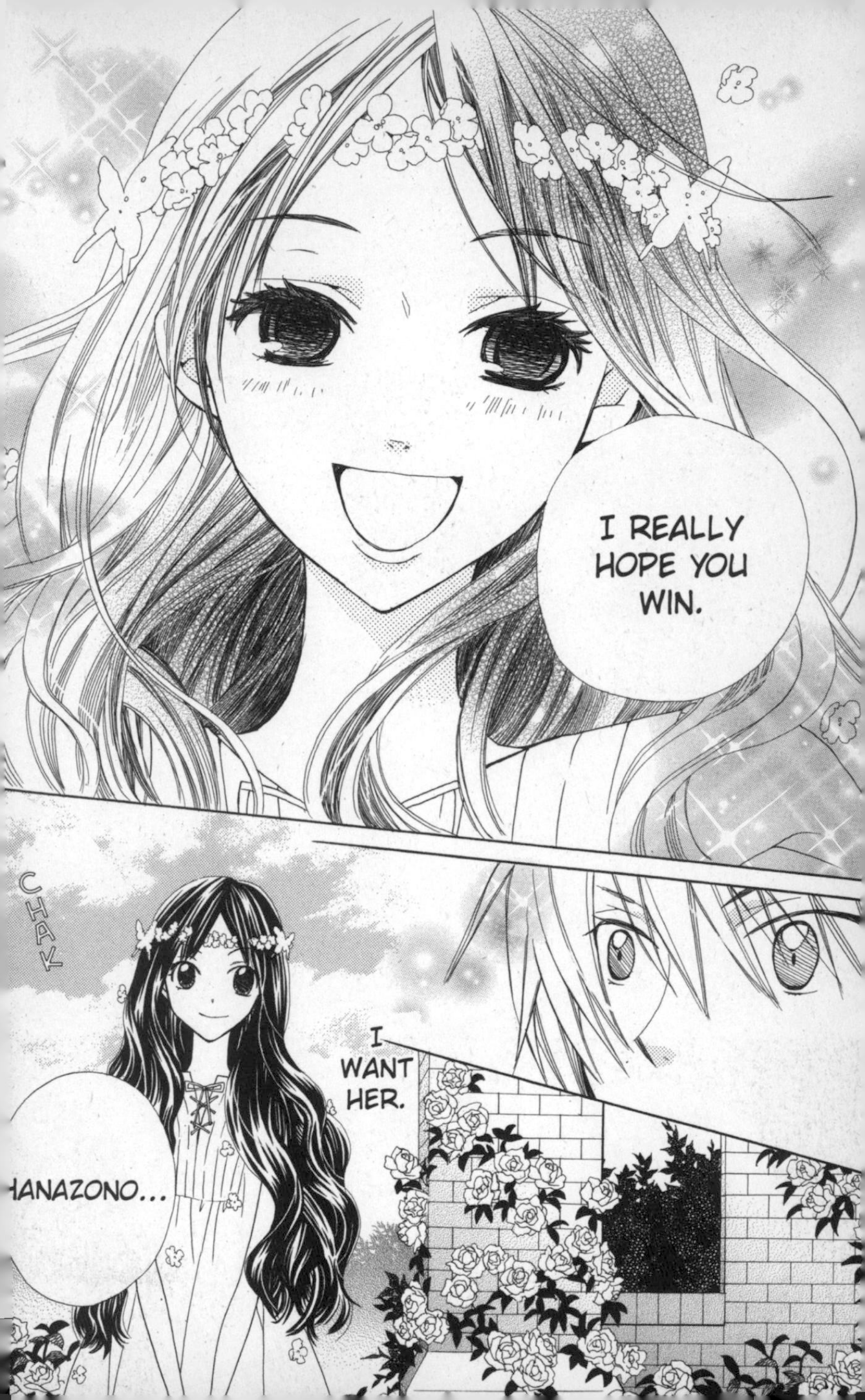
I REALLY HOPE YOU WIN.
I WANT HER.
CHAK
HANAZONO...

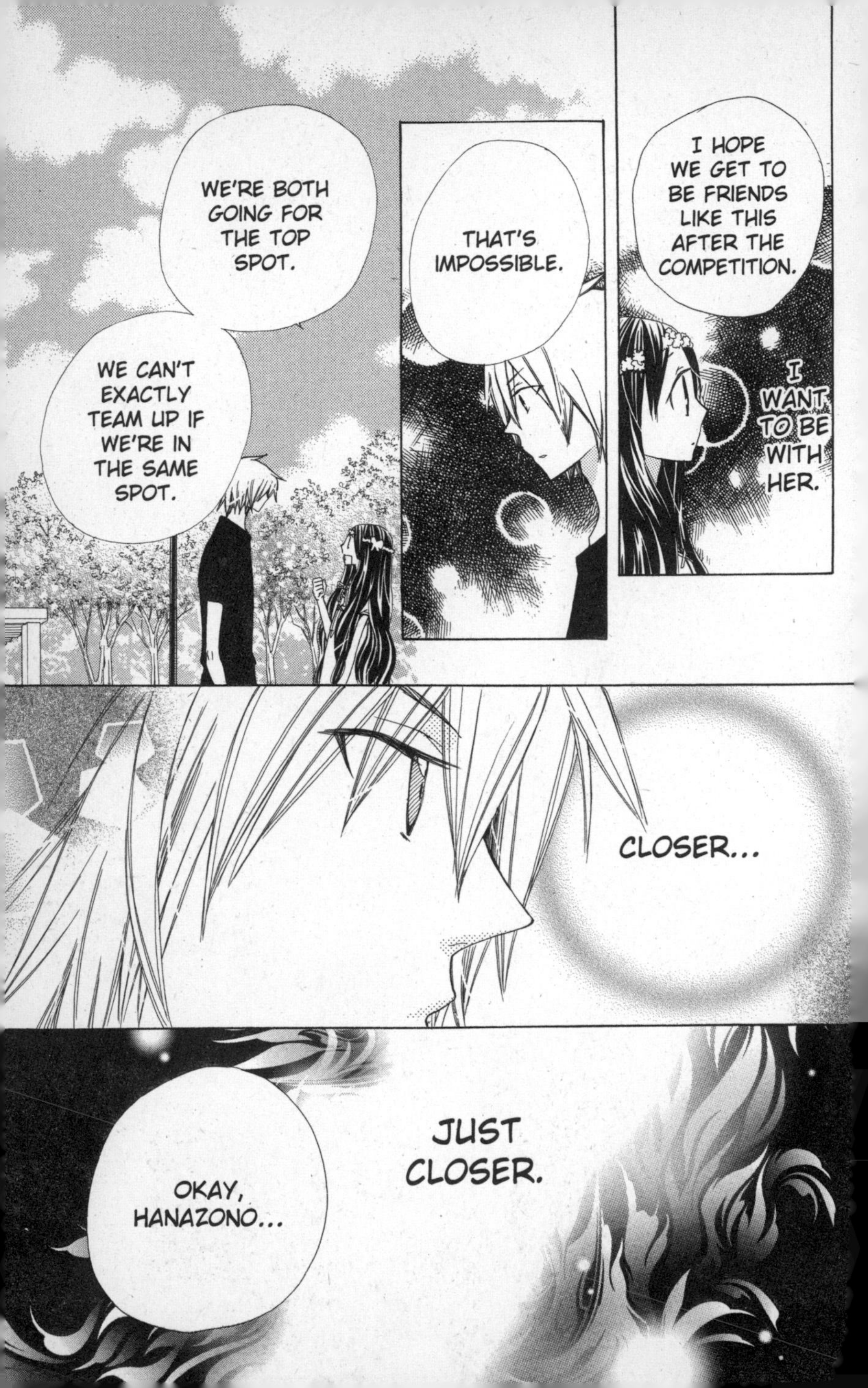
I HOPE WE GET TO BE FRIENDS LIKE THIS AFTER THE COMPETITION.
I WANT TO BE WITH HER.
THAT'S IMPOSSIBLE.
WE'RE BOTH GOING FOR THE TOP SPOT.
WE CAN'T EXACTLY TEAM UP IF WE'RE IN THE SAME SPOT.
CLOSER...
JUST CLOSER.
OKAY, HANAZONO...

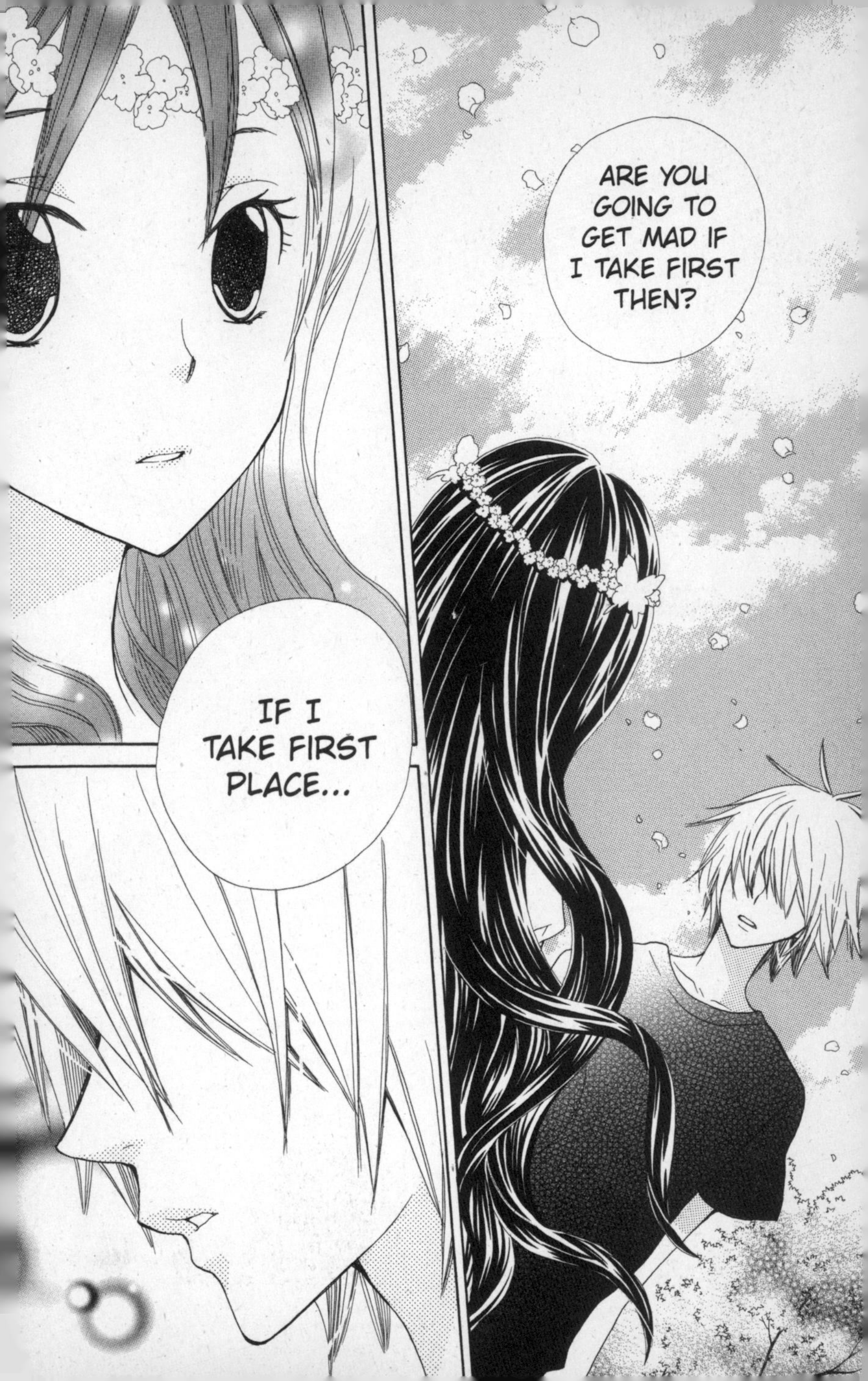
ARE YOU GOING TO GET MAD IF I TAKE FIRST THEN?
IF I TAKE FIRST PLACE...

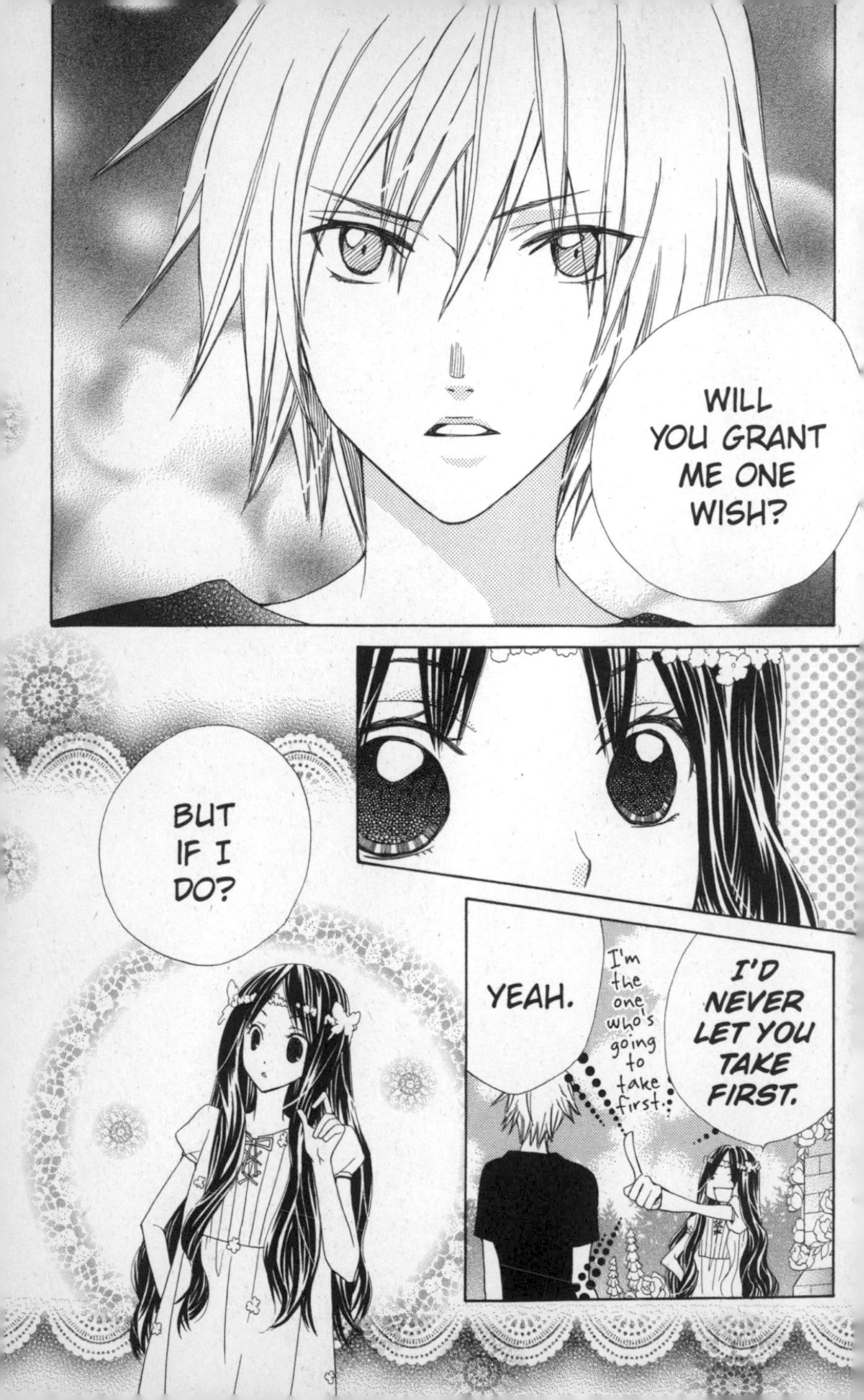
WILL YOU GRANT ME ONE WISH?
I'D NEVER LET YOU TAKE FIRST.
I'm the one who's going to take first.
YEAH.
BUT IF I DO?

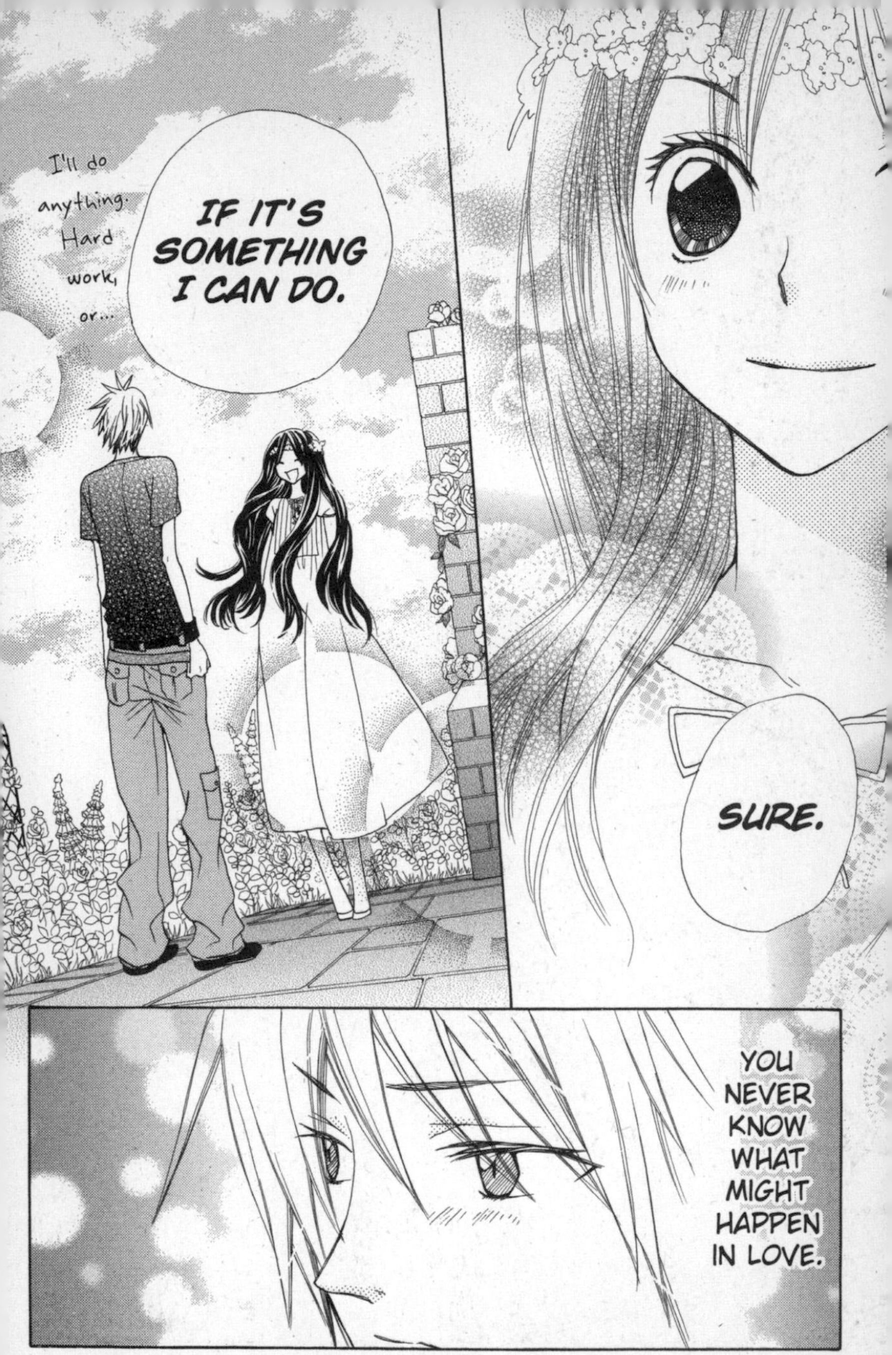
SURE.
IF IT'S SOMETHING I CAN DO.
I'll do anything. Hard work, or...
YOU NEVER KNOW WHAT MIGHT HAPPEN IN LOVE.

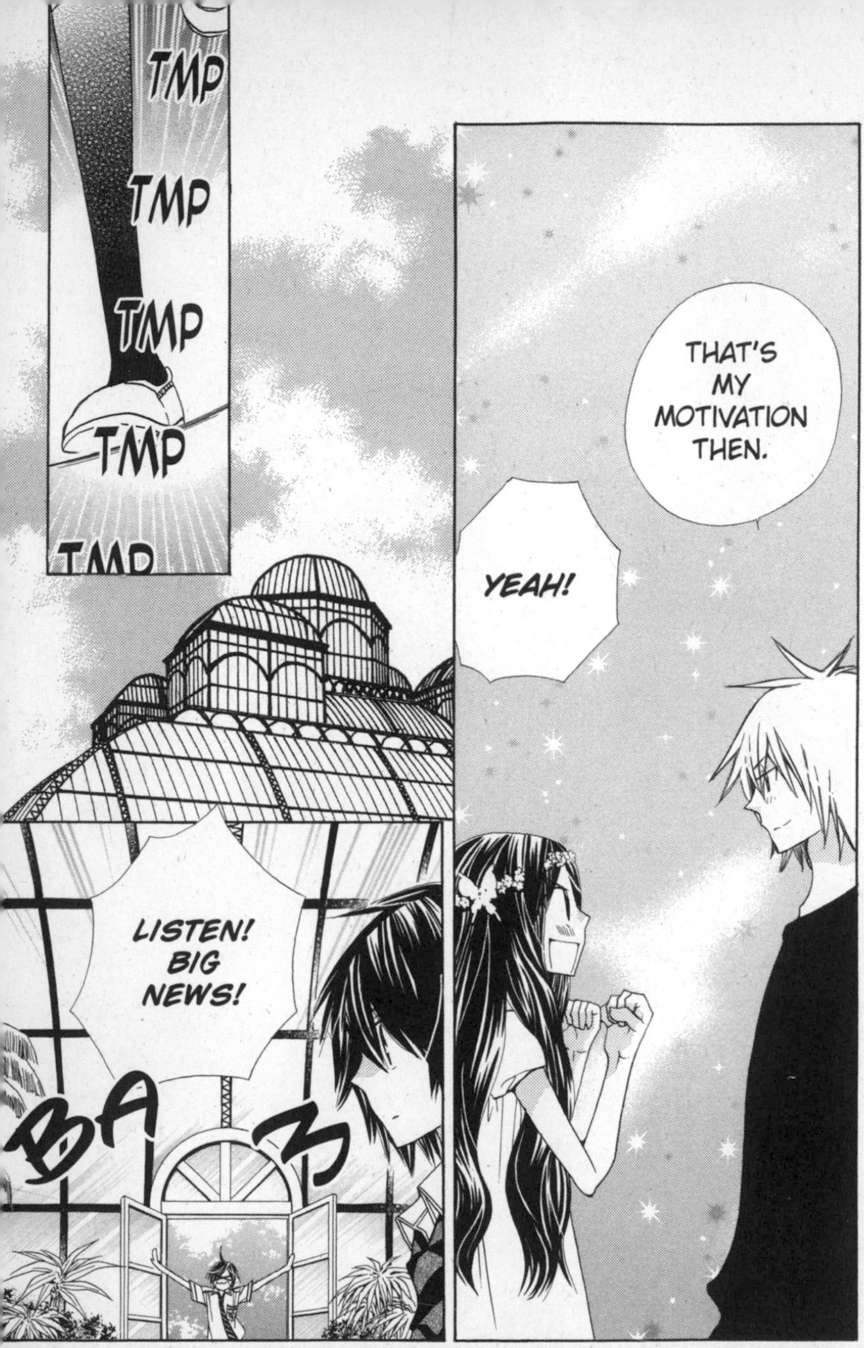
THAT'S MY MOTIVATION THEN.
YEAH!
TMP
TMP
TMP
TMP
LISTEN! BIG NEWS!
BAM

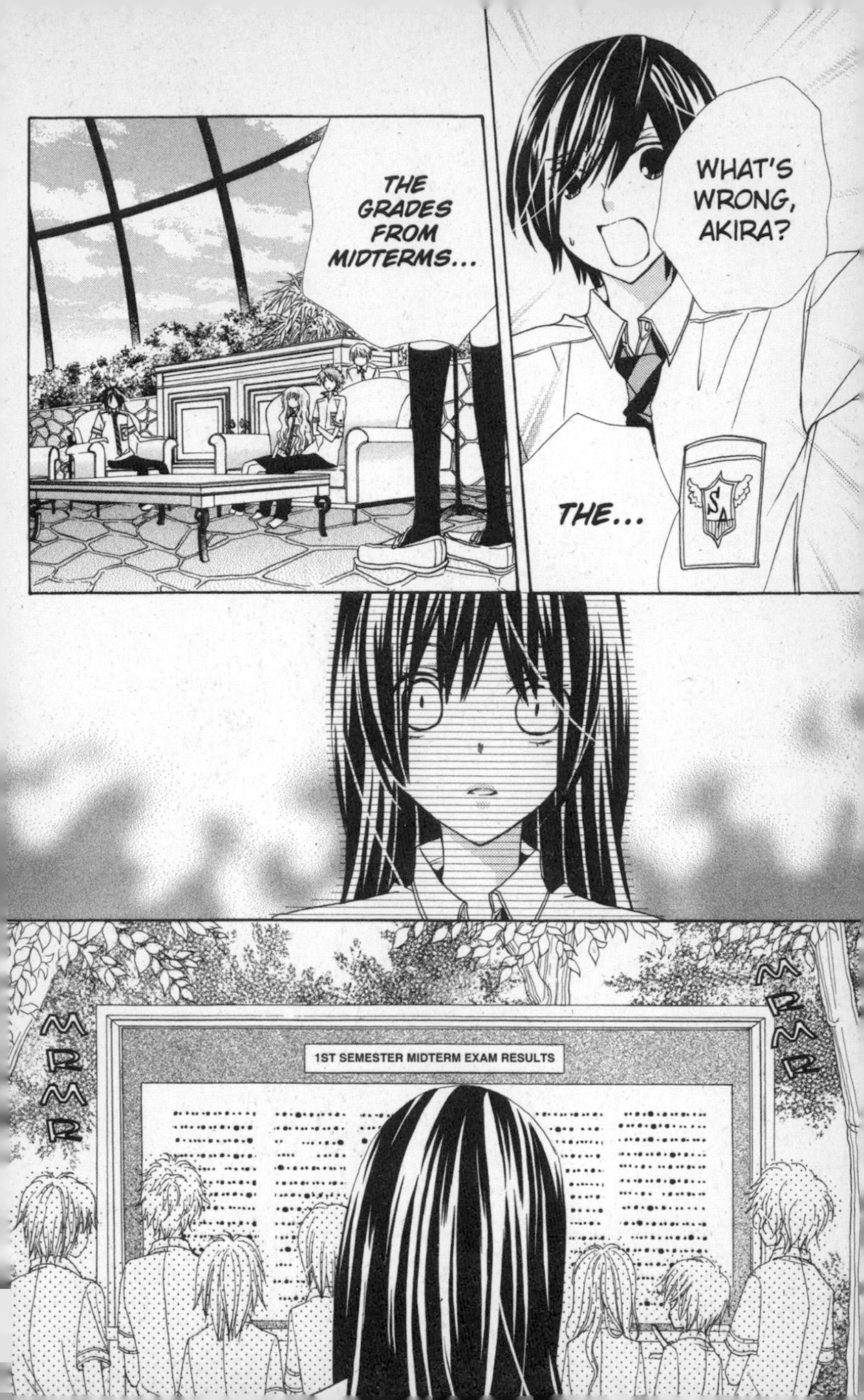
WHAT'S WRONG, AKIRA?
THE...
THE GRADES FROM MIDTERMS...
MRMR
1ST SEMESTER MIDTERM EXAM RESULTS
MRMR

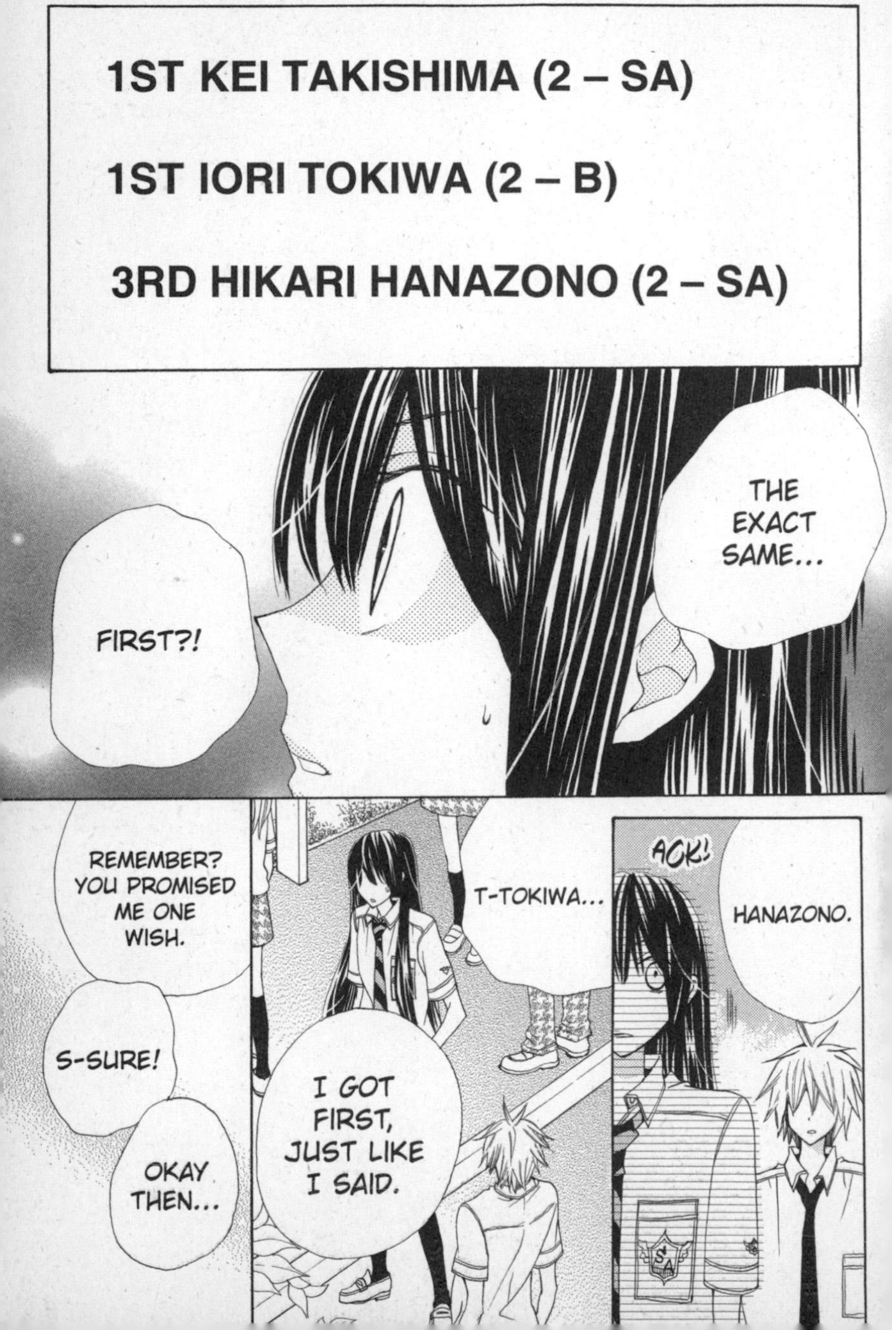
1ST KEI TAKISHIMA (2 – SA)
1ST IORI TOKIWA (2 – B)
3RD HIKARI HANAZONO (2 – SA)
THE EXACT SAME...
FIRST?!
ACK!
HANAZONO.
T-TOKIWA...
I GOT FIRST, JUST LIKE I SAID.
REMEMBER? YOU PROMISED ME ONE WISH.
S-SURE!
OKAY THEN...

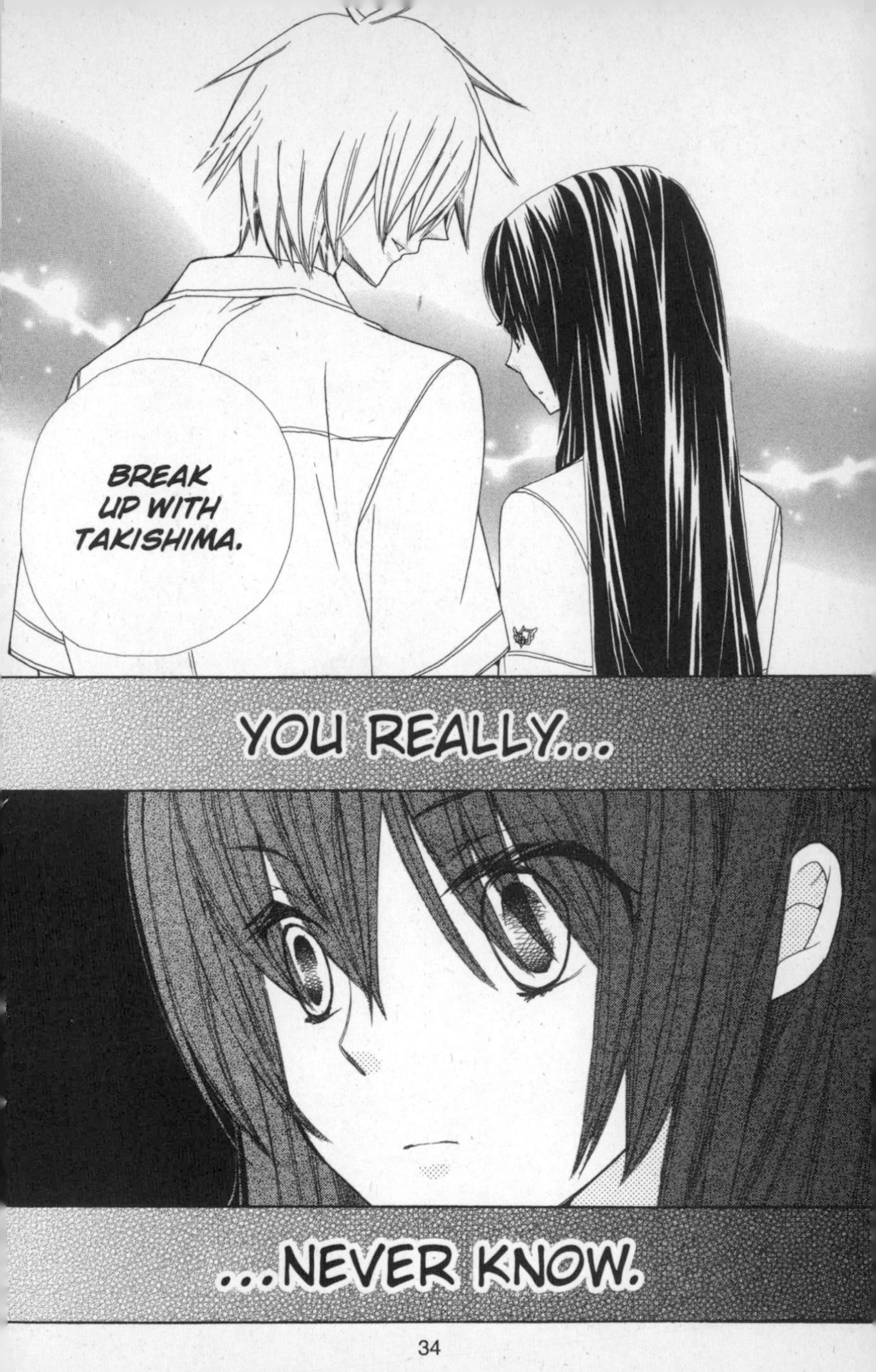
BREAK UP WITH TAKISHIMA.
YOU REALLY...
...NEVER KNOW.

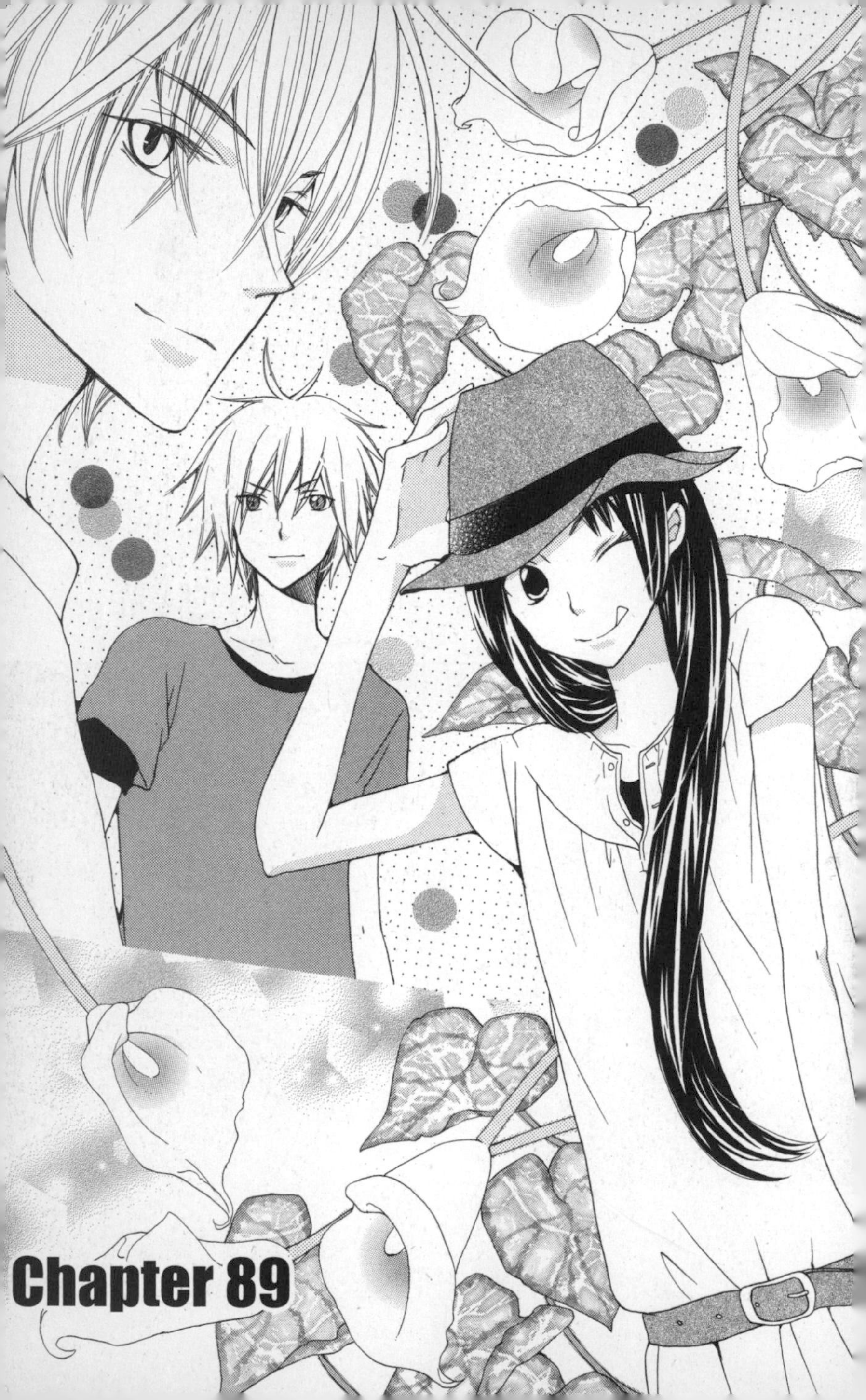
Chapter 89

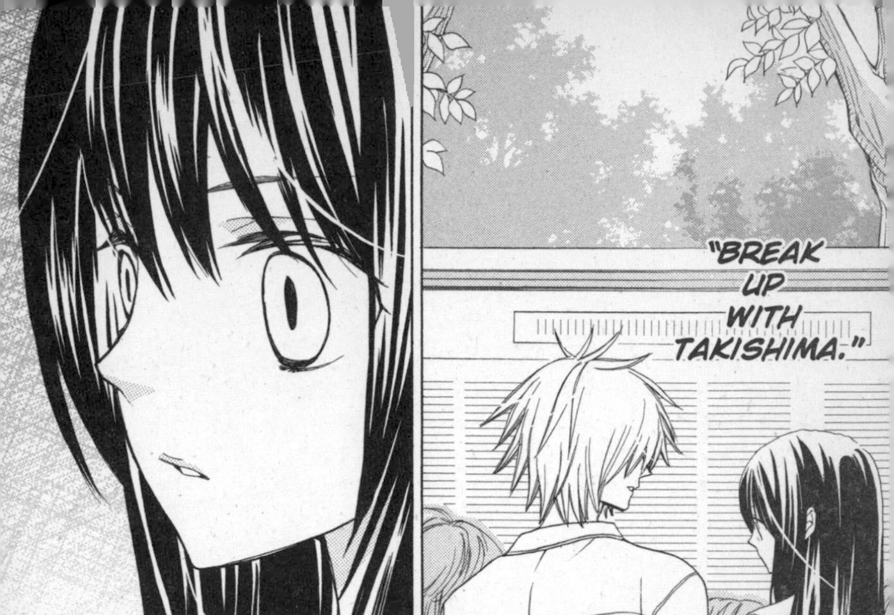
"BREAK UP WITH TAKISHIMA."

• THE OFFICE •

IN VOLUME 14, I TOLD YOU HOW MY ASSISTANT GLUED EYES ON THE PRINTER...

THIS TIME, THE HEATERS GOT SOME. WHAT IN THE WORLD?! IT'S SO CUTE, YOU LITTLE DEVIL! HA HA! IT TURNED OUT TO BE ASSISTANT E.

EVERYONE HAS SUCH A GREAT SENSE OF HUMOR. I WONDER WHAT'LL GET A FACE NEXT.

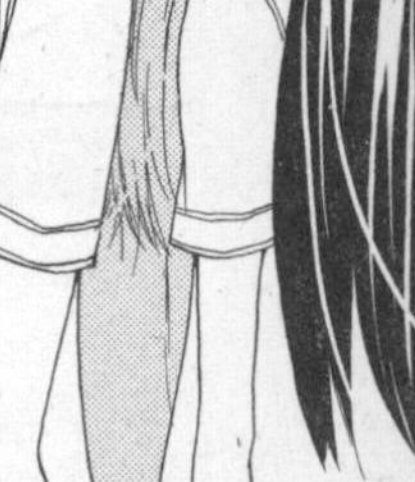
B
LOOKS LIKE A MOB BOSS AND HIS LACKEY.

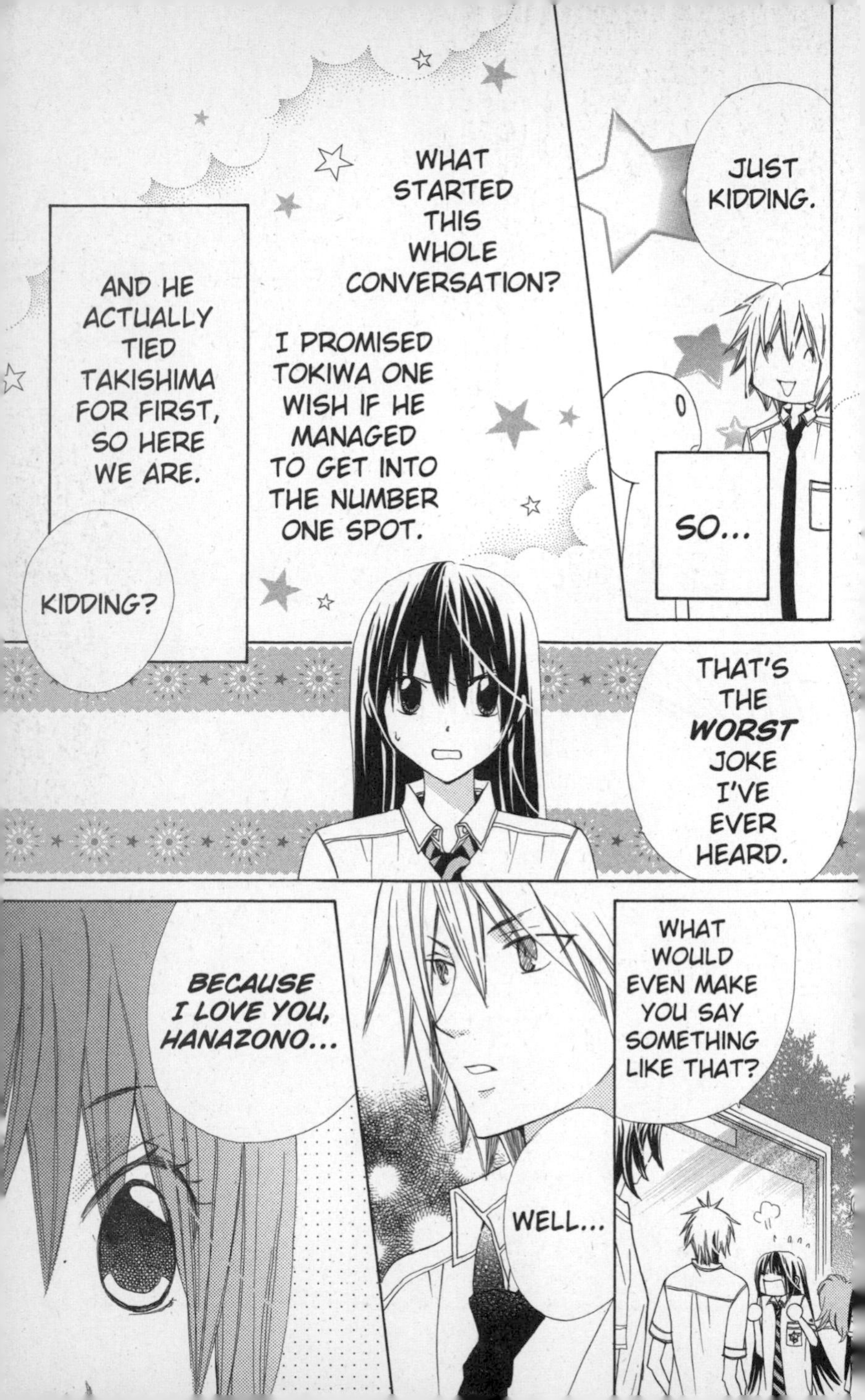
JUST KIDDING.
SO...
WHAT STARTED THIS WHOLE CONVERSATION?
I PROMISED TOKIWA ONE WISH IF HE MANAGED TO GET INTO THE NUMBER ONE SPOT.
AND HE ACTUALLY TIED TAKISHIMA FOR FIRST, SO HERE WE ARE.
KIDDING?
THAT'S THE *WORST* JOKE I'VE EVER HEARD.
WHAT WOULD EVEN MAKE YOU SAY SOMETHING LIKE THAT?
WELL...
BECAUSE I LOVE YOU, HANAZONO...

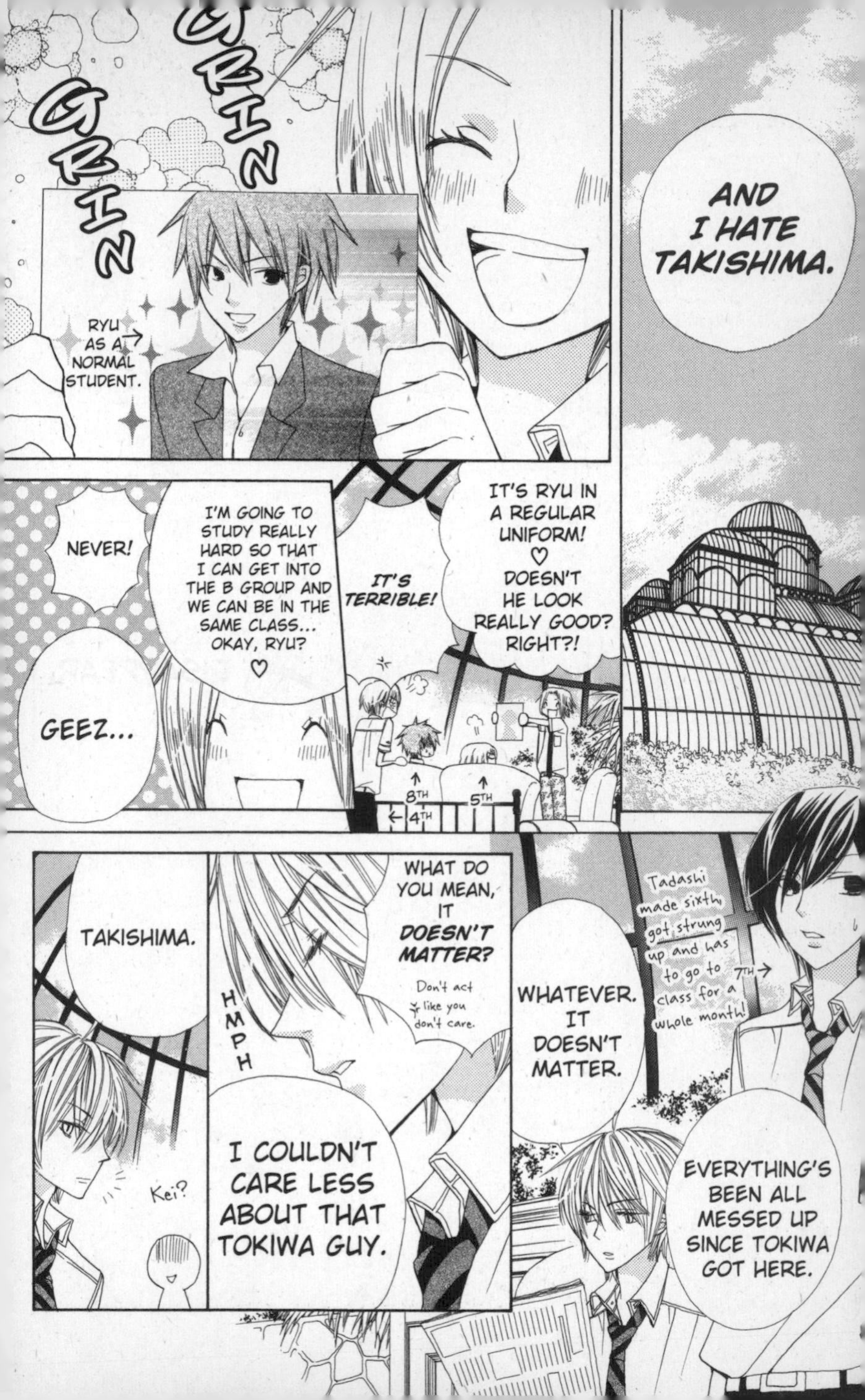
AND I HATE TAKISHIMA.
GRIN
GRIN
RYU AS A NORMAL STUDENT.
IT'S RYU IN A REGULAR UNIFORM! ♡ DOESN'T HE LOOK REALLY GOOD? RIGHT?!
IT'S TERRIBLE!
8TH
5TH
4TH
I'M GOING TO STUDY REALLY HARD SO THAT I CAN GET INTO THE B GROUP AND WE CAN BE IN THE SAME CLASS... OKAY, RYU? ♡
NEVER!
GEEZ...
WHATEVER. IT DOESN'T MATTER.
Tadashi made sixth, got strung up and has to go to class for a whole month!
7TH
EVERYTHING'S BEEN ALL MESSED UP SINCE TOKIWA GOT HERE.
WHAT DO YOU MEAN, IT DOESN'T MATTER?
Don't act like you don't care.
HMPH
I COULDN'T CARE LESS ABOUT THAT TOKIWA GUY.
TAKISHIMA.
Kei?

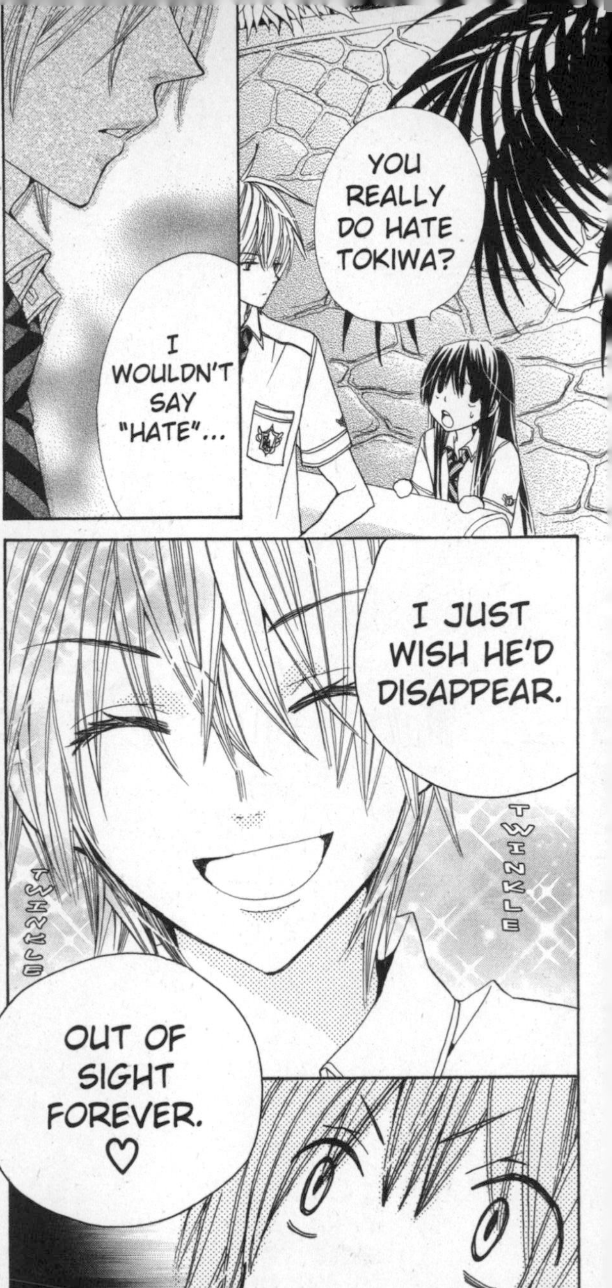
YOU REALLY DO HATE TOKIWA?
I WOULDN'T SAY "HATE"...
I JUST WISH HE'D DISAPPEAR.
TWINKLE
TWINKLE
OUT OF SIGHT FOREVER. ♡

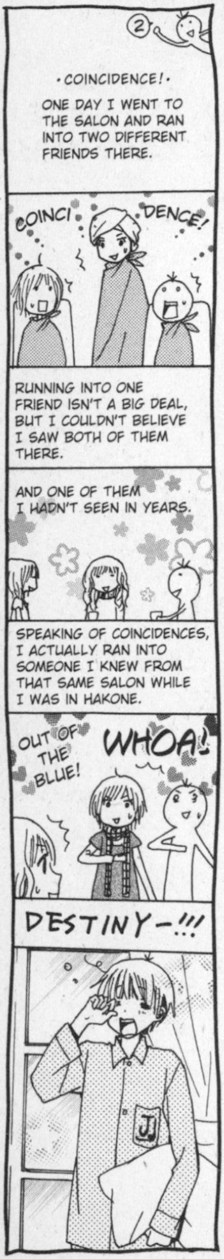
2
·COINCIDENCE!·
ONE DAY I WENT TO THE SALON AND RAN INTO TWO DIFFERENT FRIENDS THERE.
COINCI
DENCE!
RUNNING INTO ONE FRIEND ISN'T A BIG DEAL, BUT I COULDN'T BELIEVE I SAW BOTH OF THEM THERE.
AND ONE OF THEM I HADN'T SEEN IN YEARS.
SPEAKING OF COINCIDENCES, I ACTUALLY RAN INTO SOMEONE I KNEW FROM THAT SAME SALON WHILE I WAS IN HAKONE.
WHOA!
OUT OF THE BLUE!
DESTINY-!!!
J

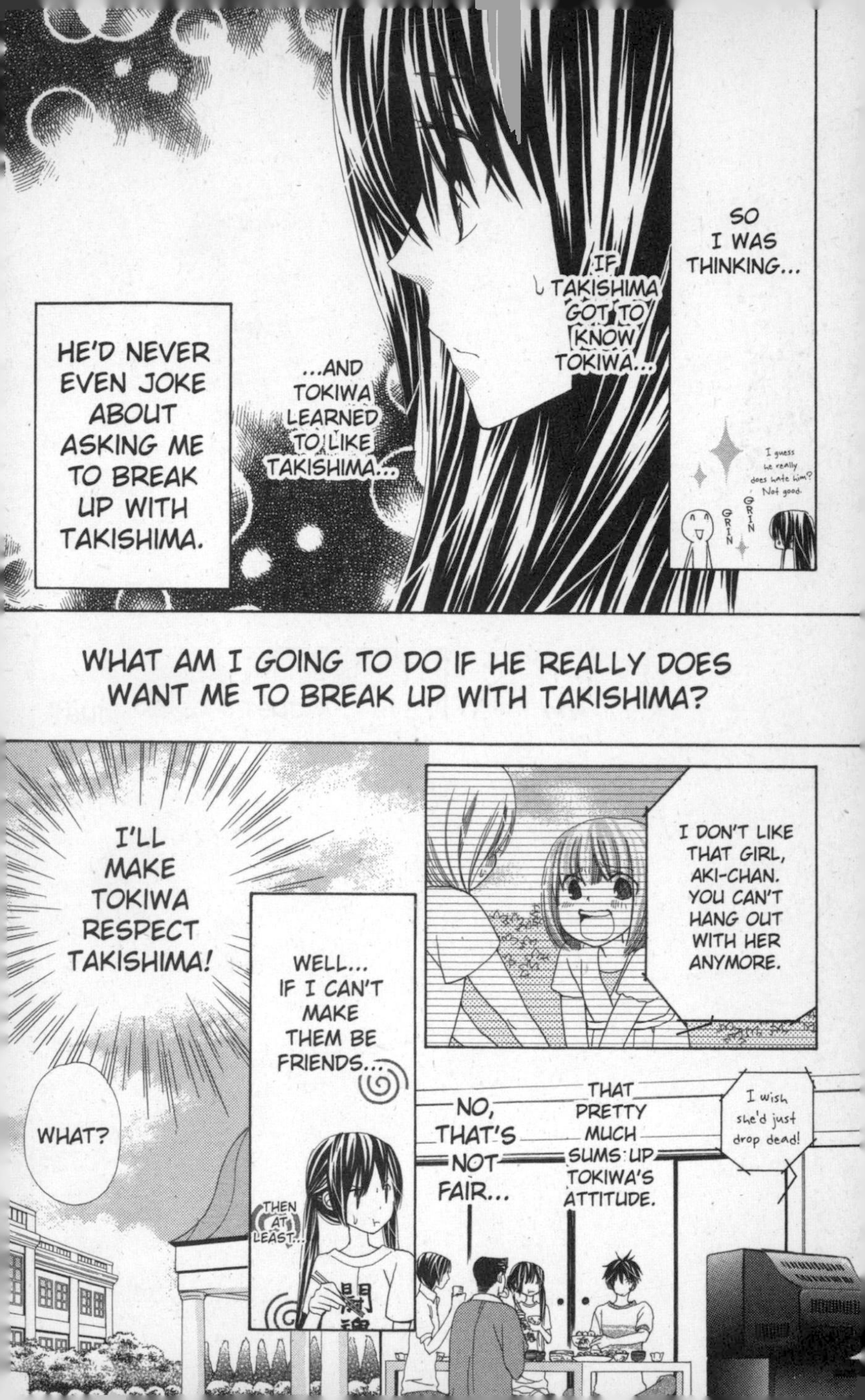
SO I WAS THINKING...
IF TAKISHIMA GOT TO KNOW TOKIWA...
I guess he really does hate him? Not good.
GRIN GRIN
...AND TOKIWA LEARNED TO LIKE TAKISHIMA...
HE'D NEVER EVEN JOKE ABOUT ASKING ME TO BREAK UP WITH TAKISHIMA.
WHAT AM I GOING TO DO IF HE REALLY DOES WANT ME TO BREAK UP WITH TAKISHIMA?
I DON'T LIKE THAT GIRL, AKI-CHAN. YOU CAN'T HANG OUT WITH HER ANYMORE.
I wish she'd just drop dead!
THAT PRETTY MUCH SUMS UP TOKIWA'S ATTITUDE.
NO, THAT'S NOT FAIR...
WELL... IF I CAN'T MAKE THEM BE FRIENDS...
THEN AT LEAST...
I'LL MAKE TOKIWA RESPECT TAKISHIMA!
WHAT?

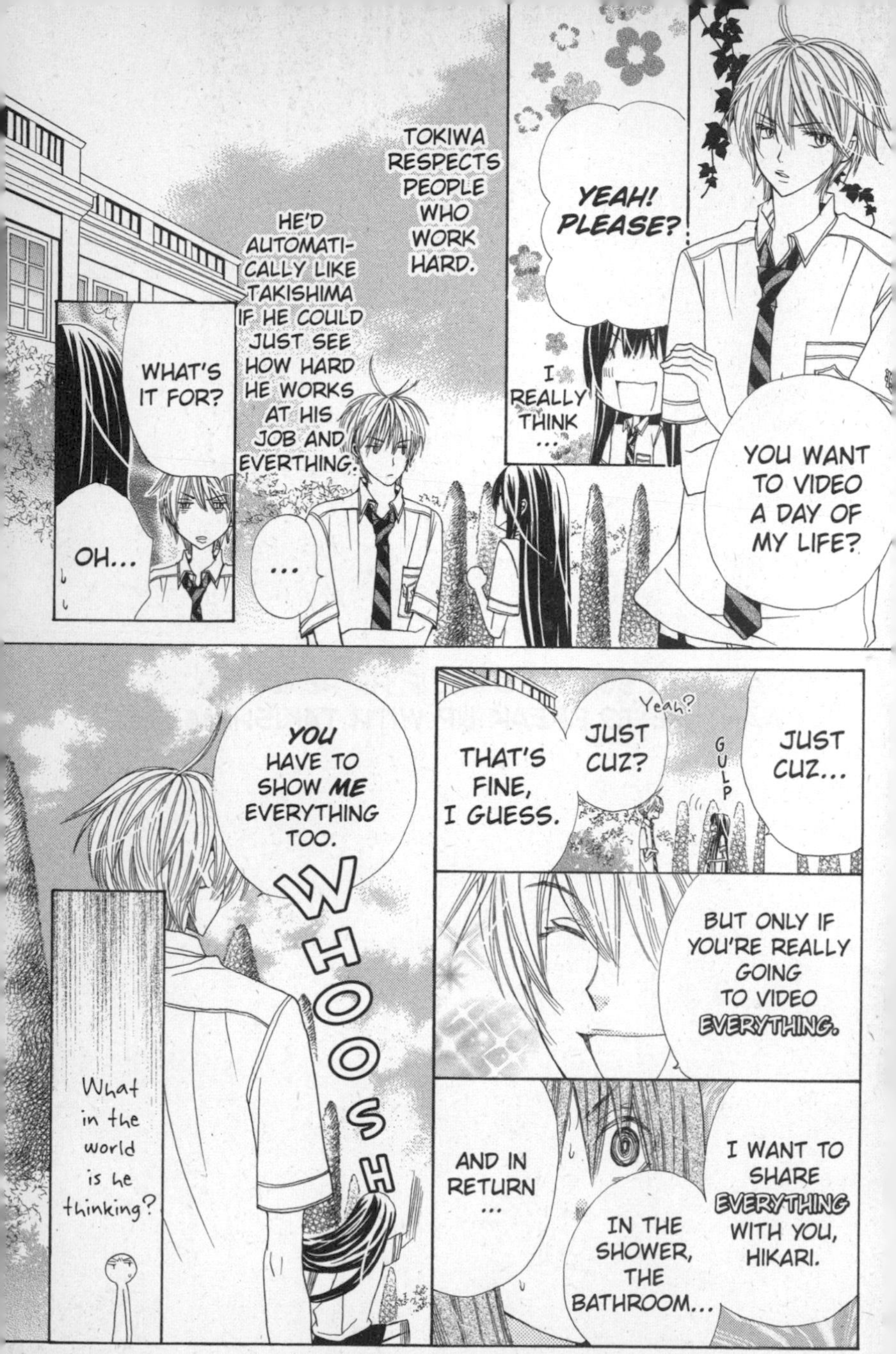
YOU WANT TO VIDEO A DAY OF MY LIFE?
YEAH! PLEASE?
I REALLY THINK...
TOKIWA RESPECTS PEOPLE WHO WORK HARD.
HE'D AUTOMATICALLY LIKE TAKISHIMA IF HE COULD JUST SEE HOW HARD HE WORKS AT HIS JOB AND EVERTHING.
...
WHAT'S IT FOR?
OH...
JUST CUZ...
GULP
Yeah?
JUST CUZ?
THAT'S FINE, I GUESS.
BUT ONLY IF YOU'RE REALLY GOING TO VIDEO EVERYTHING.
I WANT TO SHARE EVERYTHING WITH YOU, HIKARI.
IN THE SHOWER, THE BATHROOM...
AND IN RETURN...
YOU HAVE TO SHOW ME EVERYTHING TOO.
WHOOSH
What in the world is he thinking?

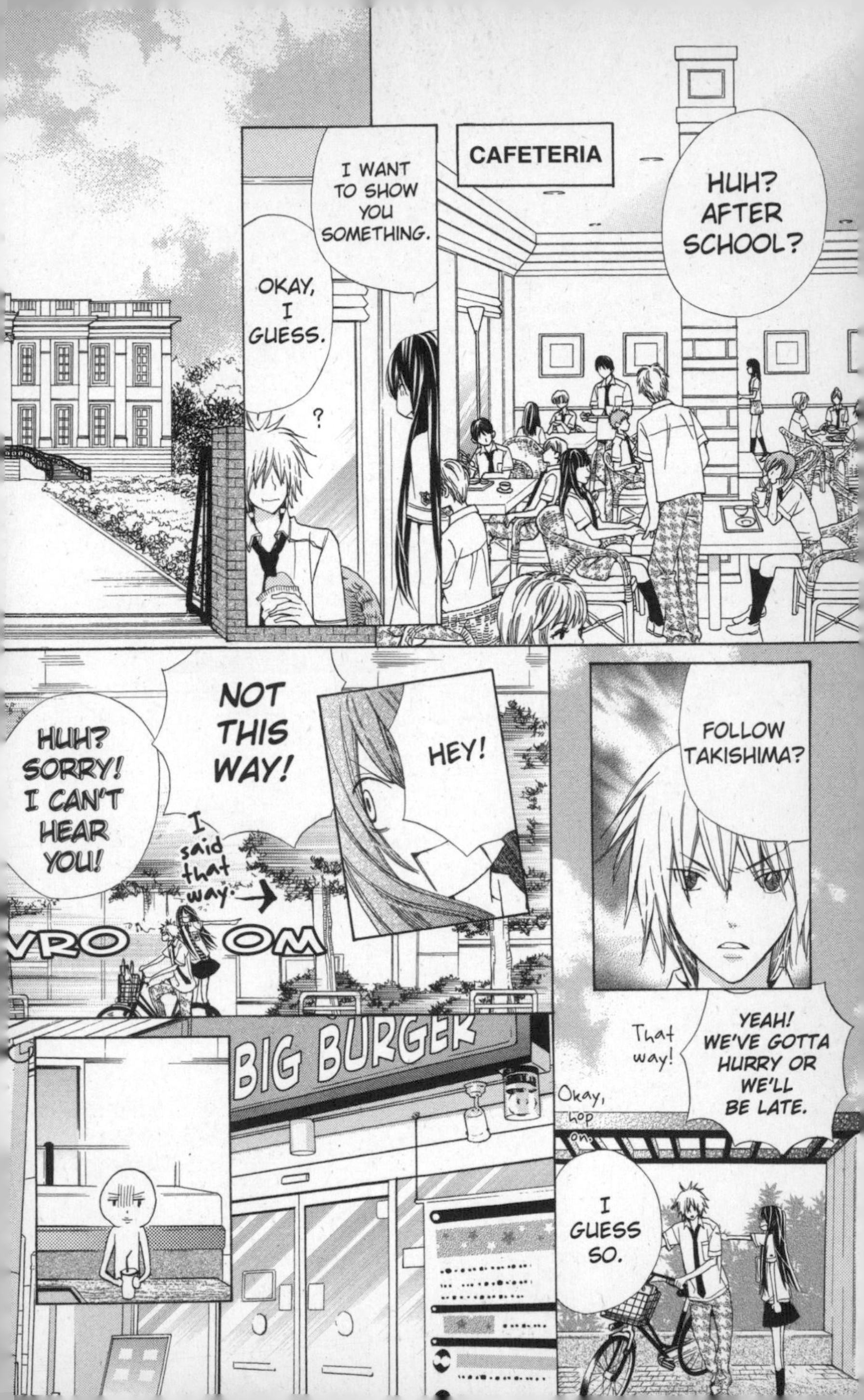
CAFETERIA
HUH? AFTER SCHOOL?
I WANT TO SHOW YOU SOMETHING.
OKAY, I GUESS.
?
FOLLOW TAKISHIMA?
YEAH! WE'VE GOTTA HURRY OR WE'LL BE LATE.
That way!
Okay, hop on.
I GUESS SO.
HEY!
NOT THIS WAY!
HUH? SORRY! I CAN'T HEAR YOU!
I said that way.
VROOM
BIG BURGER

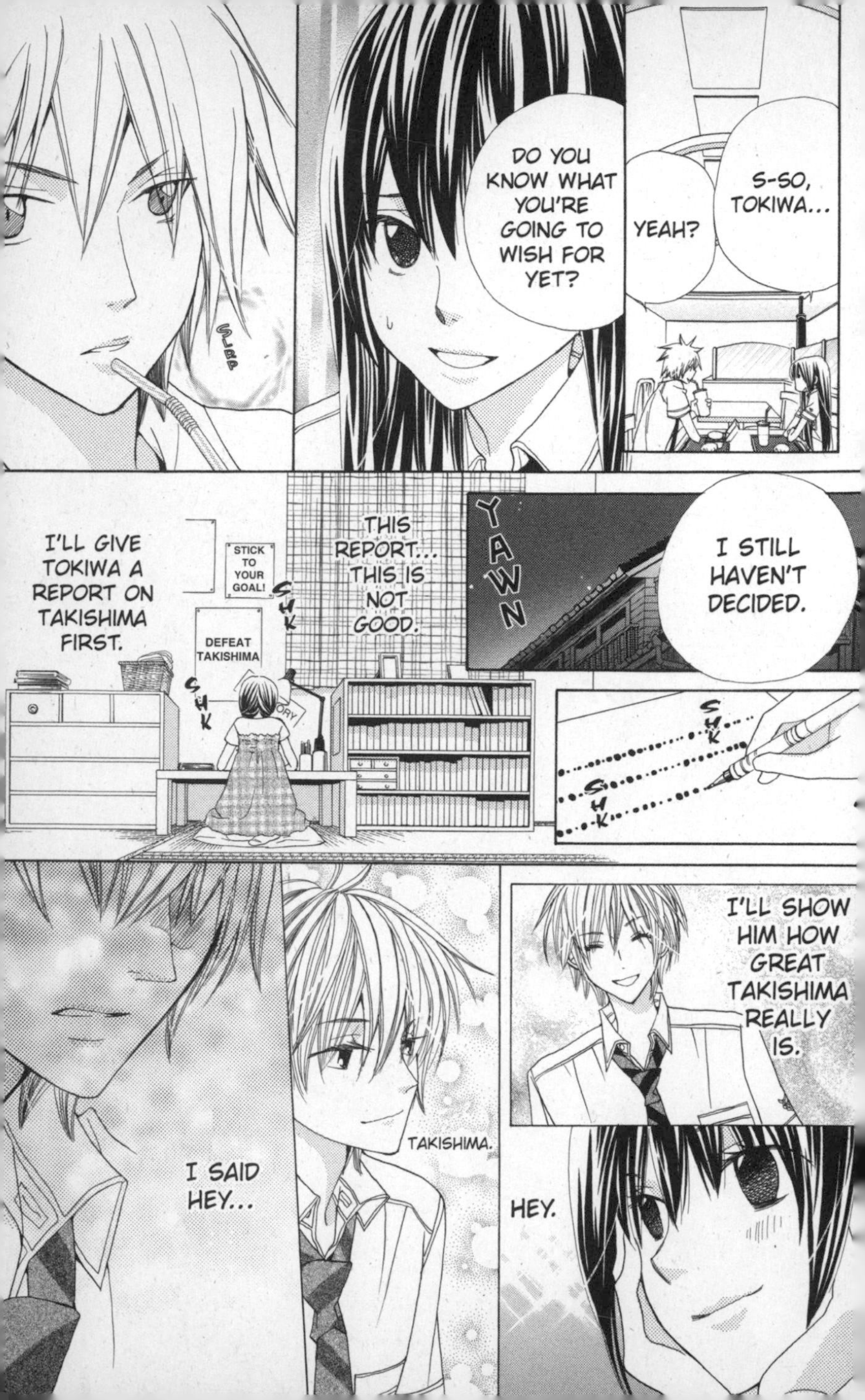
S-SO, TOKIWA...
YEAH?
DO YOU KNOW WHAT YOU'RE GOING TO WISH FOR YET?
SLRP
I STILL HAVEN'T DECIDED.
YAWN
SHK
SHK
THIS REPORT... THIS IS NOT GOOD.
STICK TO YOUR GOAL!
SHK
I'LL GIVE TOKIWA A REPORT ON TAKISHIMA FIRST.
DEFEAT TAKISHIMA
SHK
I'LL SHOW HIM HOW GREAT TAKISHIMA REALLY IS.
HEY.
TAKISHIMA.
I SAID HEY...

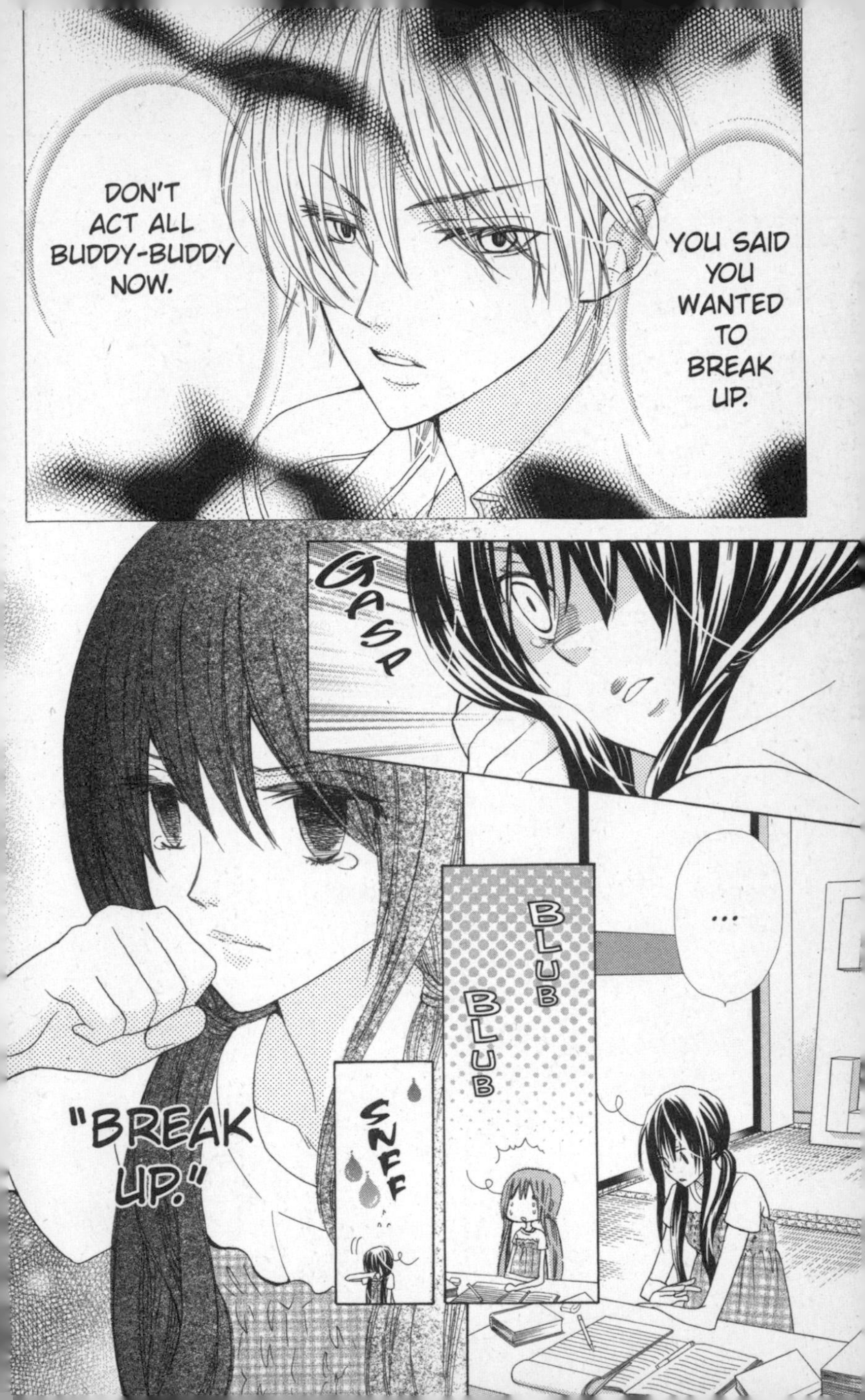
YOU SAID YOU WANTED TO BREAK UP.
DON'T ACT ALL BUDDY-BUDDY NOW.
GASP
...
BLUB
BLUB
SNFF
"BREAK UP."

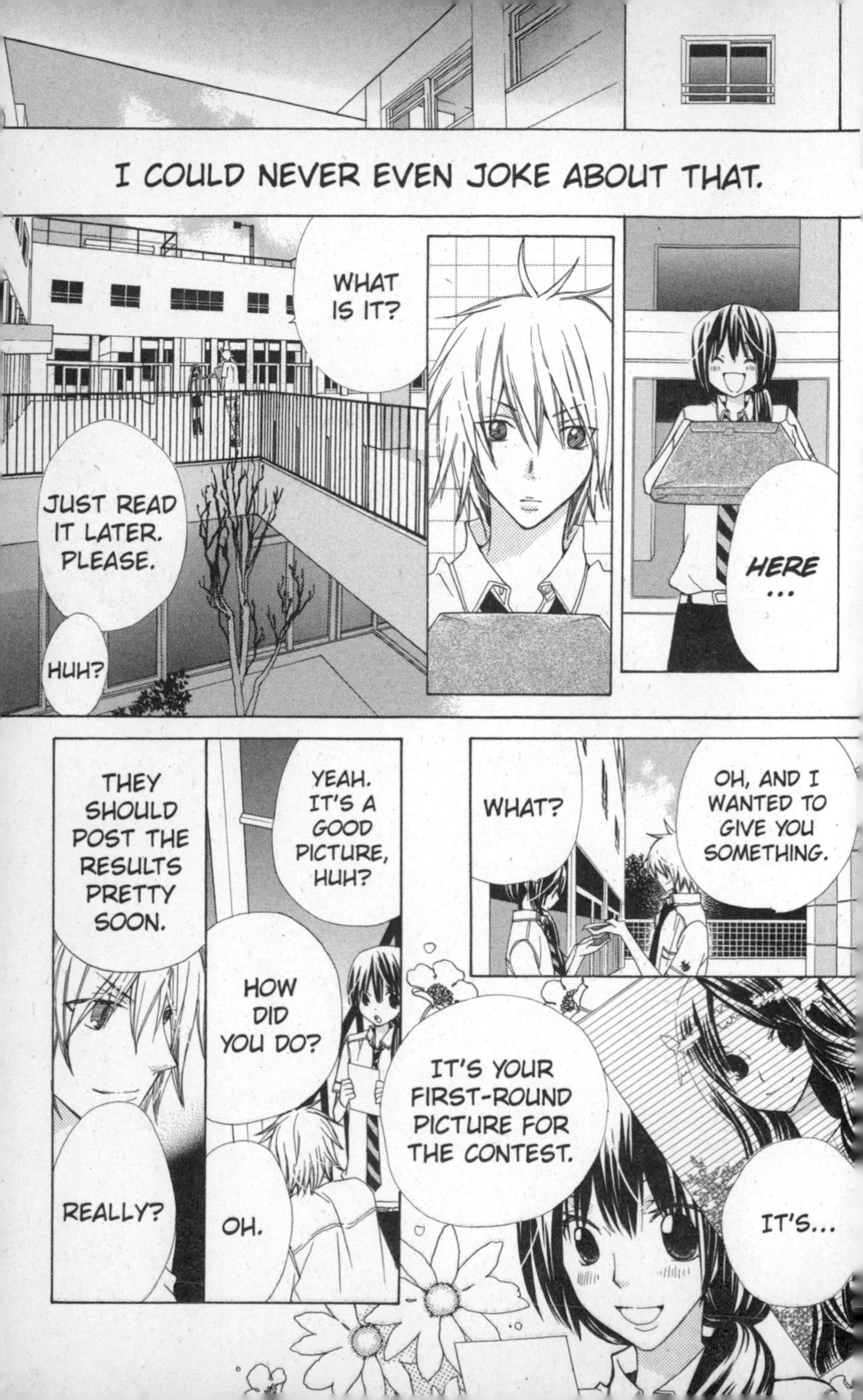
I COULD NEVER EVEN JOKE ABOUT THAT.
HERE ...
WHAT IS IT?
JUST READ IT LATER. PLEASE.
HUH?
OH, AND I WANTED TO GIVE YOU SOMETHING.
WHAT?
IT'S...
IT'S YOUR FIRST-ROUND PICTURE FOR THE CONTEST.
YEAH. IT'S A GOOD PICTURE, HUH?
HOW DID YOU DO?
OH.
THEY SHOULD POST THE RESULTS PRETTY SOON.
REALLY?

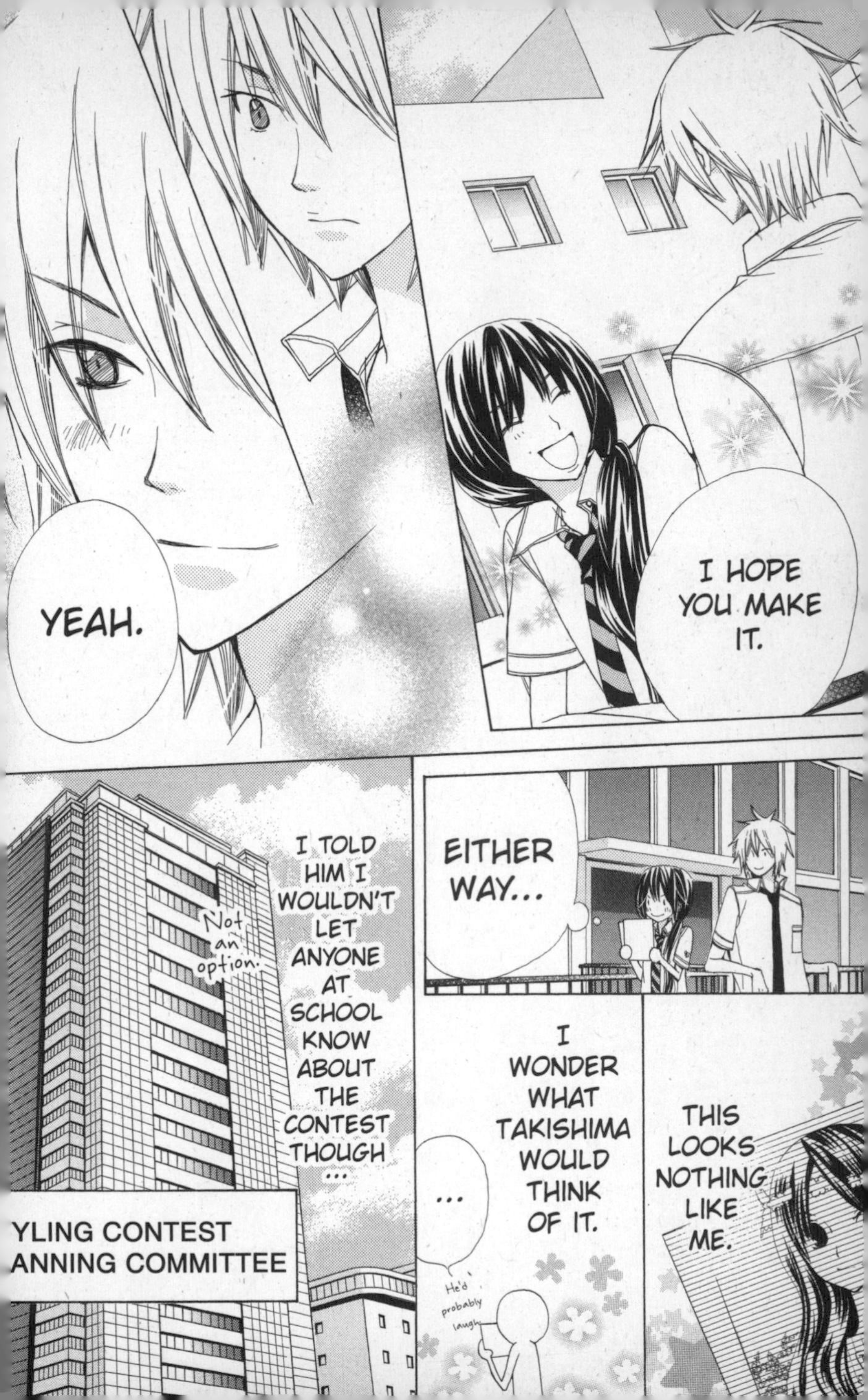
I HOPE YOU MAKE IT.
YEAH.
EITHER WAY...
THIS LOOKS NOTHING LIKE ME.
I WONDER WHAT TAKISHIMA WOULD THINK OF IT.
...
He'd probably laugh
I TOLD HIM I WOULDN'T LET ANYONE AT SCHOOL KNOW ABOUT THE CONTEST THOUGH...
Not an option.
YLING CONTEST
ANNING COMMITTEE

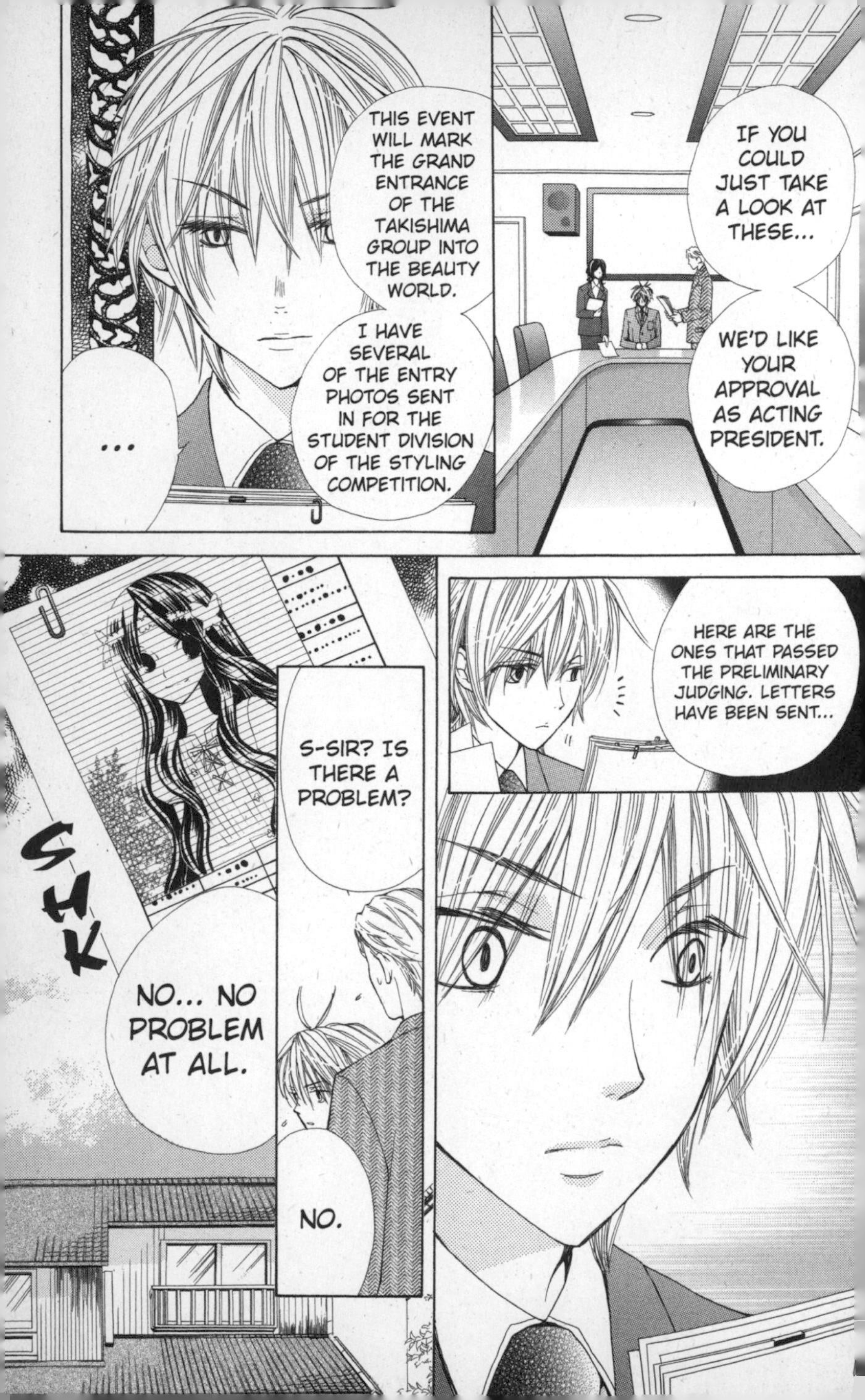
IF YOU COULD JUST TAKE A LOOK AT THESE...
WE'D LIKE YOUR APPROVAL AS ACTING PRESIDENT.
THIS EVENT WILL MARK THE GRAND ENTRANCE OF THE TAKISHIMA GROUP INTO THE BEAUTY WORLD.
I HAVE SEVERAL OF THE ENTRY PHOTOS SENT IN FOR THE STUDENT DIVISION OF THE STYLING COMPETITION.
...
HERE ARE THE ONES THAT PASSED THE PRELIMINARY JUDGING. LETTERS HAVE BEEN SENT...
S-SIR? IS THERE A PROBLEM?
NO.
SHK
NO... NO PROBLEM AT ALL.

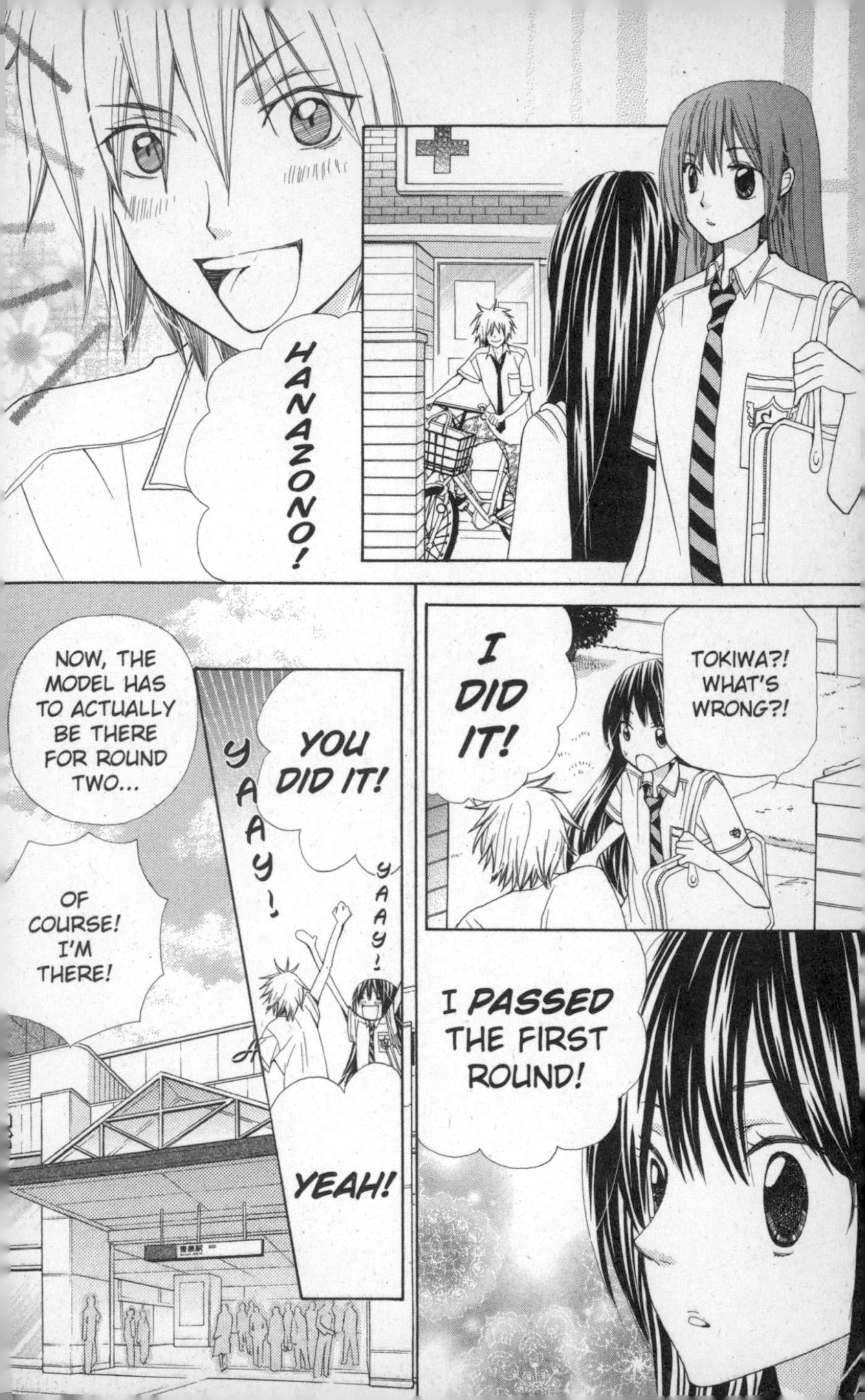
HANAZONO!
TOKIWA?! WHAT'S WRONG?!
I DID IT!
I PASSED THE FIRST ROUND!
YOU DID IT!
YAAAY!
YAAY!
YEAH!
NOW, THE MODEL HAS TO ACTUALLY BE THERE FOR ROUND TWO...
OF COURSE! I'M THERE!

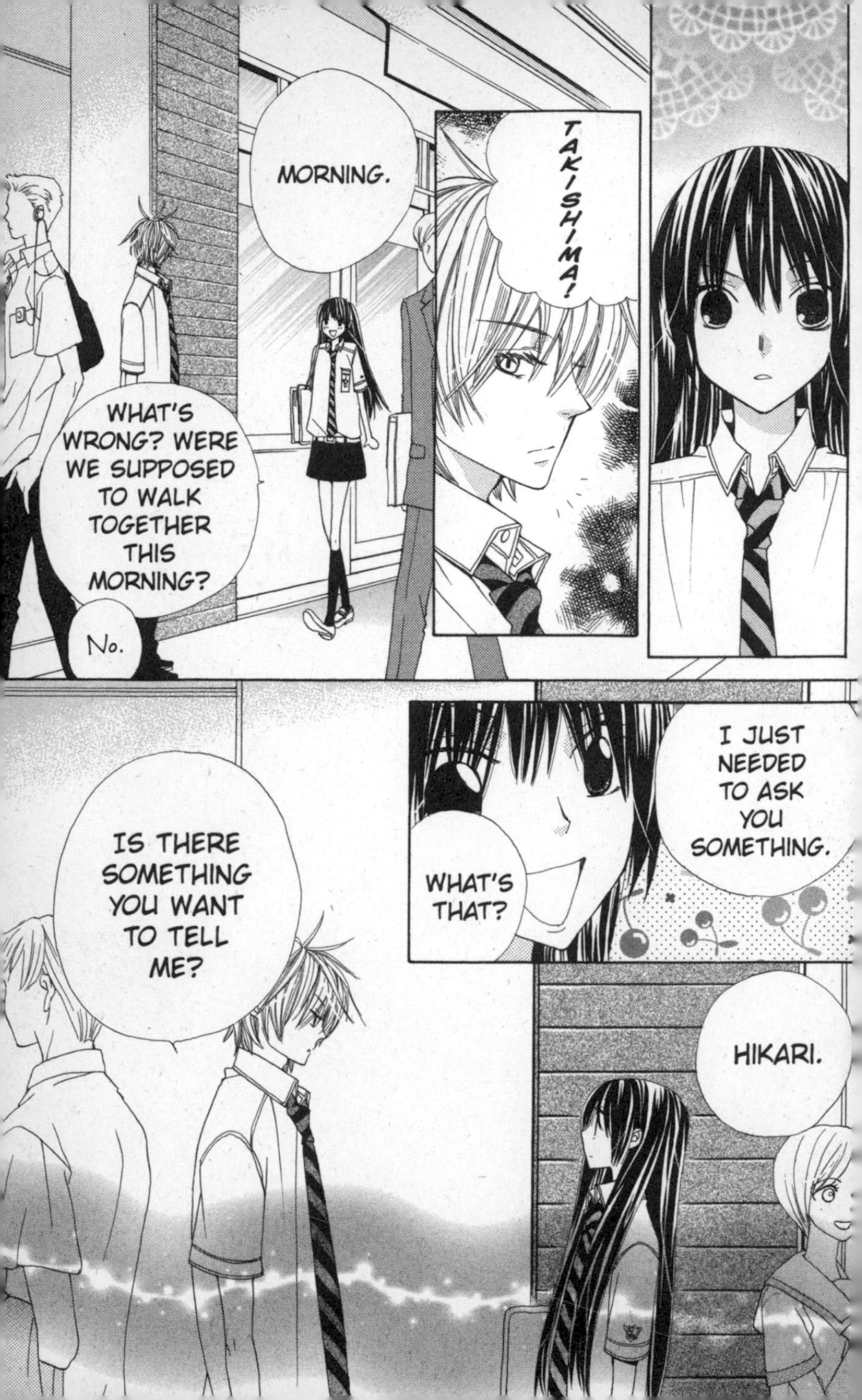
TAKISHIMA!
MORNING.
WHAT'S WRONG? WERE WE SUPPOSED TO WALK TOGETHER THIS MORNING?
No.
I JUST NEEDED TO ASK YOU SOMETHING.
WHAT'S THAT?
HIKARI.
IS THERE SOMETHING YOU WANT TO TELL ME?

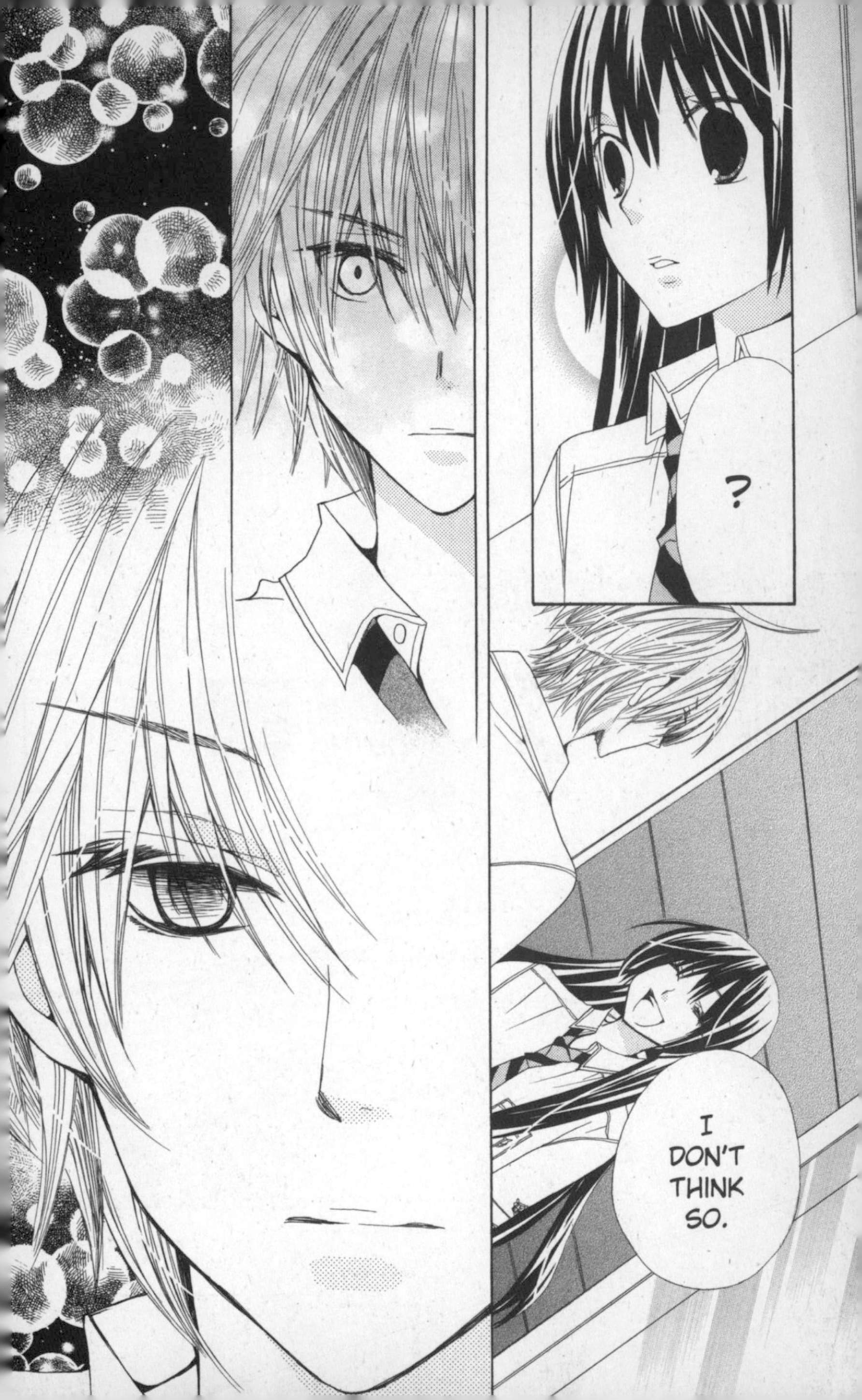
?
I DON'T THINK SO.

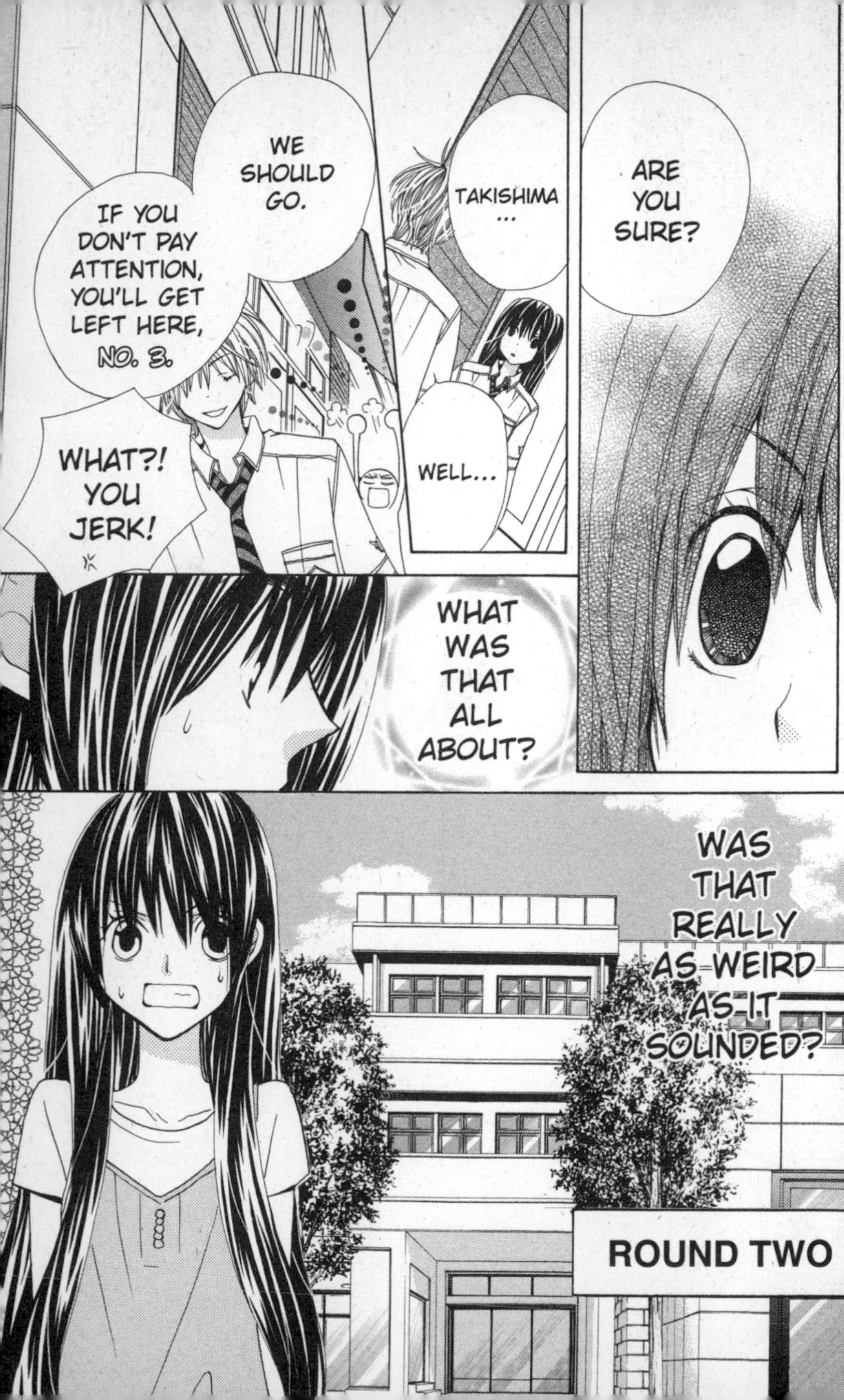
ARE YOU SURE?
TAKISHIMA...
WELL...
WE SHOULD GO.
IF YOU DON'T PAY ATTENTION, YOU'LL GET LEFT HERE, NO. 3.
WHAT?! YOU JERK!
WHAT WAS THAT ALL ABOUT?
WAS THAT REALLY AS WEIRD AS IT SOUNDED?
ROUND TWO

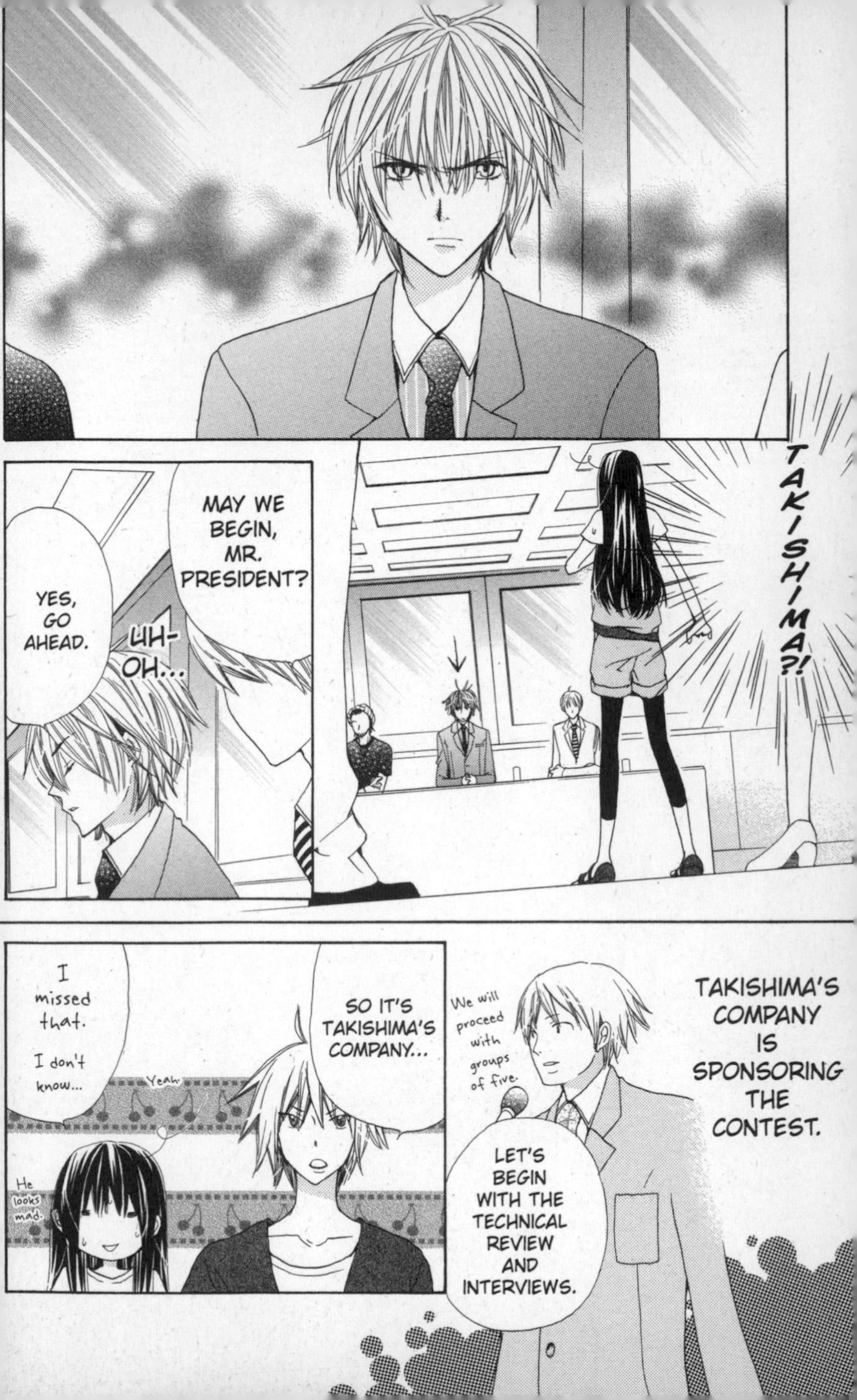
TAKISHIMA?!
MAY WE BEGIN, MR. PRESIDENT?
UH-OH...
YES, GO AHEAD.
TAKISHIMA'S COMPANY IS SPONSORING THE CONTEST.
We will proceed with groups of five.
LET'S BEGIN WITH THE TECHNICAL REVIEW AND INTERVIEWS.
SO IT'S TAKISHIMA'S COMPANY...
I missed that.
I don't know...
Yeah.
He looks mad.

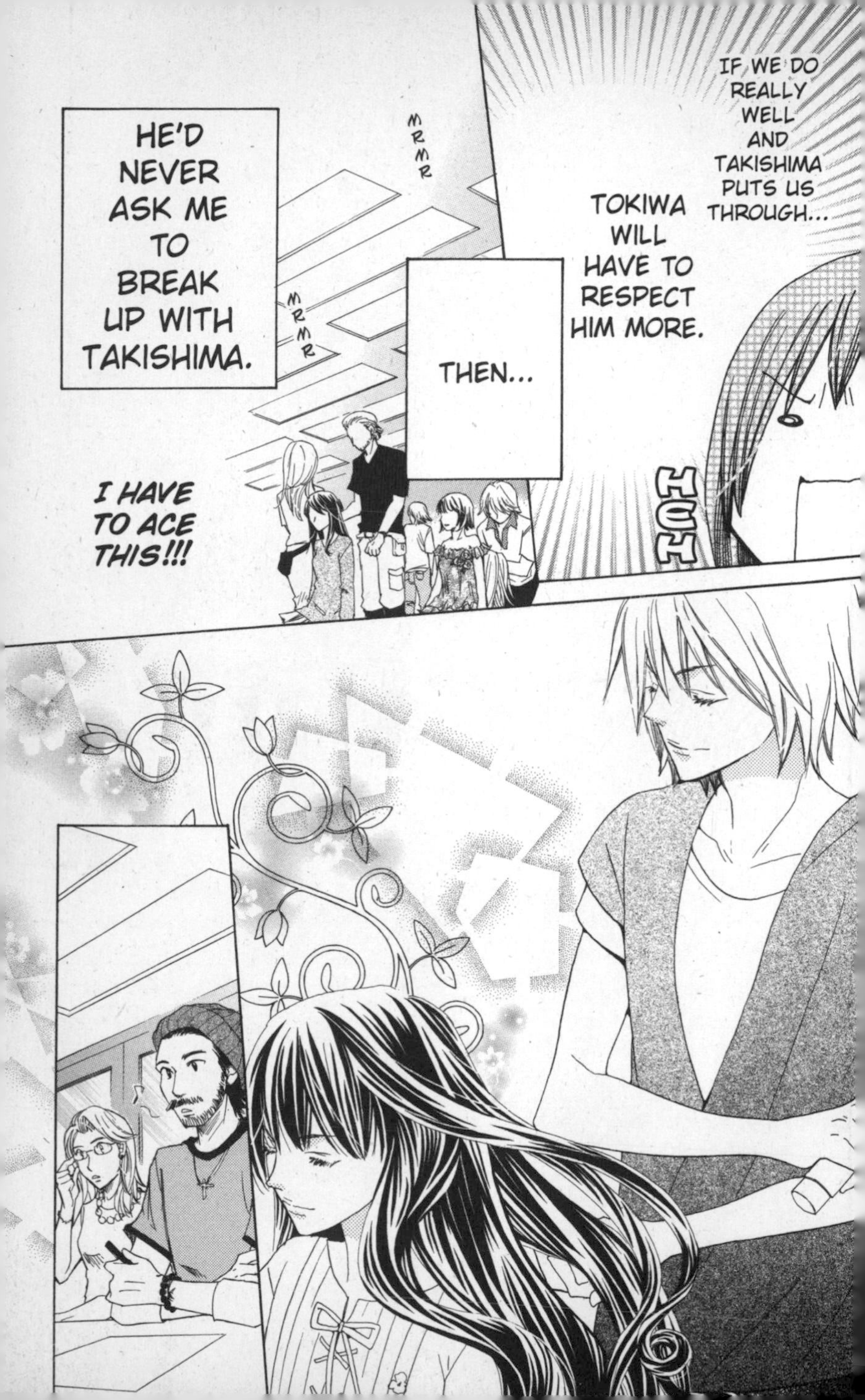
IF WE DO REALLY WELL AND TAKISHIMA PUTS US THROUGH...
TOKIWA WILL HAVE TO RESPECT HIM MORE.
HEH
THEN...
MRMR
HE'D NEVER ASK ME TO BREAK UP WITH TAKISHIMA.
MRMR
I HAVE TO ACE THIS!!!

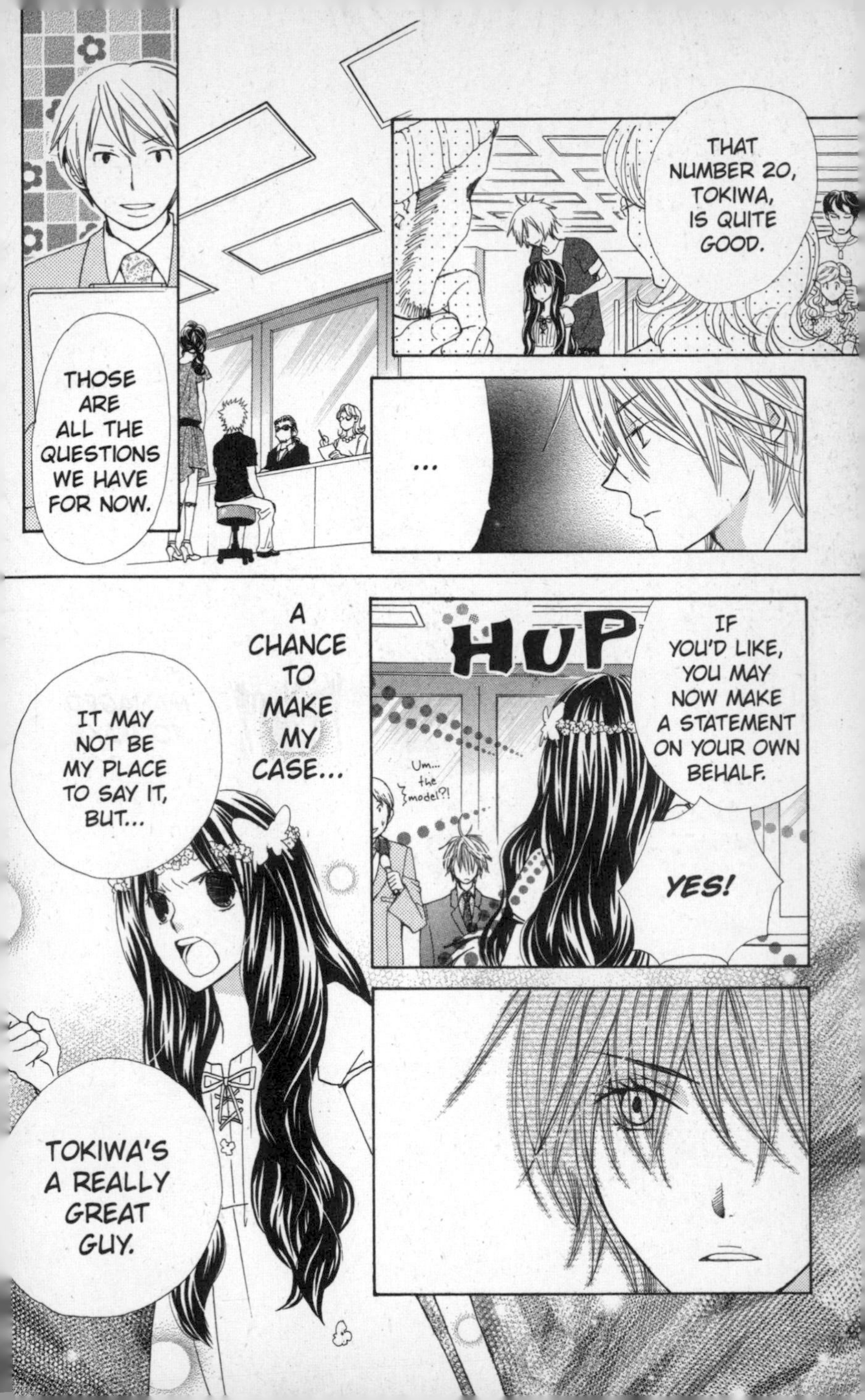
THAT NUMBER 20, TOKIWA, IS QUITE GOOD.
...
THOSE ARE ALL THE QUESTIONS WE HAVE FOR NOW.
HUP
IF YOU'D LIKE, YOU MAY NOW MAKE A STATEMENT ON YOUR OWN BEHALF.
Um... the model?!
YES!
A CHANCE TO MAKE MY CASE...
IT MAY NOT BE MY PLACE TO SAY IT, BUT...
TOKIWA'S A REALLY GREAT GUY.

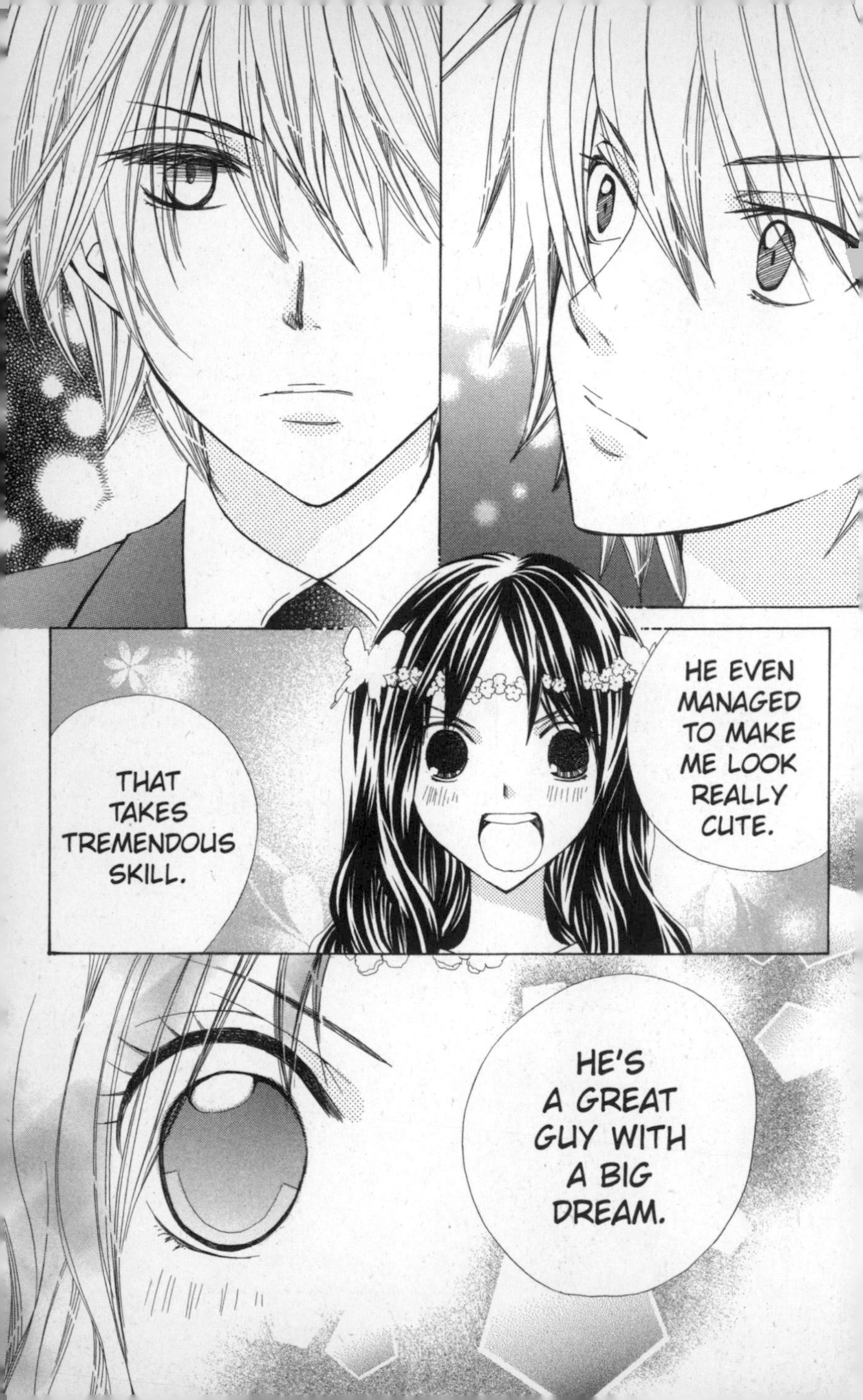
HE EVEN MANAGED TO MAKE ME LOOK REALLY CUTE.
THAT TAKES TREMENDOUS SKILL.
HE'S A GREAT GUY WITH A BIG DREAM.

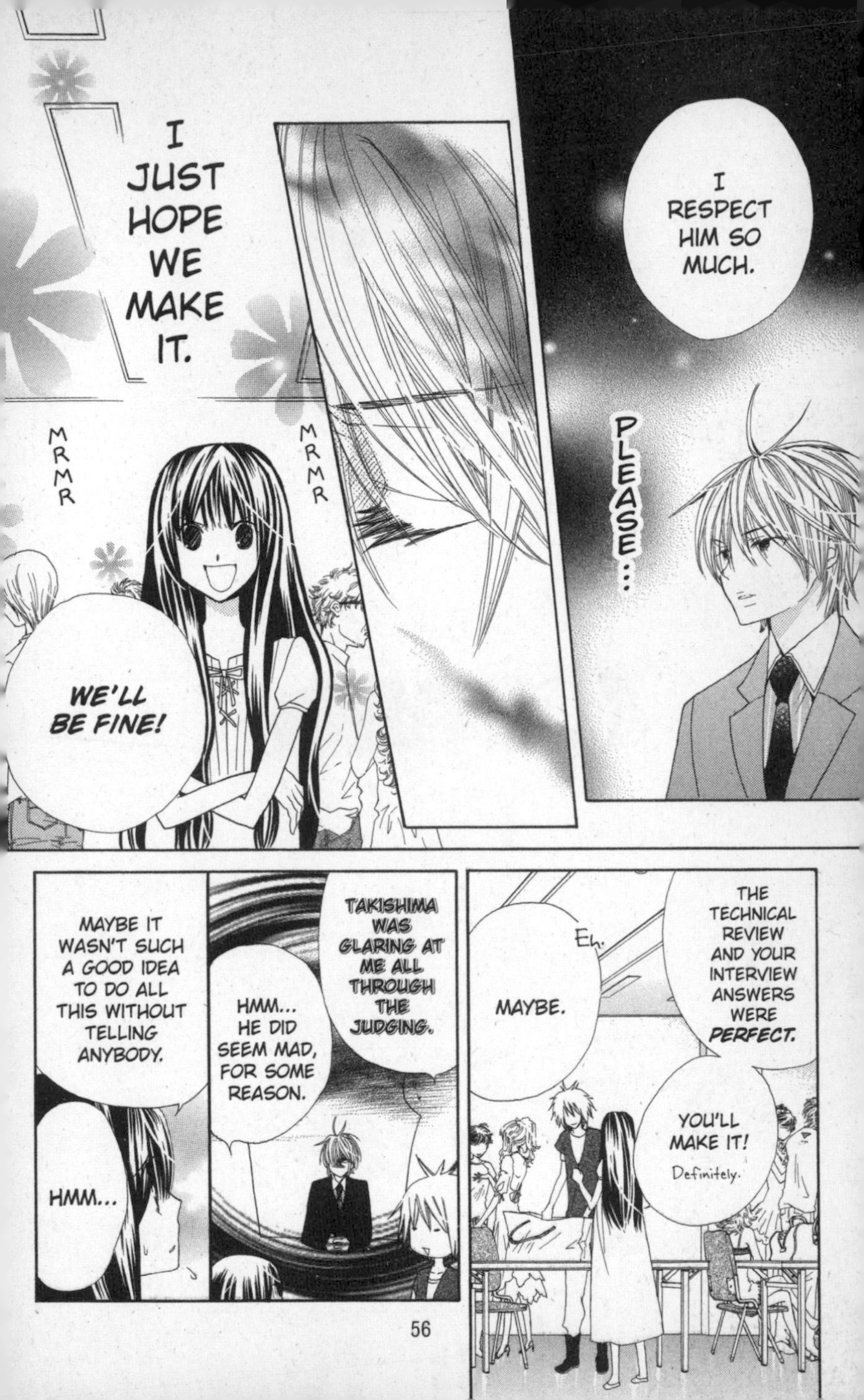
I RESPECT HIM SO MUCH.
PLEASE...
I JUST HOPE WE MAKE IT.
MRMR
MRMR
WE'LL BE FINE!
THE TECHNICAL REVIEW AND YOUR INTERVIEW ANSWERS WERE PERFECT.
Eh.
MAYBE.
YOU'LL MAKE IT!
Definitely.
TAKISHIMA WAS GLARING AT ME ALL THROUGH THE JUDGING.
HMM... HE DID SEEM MAD, FOR SOME REASON.
MAYBE IT WASN'T SUCH A GOOD IDEA TO DO ALL THIS WITHOUT TELLING ANYBODY.
HMM...

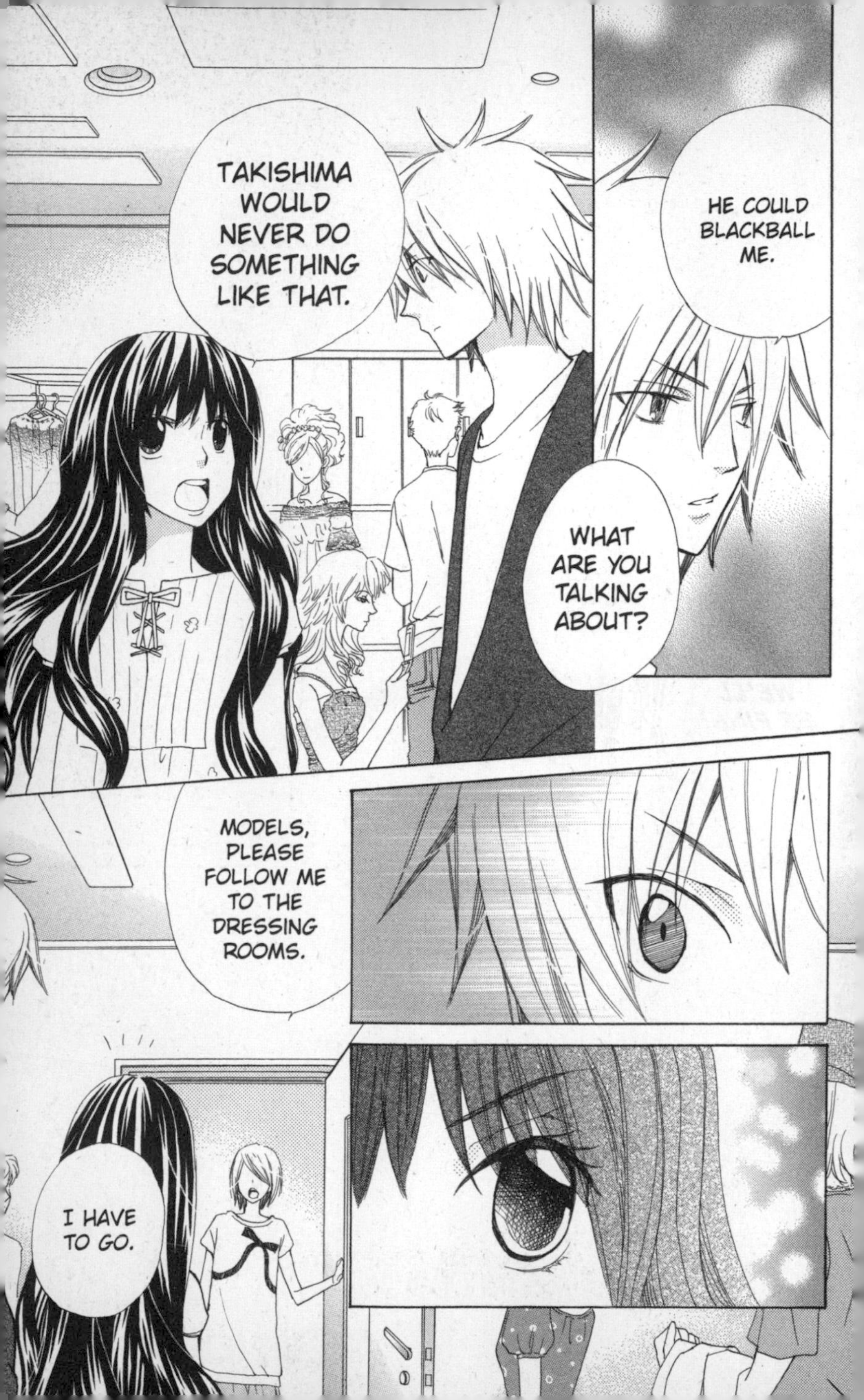
HE COULD BLACKBALL ME.
WHAT ARE YOU TALKING ABOUT?
TAKISHIMA WOULD NEVER DO SOMETHING LIKE THAT.
MODELS, PLEASE FOLLOW ME TO THE DRESSING ROOMS.
I HAVE TO GO.

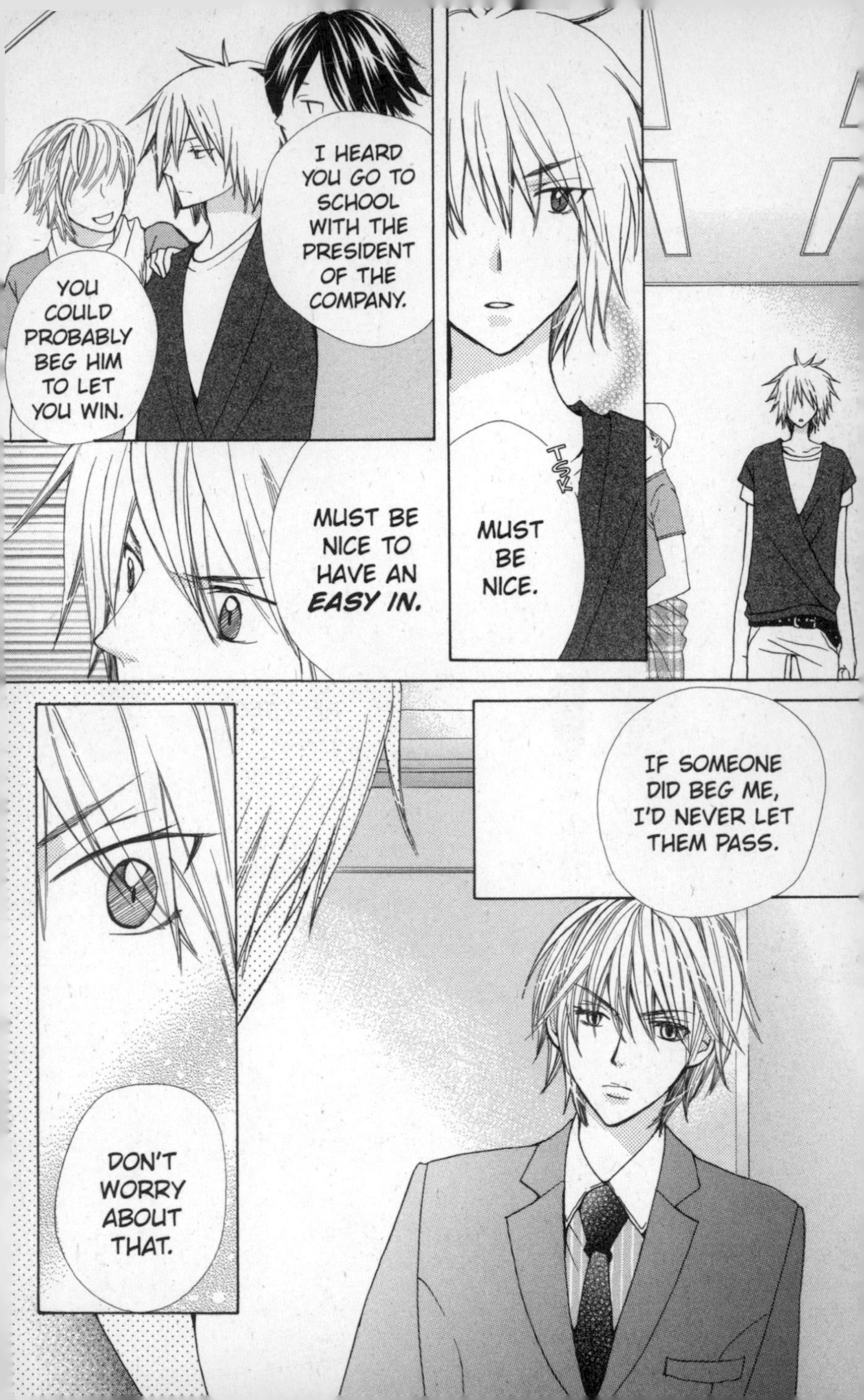
TSK
MUST BE NICE.
I HEARD YOU GO TO SCHOOL WITH THE PRESIDENT OF THE COMPANY.
YOU COULD PROBABLY BEG HIM TO LET YOU WIN.
MUST BE NICE TO HAVE AN *EASY IN.*
IF SOMEONE DID BEG ME, I'D NEVER LET THEM PASS.
DON'T WORRY ABOUT THAT.

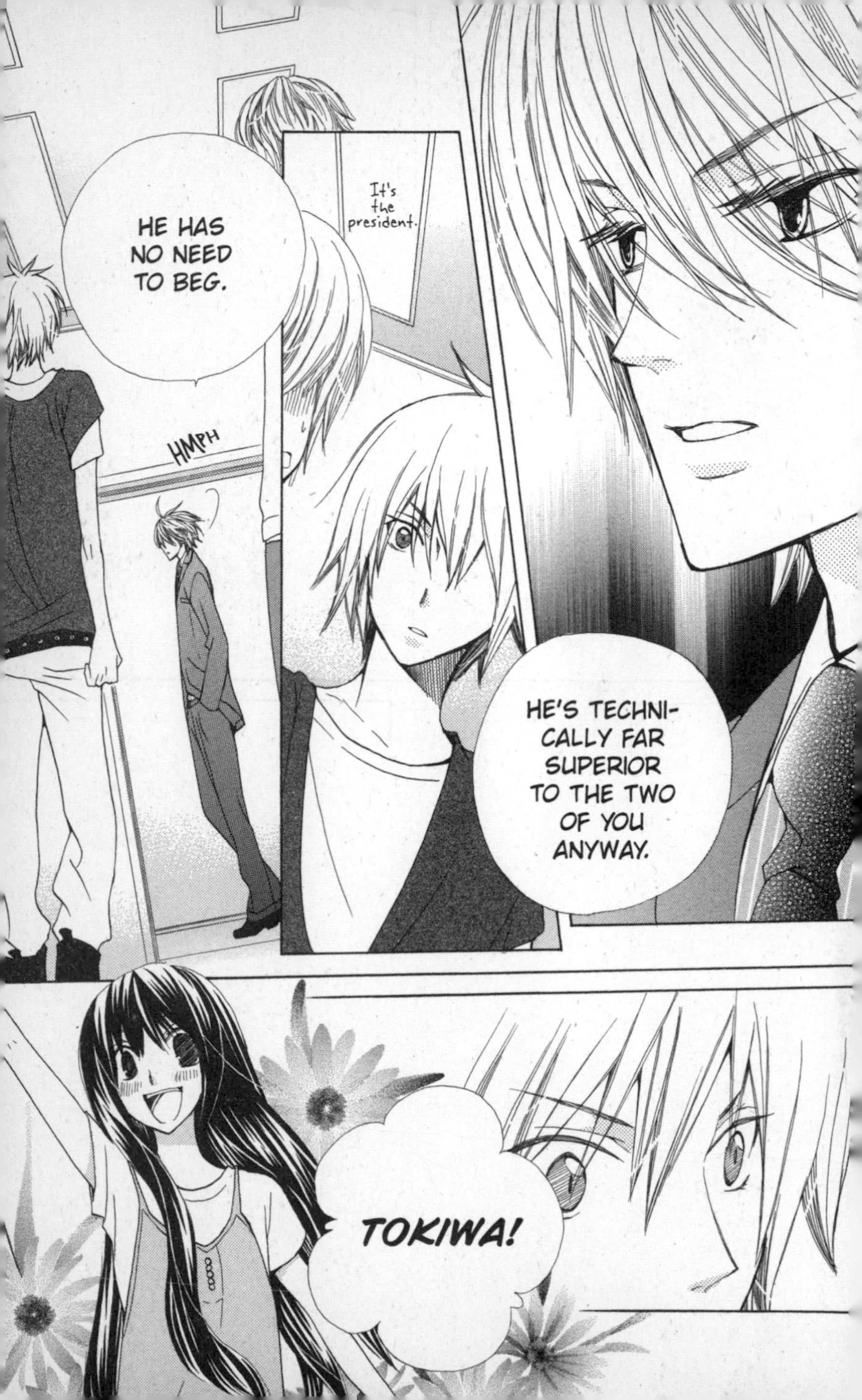
HE'S TECHNI-CALLY FAR SUPERIOR TO THE TWO OF YOU ANYWAY.
It's the president.
HE HAS NO NEED TO BEG.
HMPH
TOKIWA!

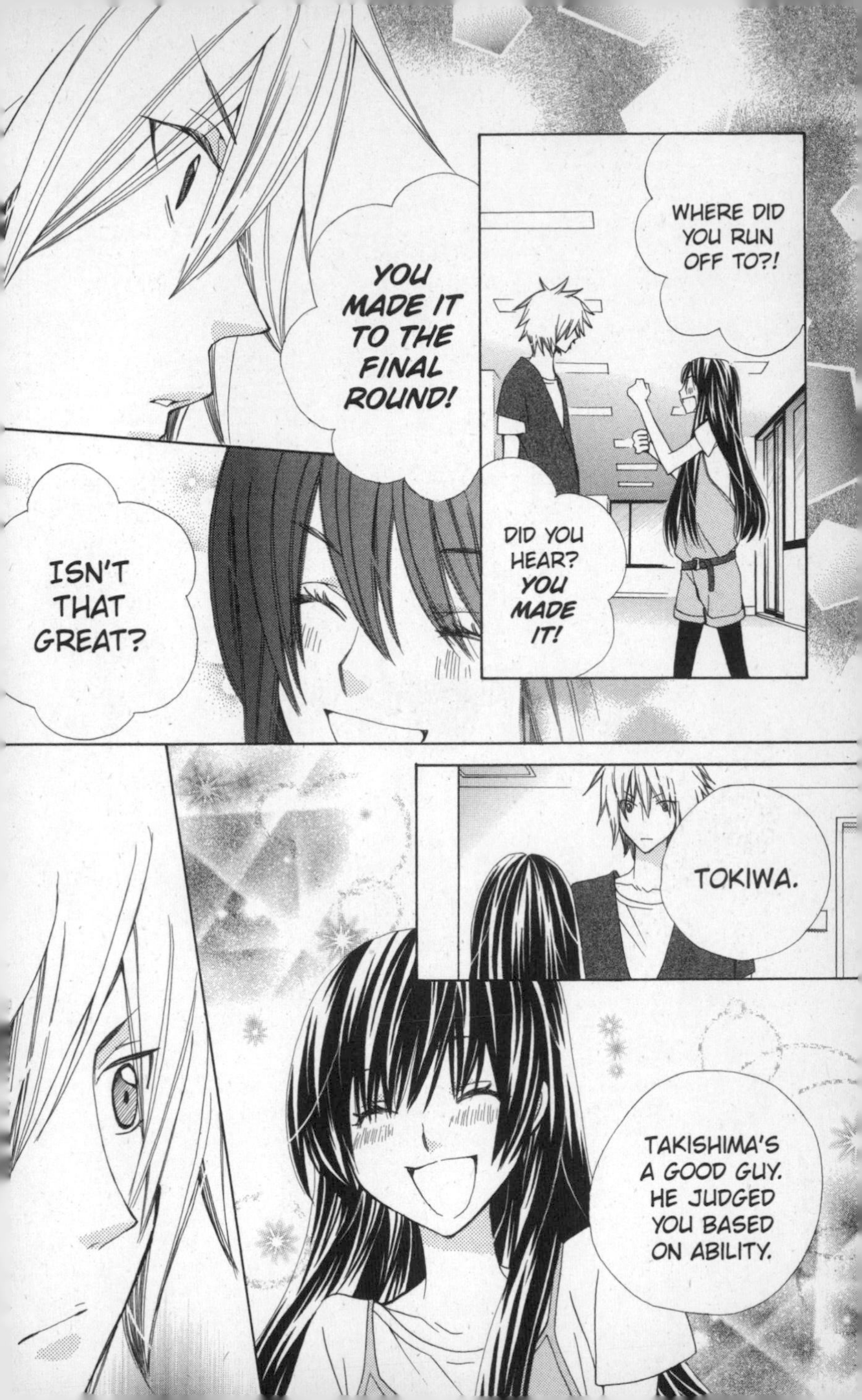
WHERE DID YOU RUN OFF TO?!
DID YOU HEAR? YOU MADE IT!
YOU MADE IT TO THE FINAL ROUND!
ISN'T THAT GREAT?
TOKIWA.
TAKISHIMA'S A GOOD GUY. HE JUDGED YOU BASED ON ABILITY.

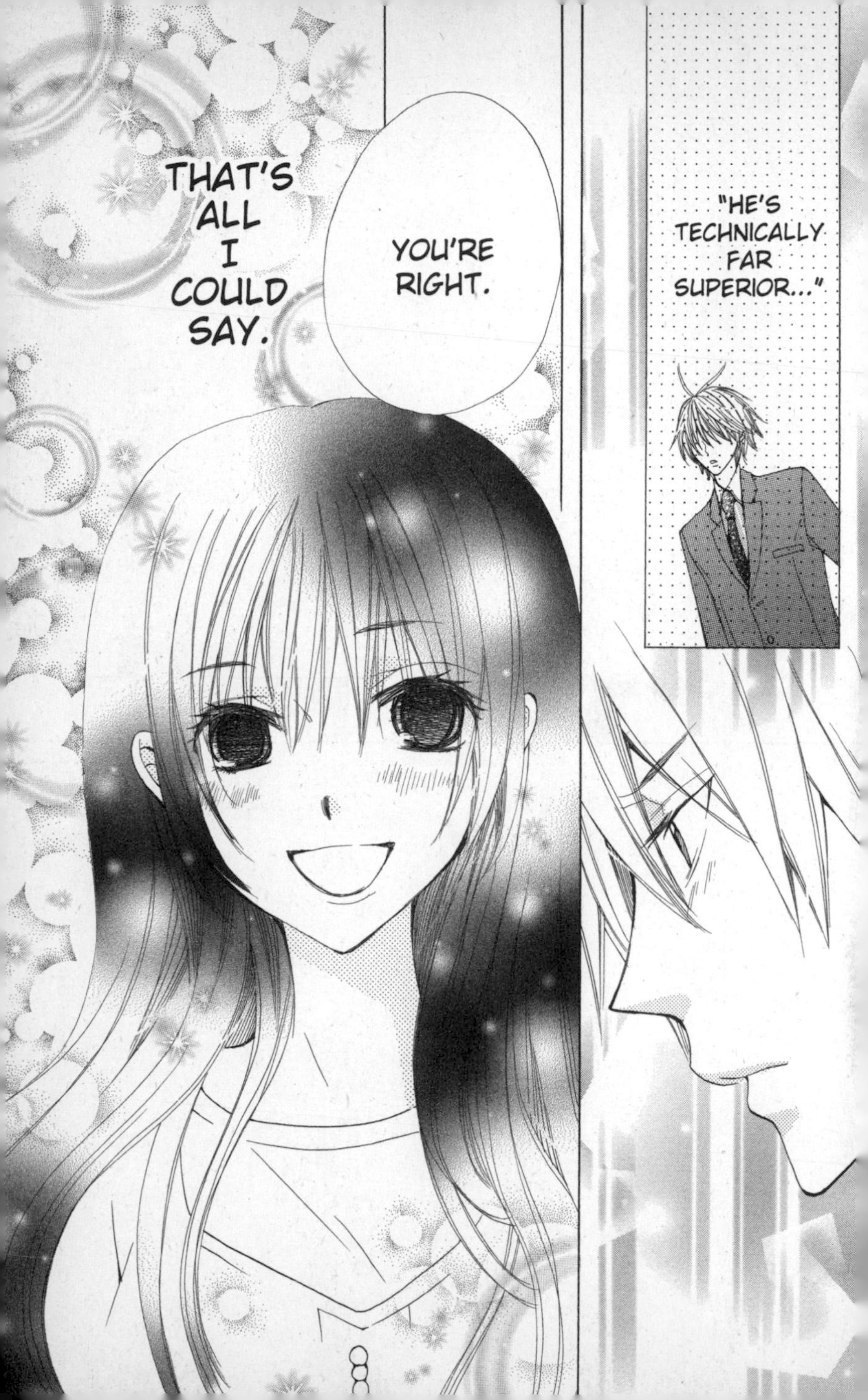
"HE'S TECHNICALLY FAR SUPERIOR..."
YOU'RE RIGHT.
THAT'S ALL I COULD SAY.

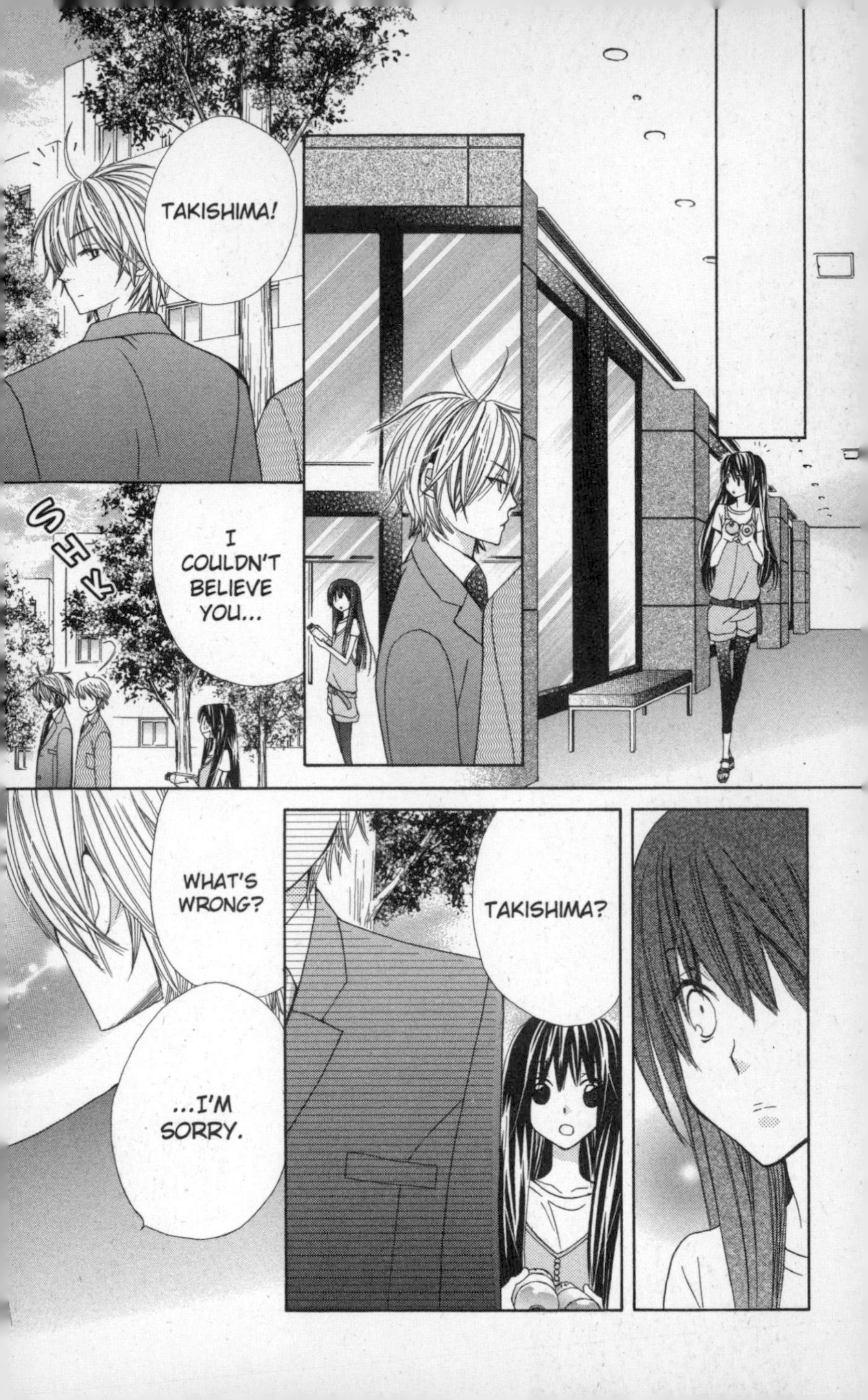
TAKISHIMA!
SHK
I COULDN'T BELIEVE YOU...
TAKISHIMA?
WHAT'S WRONG?
...I'M SORRY.

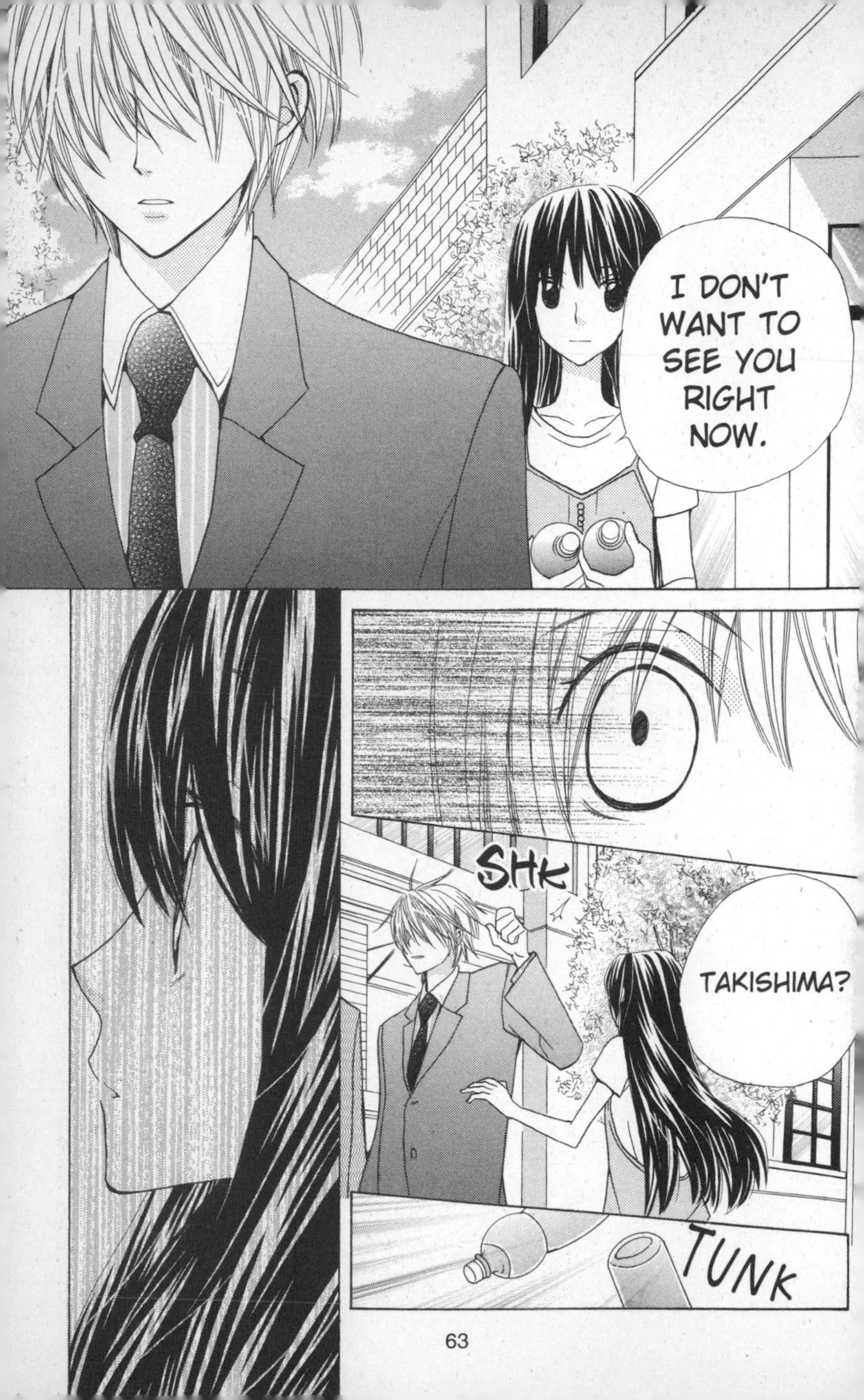
I DON'T WANT TO SEE YOU RIGHT NOW.
SHK
TAKISHIMA?
TUNK

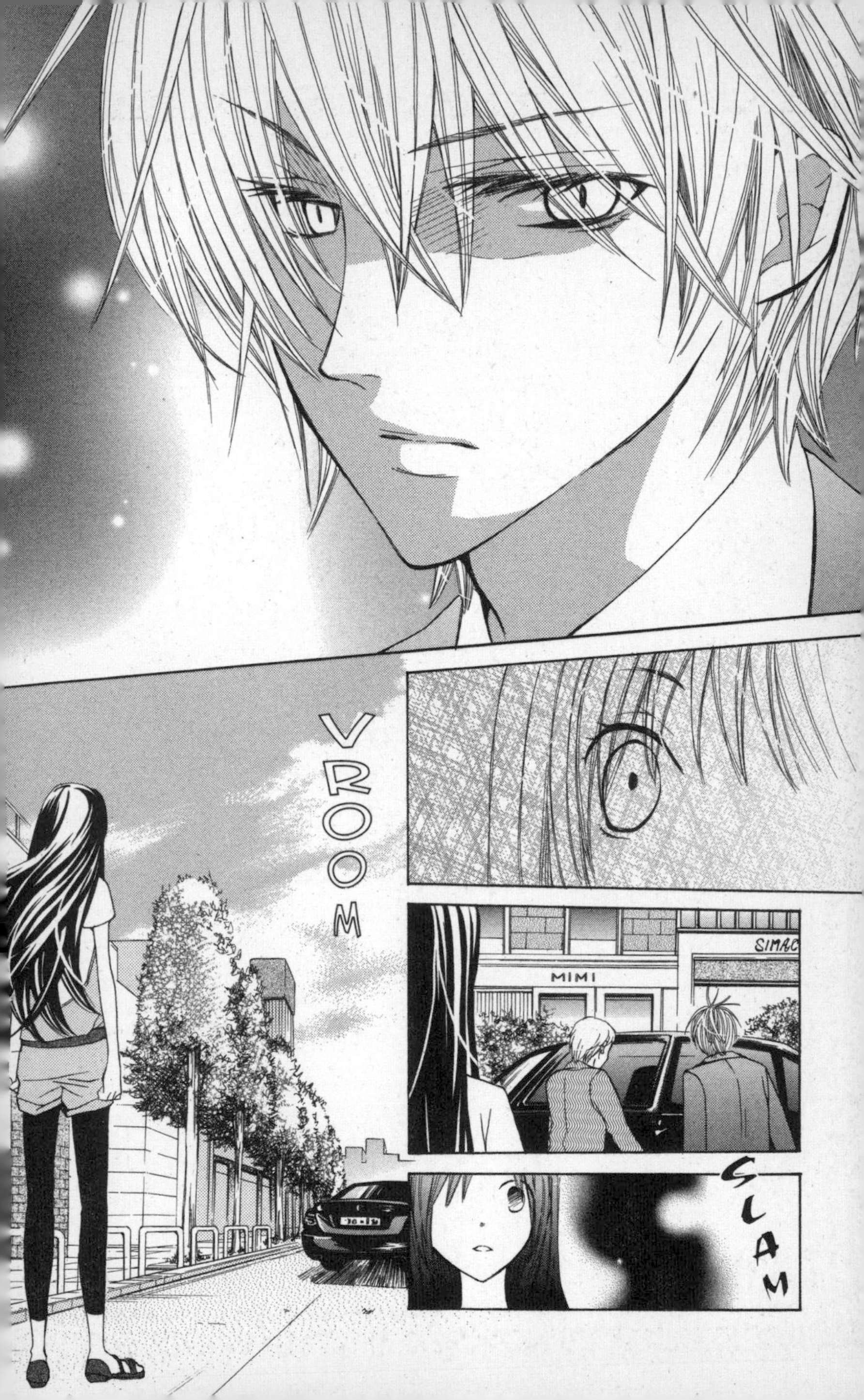
SIMAC
MIMI
SLAM
VROOM

Chapter 90

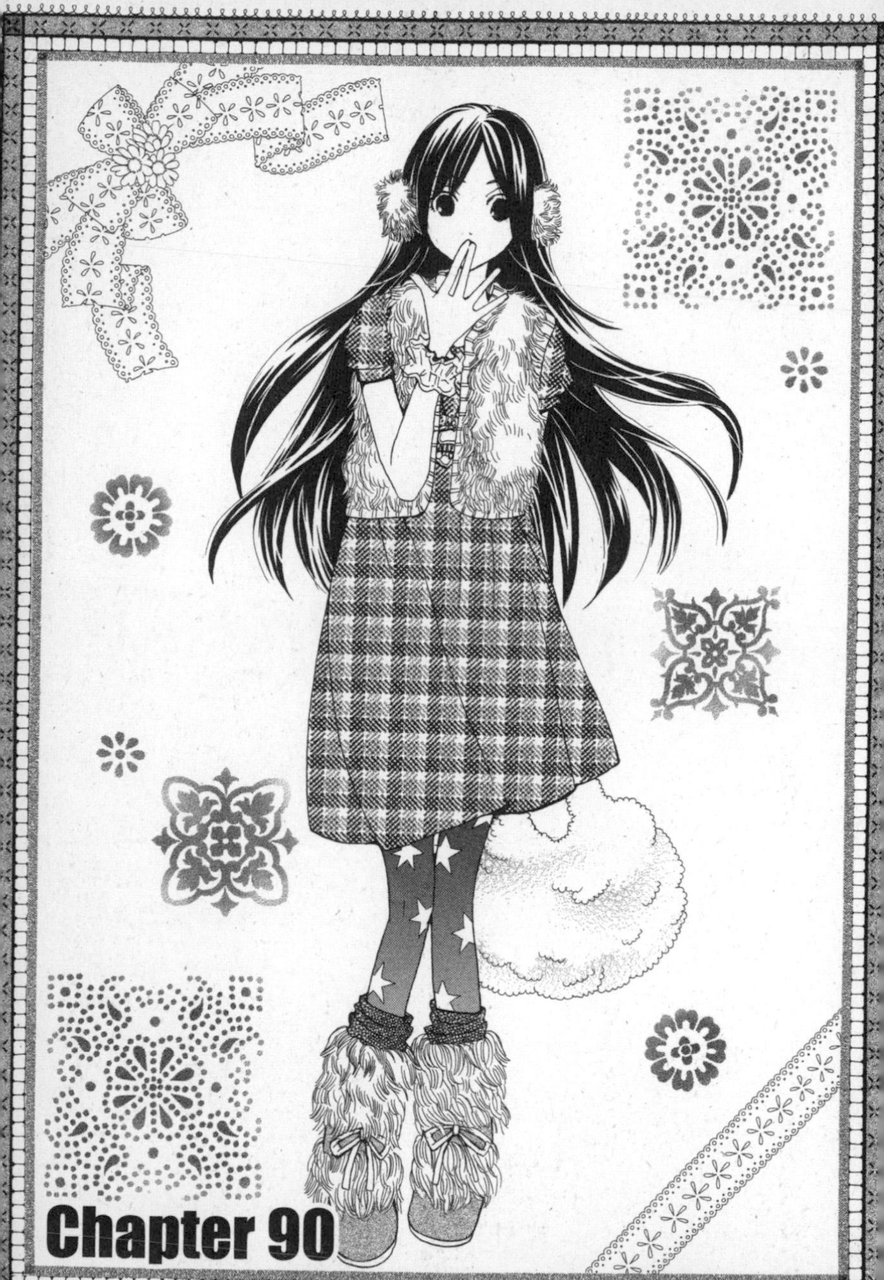

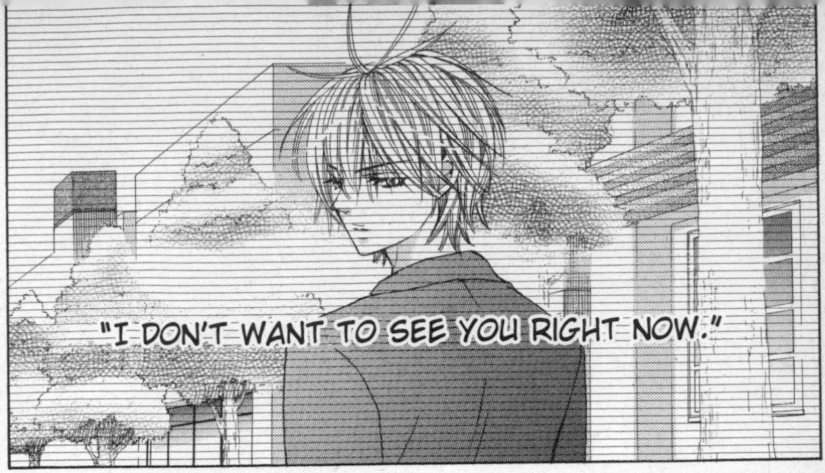
"I DON'T WANT TO SEE YOU RIGHT NOW."

COLD WORDS. COLD EYES.

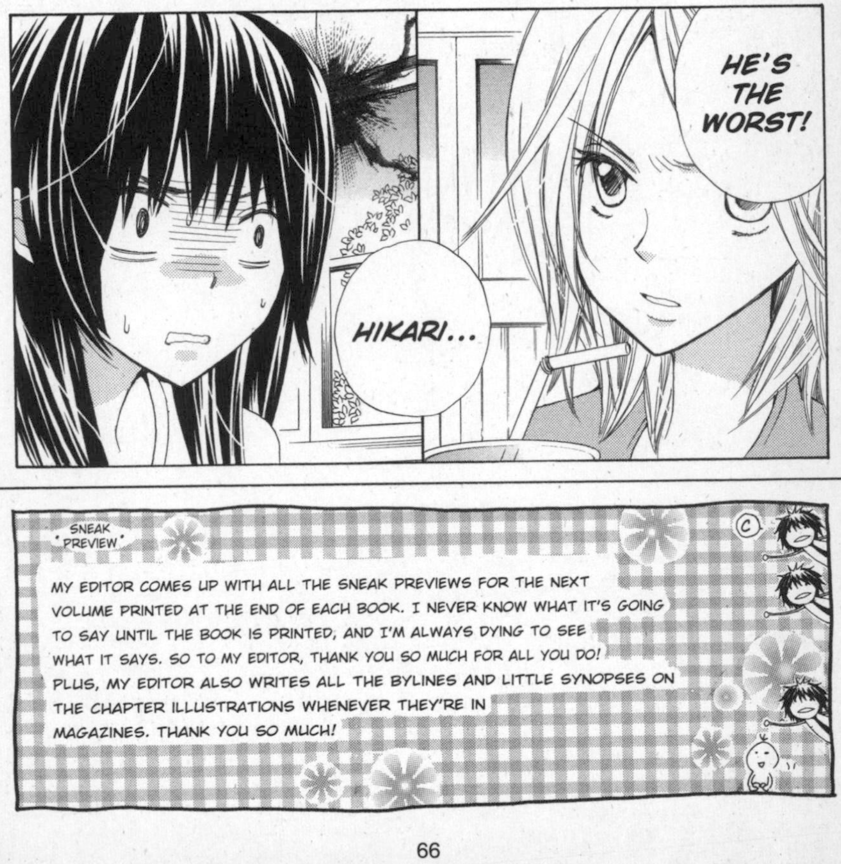
HE'S THE WORST!
HIKARI...

SNEAK PREVIEW

MY EDITOR COMES UP WITH ALL THE SNEAK PREVIEWS FOR THE NEXT VOLUME PRINTED AT THE END OF EACH BOOK. I NEVER KNOW WHAT IT'S GOING TO SAY UNTIL THE BOOK IS PRINTED, AND I'M ALWAYS DYING TO SEE WHAT IT SAYS. SO TO MY EDITOR, THANK YOU SO MUCH FOR ALL YOU DO! PLUS, MY EDITOR ALSO WRITES ALL THE BYLINES AND LITTLE SYNOPSES ON THE CHAPTER ILLUSTRATIONS WHENEVER THEY'RE IN MAGAZINES. THANK YOU SO MUCH!

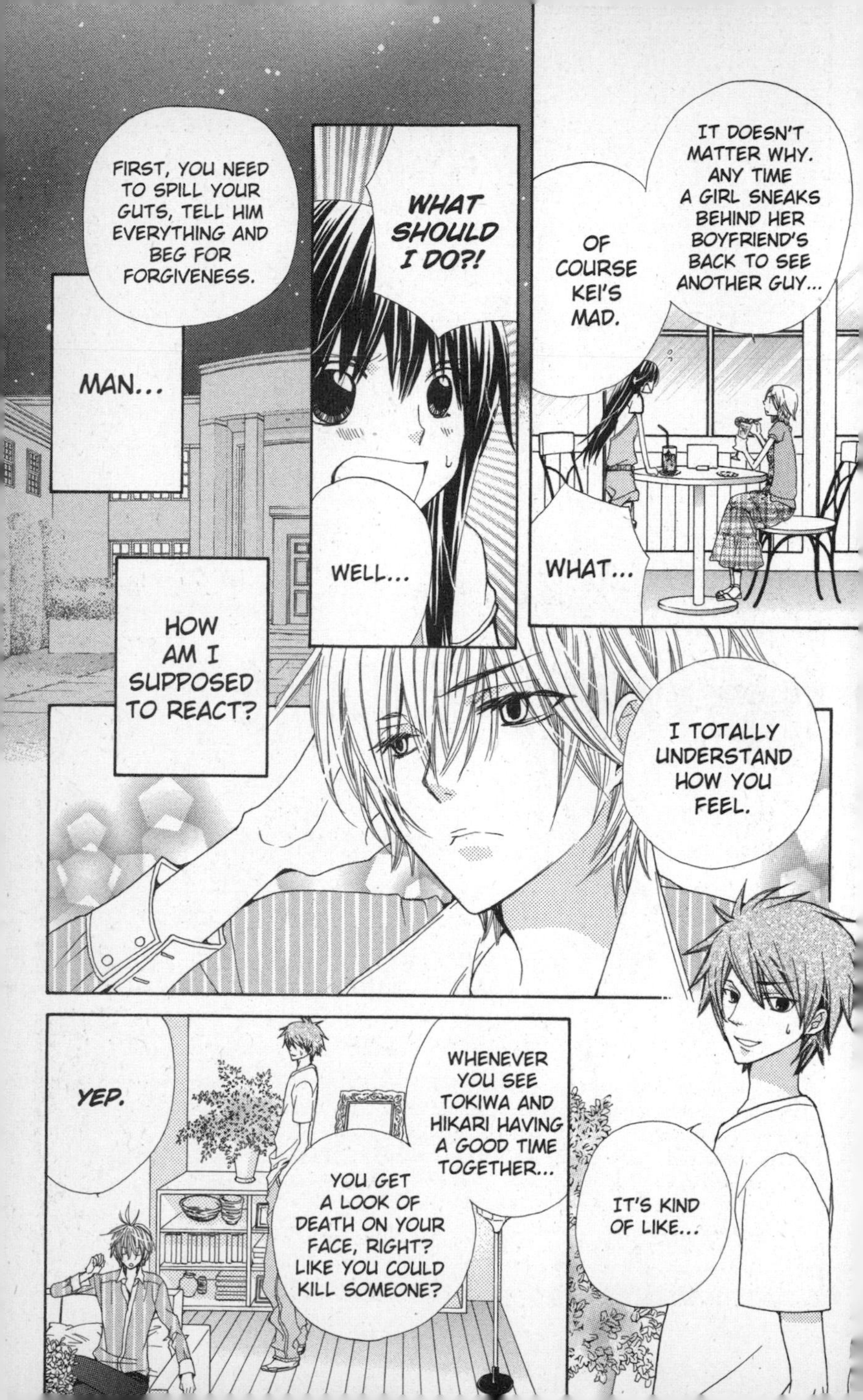
IT DOESN'T MATTER WHY. ANY TIME A GIRL SNEAKS BEHIND HER BOYFRIEND'S BACK TO SEE ANOTHER GUY...
OF COURSE KEI'S MAD.
WHAT...
WHAT SHOULD I DO?!
WELL...
FIRST, YOU NEED TO SPILL YOUR GUTS, TELL HIM EVERYTHING AND BEG FOR FORGIVENESS.
MAN...
HOW AM I SUPPOSED TO REACT?
I TOTALLY UNDERSTAND HOW YOU FEEL.
IT'S KIND OF LIKE...
WHENEVER YOU SEE TOKIWA AND HIKARI HAVING A GOOD TIME TOGETHER...
YOU GET A LOOK OF DEATH ON YOUR FACE, RIGHT? LIKE YOU COULD KILL SOMEONE?
YEP.

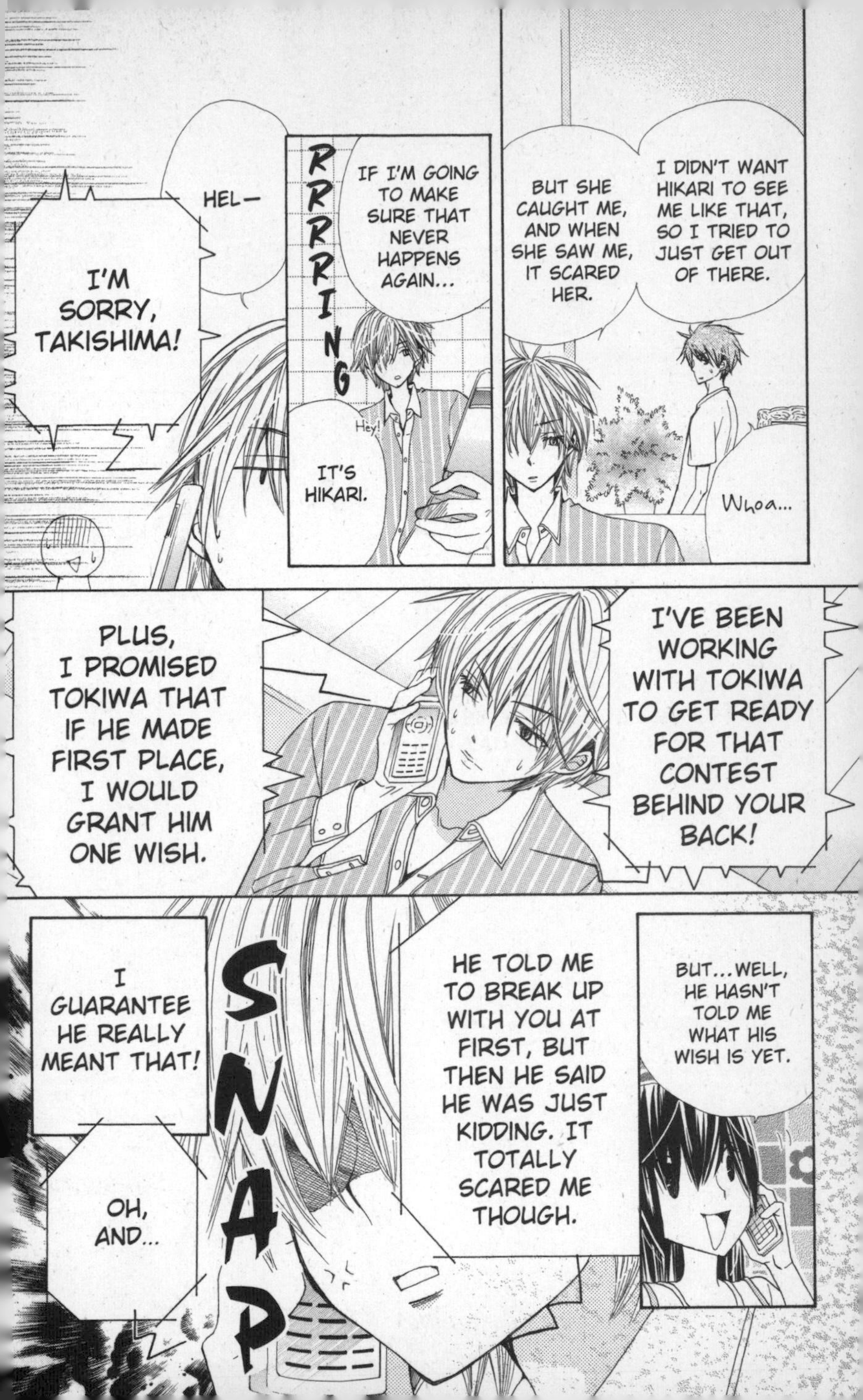
I DIDN'T WANT HIKARI TO SEE ME LIKE THAT, SO I TRIED TO JUST GET OUT OF THERE.
BUT SHE CAUGHT ME, AND WHEN SHE SAW ME, IT SCARED HER.
Whoa...
IF I'M GOING TO MAKE SURE THAT NEVER HAPPENS AGAIN...
RRRRING
Hey!
IT'S HIKARI.
HEL—
I'M SORRY, TAKISHIMA!
I'VE BEEN WORKING WITH TOKIWA TO GET READY FOR THAT CONTEST BEHIND YOUR BACK!
PLUS, I PROMISED TOKIWA THAT IF HE MADE FIRST PLACE, I WOULD GRANT HIM ONE WISH.
BUT...WELL, HE HASN'T TOLD ME WHAT HIS WISH IS YET.
HE TOLD ME TO BREAK UP WITH YOU AT FIRST, BUT THEN HE SAID HE WAS JUST KIDDING. IT TOTALLY SCARED ME THOUGH.
I GUARANTEE HE REALLY MEANT THAT!
OH, AND...
SNAP

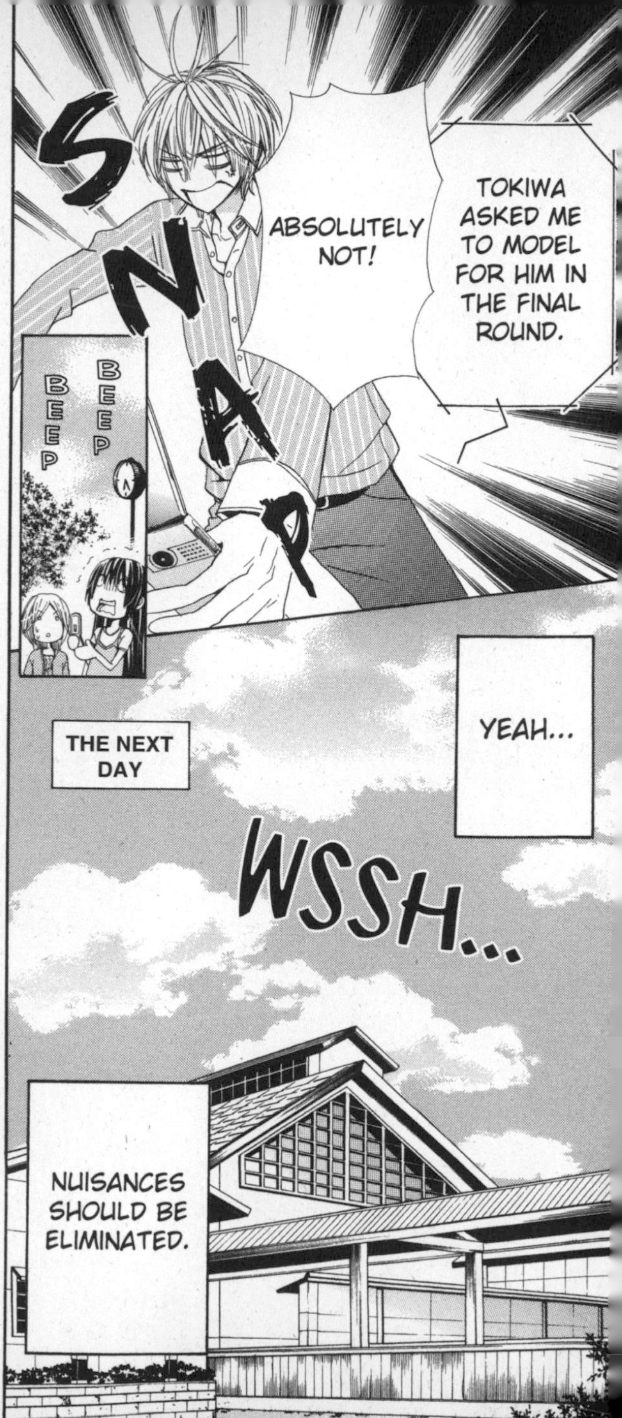
TOKIWA ASKED ME TO MODEL FOR HIM IN THE FINAL ROUND.
ABSOLUTELY NOT!
SNAP
BEEP BEEP
BEEP
YEAH...
THE NEXT DAY
WSSH...
NUISANCES SHOULD BE ELIMINATED.

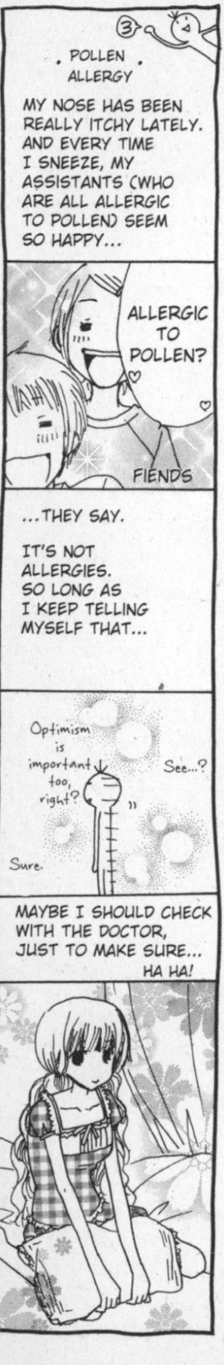
3
POLLEN ALLERGY
MY NOSE HAS BEEN REALLY ITCHY LATELY. AND EVERY TIME I SNEEZE, MY ASSISTANTS (WHO ARE ALL ALLERGIC TO POLLEN) SEEM SO HAPPY...
ALLERGIC TO POLLEN?
FIENDS
...THEY SAY.
IT'S NOT ALLERGIES. SO LONG AS I KEEP TELLING MYSELF THAT...
Optimism is important too, right?
See...?
Sure.
MAYBE I SHOULD CHECK WITH THE DOCTOR, JUST TO MAKE SURE...
HA HA!

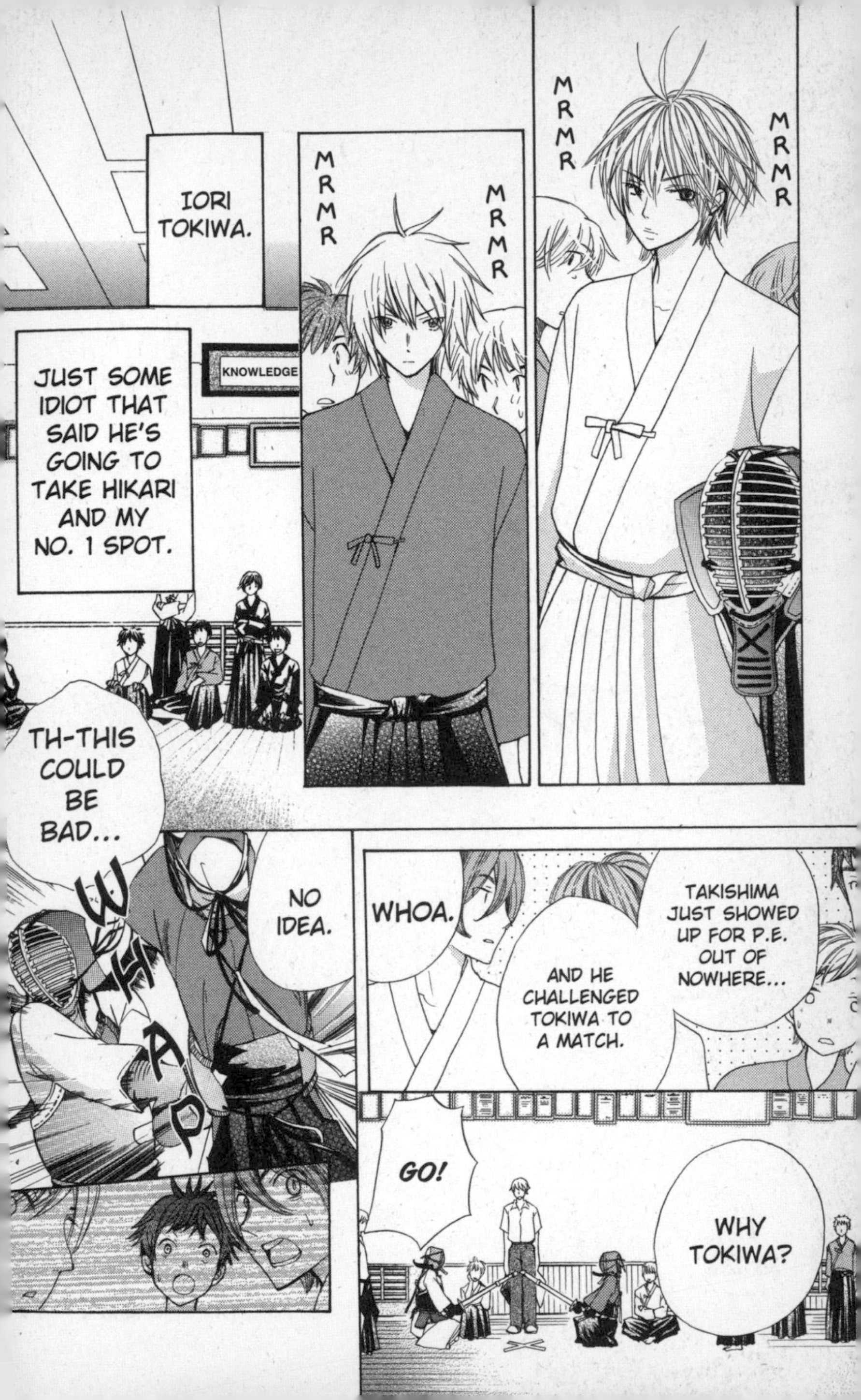
MRMR
MRMR
MRMR
MRMR
IORI TOKIWA.
JUST SOME IDIOT THAT SAID HE'S GOING TO TAKE HIKARI AND MY NO. 1 SPOT.
KNOWLEDGE
TAKISHIMA JUST SHOWED UP FOR P.E. OUT OF NOWHERE...
AND HE CHALLENGED TOKIWA TO A MATCH.
WHOA.
WHY TOKIWA?
GO!
NO IDEA.
TH-THIS COULD BE BAD...
WHAP

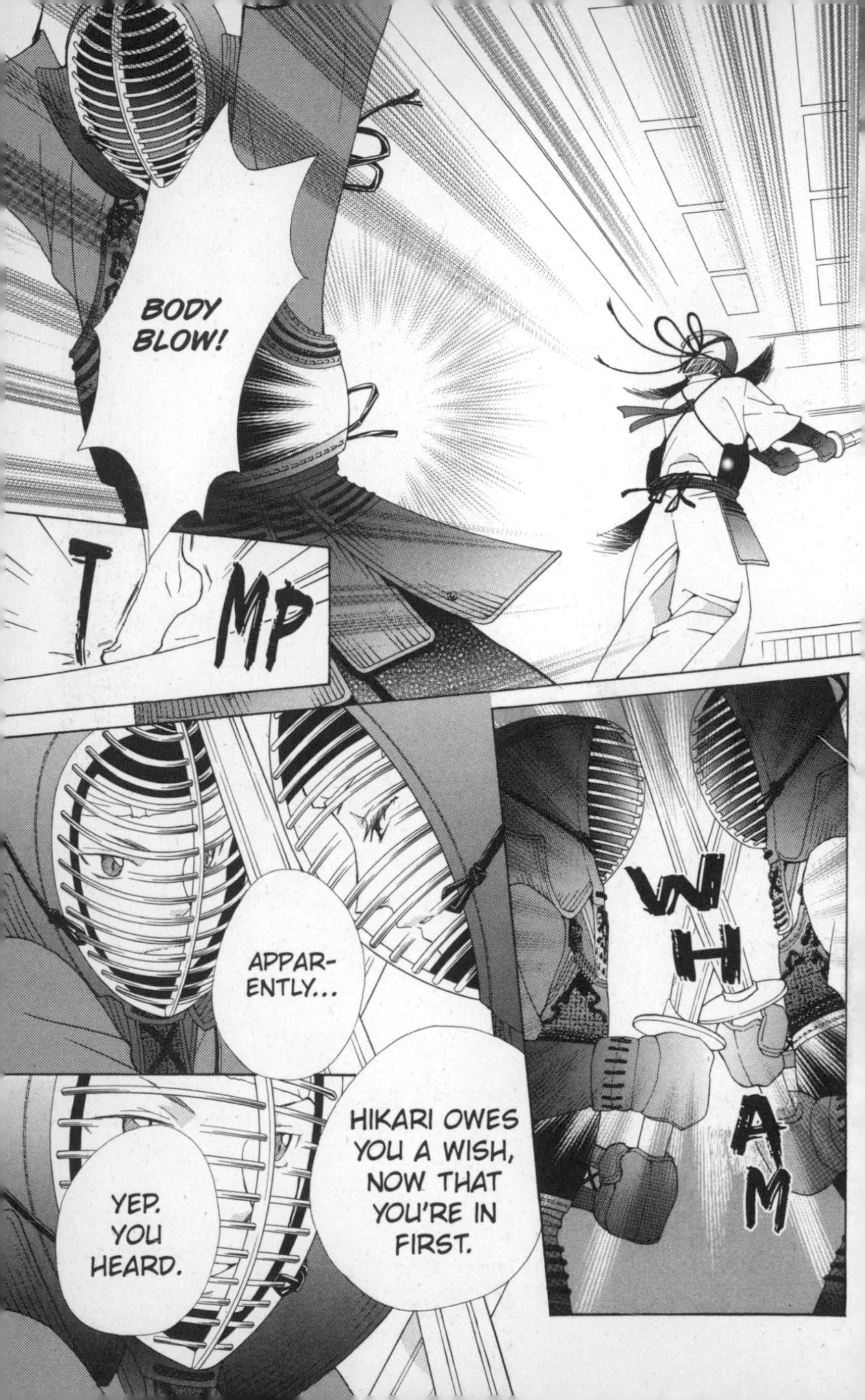
BODY BLOW!
T MP
WHAM
APPAR-ENTLY...
HIKARI OWES YOU A WISH, NOW THAT YOU'RE IN FIRST.
YEP. YOU HEARD.

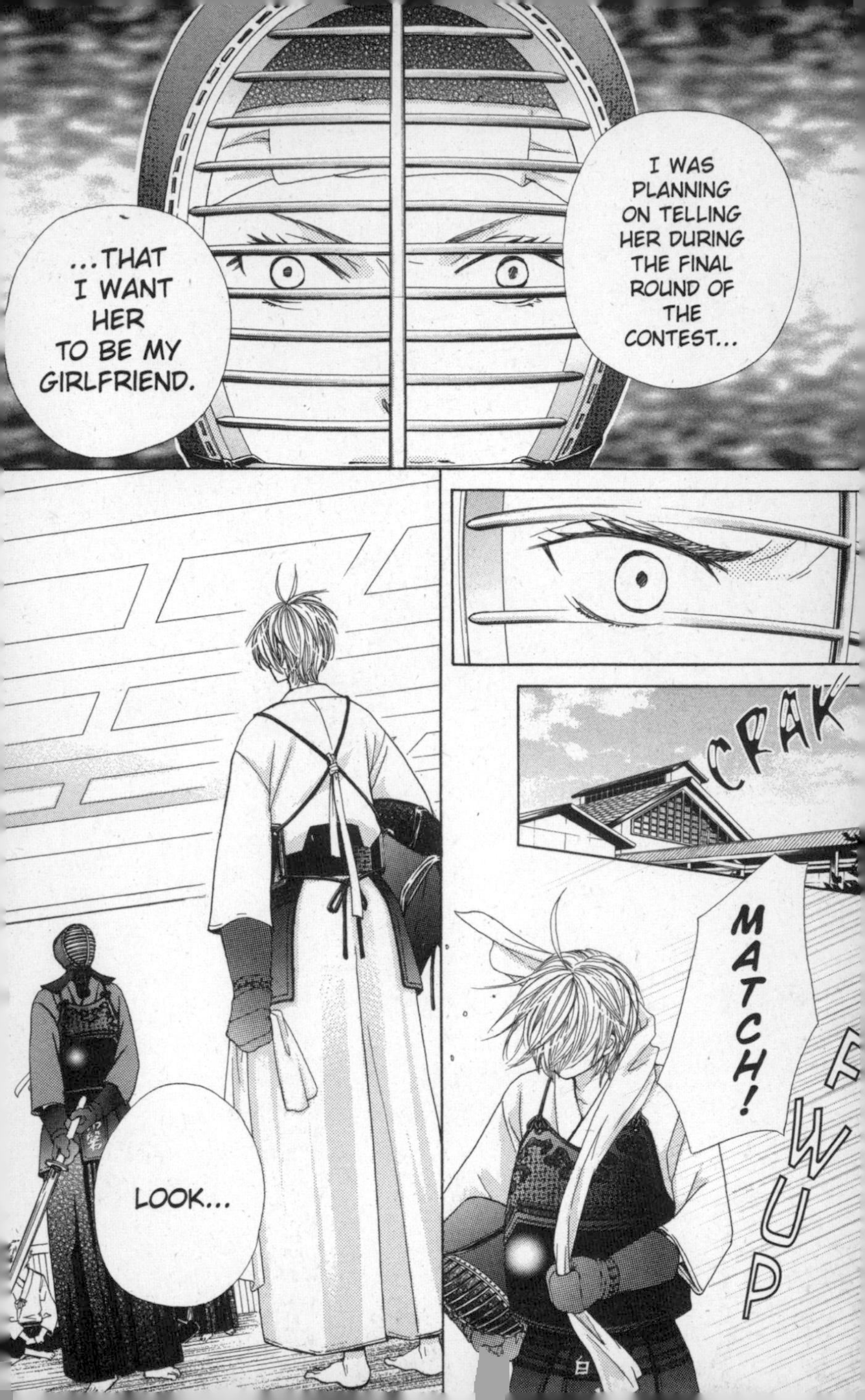
I WAS PLANNING ON TELLING HER DURING THE FINAL ROUND OF THE CONTEST...
...THAT I WANT HER TO BE MY GIRLFRIEND.
CRAK
MATCH!
FWUP
LOOK...

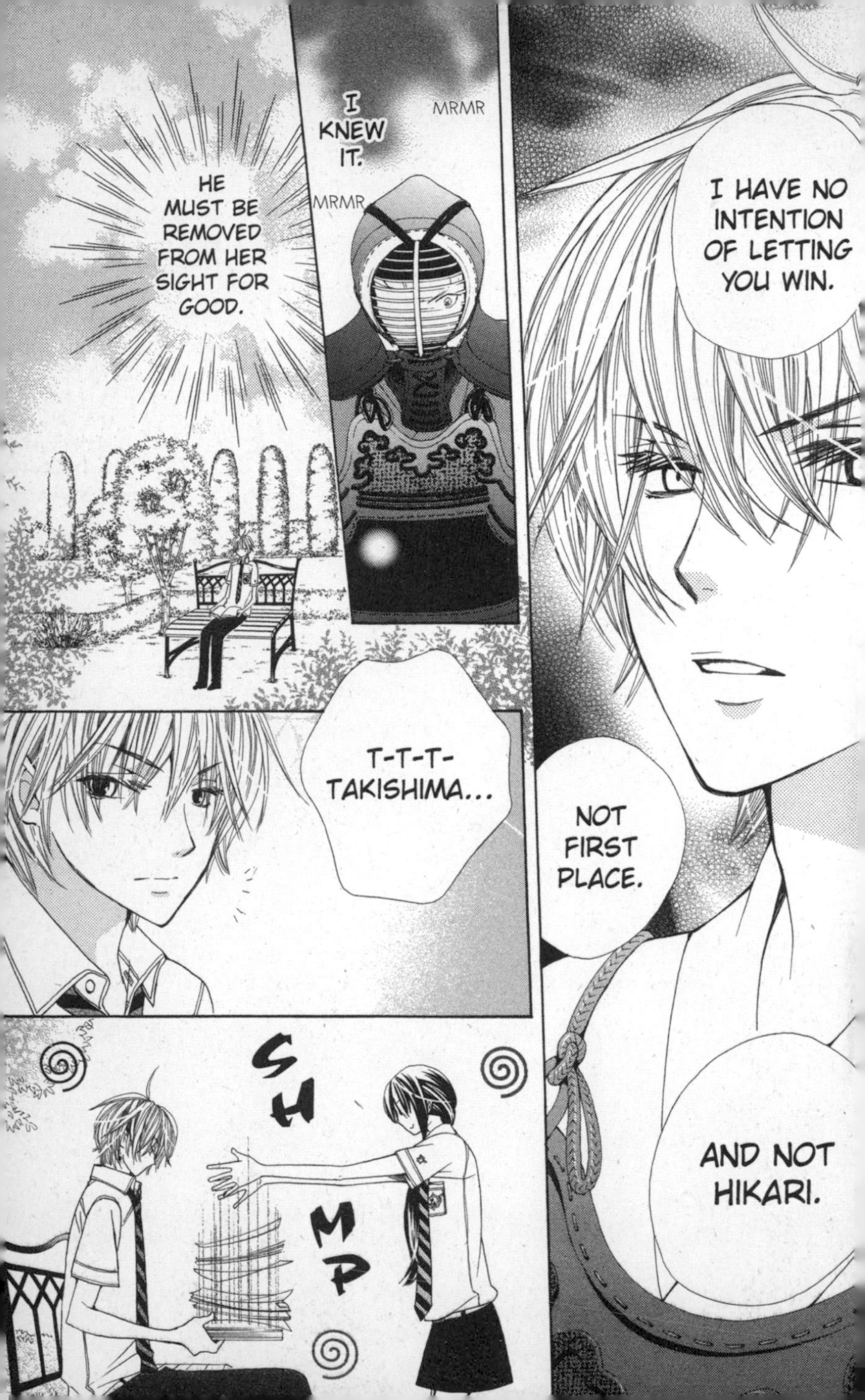
I HAVE NO INTENTION OF LETTING YOU WIN.
NOT FIRST PLACE.
AND NOT HIKARI.
MRMR
I KNEW IT.
MRMR
HE MUST BE REMOVED FROM HER SIGHT FOR GOOD.
T-T-T-TAKISHIMA...
SHUMP

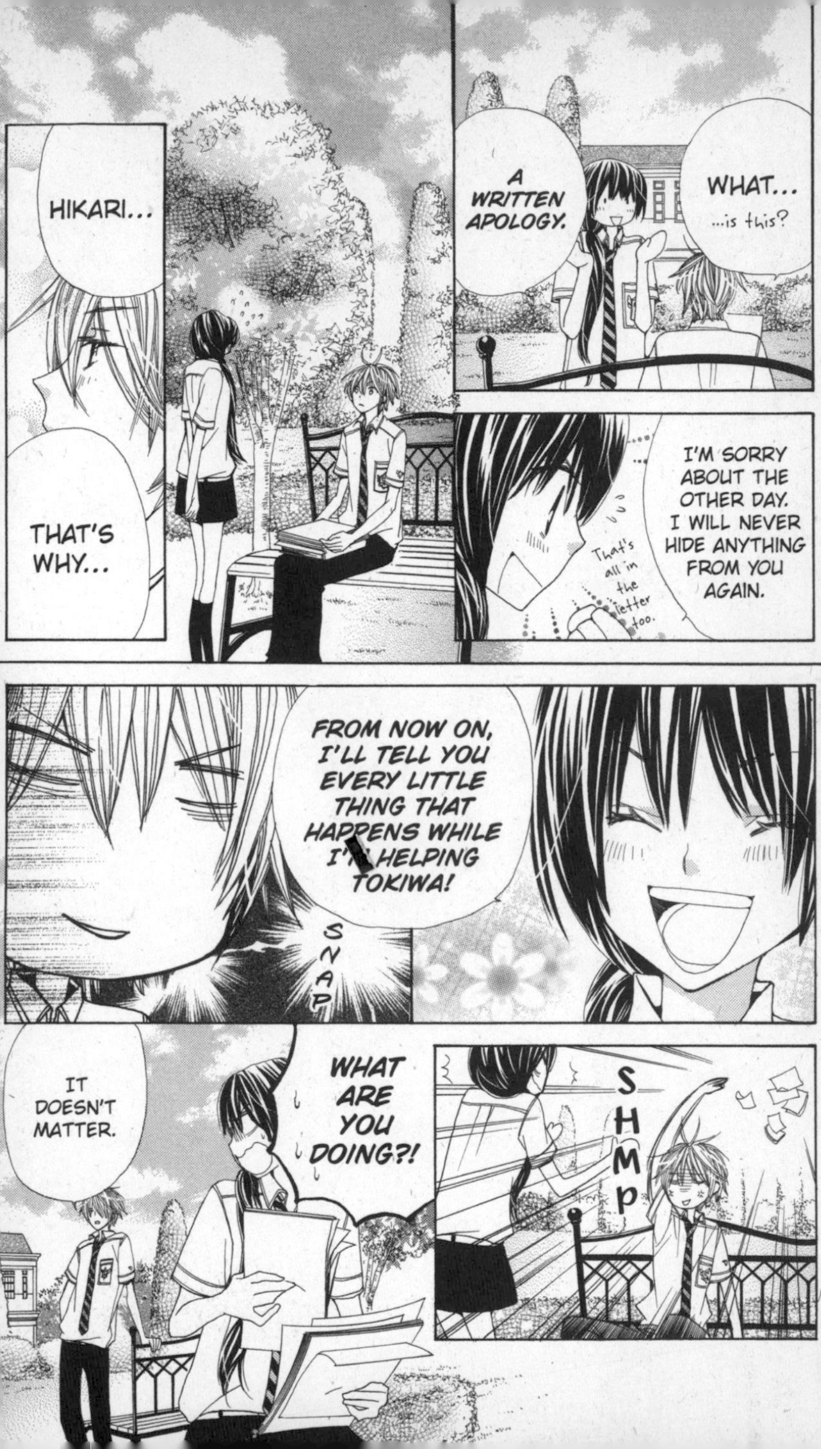
WHAT... ...is this?
A WRITTEN APOLOGY.
I'M SORRY ABOUT THE OTHER DAY. I WILL NEVER HIDE ANYTHING FROM YOU AGAIN.
That's all in the letter too.
HIKARI...
THAT'S WHY...
FROM NOW ON, I'LL TELL YOU EVERY LITTLE THING THAT HAPPENS WHILE I'M HELPING TOKIWA!
SNAP
SHMP
WHAT ARE YOU DOING?!
IT DOESN'T MATTER.

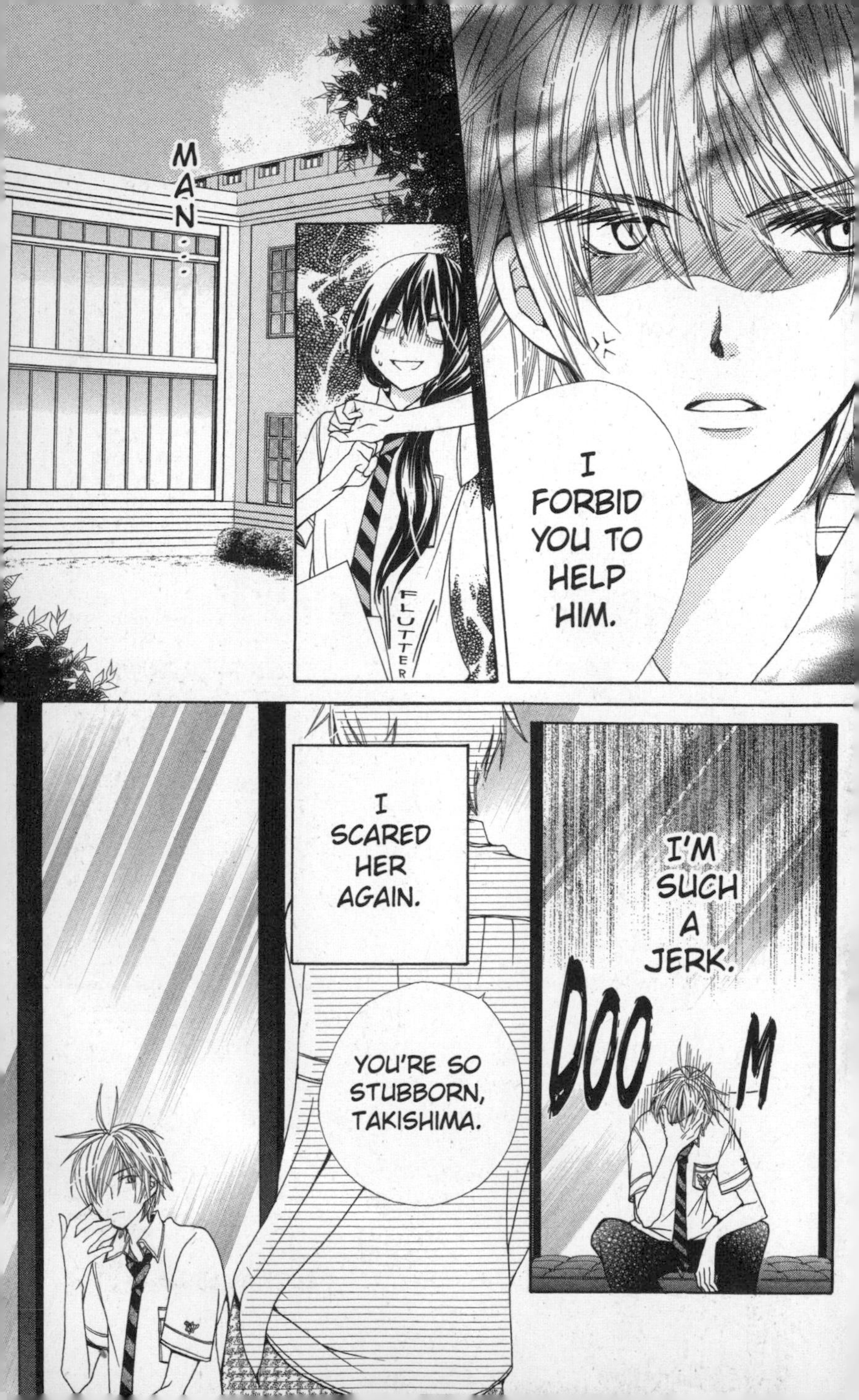
I FORBID YOU TO HELP HIM.
FLUTTER
MAN...
I'M SUCH A JERK.
DOOM
I SCARED HER AGAIN.
YOU'RE SO STUBBORN, TAKISHIMA.

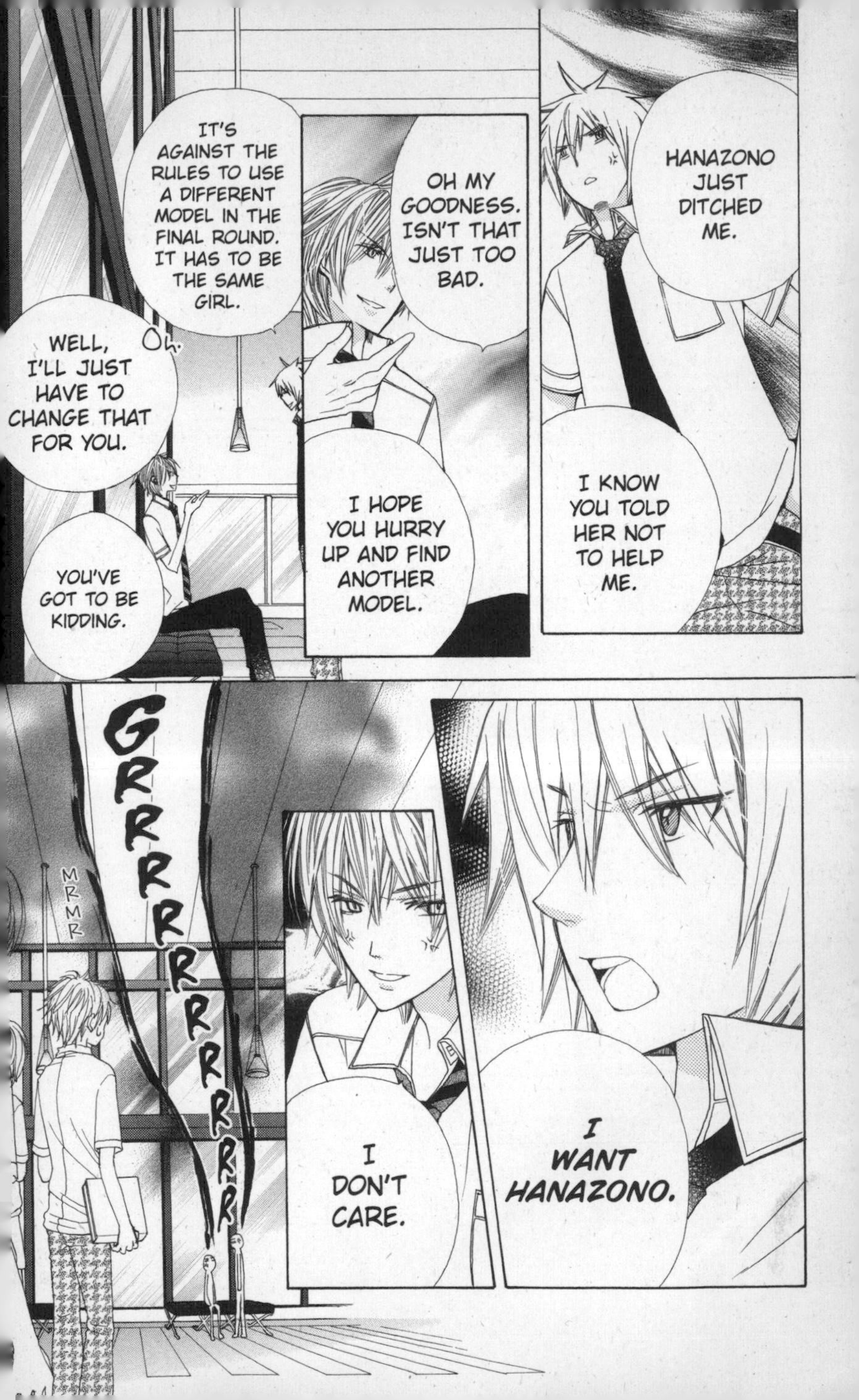
HANAZONO JUST DITCHED ME.
I KNOW YOU TOLD HER NOT TO HELP ME.
OH MY GOODNESS. ISN'T THAT JUST TOO BAD.
I HOPE YOU HURRY UP AND FIND ANOTHER MODEL.
IT'S AGAINST THE RULES TO USE A DIFFERENT MODEL IN THE FINAL ROUND. IT HAS TO BE THE SAME GIRL.
Oh.
WELL, I'LL JUST HAVE TO CHANGE THAT FOR YOU.
YOU'VE GOT TO BE KIDDING.
I WANT HANAZONO.
I DON'T CARE.
GRRRRRRRRRRR
MRMR

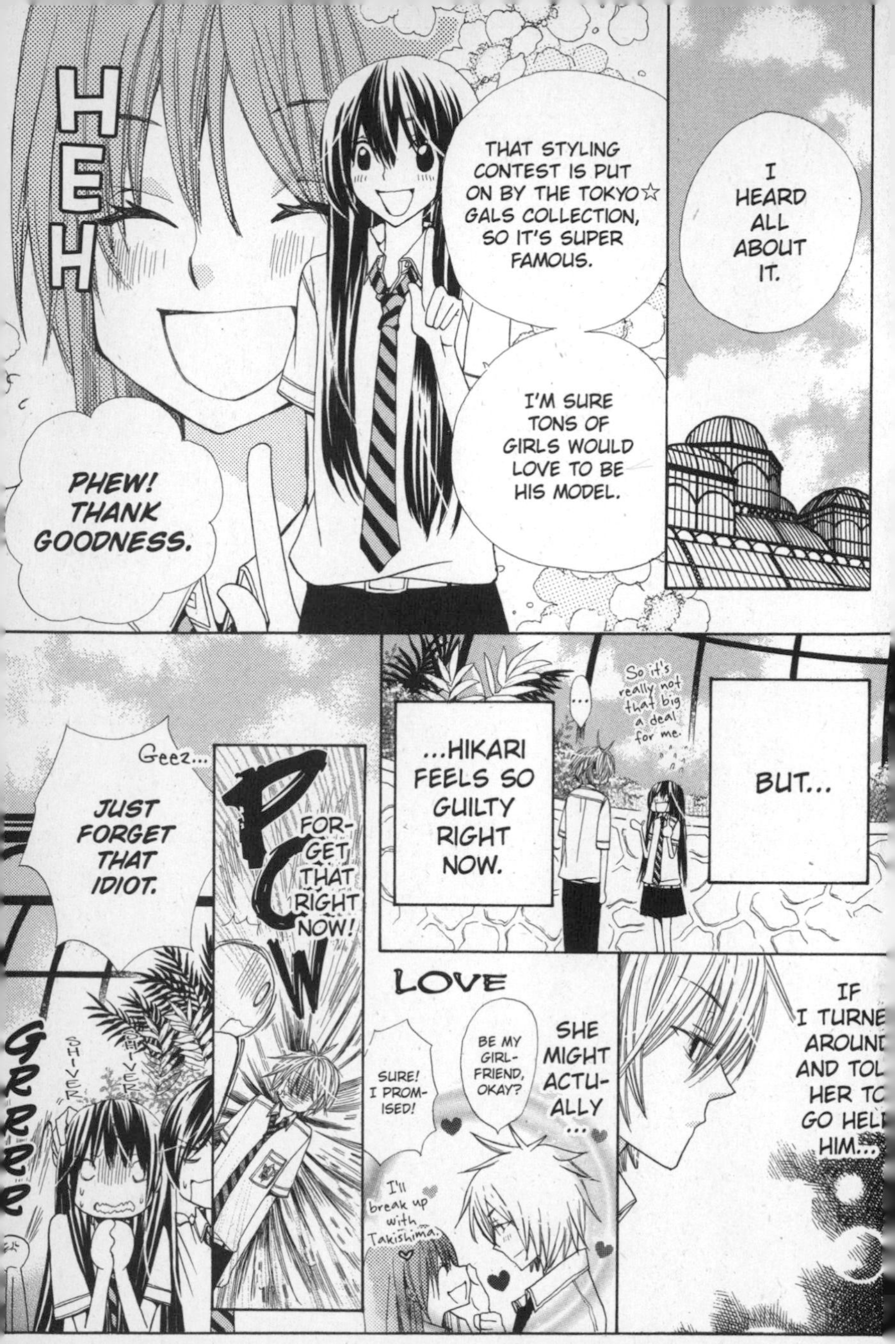
I HEARD ALL ABOUT IT.
THAT STYLING CONTEST IS PUT ON BY THE TOKYO☆GALS COLLECTION, SO IT'S SUPER FAMOUS.
I'M SURE TONS OF GIRLS WOULD LOVE TO BE HIS MODEL.
HEH
PHEW! THANK GOODNESS.
BUT...
So it's really not that big a deal for me.
...
...HIKARI FEELS SO GUILTY RIGHT NOW.
IF I TURNE AROUN AND TOL HER TO GO HEL HIM...
SHE MIGHT ACTU-ALLY...
BE MY GIRL-FRIEND, OKAY?
SURE! I PROM-ISED!
LOVE
I'll break up with Takishima.
POW
FOR-GET THAT RIGHT NOW!
Geez...
JUST FORGET THAT IDIOT.
SHIVER
SHIVER

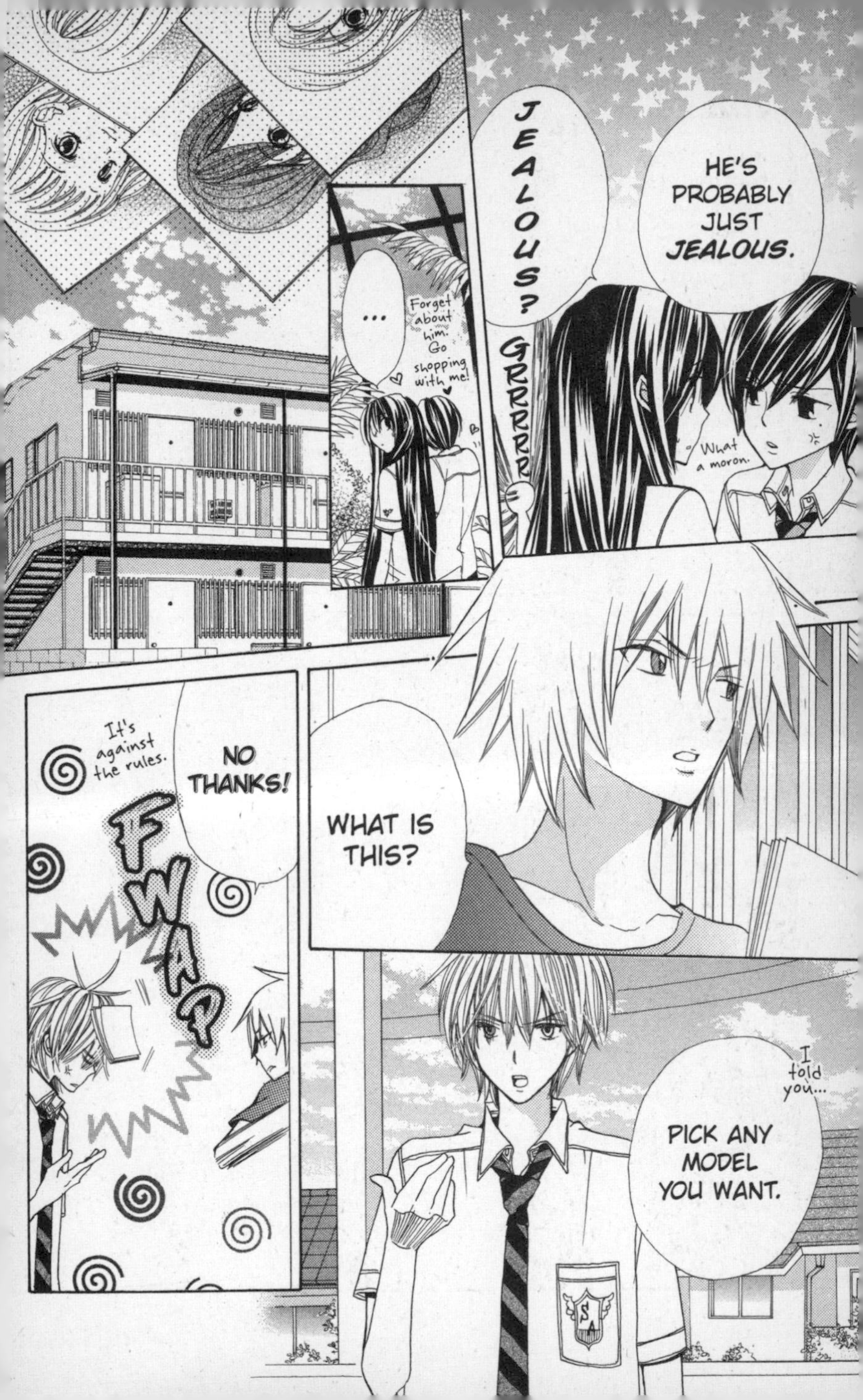
HE'S PROBABLY JUST JEALOUS.
JEALOUS?
GRRRRR
What a moron.
...
Forget about him. Go shopping with me!
WHAT IS THIS?
I told you...
PICK ANY MODEL YOU WANT.
NO THANKS!
It's against the rules.
FWAP

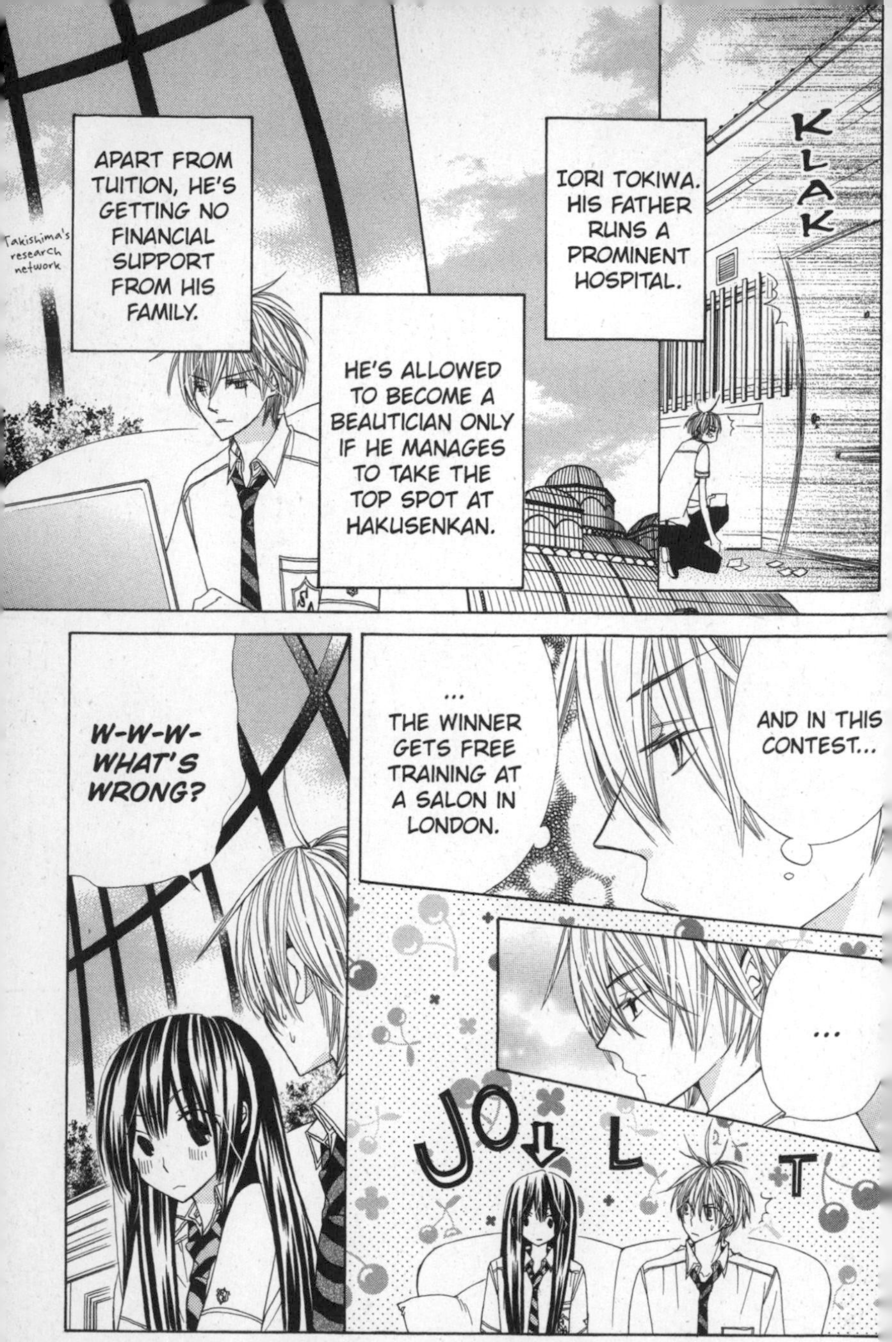
KLAK
IORI TOKIWA. HIS FATHER RUNS A PROMINENT HOSPITAL.
Takishima's research network
APART FROM TUITION, HE'S GETTING NO FINANCIAL SUPPORT FROM HIS FAMILY.
HE'S ALLOWED TO BECOME A BEAUTICIAN ONLY IF HE MANAGES TO TAKE THE TOP SPOT AT HAKUSENKAN.
AND IN THIS CONTEST...
... THE WINNER GETS FREE TRAINING AT A SALON IN LONDON.
...
JOLT
W-W-W-WHAT'S WRONG?

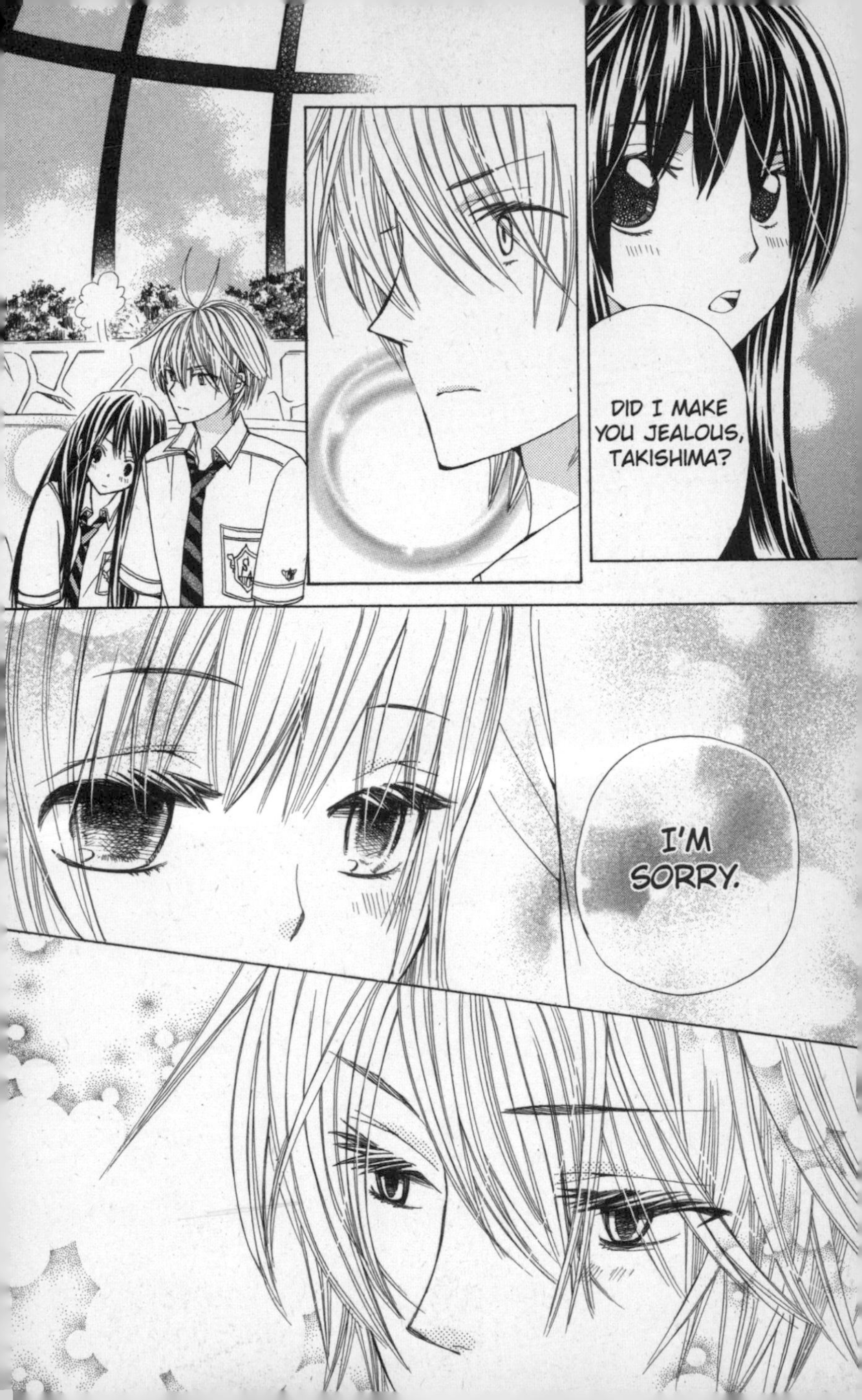
DID I MAKE YOU JEALOUS, TAKISHIMA?
I'M SORRY.

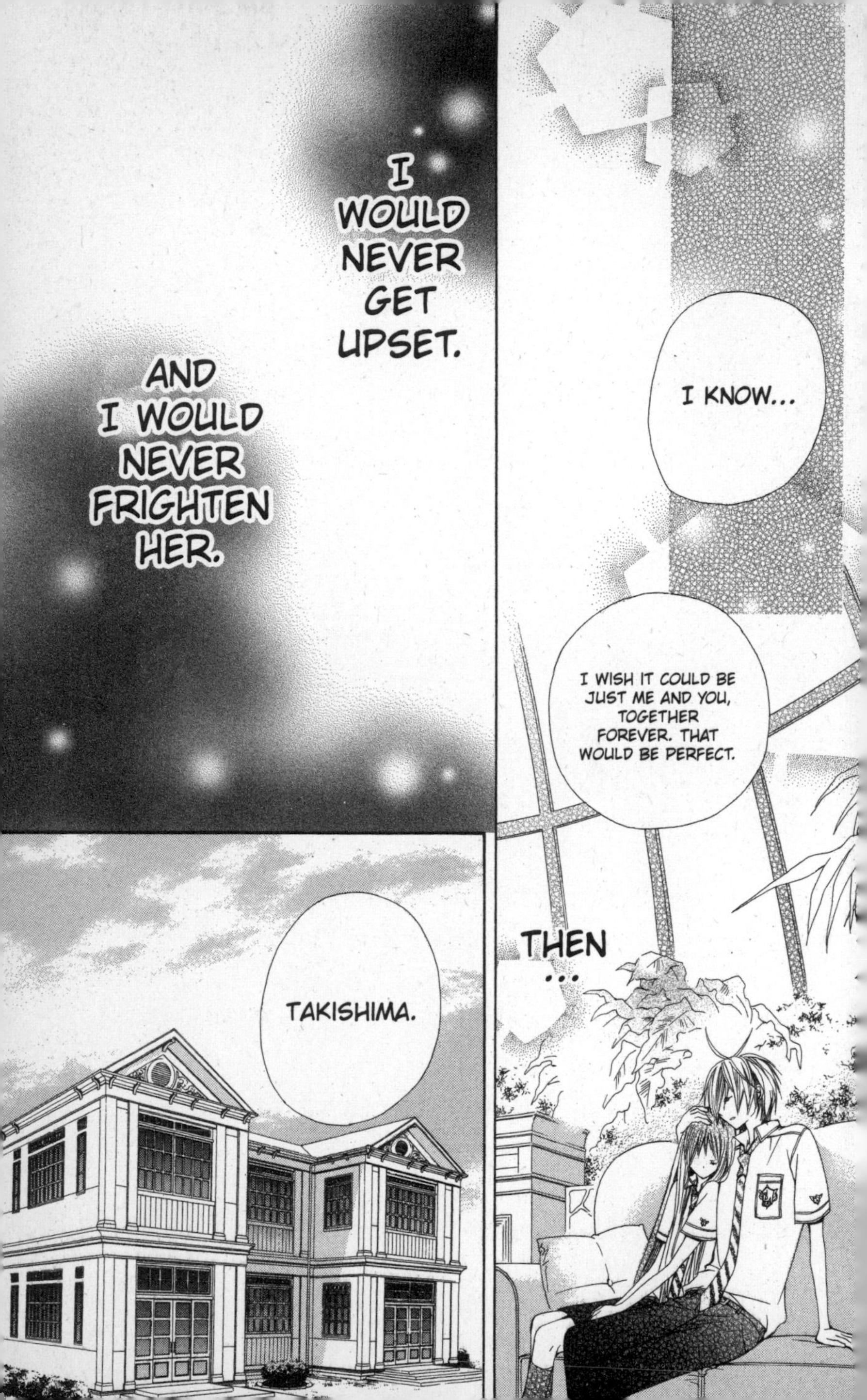
I KNOW...
I WISH IT COULD BE JUST ME AND YOU, TOGETHER FOREVER. THAT WOULD BE PERFECT.
THEN...
I WOULD NEVER GET UPSET.
AND I WOULD NEVER FRIGHTEN HER.
TAKISHIMA.

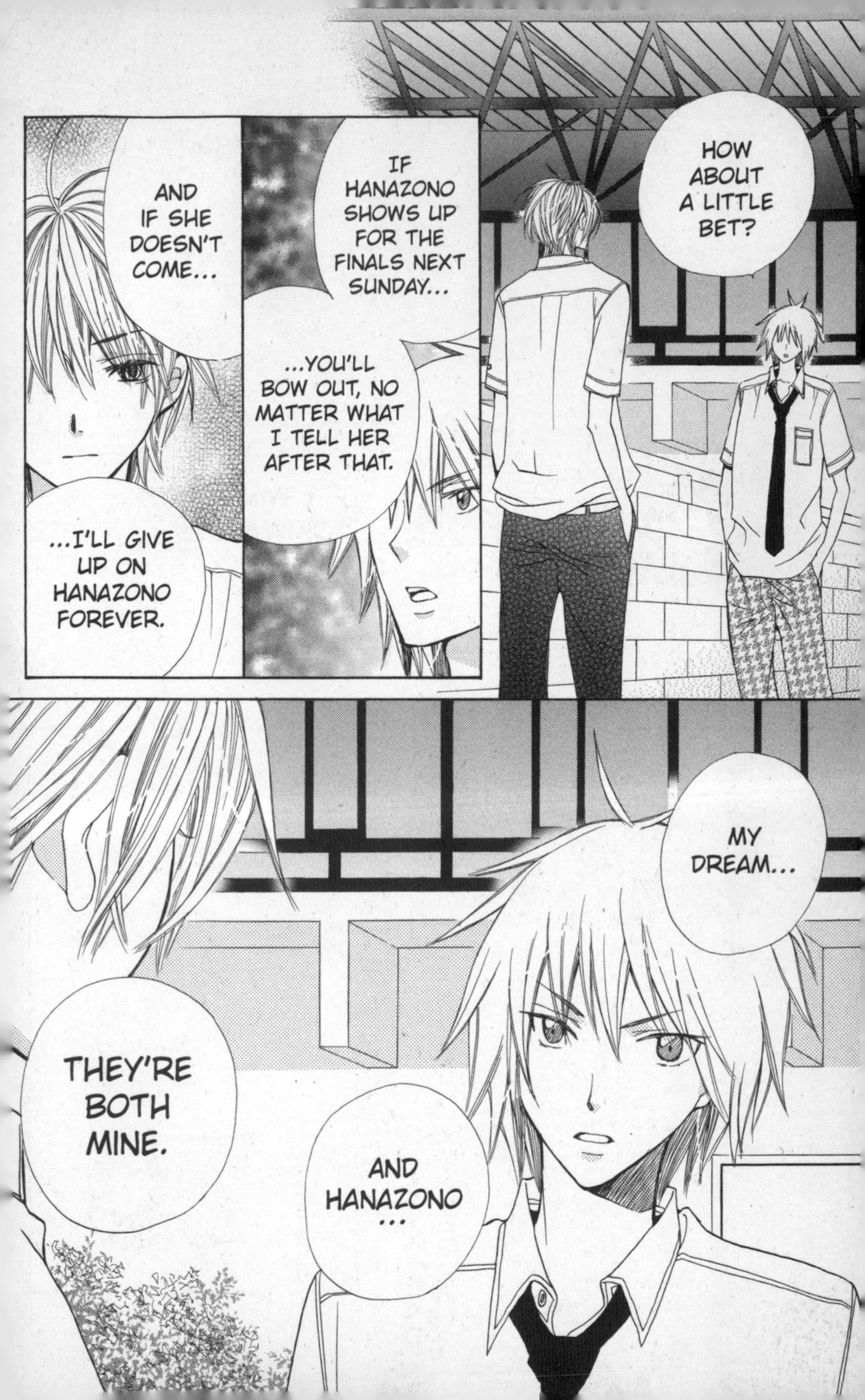
HOW ABOUT A LITTLE BET?
IF HANAZONO SHOWS UP FOR THE FINALS NEXT SUNDAY...
...YOU'LL BOW OUT, NO MATTER WHAT I TELL HER AFTER THAT.
AND IF SHE DOESN'T COME...
...I'LL GIVE UP ON HANAZONO FOREVER.
MY DREAM...
AND HANAZONO...
THEY'RE BOTH MINE.

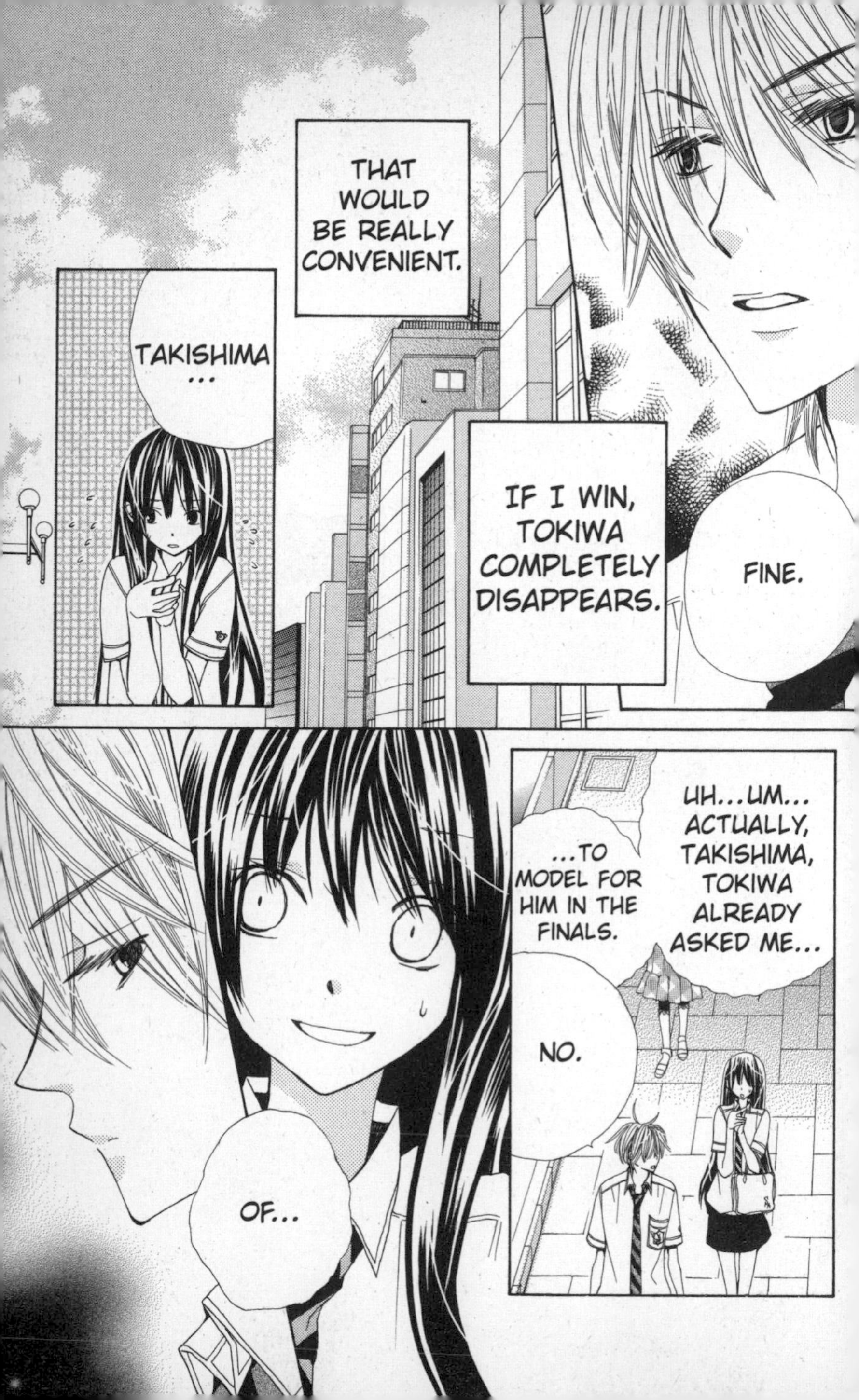
FINE.
IF I WIN, TOKIWA COMPLETELY DISAPPEARS.
THAT WOULD BE REALLY CONVENIENT.
TAKISHIMA...
UH...UM... ACTUALLY, TAKISHIMA, TOKIWA ALREADY ASKED ME...
...TO MODEL FOR HIM IN THE FINALS.
NO.
OF...

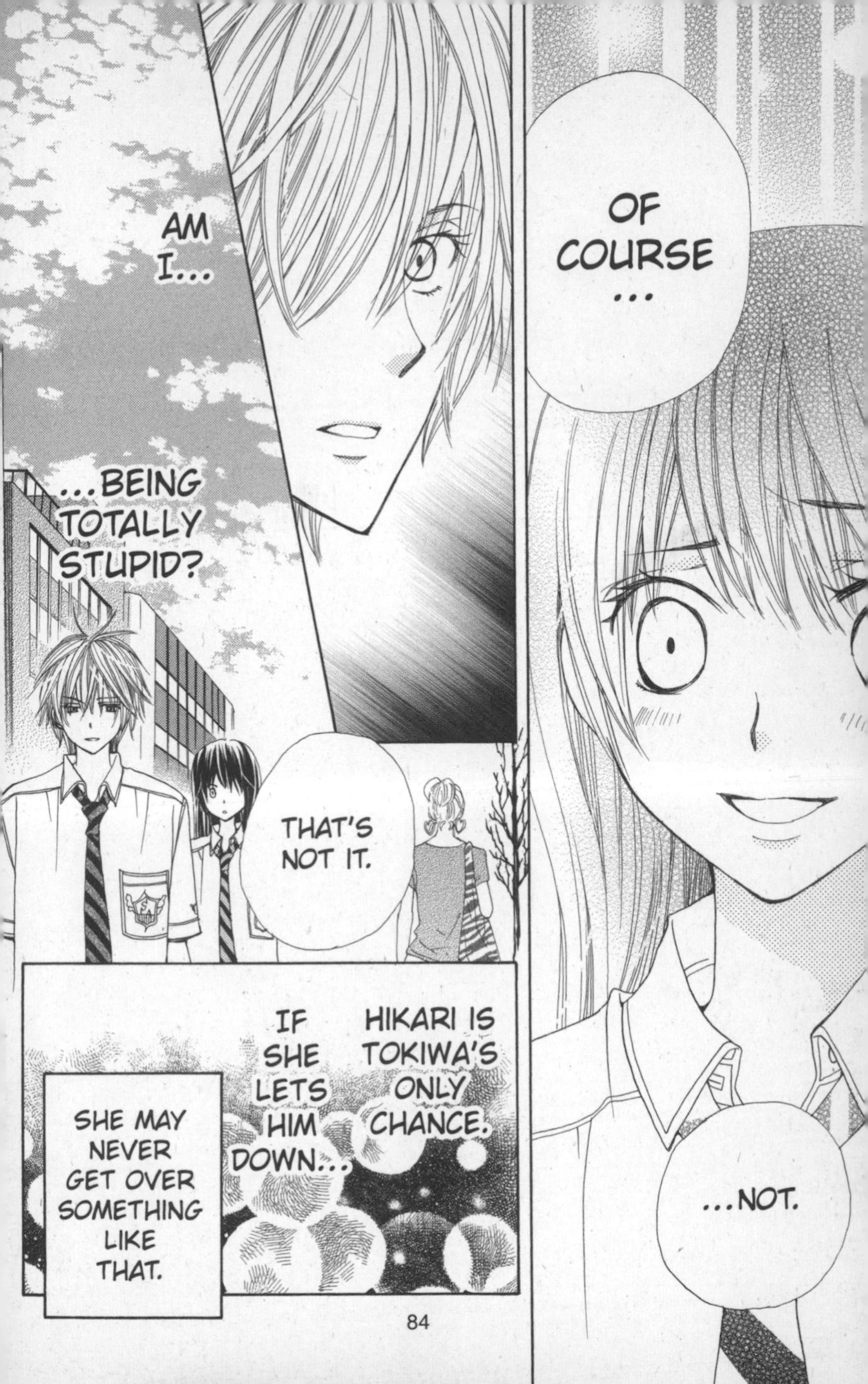
OF COURSE ...
...NOT.
AM I...
...BEING TOTALLY STUPID?
THAT'S NOT IT.
HIKARI IS TOKIWA'S ONLY CHANCE.
IF SHE LETS HIM DOWN...
SHE MAY NEVER GET OVER SOMETHING LIKE THAT.

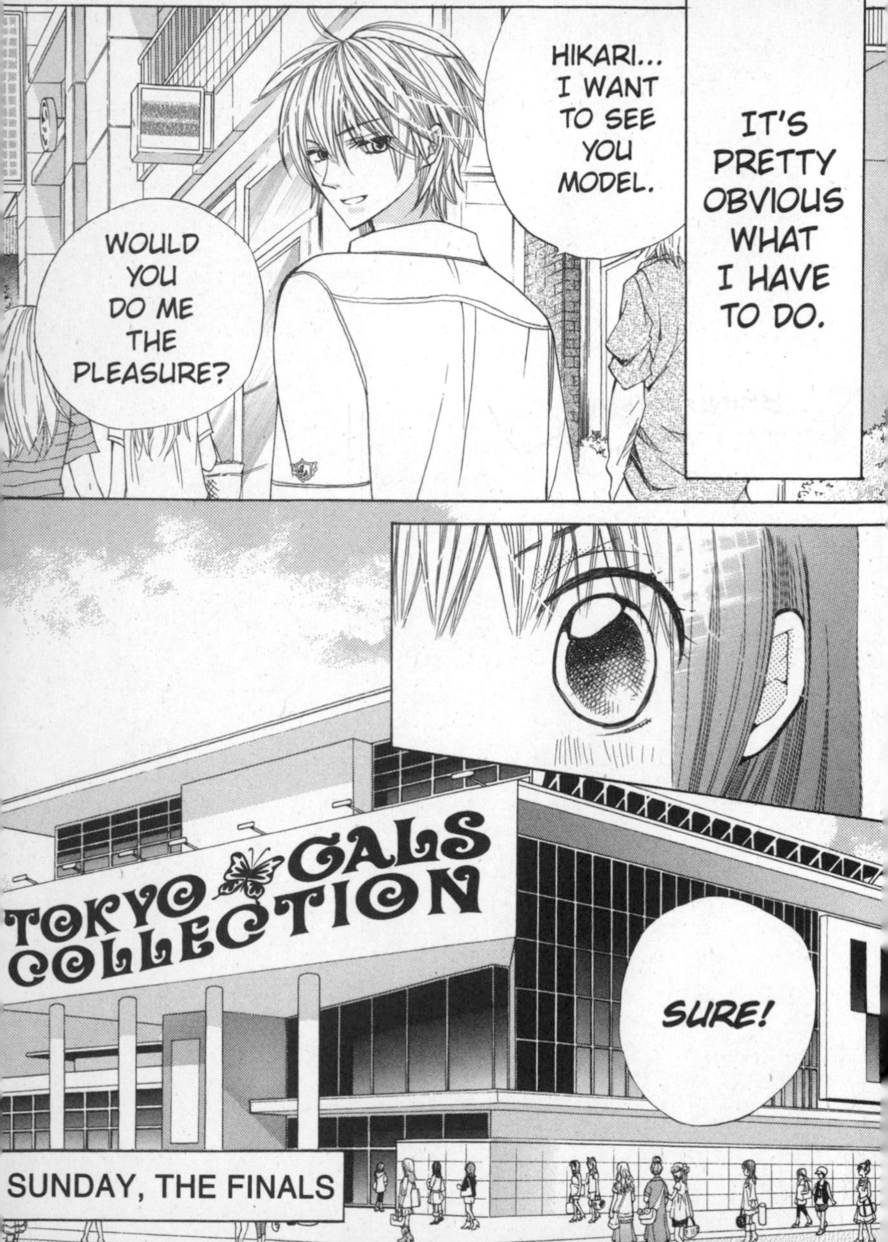
IT'S PRETTY OBVIOUS WHAT I HAVE TO DO.
HIKARI... I WANT TO SEE YOU MODEL.
WOULD YOU DO ME THE PLEASURE?
SURE!
TOKYO GALS COLLECTION
SUNDAY, THE FINALS

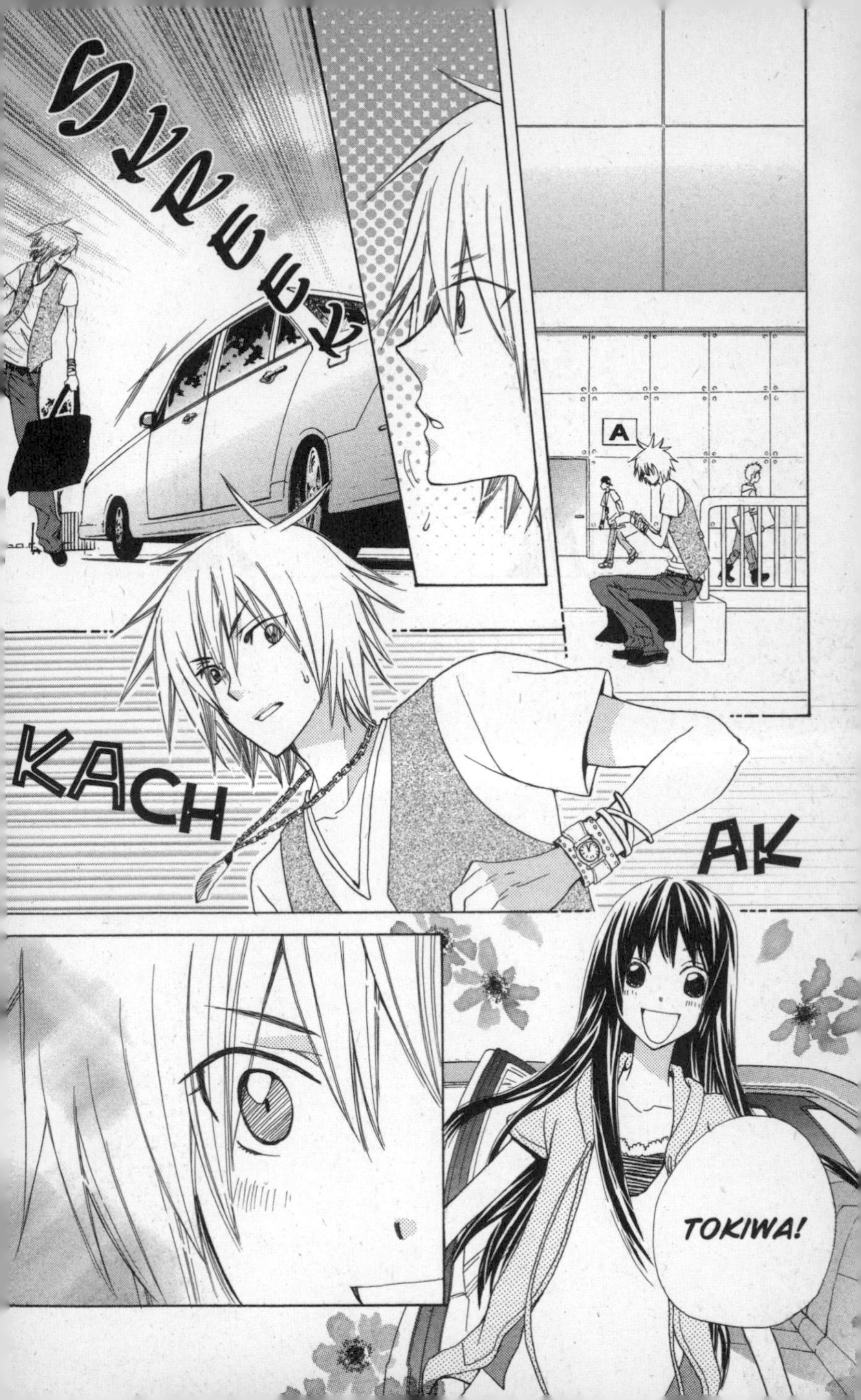
SKREEK
KACH
AK
TOKIWA!

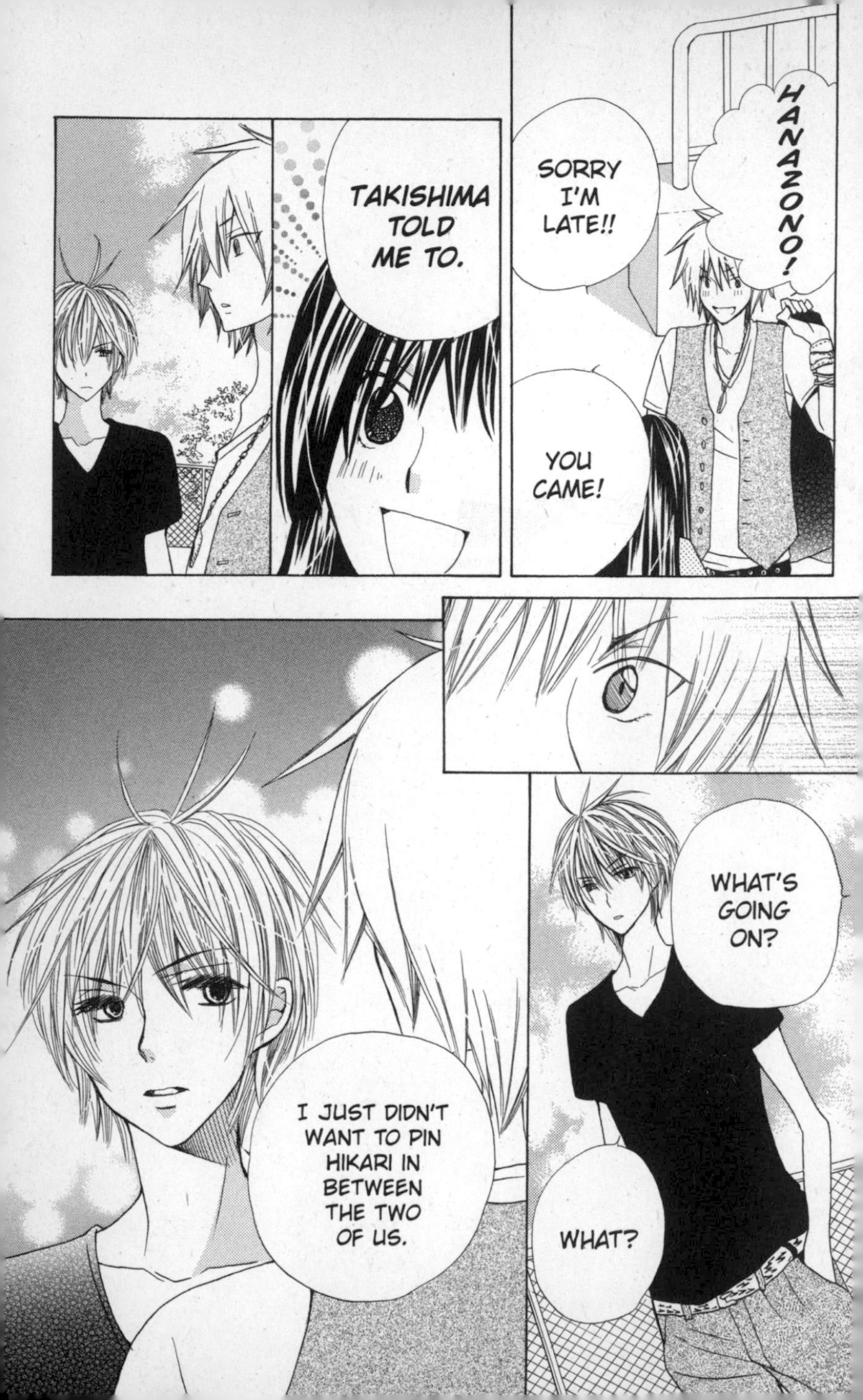
HANAZONO!
SORRY I'M LATE!!
YOU CAME!
TAKISHIMA TOLD ME TO.
WHAT'S GOING ON?
WHAT?
I JUST DIDN'T WANT TO PIN HIKARI IN BETWEEN THE TWO OF US.

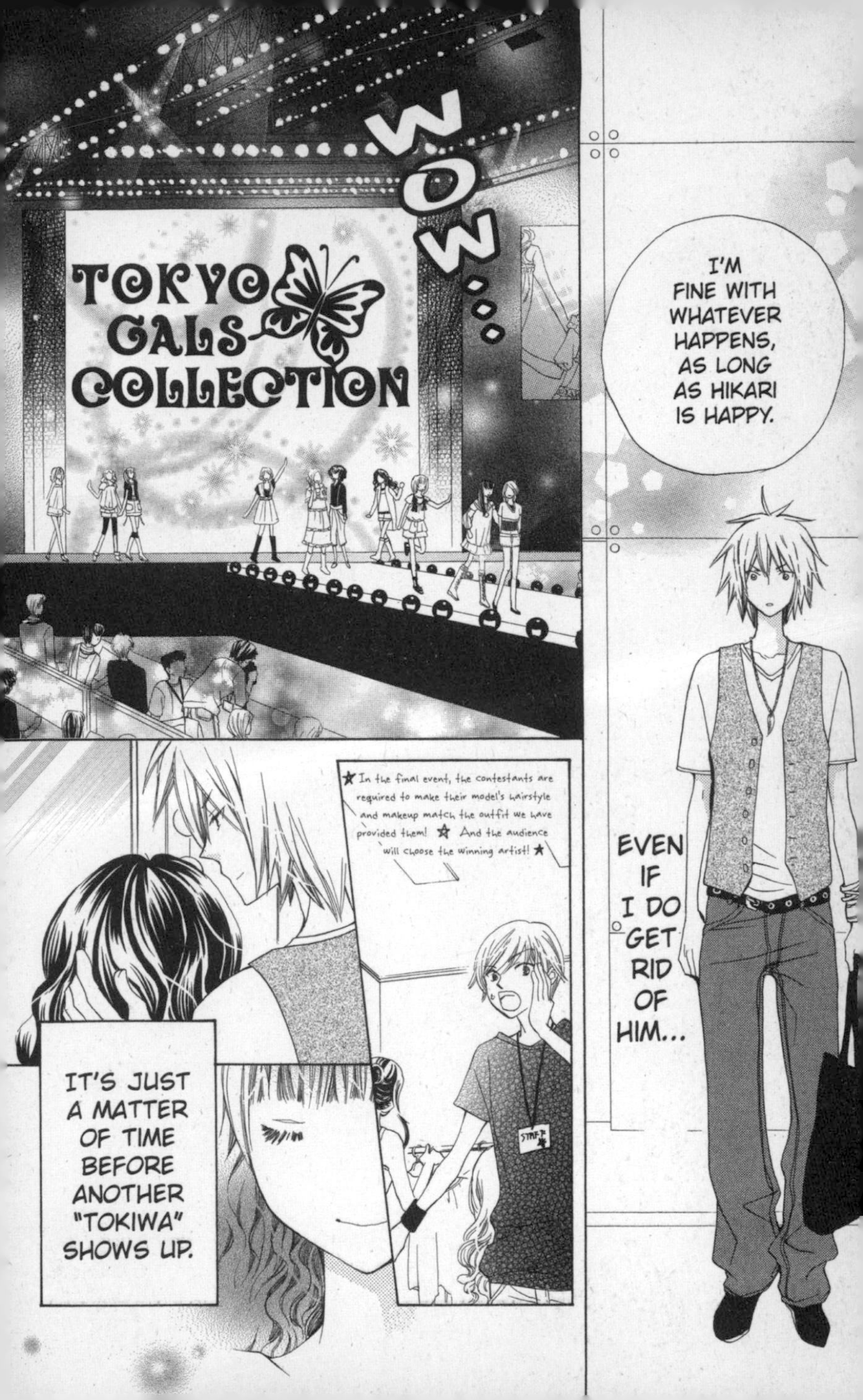
I'M FINE WITH WHATEVER HAPPENS, AS LONG AS HIKARI IS HAPPY.
EVEN IF I DO GET RID OF HIM...
WOW...
TOKYO GALS COLLECTION
★ In the final event, the contestants are required to make their model's hairstyle and makeup match the outfit we have provided them! ☆ And the audience will choose the winning artist! ★
IT'S JUST A MATTER OF TIME BEFORE ANOTHER "TOKIWA" SHOWS UP.

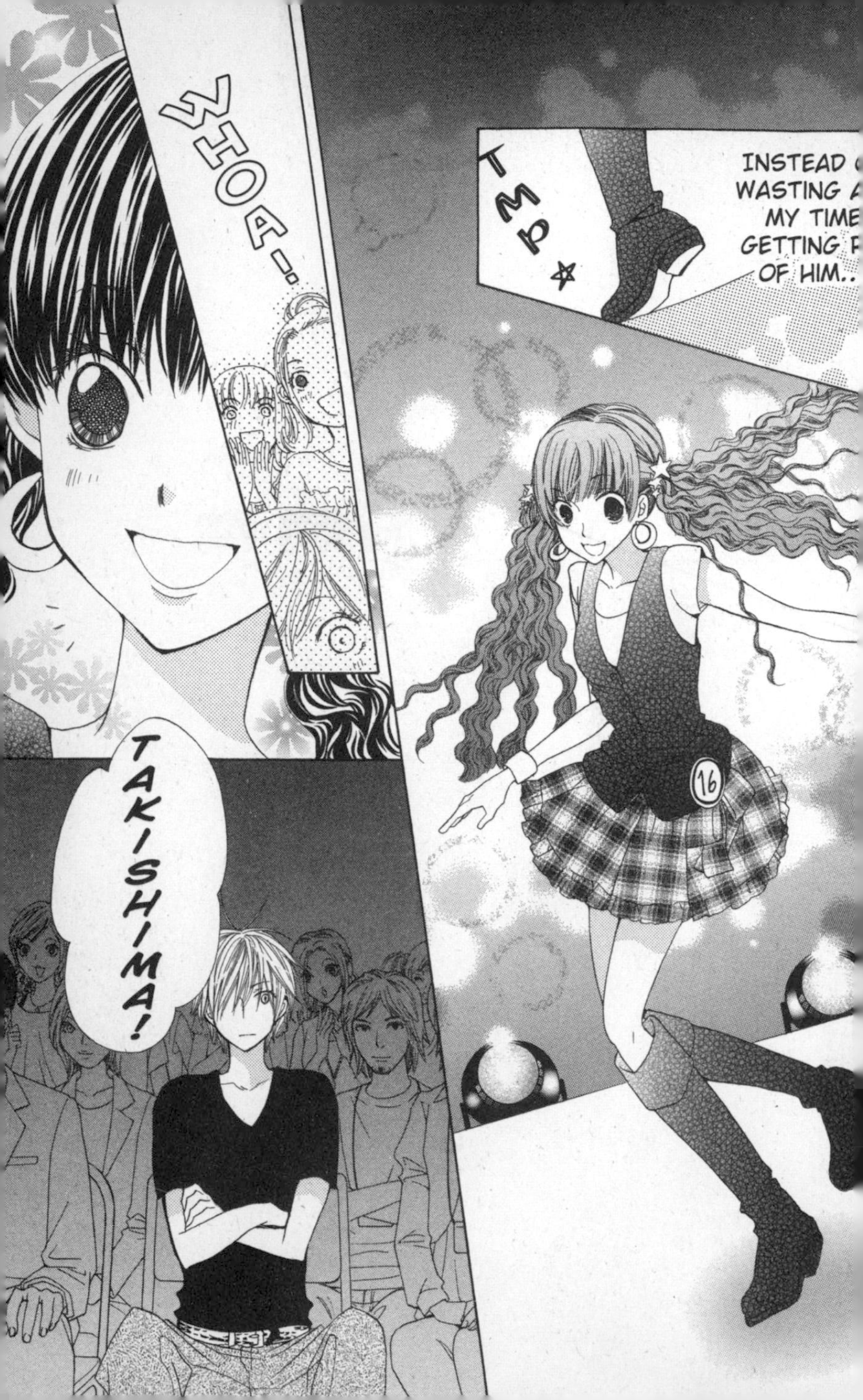
TMP☆
INSTEAD WASTING MY TIME GETTING OF HIM...
WHOA!
TAKISHIMA!

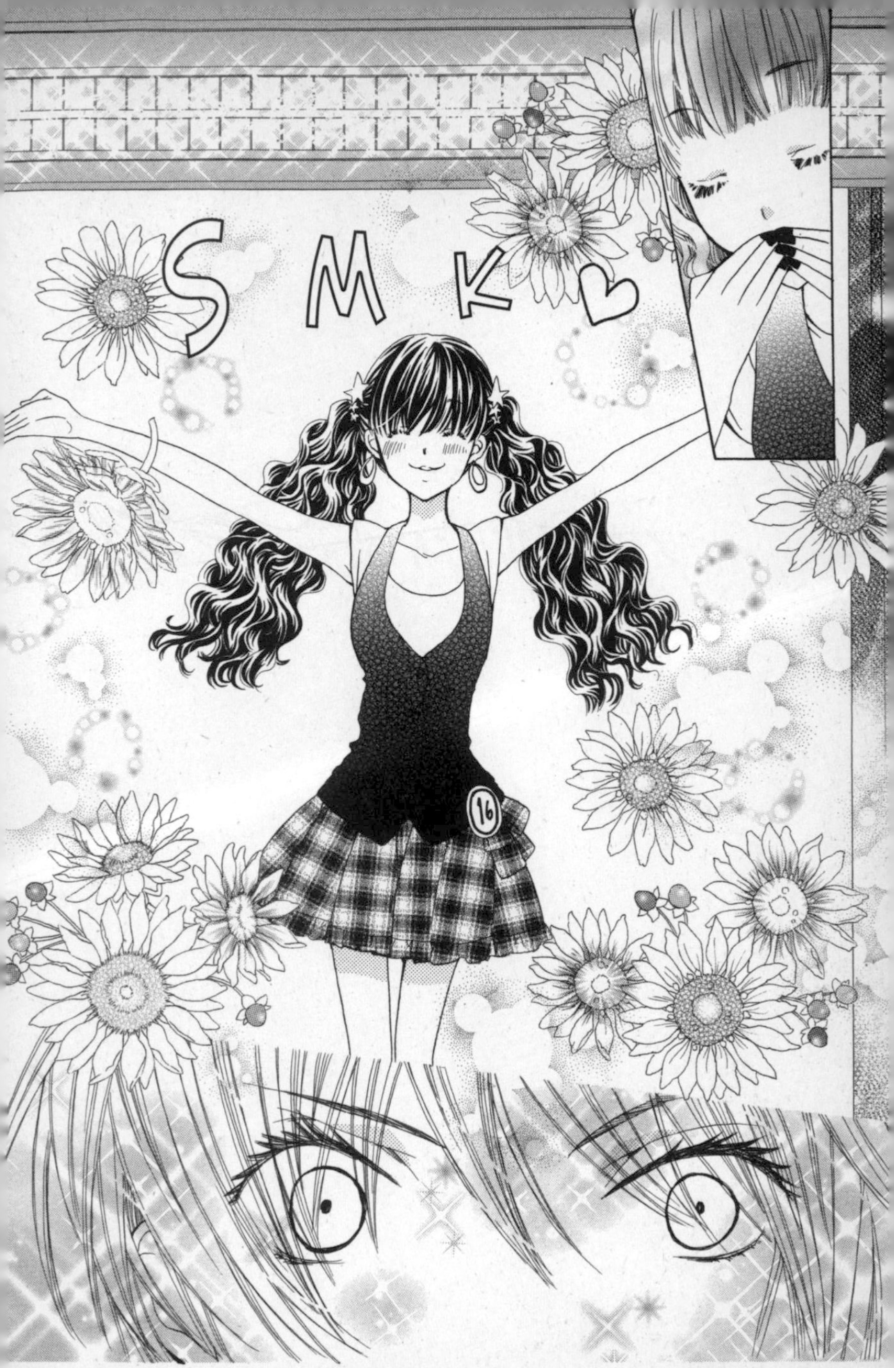
SMK♥

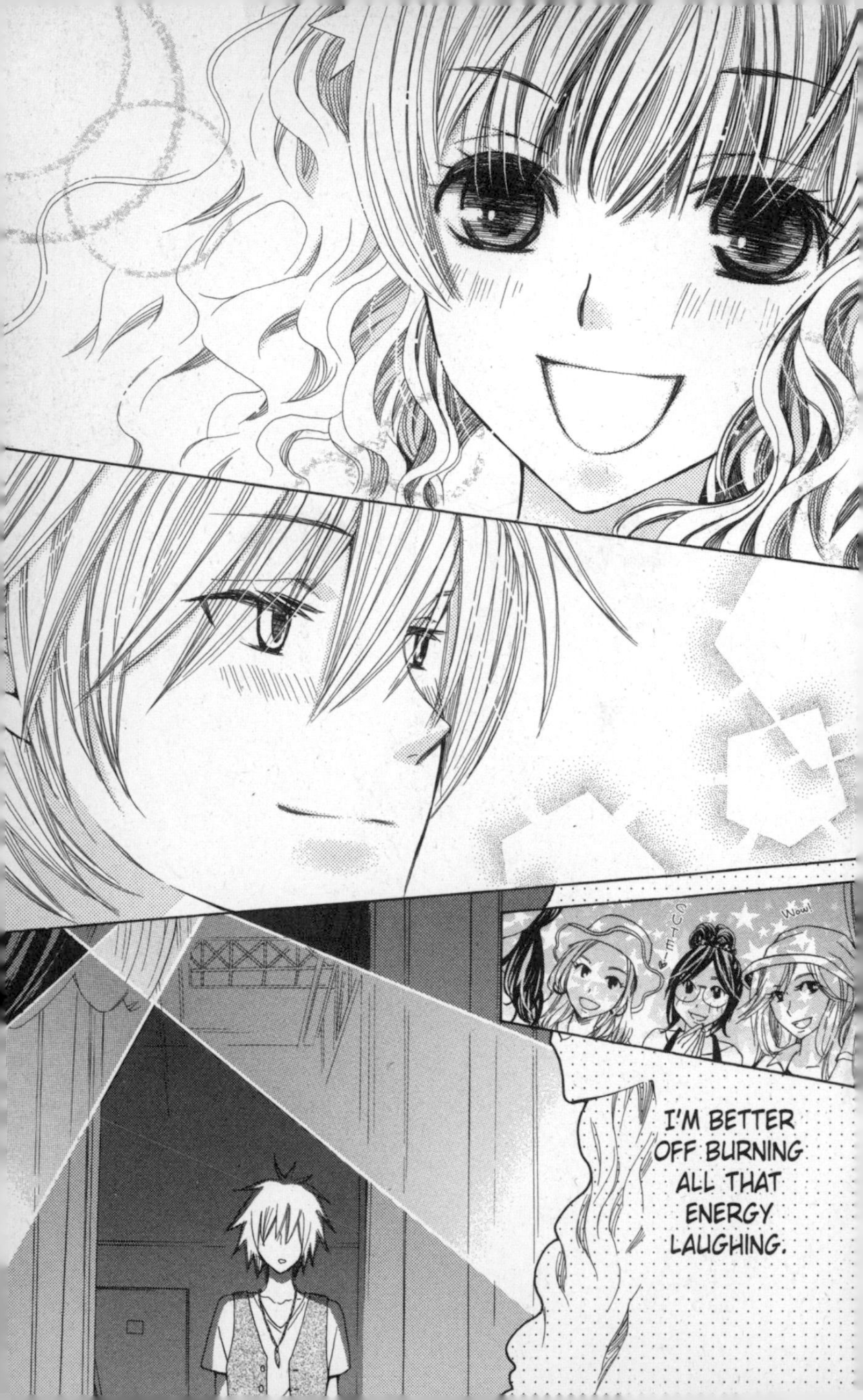
Wow!
CUTE!
I'M BETTER OFF BURNING ALL THAT ENERGY LAUGHING.

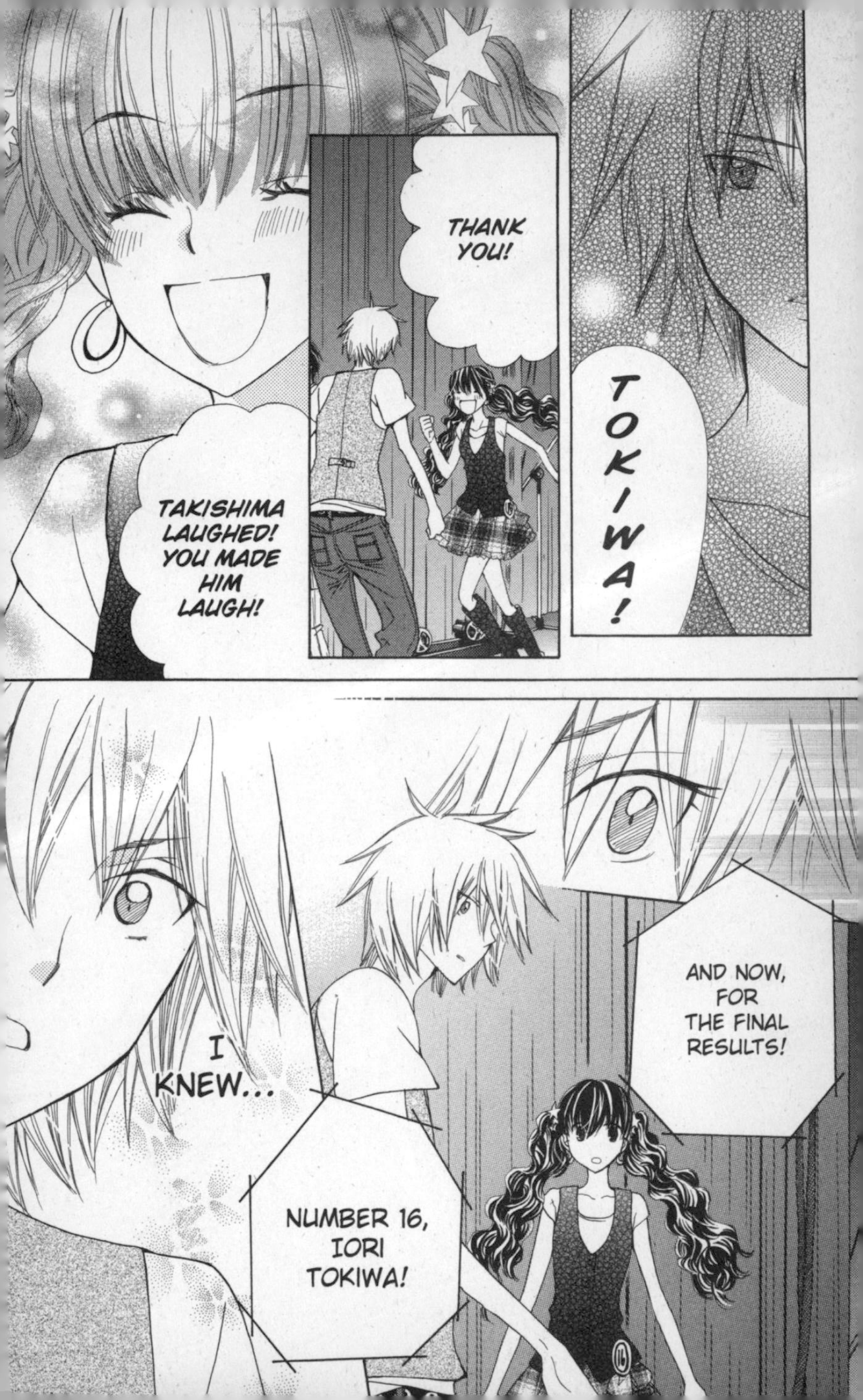
TOKIWA!
THANK YOU!
TAKISHIMA LAUGHED! YOU MADE HIM LAUGH!
AND NOW, FOR THE FINAL RESULTS!
NUMBER 16, IORI TOKIWA!
I KNEW...

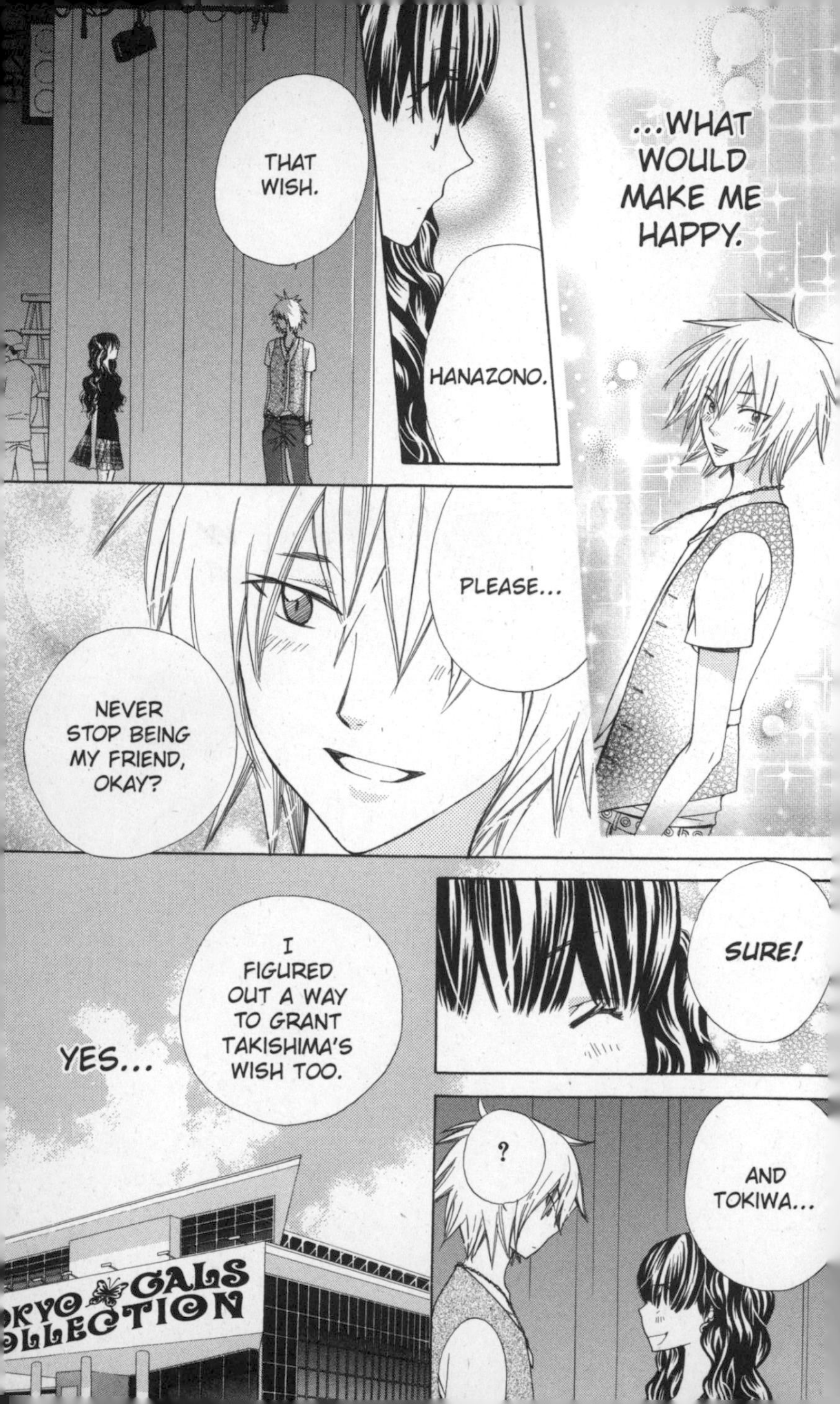
...WHAT WOULD MAKE ME HAPPY.
HANAZONO.
THAT WISH.
PLEASE...
NEVER STOP BEING MY FRIEND, OKAY?
SURE!
AND TOKIWA...
?
I FIGURED OUT A WAY TO GRANT TAKISHIMA'S WISH TOO.
YES...
OKYO GALS
OLLECTION

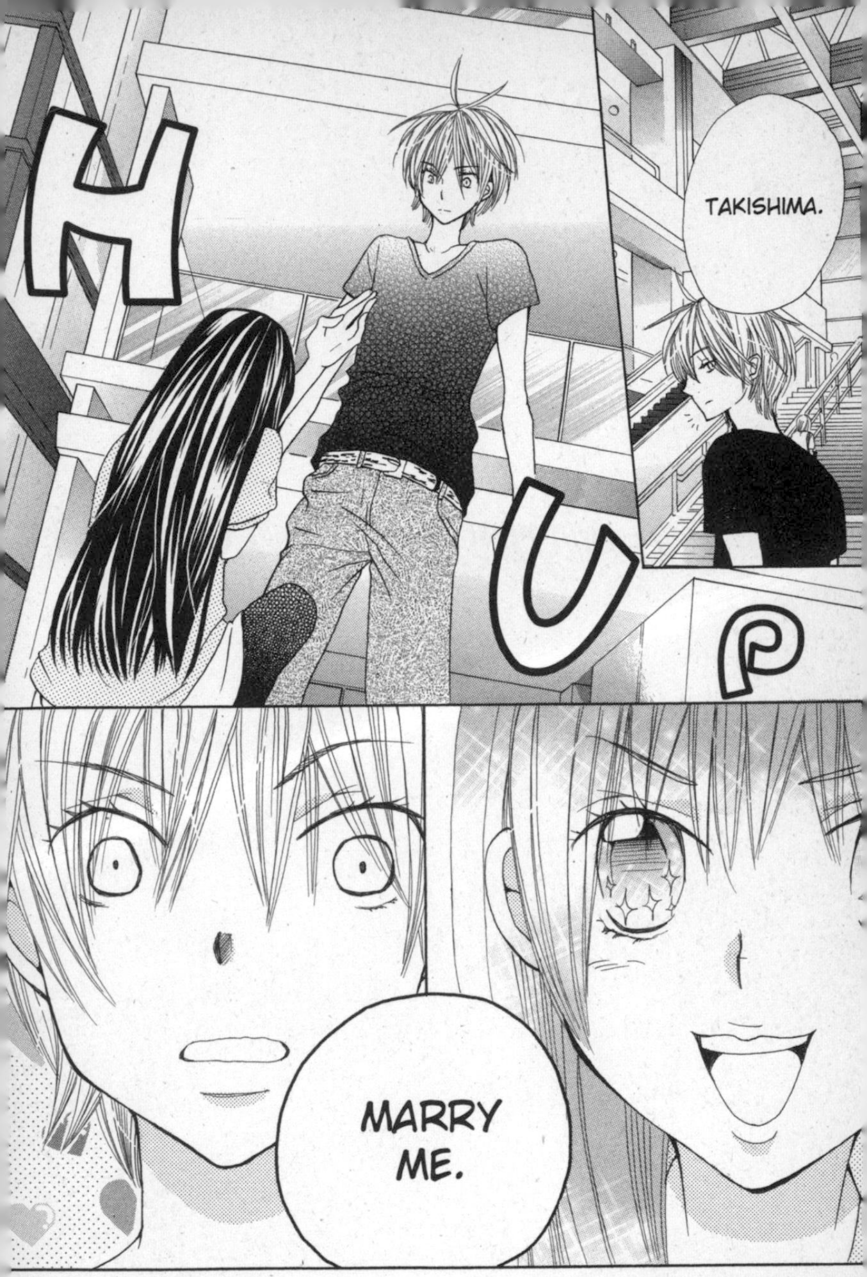
TAKISHIMA.
HUP
MARRY ME.
I'D DO ANYTHING TO MAKE YOU HAPPY.

Chapter 91

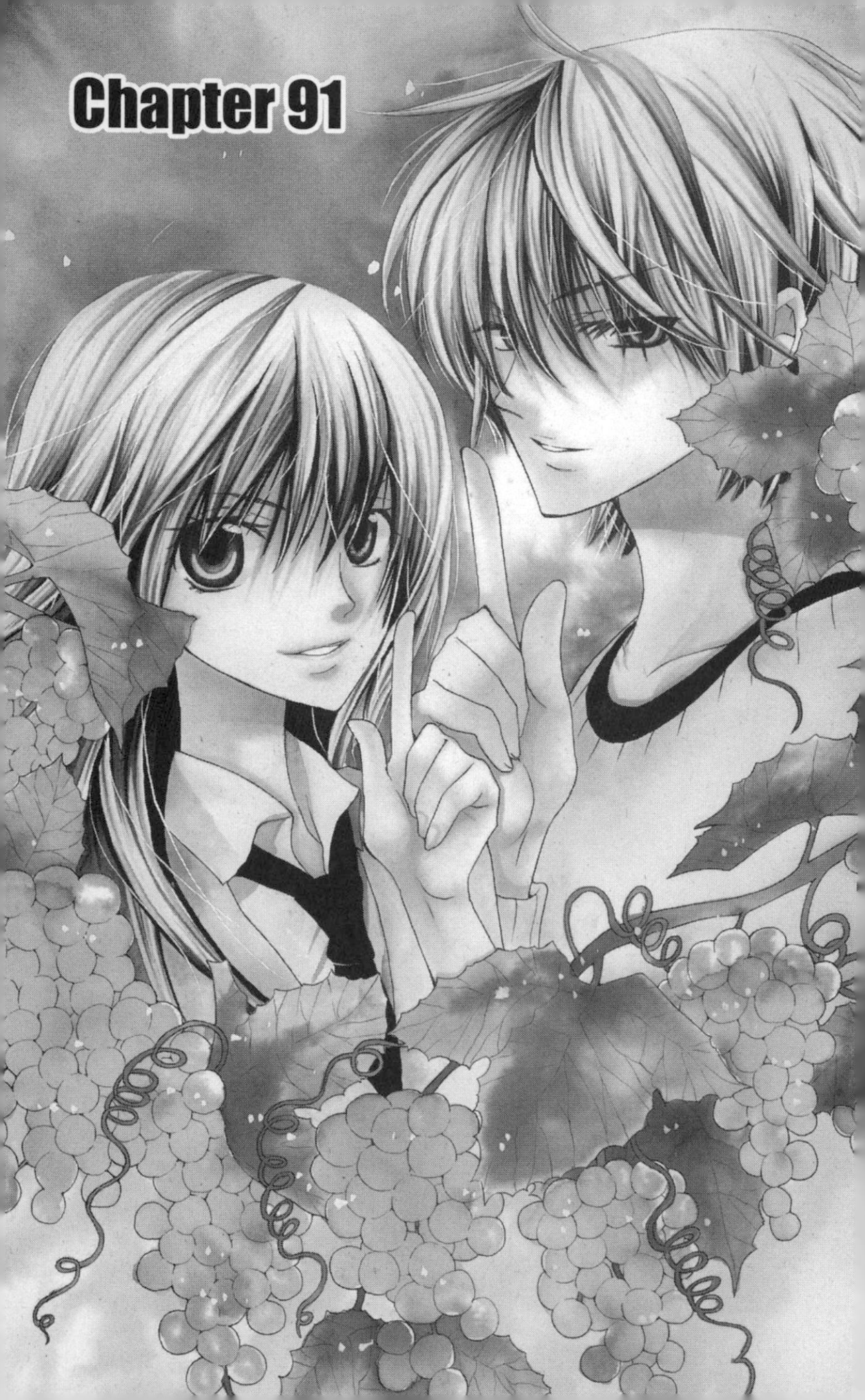

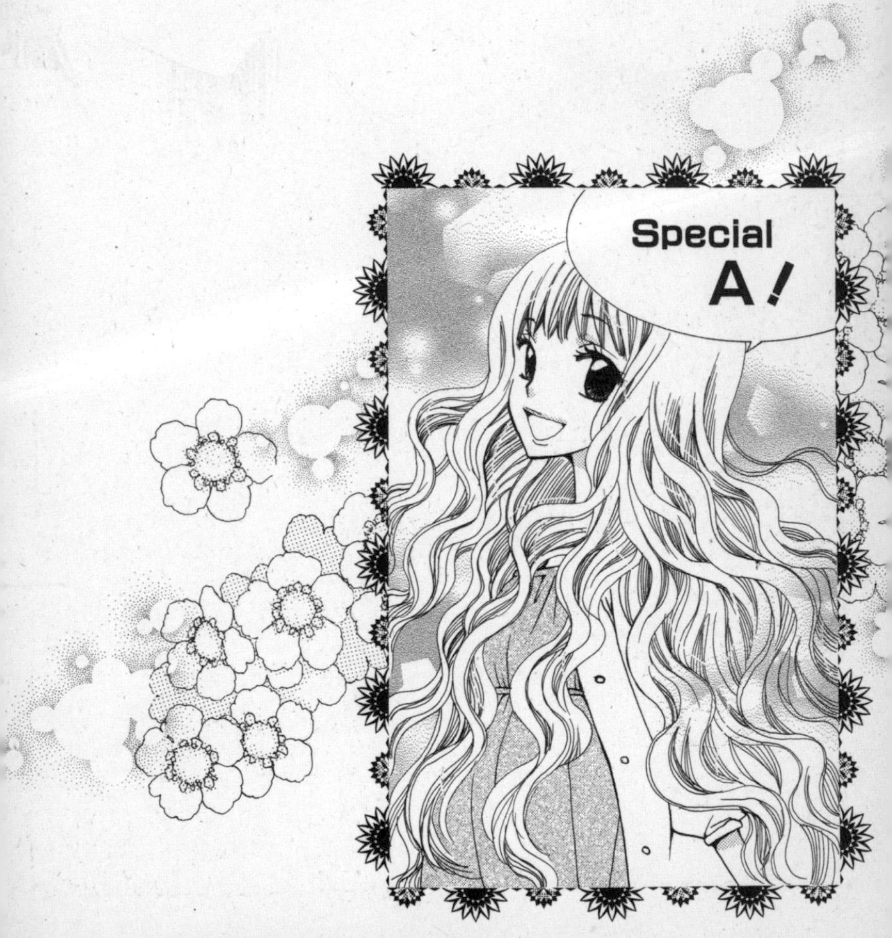
Special A!

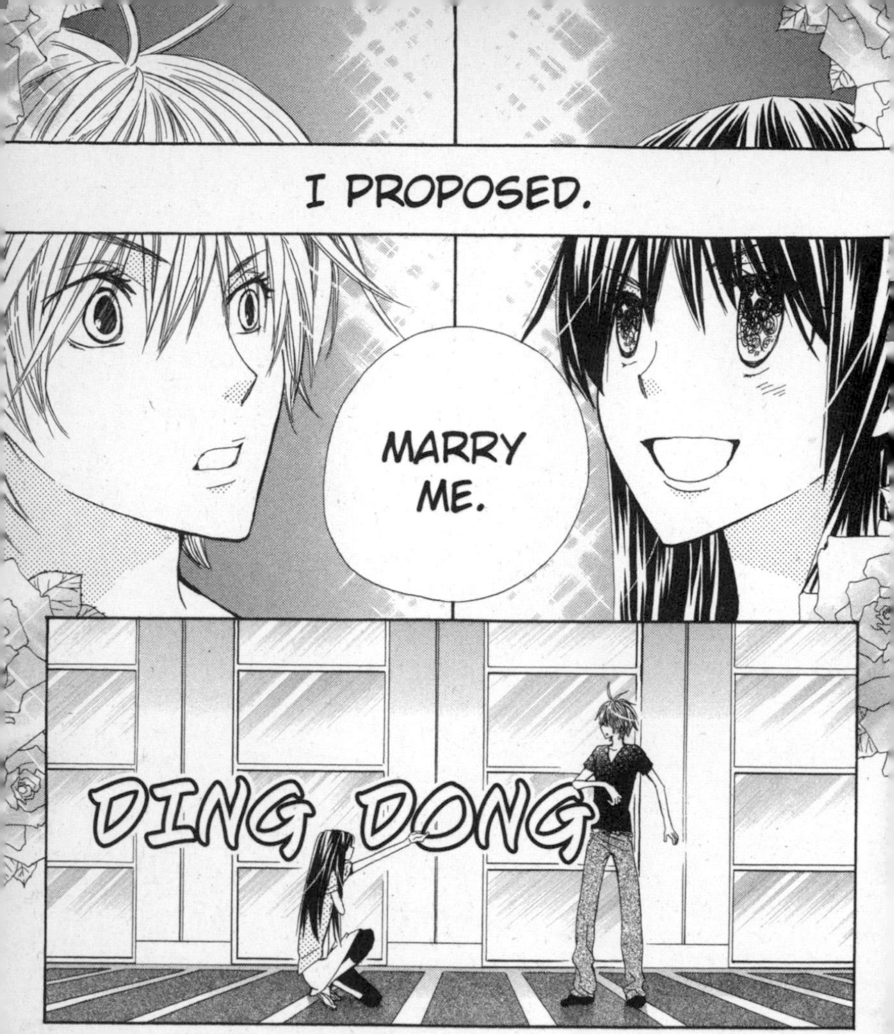
I PROPOSED.
MARRY ME.
DING DONG

• VOLUME 16 •

THERE ARE TWO MAIN STORIES IN VOL. 16, ONE ABOUT IORI AND ONE ABOUT TAKISHIMA'S GRANDFATHER.

SOME OF YOU WROTE ASKING FOR HIKARI AND IORI TO GET TOGETHER, BUT KEI REALLY IS THE ONLY GUY FOR HER. THANK YOU ALL SO MUCH!

AND I HAD A LOT OF FUN WRITING ABOUT HIKARI'S DATE WITH KEI'S GRANDFATHER IN THIS ONE!

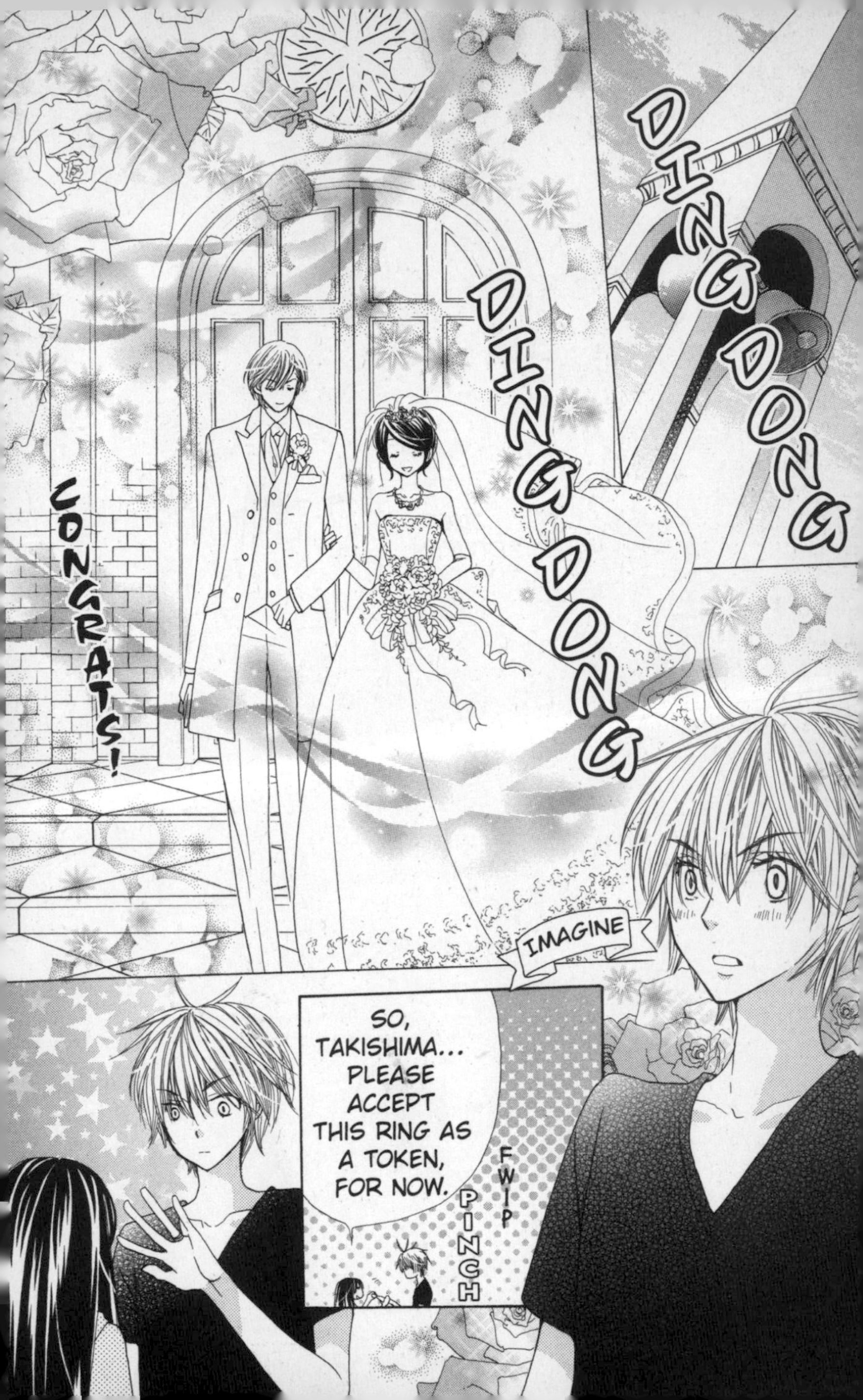
DING DONG
DING DONG
CONGRATS!
IMAGINE
SO, TAKISHIMA... PLEASE ACCEPT THIS RING AS A TOKEN, FOR NOW.
FWIP
PINCH

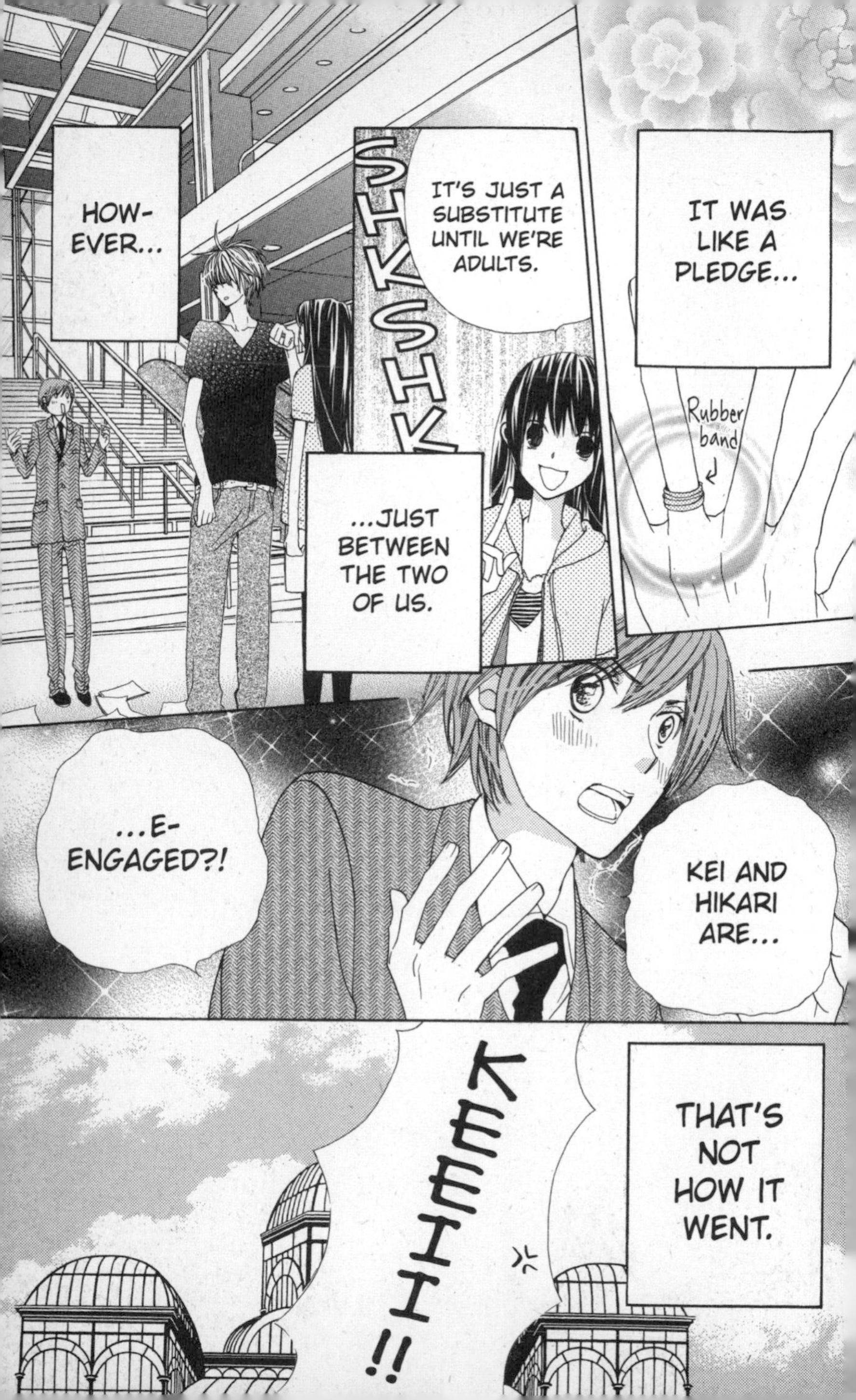
IT WAS LIKE A PLEDGE...
Rubber band
IT'S JUST A SUBSTITUTE UNTIL WE'RE ADULTS.
SHKSHK
...JUST BETWEEN THE TWO OF US.
HOW-EVER...
KEI AND HIKARI ARE...
...E-ENGAGED?!
THAT'S NOT HOW IT WENT.
KEEIII!!

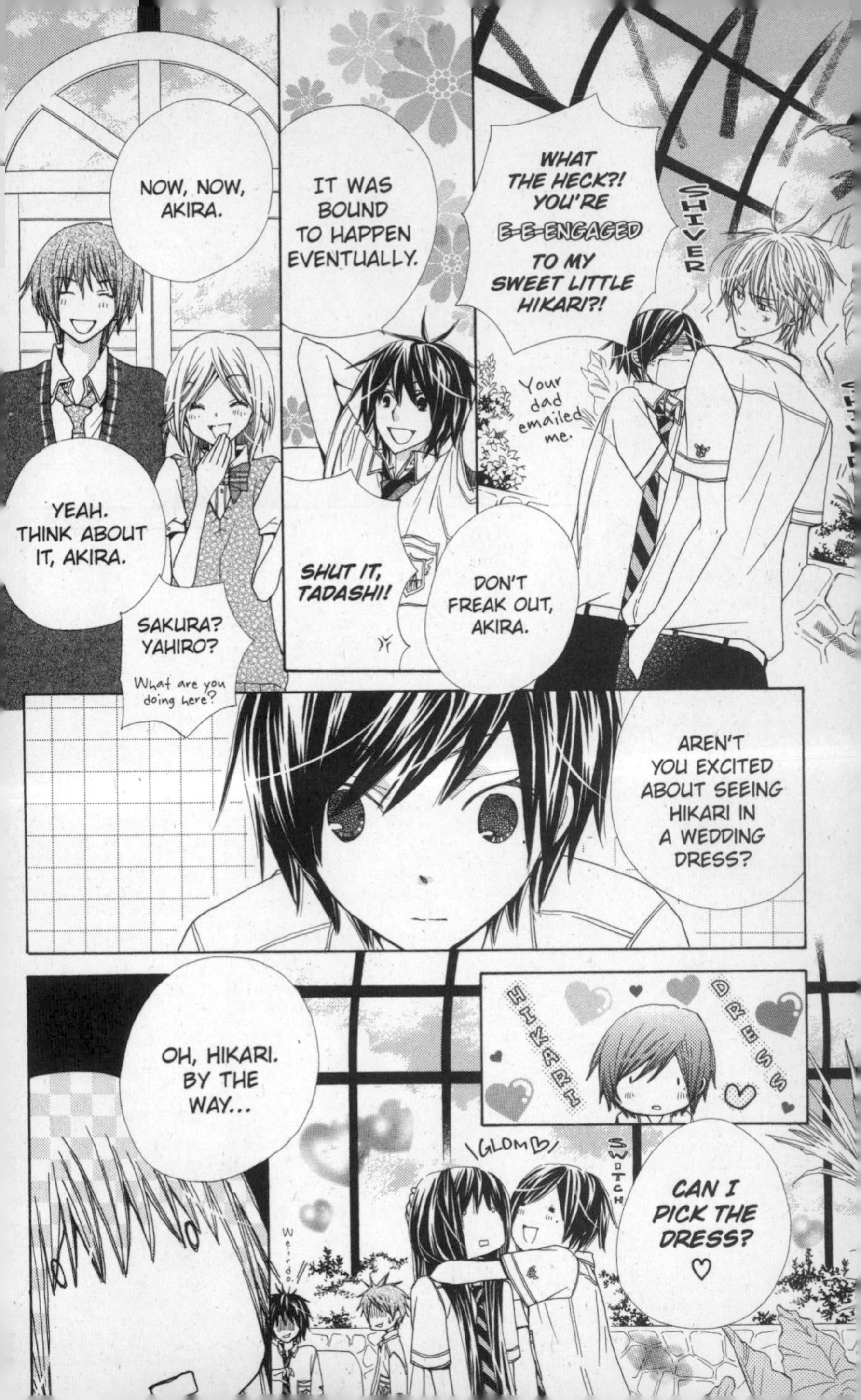
SHIVER
WHAT THE HECK?! YOU'RE E-E-ENGAGED TO MY SWEET LITTLE HIKARI?!
Your dad emailed me.
IT WAS BOUND TO HAPPEN EVENTUALLY.
DON'T FREAK OUT, AKIRA.
SHUT IT, TADASHI!
NOW, NOW, AKIRA.
YEAH. THINK ABOUT IT, AKIRA.
SAKURA? YAHIRO?
What are you doing here?
AREN'T YOU EXCITED ABOUT SEEING HIKARI IN A WEDDING DRESS?
HIKARI
DRESS
CAN I PICK THE DRESS? ♡
SWITCH
GLOM
OH, HIKARI. BY THE WAY...
Weirdo.

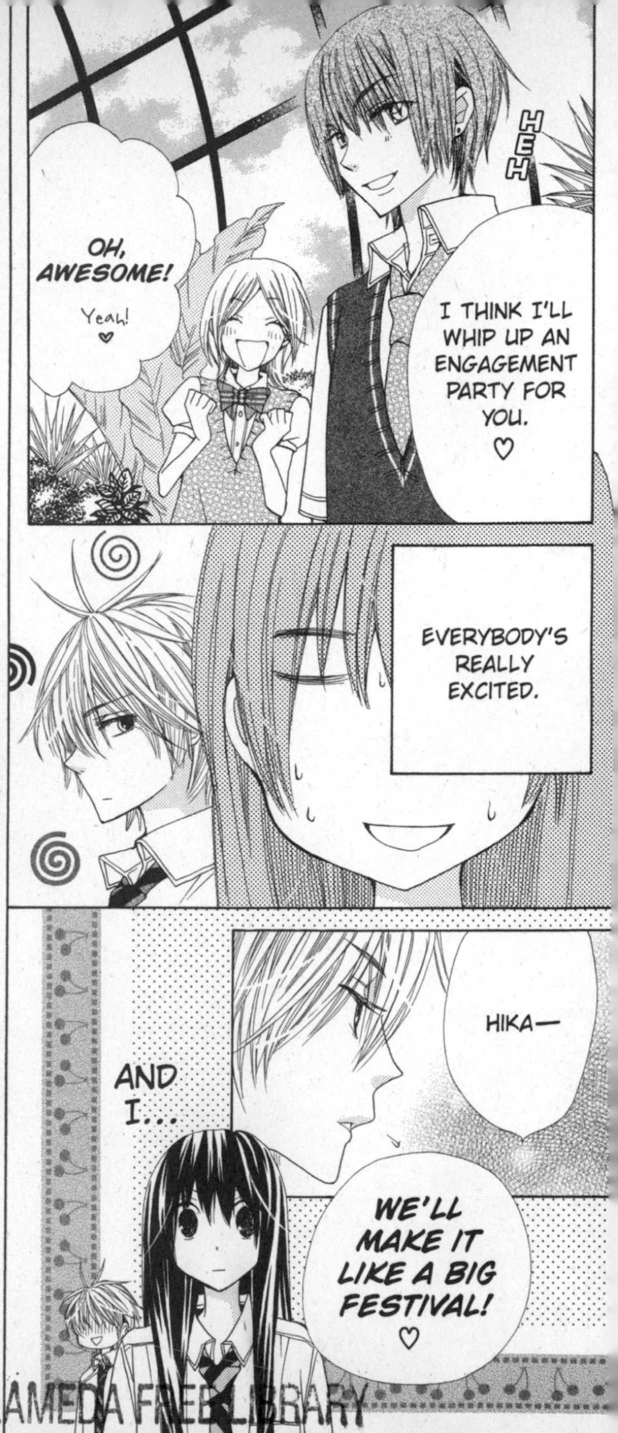
HEH
I THINK I'LL WHIP UP AN ENGAGEMENT PARTY FOR YOU. ♡
OH, AWESOME!
Yeah! ♡
EVERYBODY'S REALLY EXCITED.
HIKA—
WE'LL MAKE IT LIKE A BIG FESTIVAL! ♡
AND I...

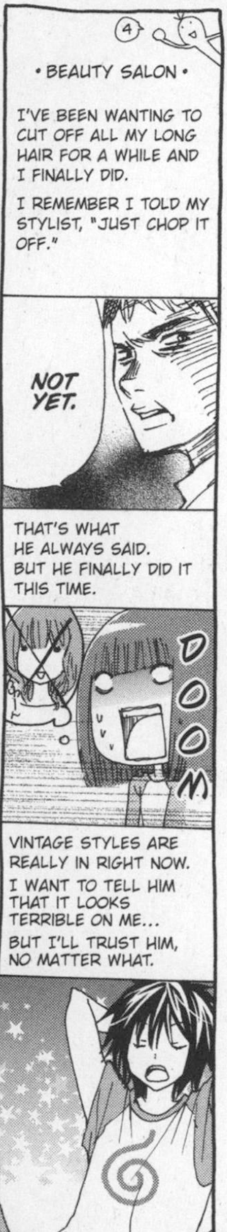
4
• BEAUTY SALON •
I'VE BEEN WANTING TO CUT OFF ALL MY LONG HAIR FOR A WHILE AND I FINALLY DID.
I REMEMBER I TOLD MY STYLIST, "JUST CHOP IT OFF."
NOT YET.
THAT'S WHAT HE ALWAYS SAID. BUT HE FINALLY DID IT THIS TIME.
DOOOM
VINTAGE STYLES ARE REALLY IN RIGHT NOW.
I WANT TO TELL HIM THAT IT LOOKS TERRIBLE ON ME...
BUT I'LL TRUST HIM, NO MATTER WHAT.

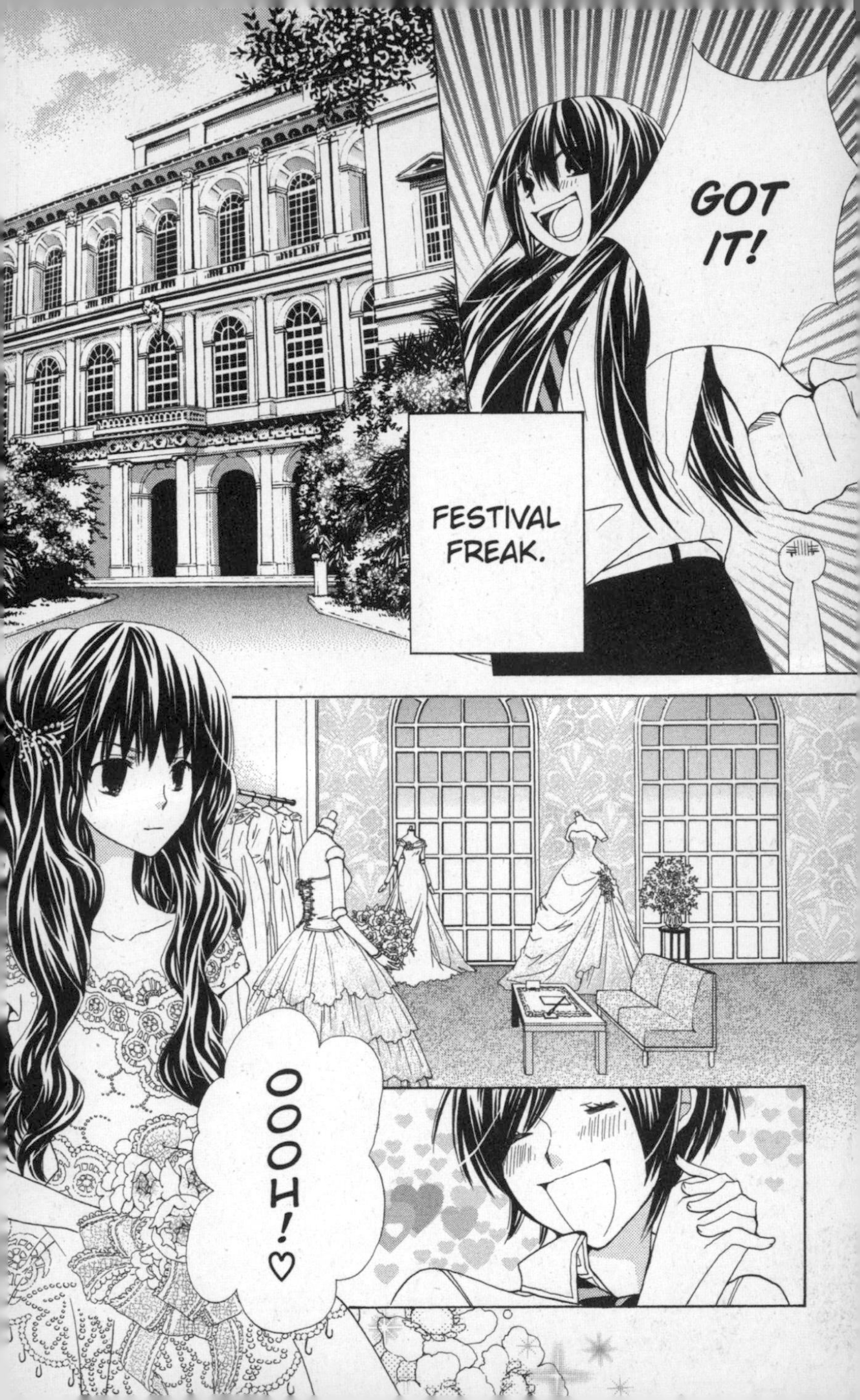
GOT IT!
FESTIVAL FREAK.
OOOH!♡

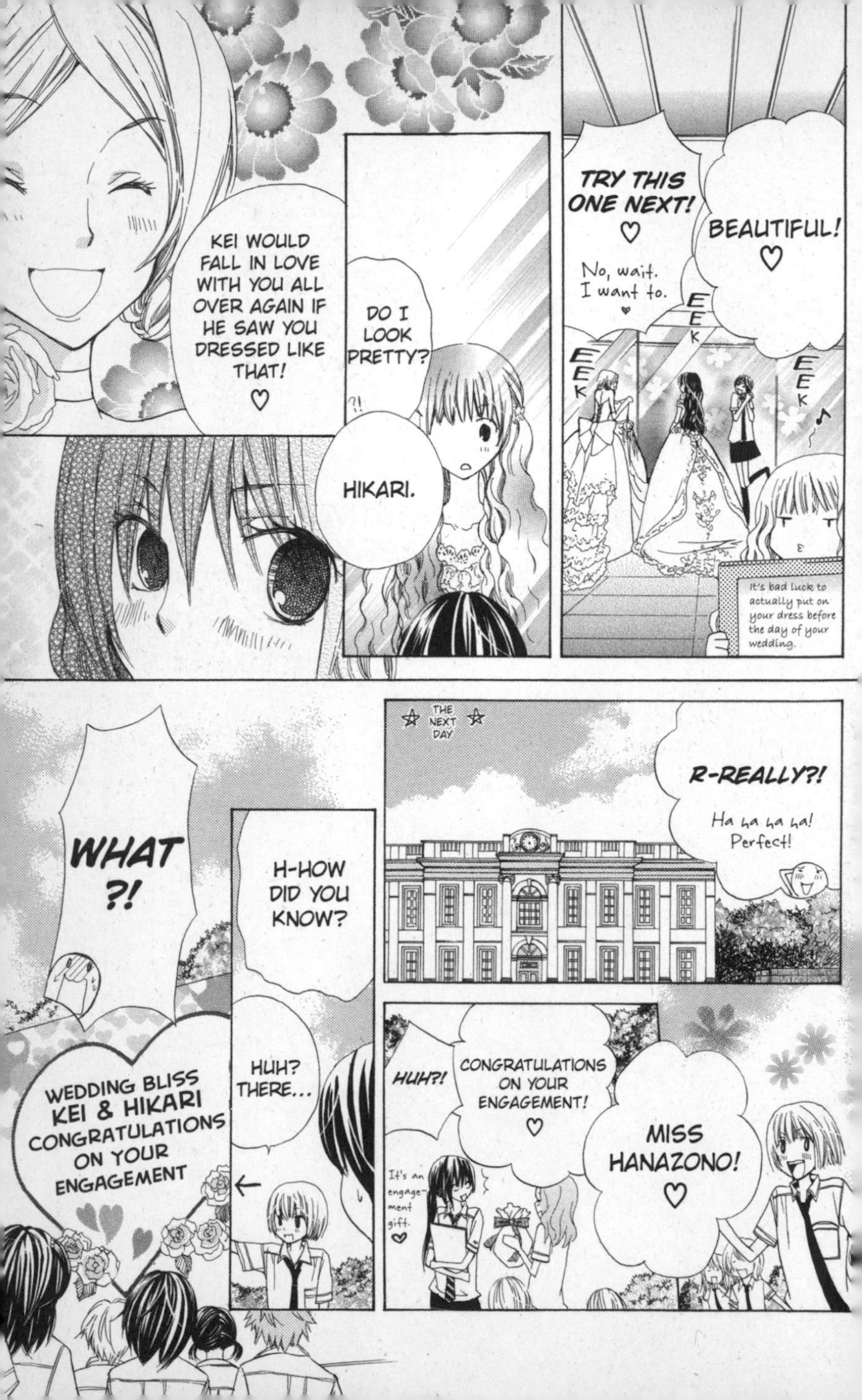
TRY THIS ONE NEXT! ♡
BEAUTIFUL! ♡
No, wait. I want to. ♡
EEK
EEK
EEK
It's bad luck to actually put on your dress before the day of your wedding.
DO I LOOK PRETTY?
?!
HIKARI.
KEI WOULD FALL IN LOVE WITH YOU ALL OVER AGAIN IF HE SAW YOU DRESSED LIKE THAT! ♡
THE NEXT DAY
R-REALLY?!
Ha ha ha ha! Perfect!
MISS HANAZONO! ♡
CONGRATULATIONS ON YOUR ENGAGEMENT! ♡
HUH?!
It's an engagement gift. ♡
H-HOW DID YOU KNOW?
HUH? THERE...
WHAT ?!
WEDDING BLISS KEI & HIKARI CONGRATULATIONS ON YOUR ENGAGEMENT

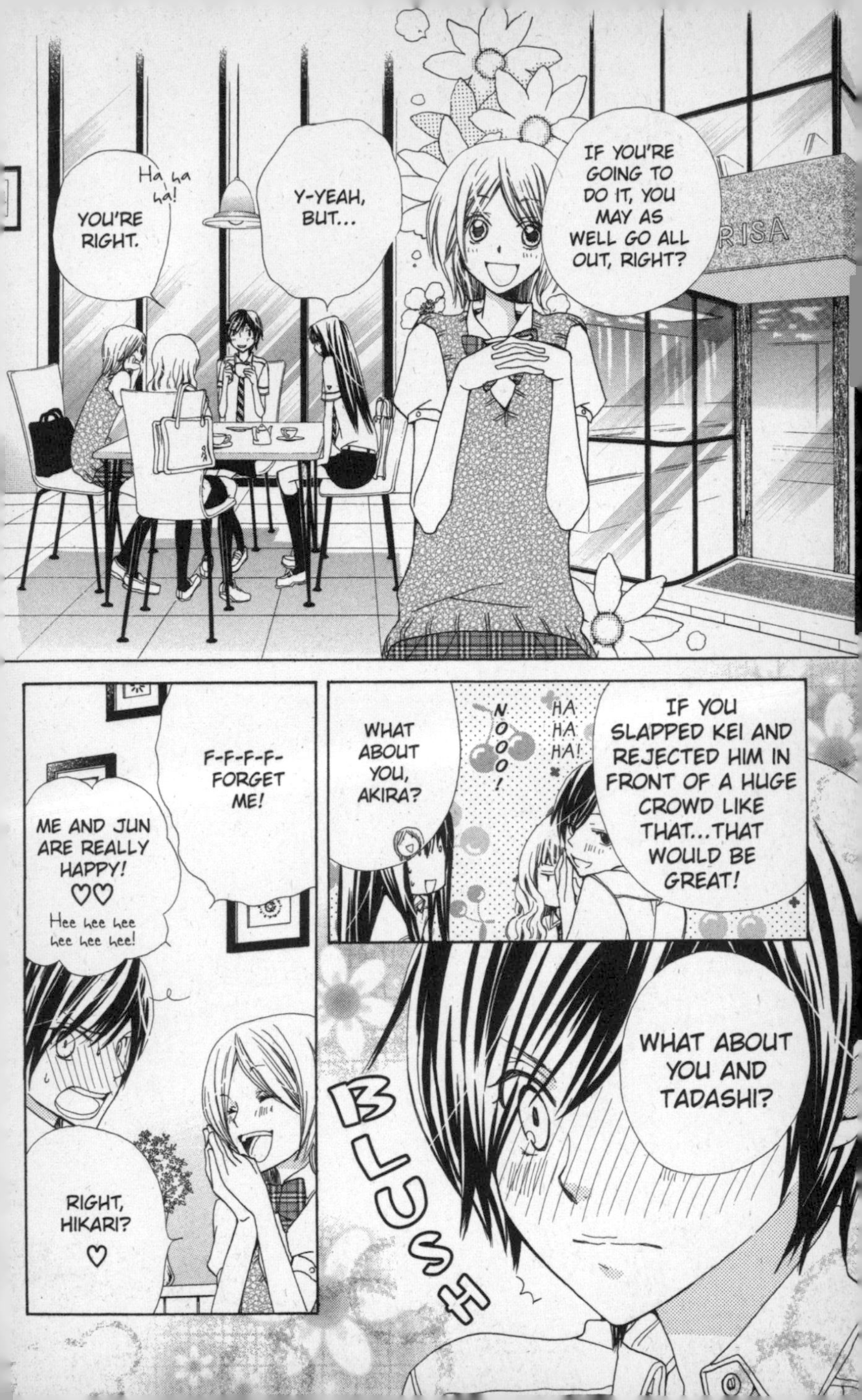
IF YOU'RE GOING TO DO IT, YOU MAY AS WELL GO ALL OUT, RIGHT?
RISA
Y-YEAH, BUT...
Ha ha ha!
YOU'RE RIGHT.
IF YOU SLAPPED KEI AND REJECTED HIM IN FRONT OF A HUGE CROWD LIKE THAT...THAT WOULD BE GREAT!
HA HA HA!
NOOOO!
WHAT ABOUT YOU, AKIRA?
WHAT ABOUT YOU AND TADASHI?
BLUSH
F-F-F-F-FORGET ME!
ME AND JUN ARE REALLY HAPPY! ♡♡
Hee hee hee hee hee hee!
RIGHT, HIKARI? ♡

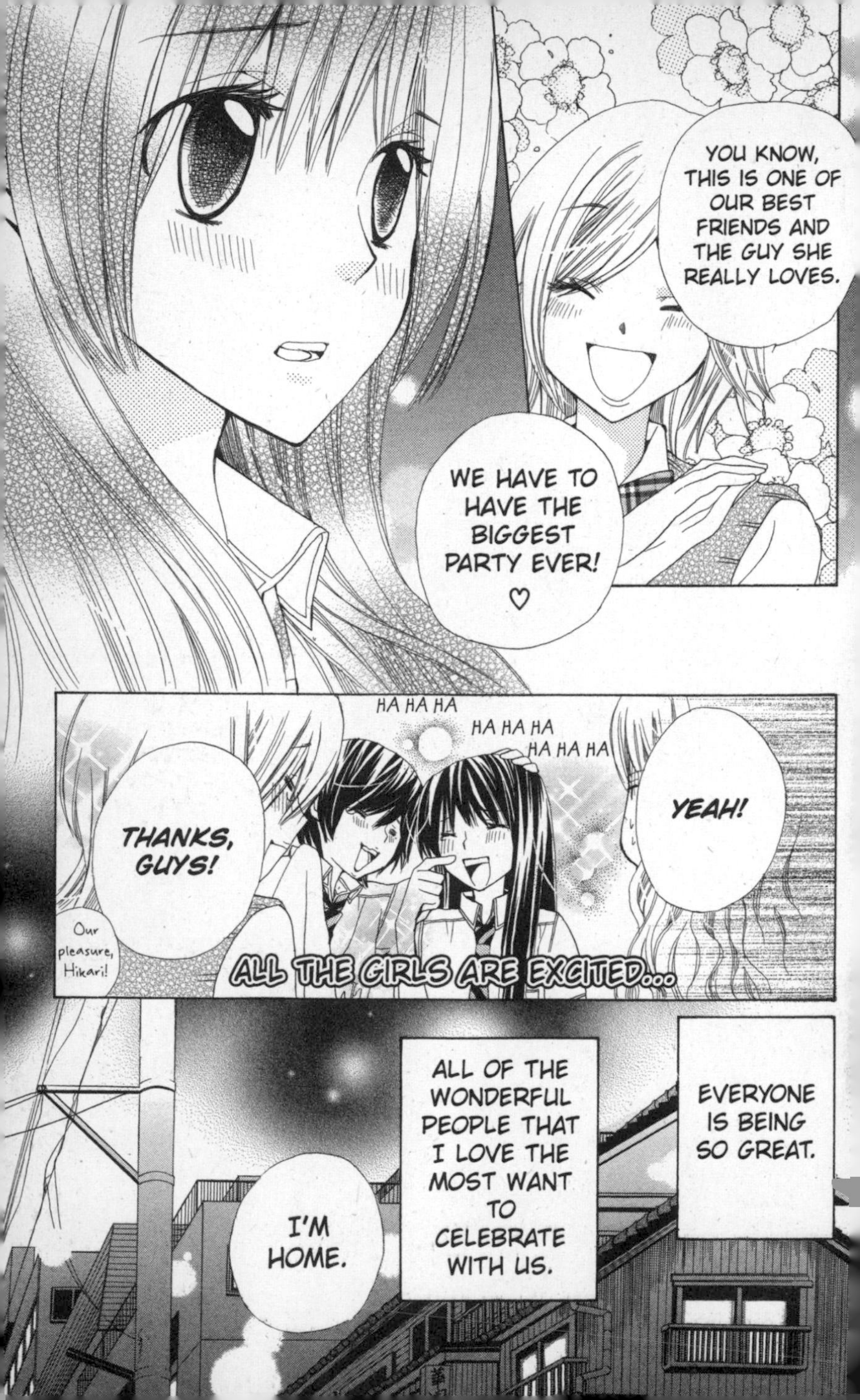
YOU KNOW, THIS IS ONE OF OUR BEST FRIENDS AND THE GUY SHE REALLY LOVES.
WE HAVE TO HAVE THE BIGGEST PARTY EVER! ♡
YEAH!
HA HA HA HA HA HA HA HA HA
THANKS, GUYS!
Our pleasure, Hikari!
ALL THE GIRLS ARE EXCITED...
EVERYONE IS BEING SO GREAT.
ALL OF THE WONDERFUL PEOPLE THAT I LOVE THE MOST WANT TO CELEBRATE WITH US.
I'M HOME.

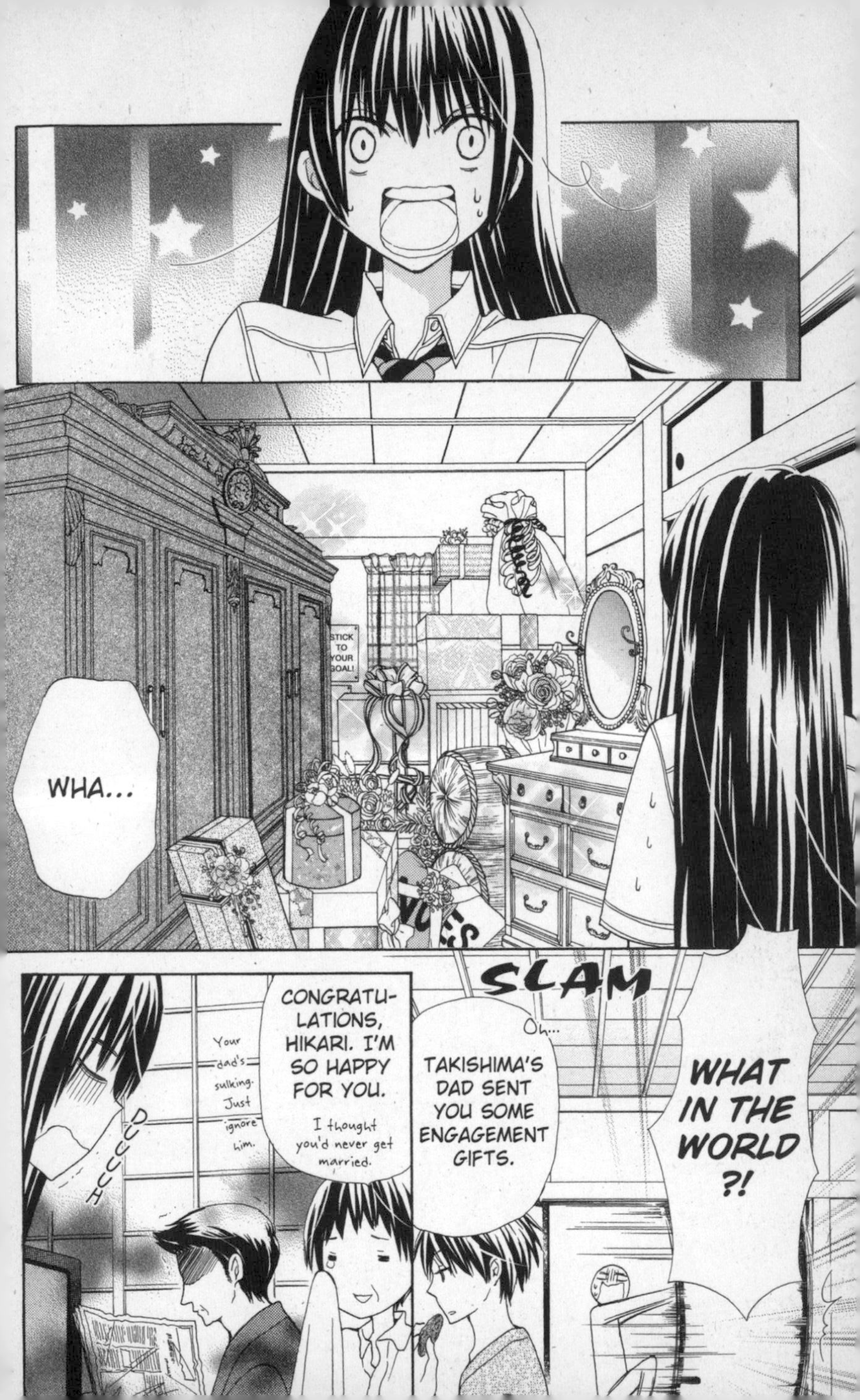
STICK TO YOUR GOAL!
WHA...
SLAM
WHAT IN THE WORLD ?!
Oh...
TAKISHIMA'S DAD SENT YOU SOME ENGAGEMENT GIFTS.
CONGRATULATIONS, HIKARI. I'M SO HAPPY FOR YOU.
I thought you'd never get married.
Your dad's sulking. Just ignore him.
DUUUUH

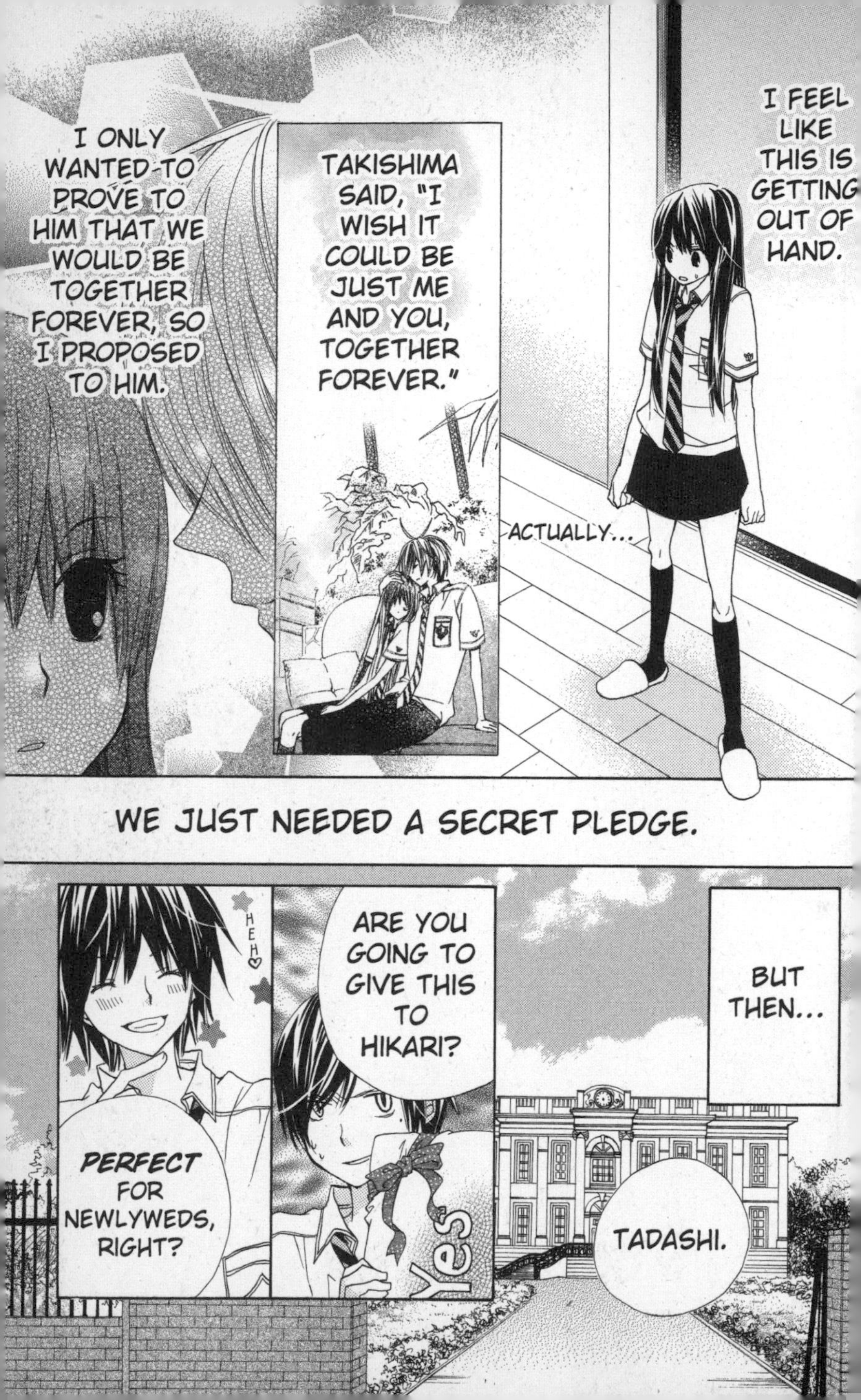
I FEEL LIKE THIS IS GETTING OUT OF HAND.
ACTUALLY...
TAKISHIMA SAID, "I WISH IT COULD BE JUST ME AND YOU, TOGETHER FOREVER."
I ONLY WANTED TO PROVE TO HIM THAT WE WOULD BE TOGETHER FOREVER, SO I PROPOSED TO HIM.
WE JUST NEEDED A SECRET PLEDGE.
BUT THEN...
TADASHI.
ARE YOU GOING TO GIVE THIS TO HIKARI?
YES
HEH ♥
PERFECT FOR NEWLYWEDS, RIGHT?

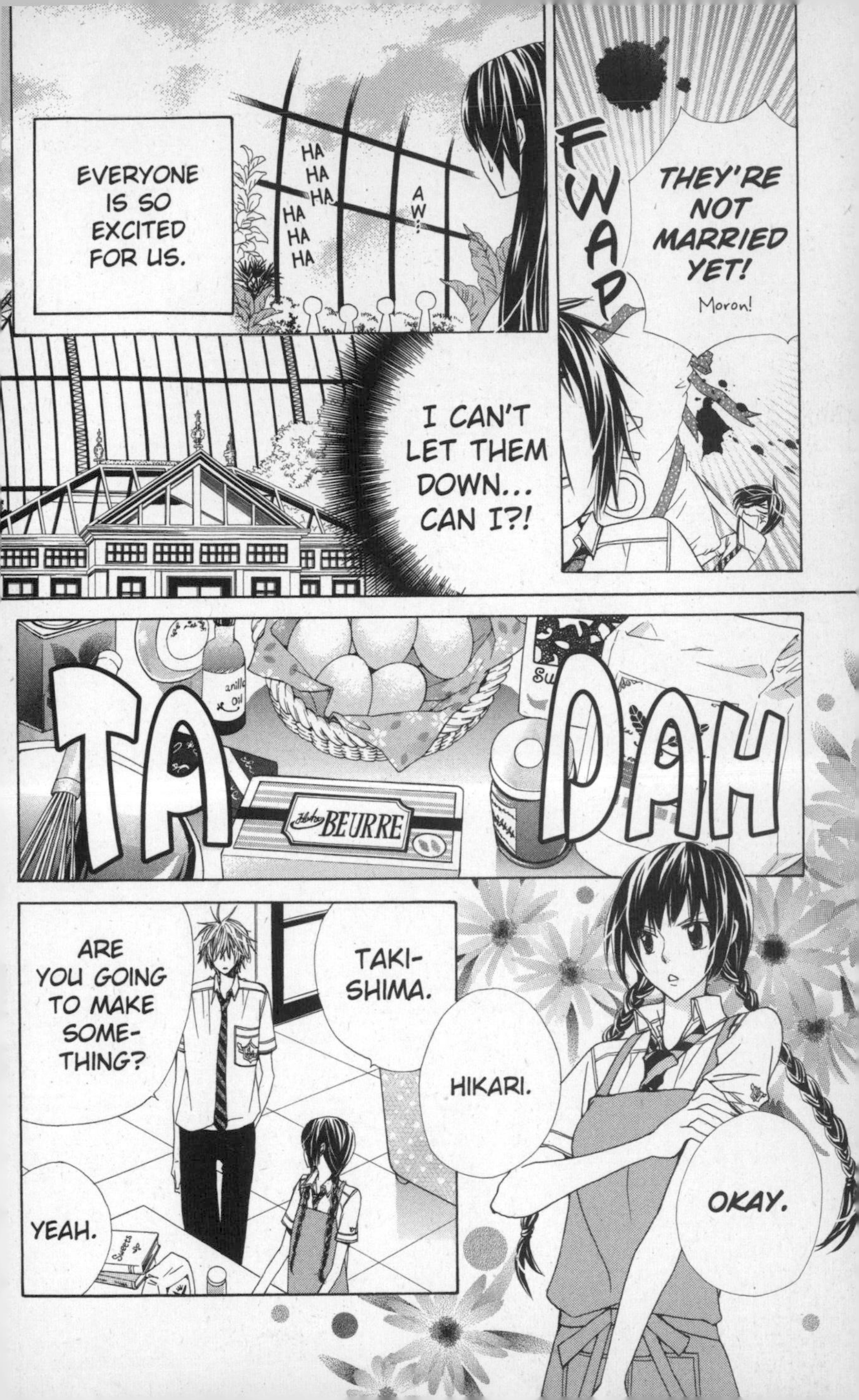
FWAP
THEY'RE NOT MARRIED YET!
Moron!
EVERYONE IS SO EXCITED FOR US.
HA HA HA
HA HA HA
AW...
I CAN'T LET THEM DOWN... CAN I?!
TA
DAH
BEURRE
TAKI-SHIMA.
HIKARI.
ARE YOU GOING TO MAKE SOME-THING?
YEAH.
OKAY.

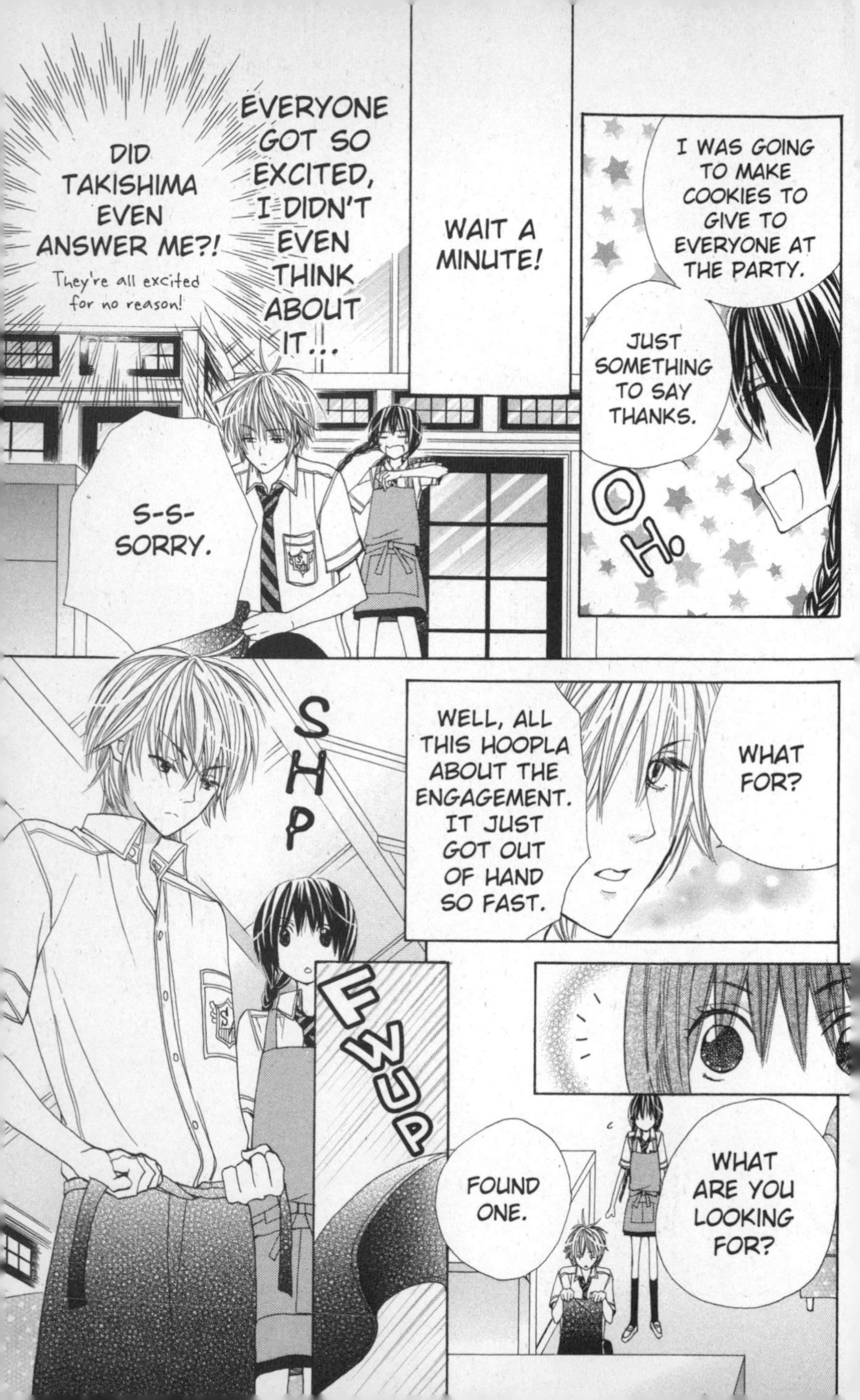
I WAS GOING TO MAKE COOKIES TO GIVE TO EVERYONE AT THE PARTY.
JUST SOMETHING TO SAY THANKS.
OH.
WAIT A MINUTE!
EVERYONE GOT SO EXCITED, I DIDN'T EVEN THINK ABOUT IT...
DID TAKISHIMA EVEN ANSWER ME?!
They're all excited for no reason!
S-S-SORRY.
WHAT FOR?
WELL, ALL THIS HOOPLA ABOUT THE ENGAGEMENT. IT JUST GOT OUT OF HAND SO FAST.
WHAT ARE YOU LOOKING FOR?
FOUND ONE.
FWUP
SHP

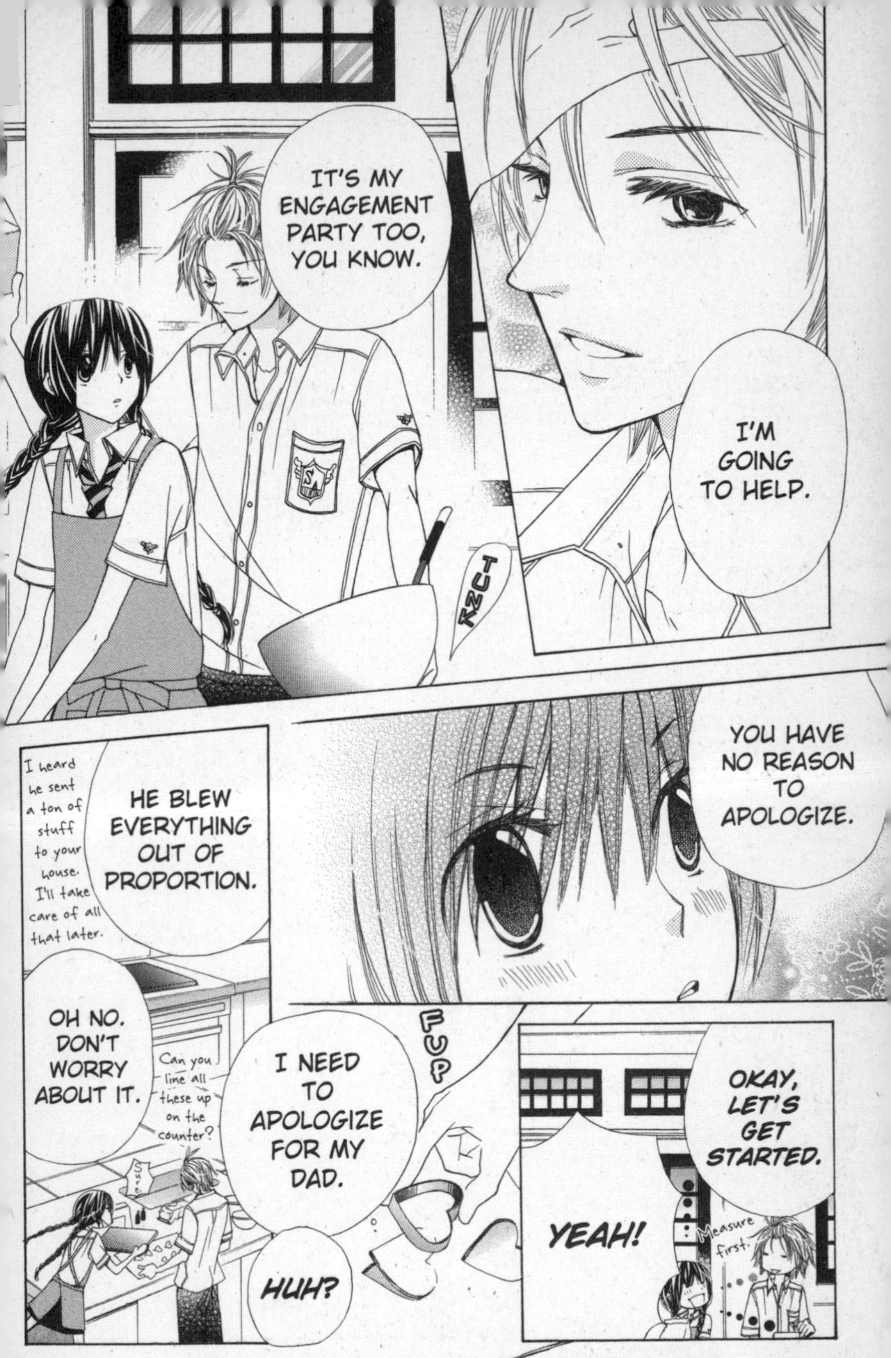
I'M GOING TO HELP.
IT'S MY ENGAGEMENT PARTY TOO, YOU KNOW.
TUNK
YOU HAVE NO REASON TO APOLOGIZE.
HE BLEW EVERYTHING OUT OF PROPORTION.
I heard he sent a ton of stuff to your house. I'll take care of all that later.
OKAY, LET'S GET STARTED.
YEAH!
Measure first.
FUP
I NEED TO APOLOGIZE FOR MY DAD.
HUH?
OH NO. DON'T WORRY ABOUT IT.
Can you line all these up on the counter?
Sure

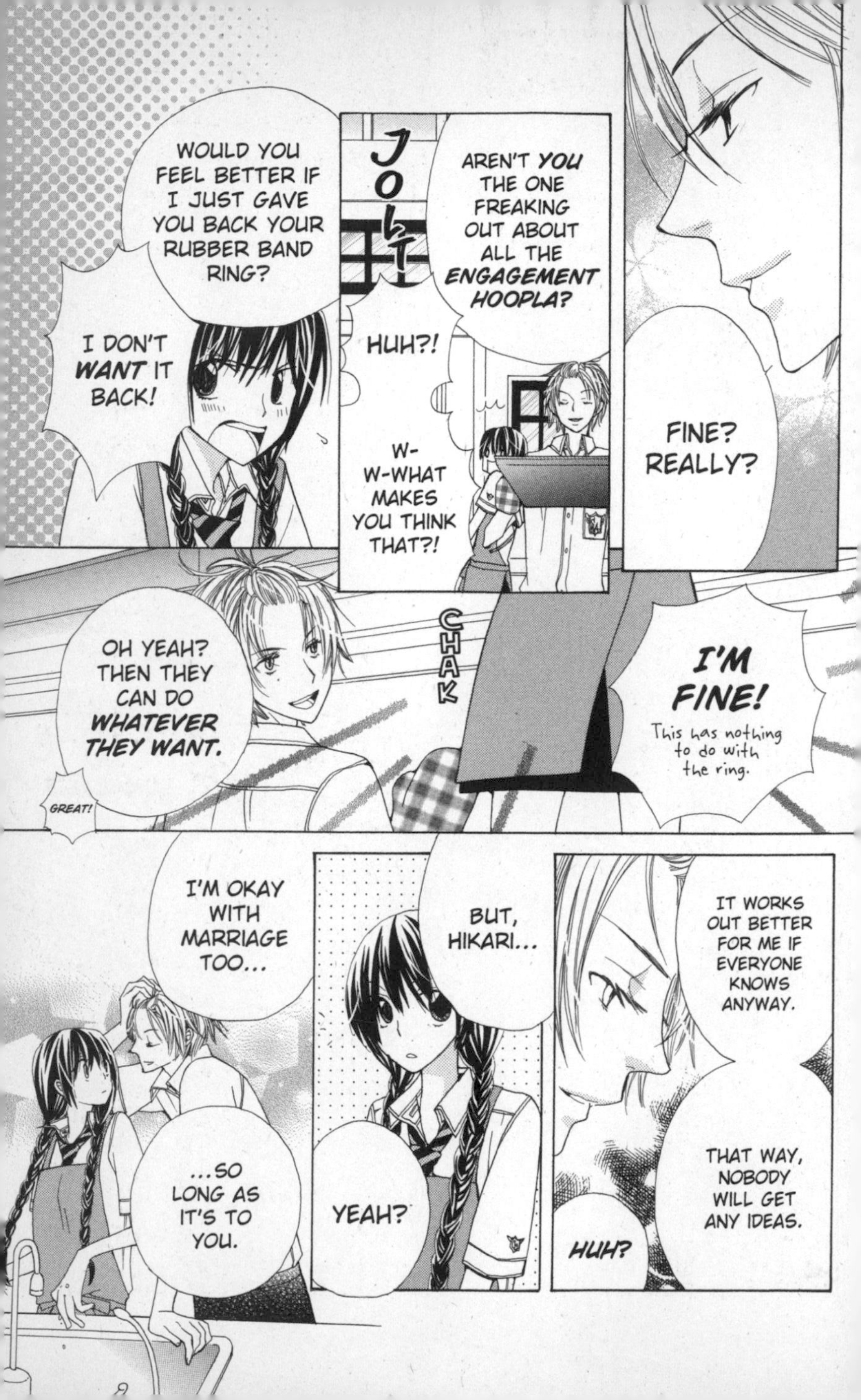
FINE? REALLY?
AREN'T YOU THE ONE FREAKING OUT ABOUT ALL THE ENGAGEMENT HOOPLA?
JOLT
HUH?!
W-W-WHAT MAKES YOU THINK THAT?!
WOULD YOU FEEL BETTER IF I JUST GAVE YOU BACK YOUR RUBBER BAND RING?
I DON'T WANT IT BACK!
I'M FINE!
This has nothing to do with the ring.
CHAK
OH YEAH? THEN THEY CAN DO WHATEVER THEY WANT.
GREAT!
IT WORKS OUT BETTER FOR ME IF EVERYONE KNOWS ANYWAY.
THAT WAY, NOBODY WILL GET ANY IDEAS.
HUH?
BUT, HIKARI...
YEAH?
I'M OKAY WITH MARRIAGE TOO...
...SO LONG AS IT'S TO YOU.

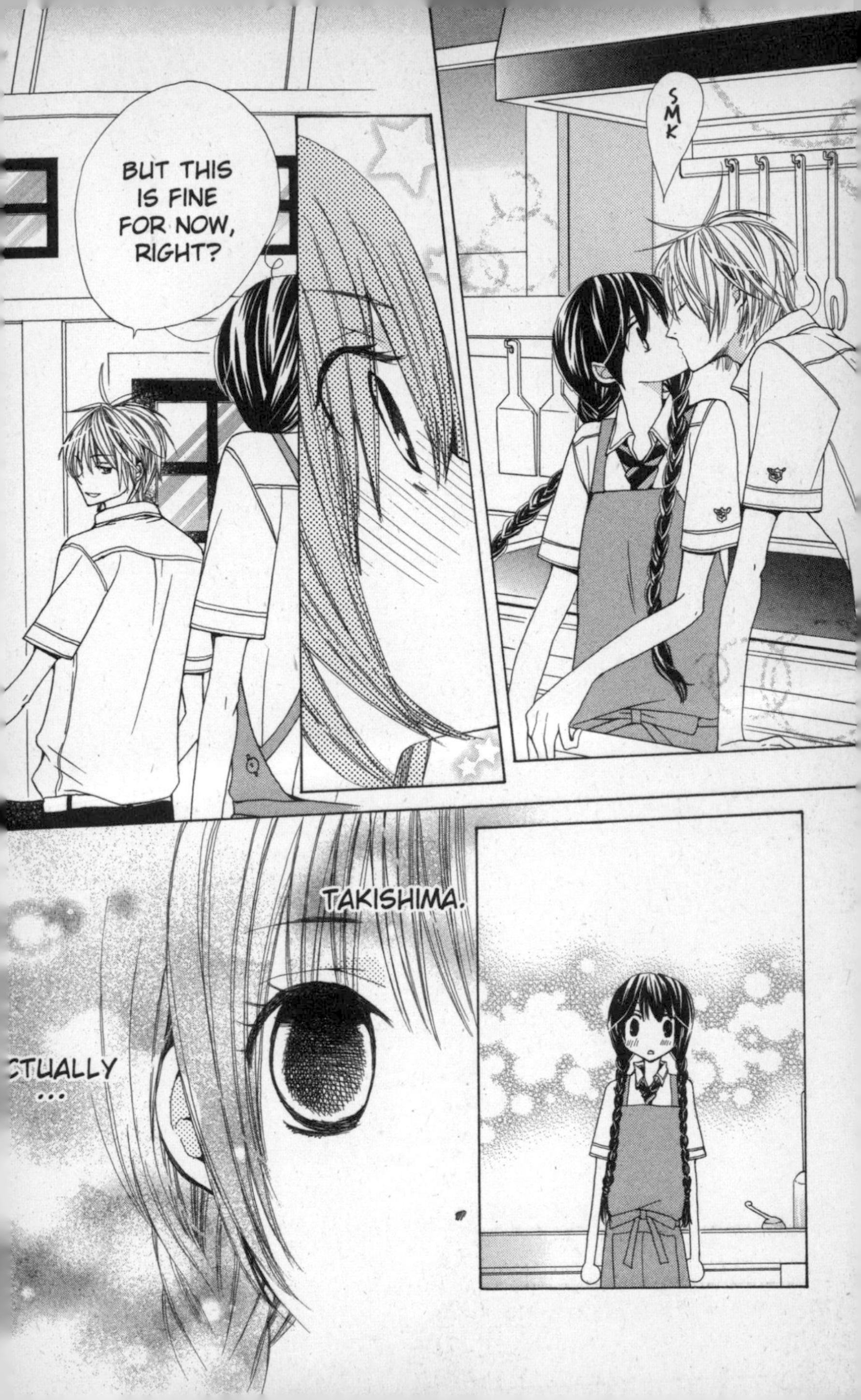
SMK
BUT THIS IS FINE FOR NOW, RIGHT?
TAKISHIMA.
CTUALLY ...

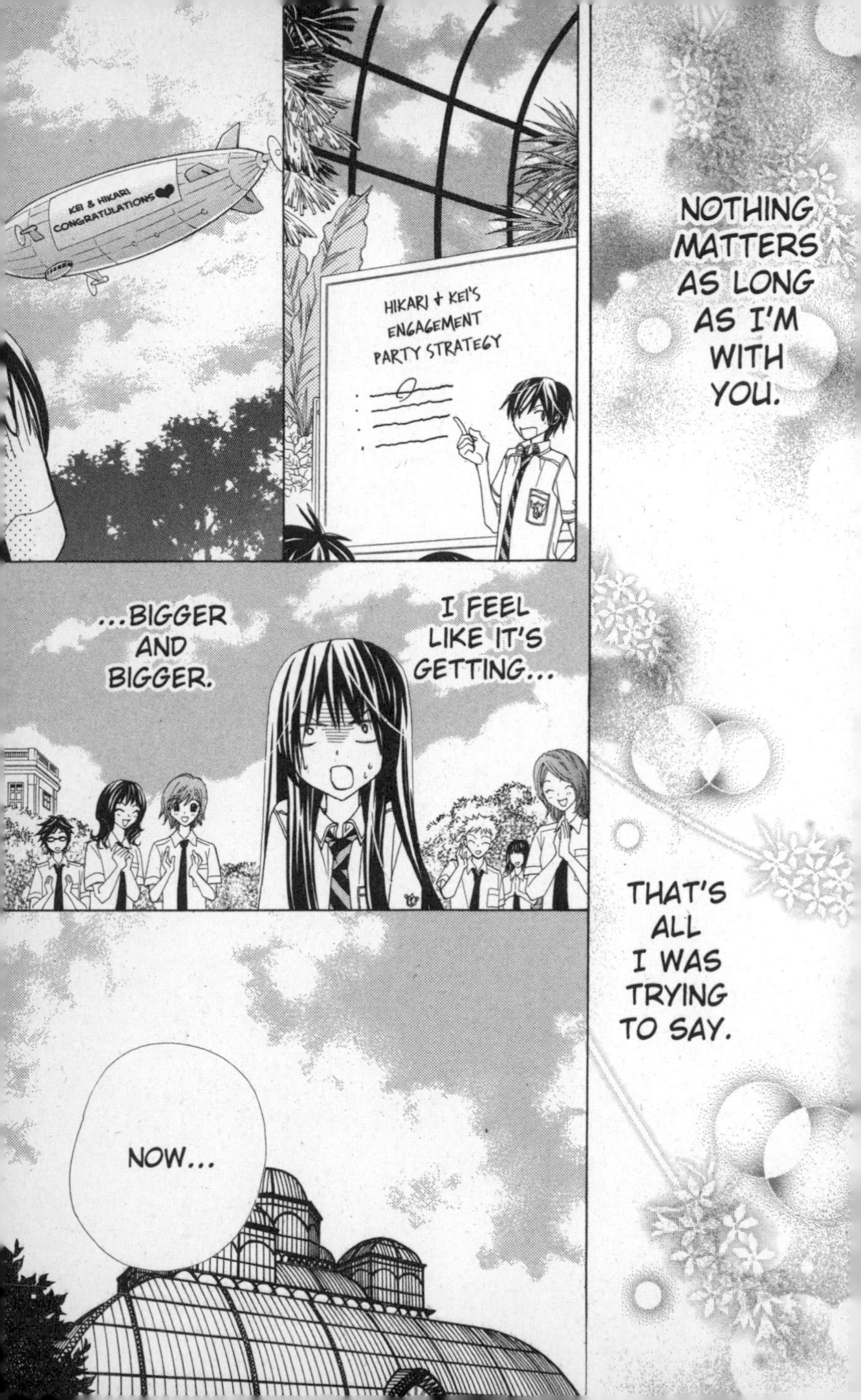
NOTHING MATTERS AS LONG AS I'M WITH YOU.
THAT'S ALL I WAS TRYING TO SAY.
HIKARI + KEI'S ENGAGEMENT PARTY STRATEGY
KEI & HIKARI CONGRATULATIONS
I FEEL LIKE IT'S GETTING...
...BIGGER AND BIGGER.
NOW...

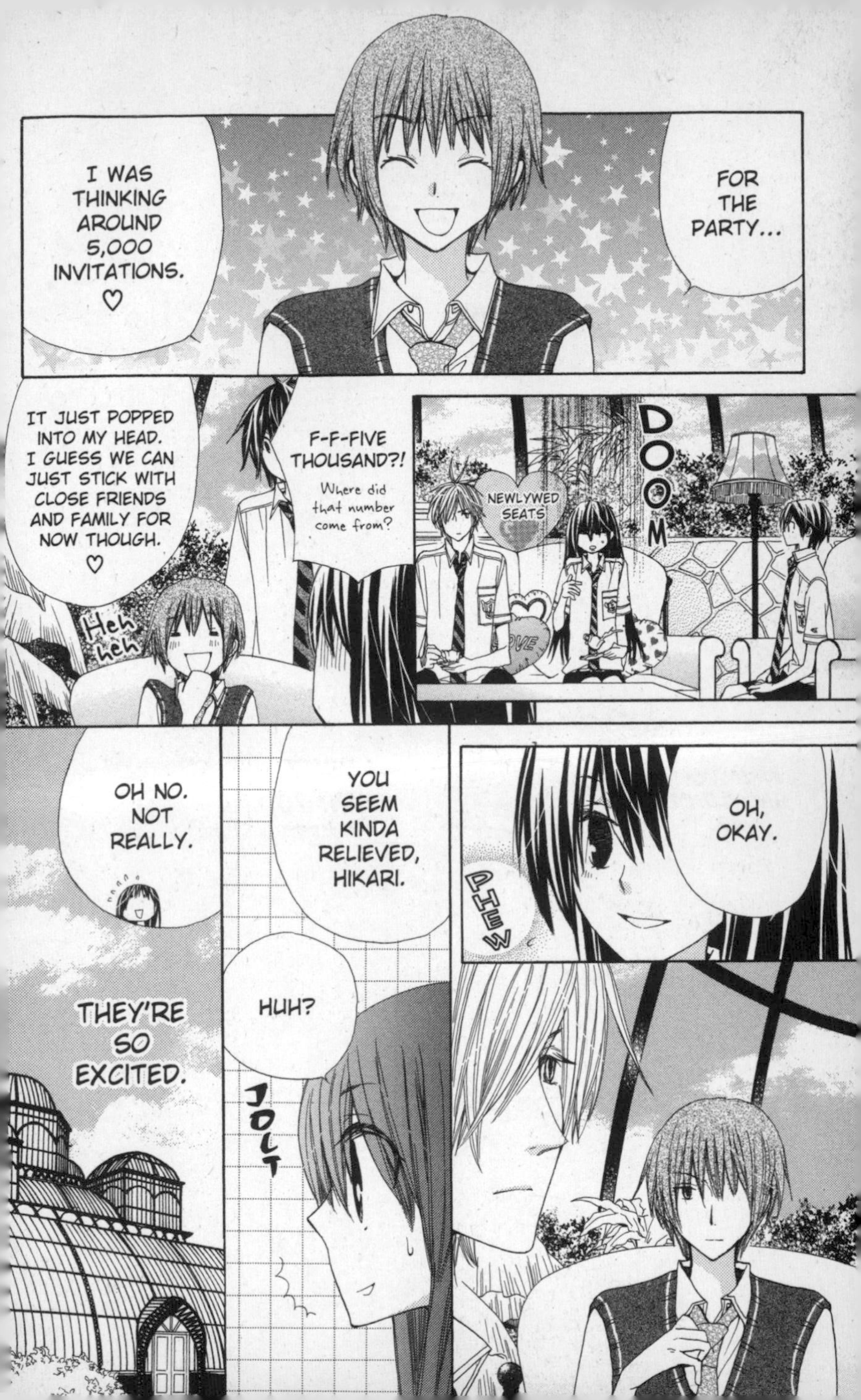

FOR THE PARTY...
I WAS THINKING AROUND 5,000 INVITATIONS. ♡
DOOM
NEWLYWED SEATS
LOVE
F-F-FIVE THOUSAND?!
Where did that number come from?
IT JUST POPPED INTO MY HEAD. I GUESS WE CAN JUST STICK WITH CLOSE FRIENDS AND FAMILY FOR NOW THOUGH. ♡
Heh heh
OH, OKAY.
PHEW
YOU SEEM KINDA RELIEVED, HIKARI.
HUH?
JOLT
OH NO. NOT REALLY.
THEY'RE SO EXCITED.

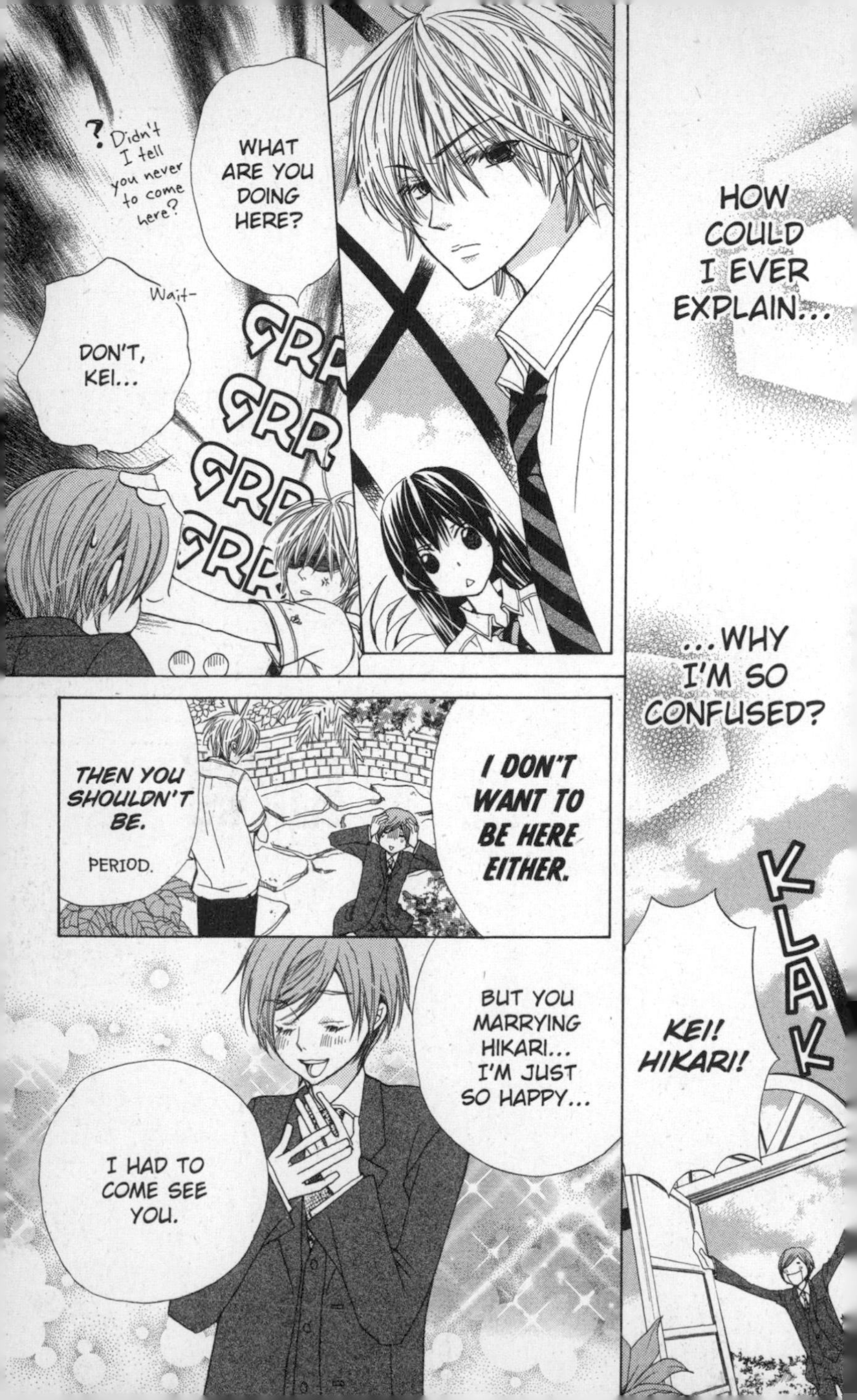
HOW COULD I EVER EXPLAIN...
...WHY I'M SO CONFUSED?
KLAK
KEI! HIKARI!
WHAT ARE YOU DOING HERE?
Didn't I tell you never to come here?
Wait-
DON'T, KEI...
GRR GRR GRR GRR
I DON'T WANT TO BE HERE EITHER.
THEN YOU SHOULDN'T BE.
PERIOD.
BUT YOU MARRYING HIKARI... I'M JUST SO HAPPY...
I HAD TO COME SEE YOU.

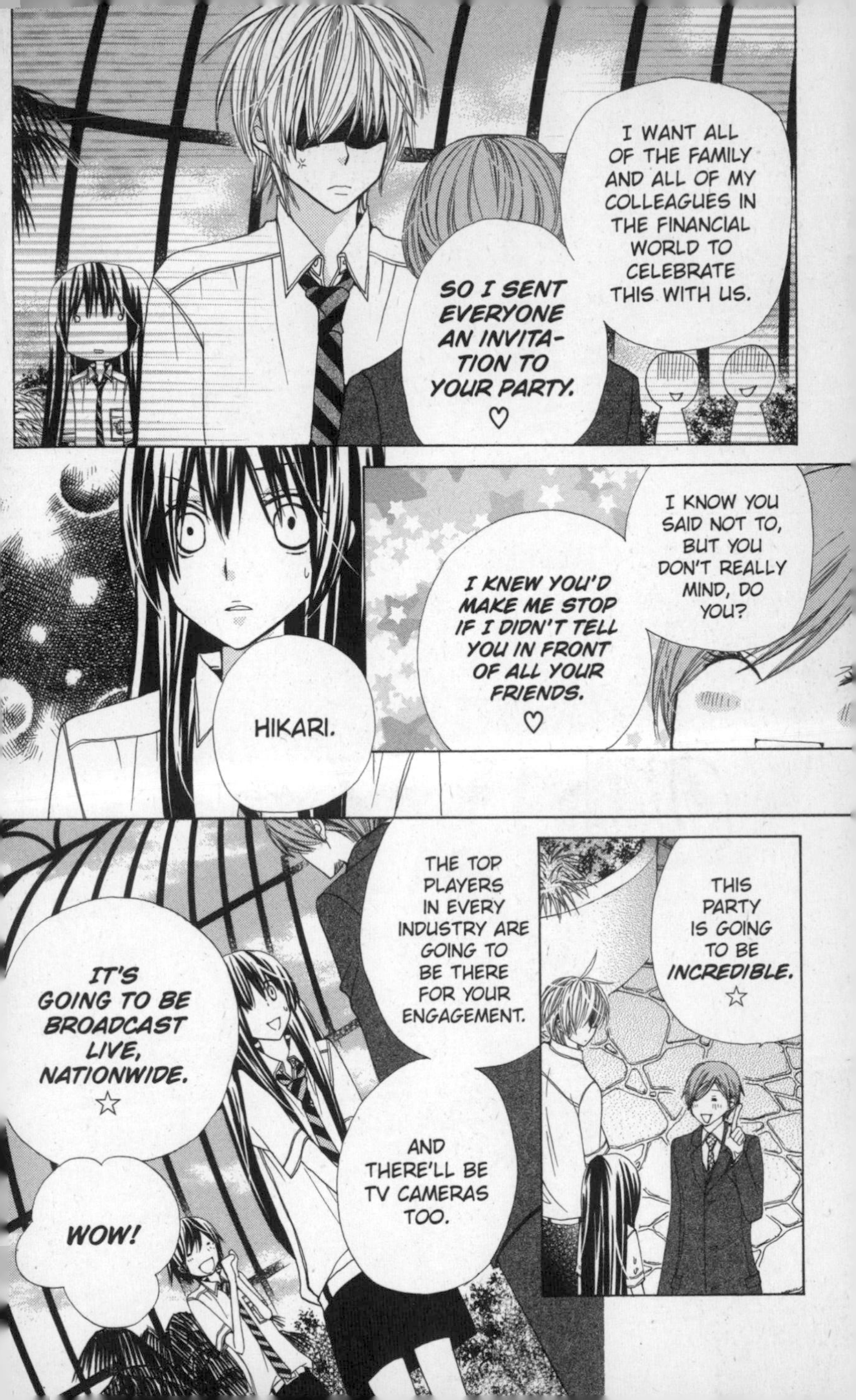
I WANT ALL OF THE FAMILY AND ALL OF MY COLLEAGUES IN THE FINANCIAL WORLD TO CELEBRATE THIS WITH US.
SO I SENT EVERYONE AN INVITATION TO YOUR PARTY. ♡
I KNOW YOU SAID NOT TO, BUT YOU DON'T REALLY MIND, DO YOU?
I KNEW YOU'D MAKE ME STOP IF I DIDN'T TELL YOU IN FRONT OF ALL YOUR FRIENDS. ♡
HIKARI.
THIS PARTY IS GOING TO BE INCREDIBLE. ☆
THE TOP PLAYERS IN EVERY INDUSTRY ARE GOING TO BE THERE FOR YOUR ENGAGEMENT.
AND THERE'LL BE TV CAMERAS TOO.
IT'S GOING TO BE BROADCAST LIVE, NATIONWIDE. ☆
WOW!

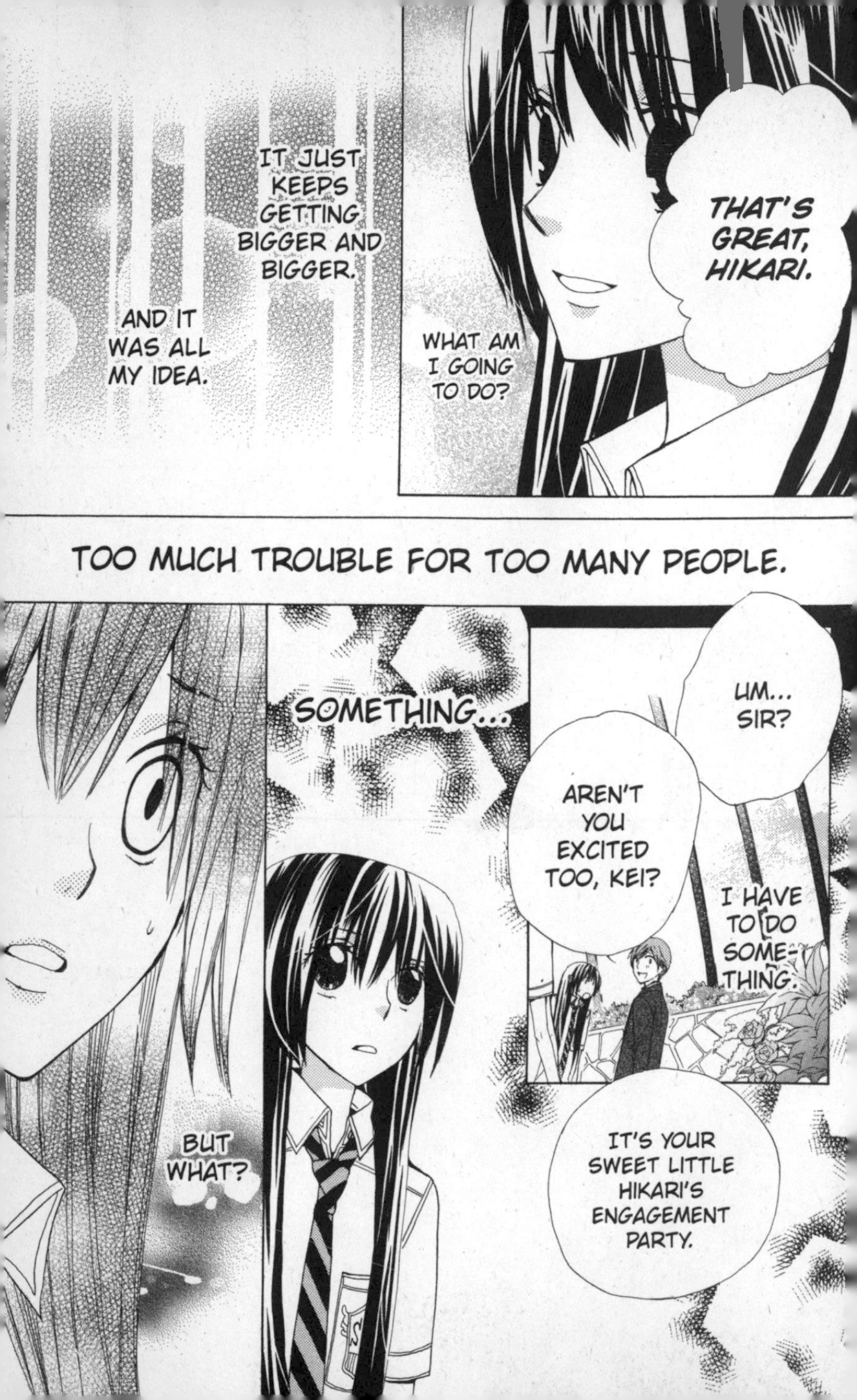
THAT'S GREAT, HIKARI.
WHAT AM I GOING TO DO?
IT JUST KEEPS GETTING BIGGER AND BIGGER.
AND IT WAS ALL MY IDEA.
TOO MUCH TROUBLE FOR TOO MANY PEOPLE.
UM... SIR?
AREN'T YOU EXCITED TOO, KEI?
I HAVE TO DO SOME-THING.
IT'S YOUR SWEET LITTLE HIKARI'S ENGAGEMENT PARTY.
SOMETHING...
BUT WHAT?

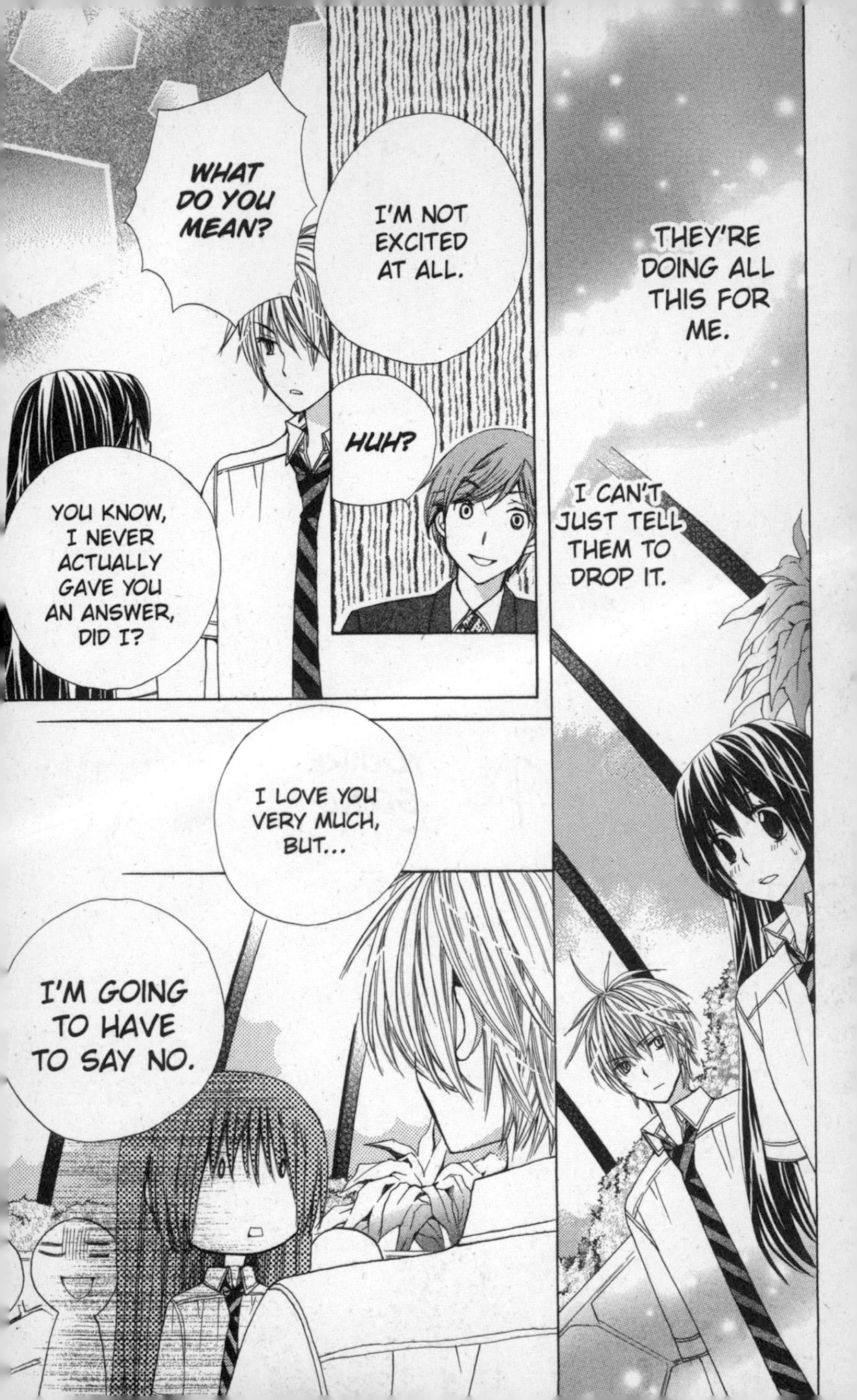
THEY'RE DOING ALL THIS FOR ME.
I CAN'T JUST TELL THEM TO DROP IT.
I'M NOT EXCITED AT ALL.
HUH?
WHAT DO YOU MEAN?
YOU KNOW, I NEVER ACTUALLY GAVE YOU AN ANSWER, DID I?
I LOVE YOU VERY MUCH, BUT...
I'M GOING TO HAVE TO SAY NO.

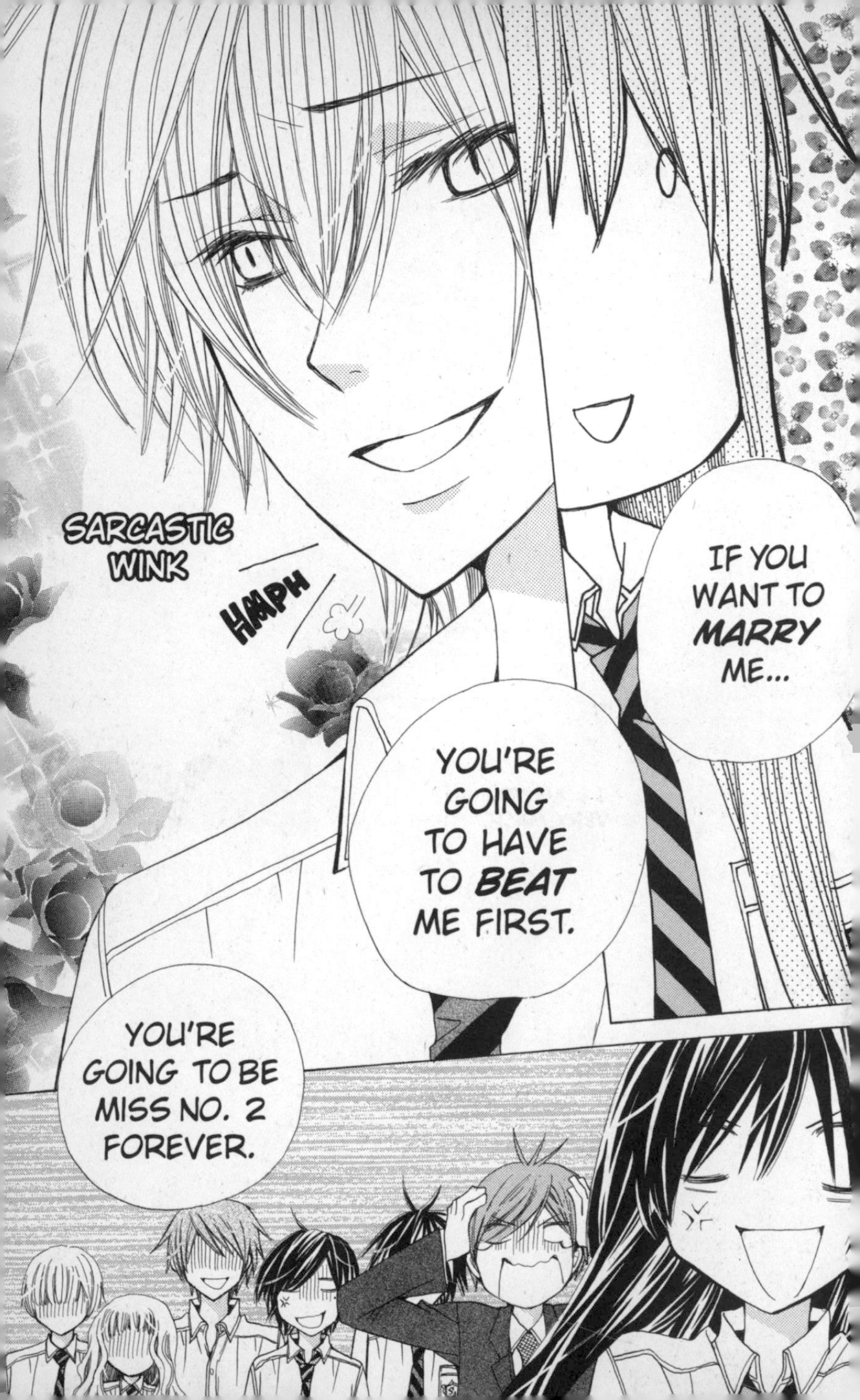

IF YOU WANT TO MARRY ME...
SARCASTIC WINK
HMPH
YOU'RE GOING TO HAVE TO BEAT ME FIRST.
YOU'RE GOING TO BE MISS NO. 2 FOREVER.

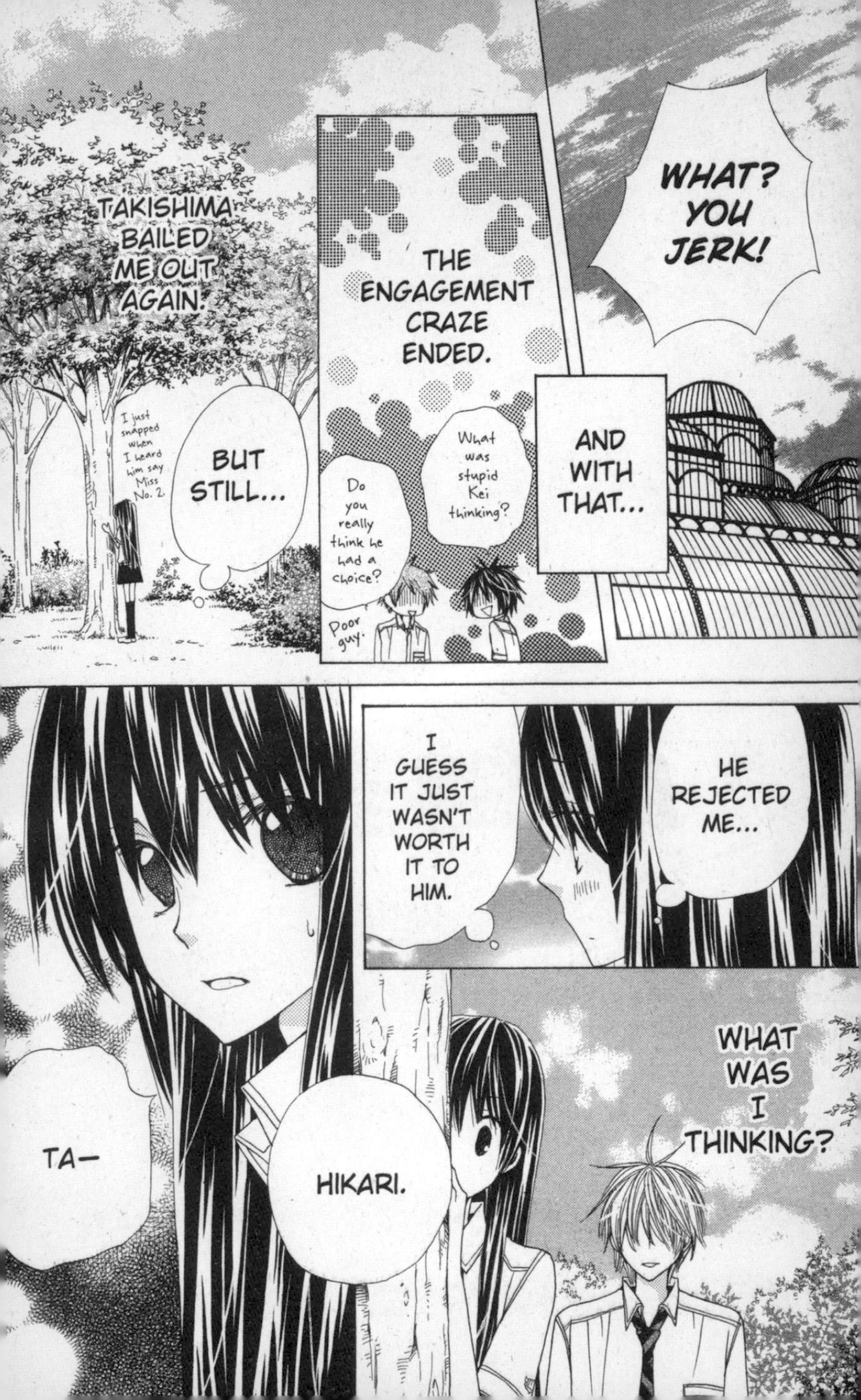
WHAT? YOU JERK!
AND WITH THAT...
THE ENGAGEMENT CRAZE ENDED.
What was stupid Kei thinking?
Do you really think he had a choice?
Poor guy.
TAKISHIMA BAILED ME OUT AGAIN.
BUT STILL...
I just snapped when I heard him say Miss No. 2.
HE REJECTED ME...
I GUESS IT JUST WASN'T WORTH IT TO HIM.
WHAT WAS I THINKING?
HIKARI.
TA—

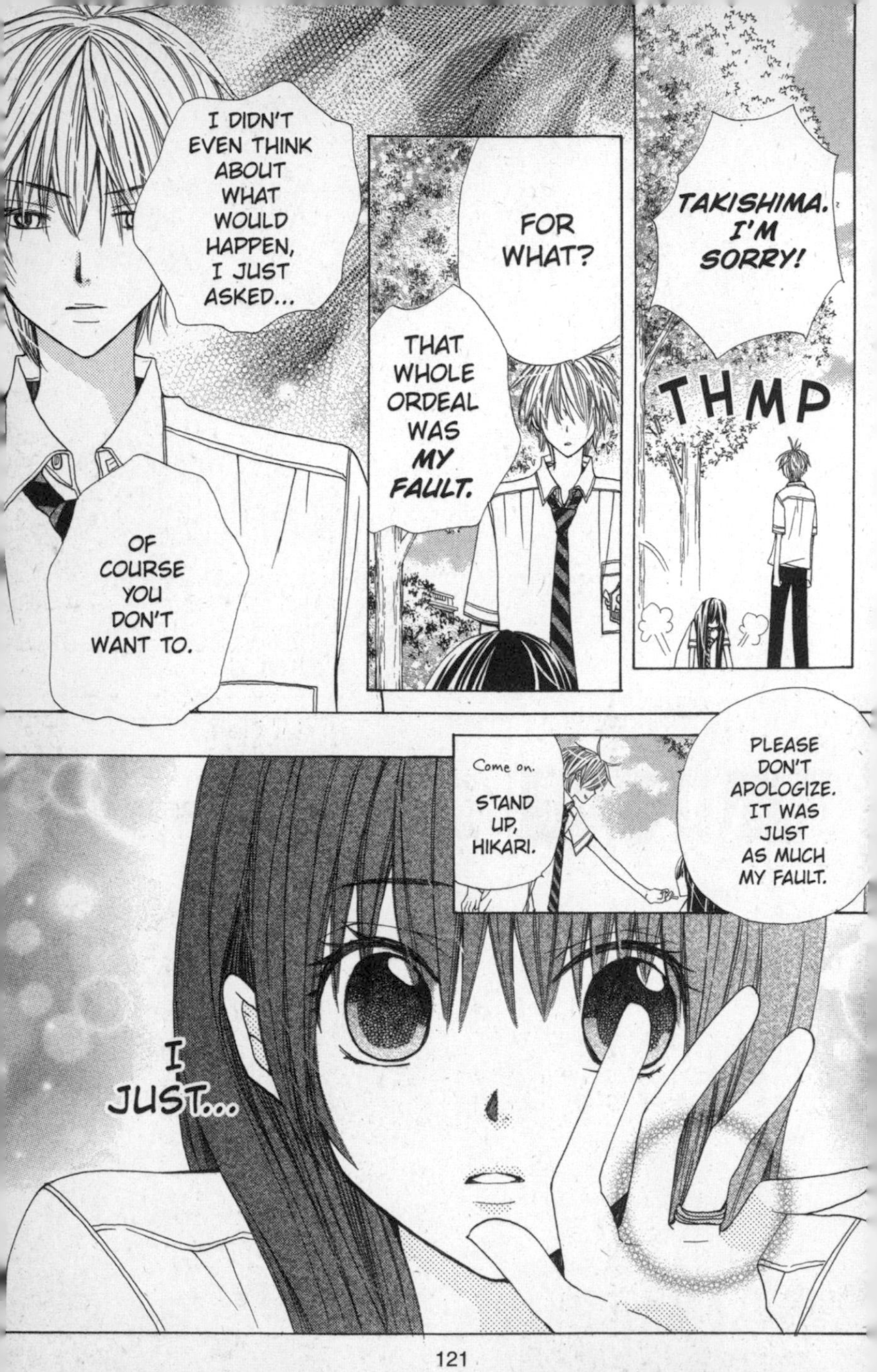
TAKISHIMA. I'M SORRY!
THMP
FOR WHAT?
THAT WHOLE ORDEAL WAS *MY FAULT.*
I DIDN'T EVEN THINK ABOUT WHAT WOULD HAPPEN, I JUST ASKED...
OF COURSE YOU DON'T WANT TO.
PLEASE DON'T APOLOGIZE. IT WAS JUST AS MUCH MY FAULT.
Come on.
STAND UP, HIKARI.
I JUST...

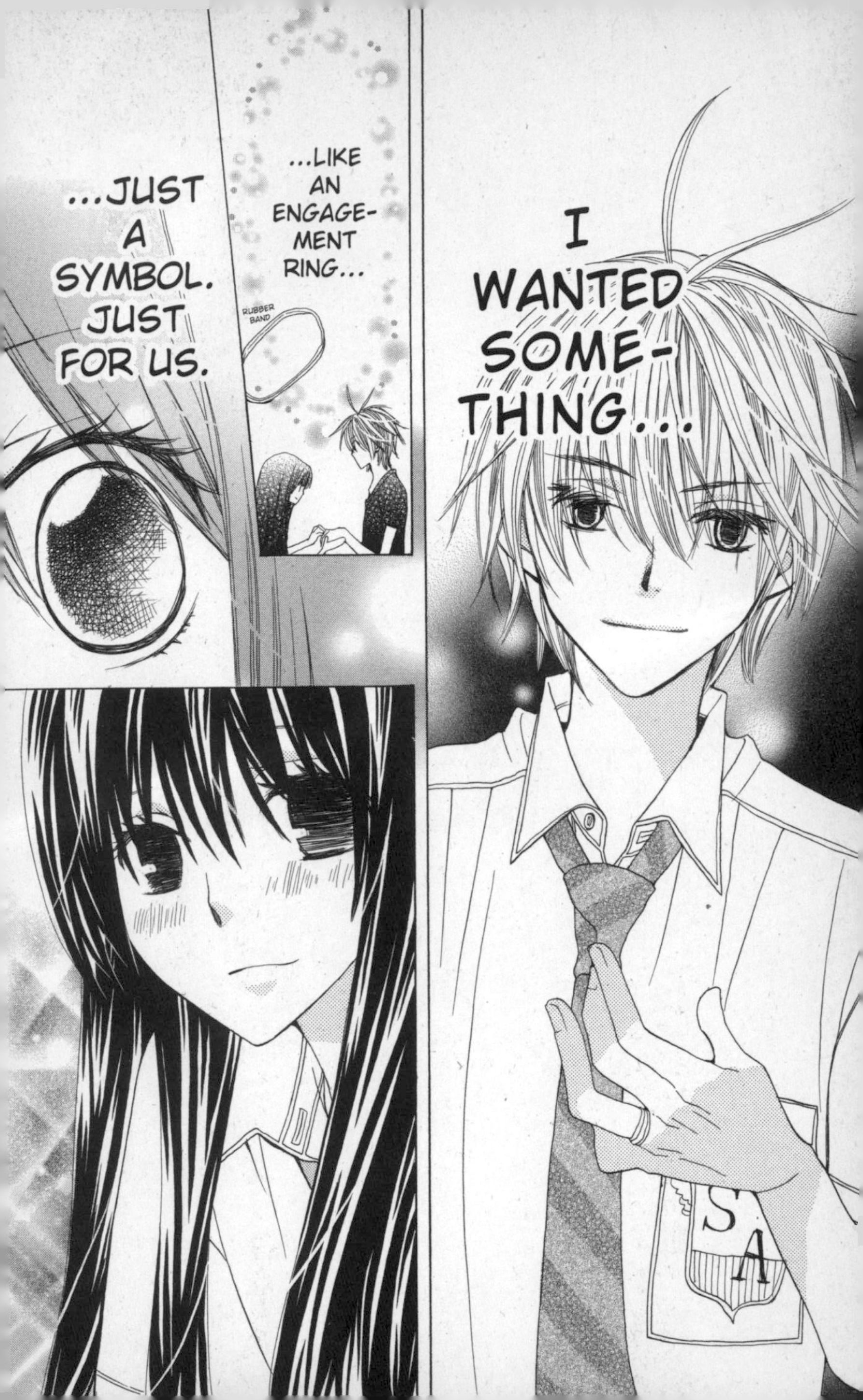
I WANTED SOME-THING...
...LIKE AN ENGAGE-MENT RING...
RUBBER BAND
...JUST A SYMBOL. JUST FOR US.

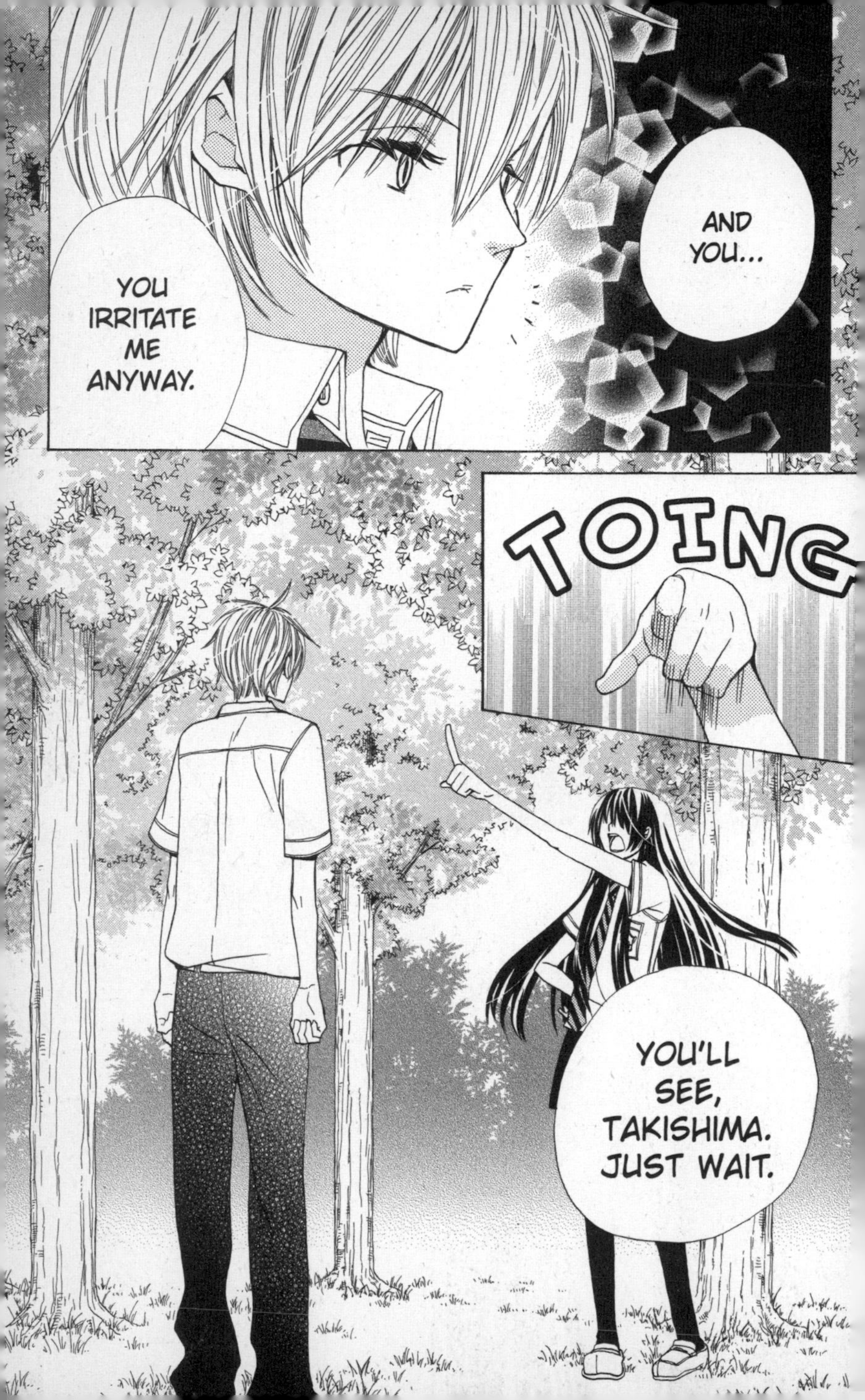
AND YOU...
YOU IRRITATE ME ANYWAY.
TOING
YOU'LL SEE, TAKISHIMA. JUST WAIT.

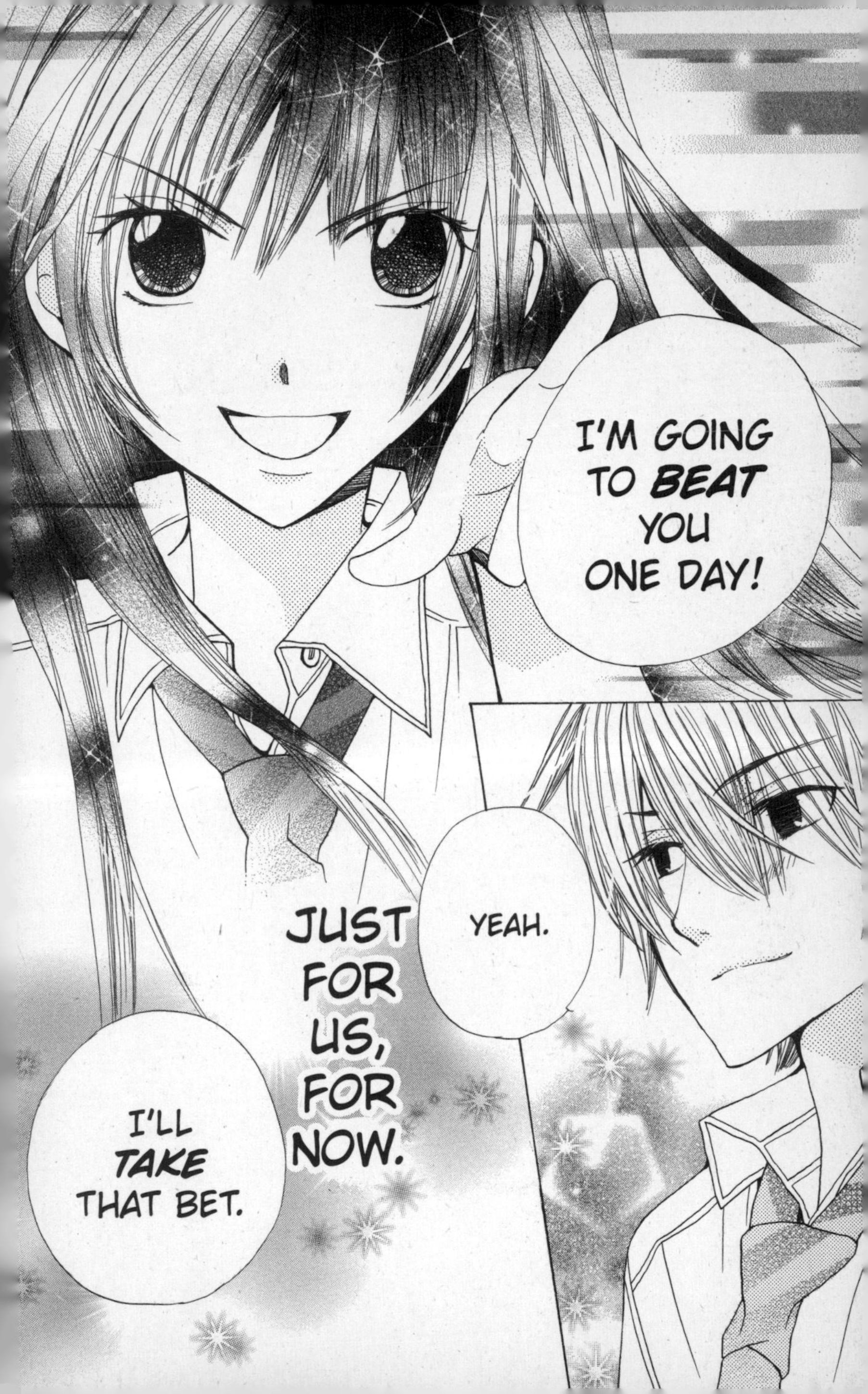
I'M GOING TO *BEAT* YOU ONE DAY!
YEAH.
JUST FOR US, FOR NOW.
I'LL *TAKE* THAT BET.

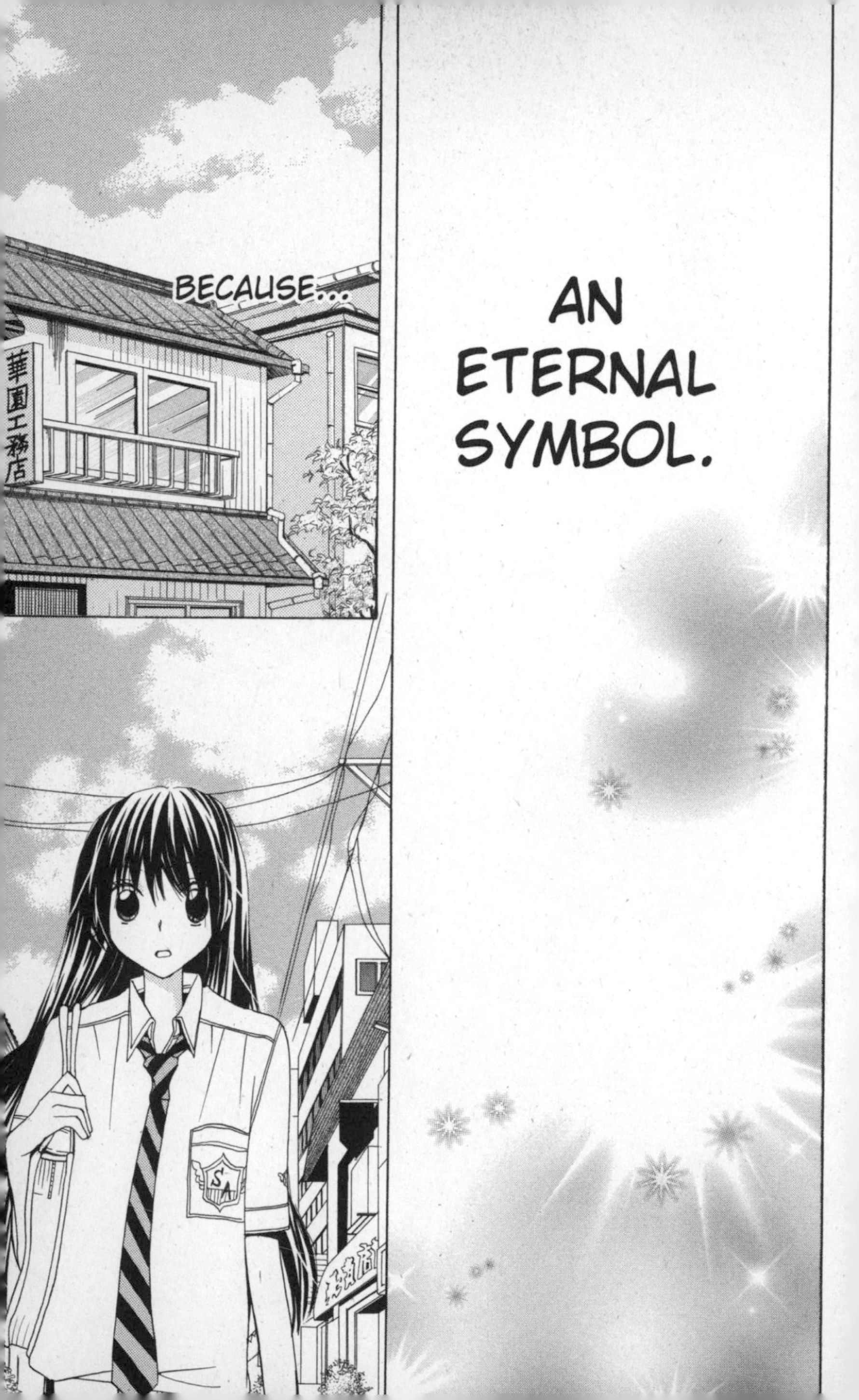
AN ETERNAL SYMBOL.
BECAUSE...
華園工務店

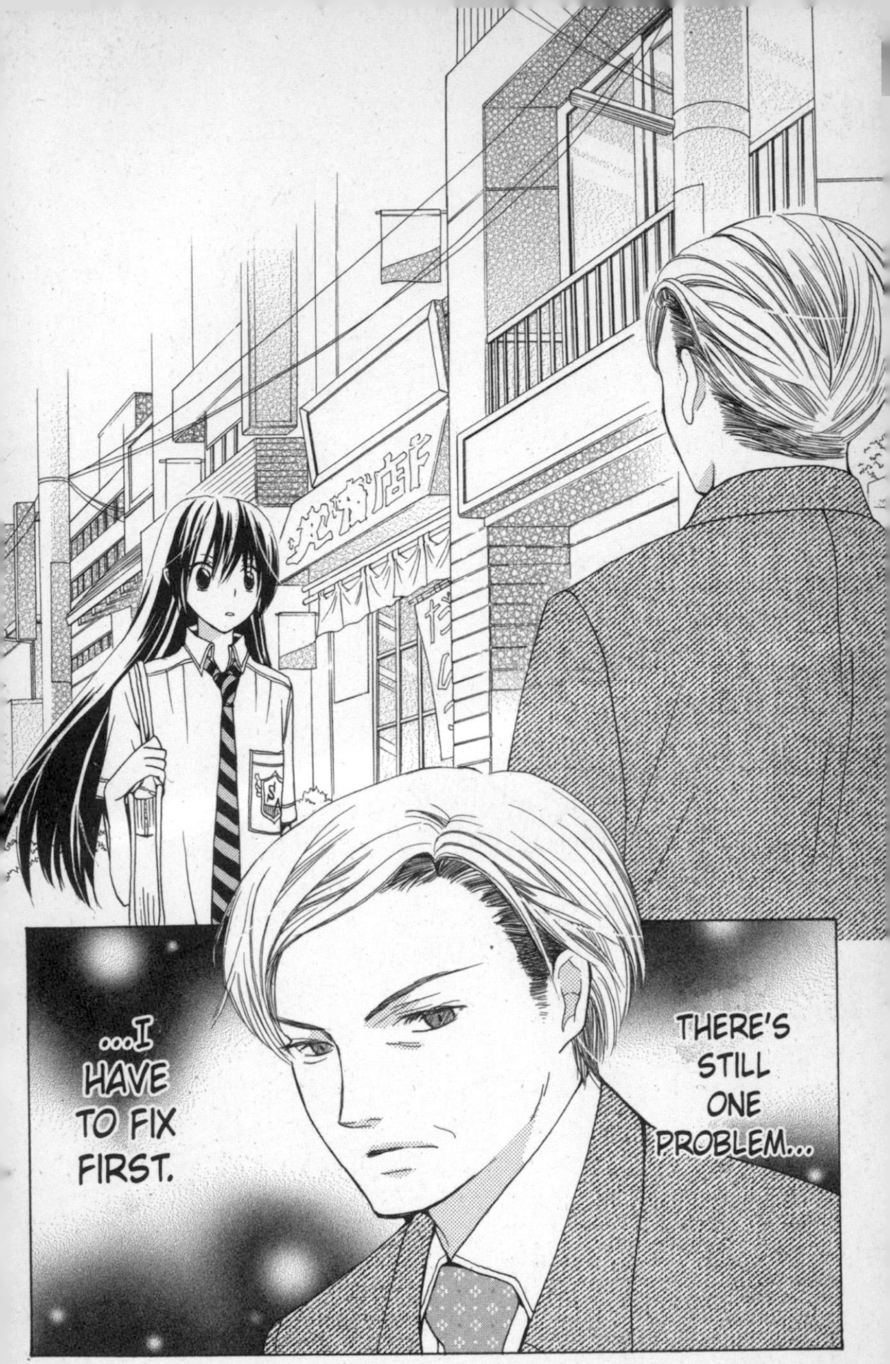
THERE'S STILL ONE PROBLEM...
...I HAVE TO FIX FIRST.

Chapter 92

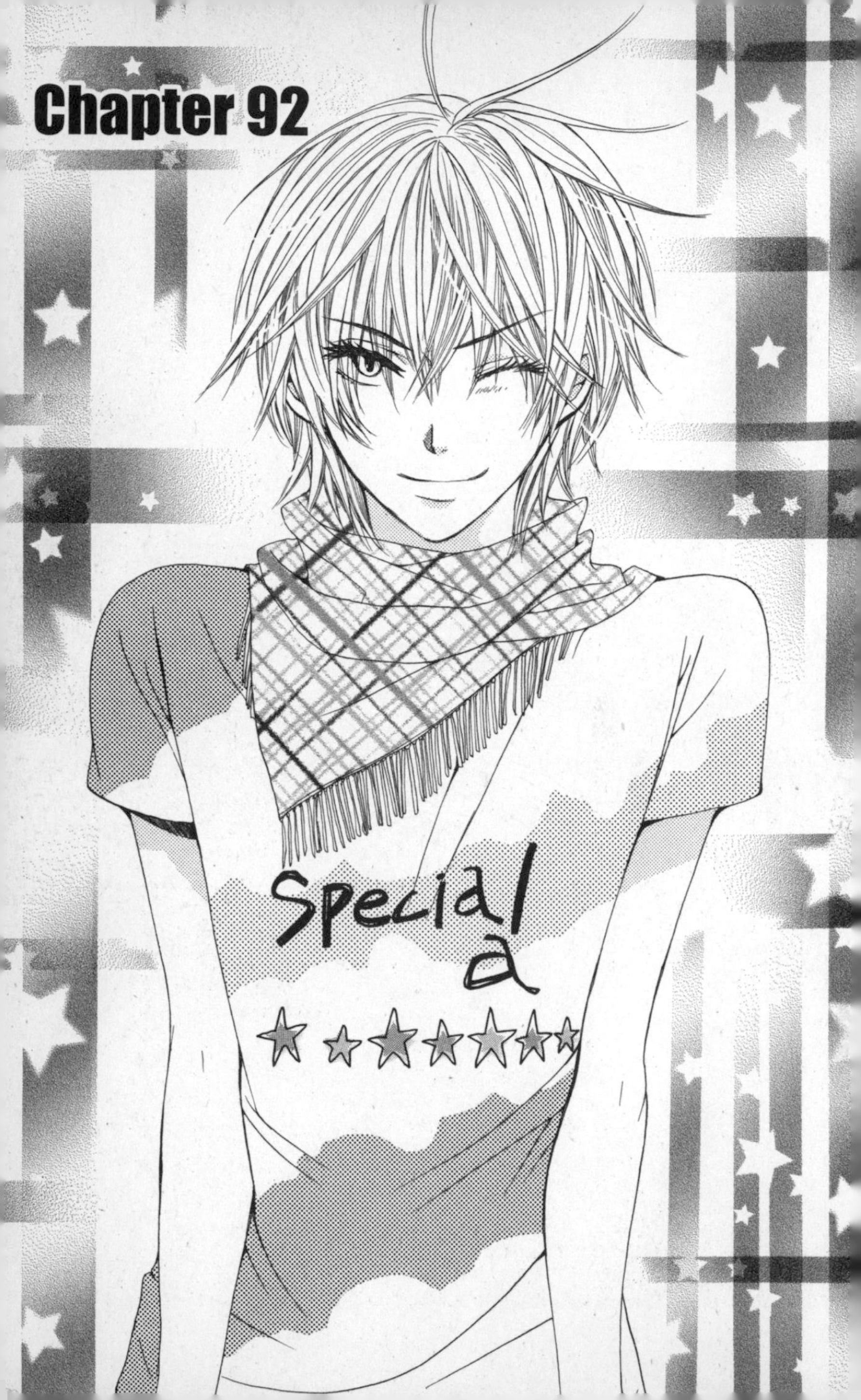
Special a

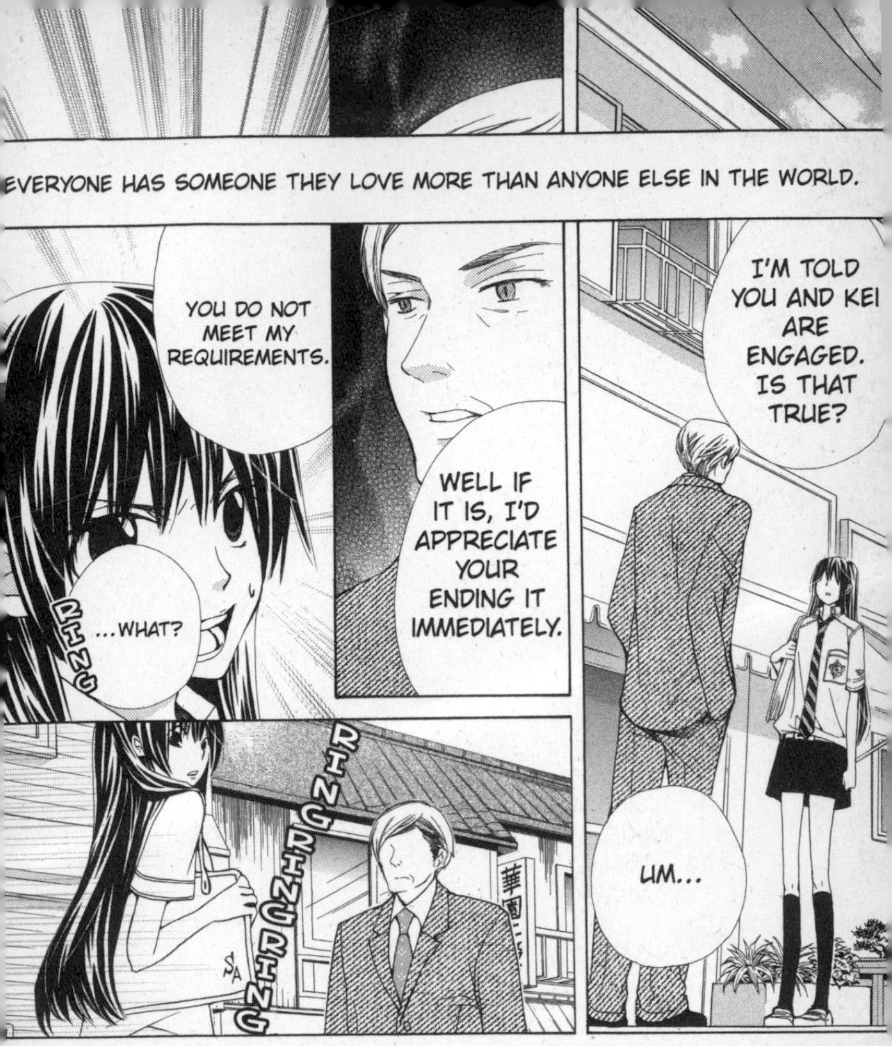
EVERYONE HAS SOMEONE THEY LOVE MORE THAN ANYONE ELSE IN THE WORLD.
I'M TOLD YOU AND KEI ARE ENGAGED. IS THAT TRUE?
UM...
WELL IF IT IS, I'D APPRECIATE YOUR ENDING IT IMMEDIATELY.
YOU DO NOT MEET MY REQUIREMENTS.
...WHAT?
RING
RINGRINGRING

·ART SUPPLIES·

THERE'S A SIGN HANGING UP AT THE CONVENIENCE STORE I USUALLY GO TO THAT SAYS, "1.0 MM LEAD PENCILS. SO POPULAR WITH YOUNG PEOPLE!" I WANT TO TRY ONE. I LIKE TO USE THICKER LEAD WHEN I DRAW BIG FACES, SO THAT MIGHT BE A GOOD THING TO TRY THEM ON. HA HA! I USUALLY USE A 0.3 MM LEAD WHEN I DRAW LITTLE PEOPLE OR BACKGROUND SCENES, BUT I DO MOST OF THE NORMAL STUFF WITH A 0.4 MM. ANY TIME I DO CLOSE-UPS, I USE A 0.7 MM POINT. IT JUST SEEMS EASIER TO DRAW THAT WAY... HA HA!

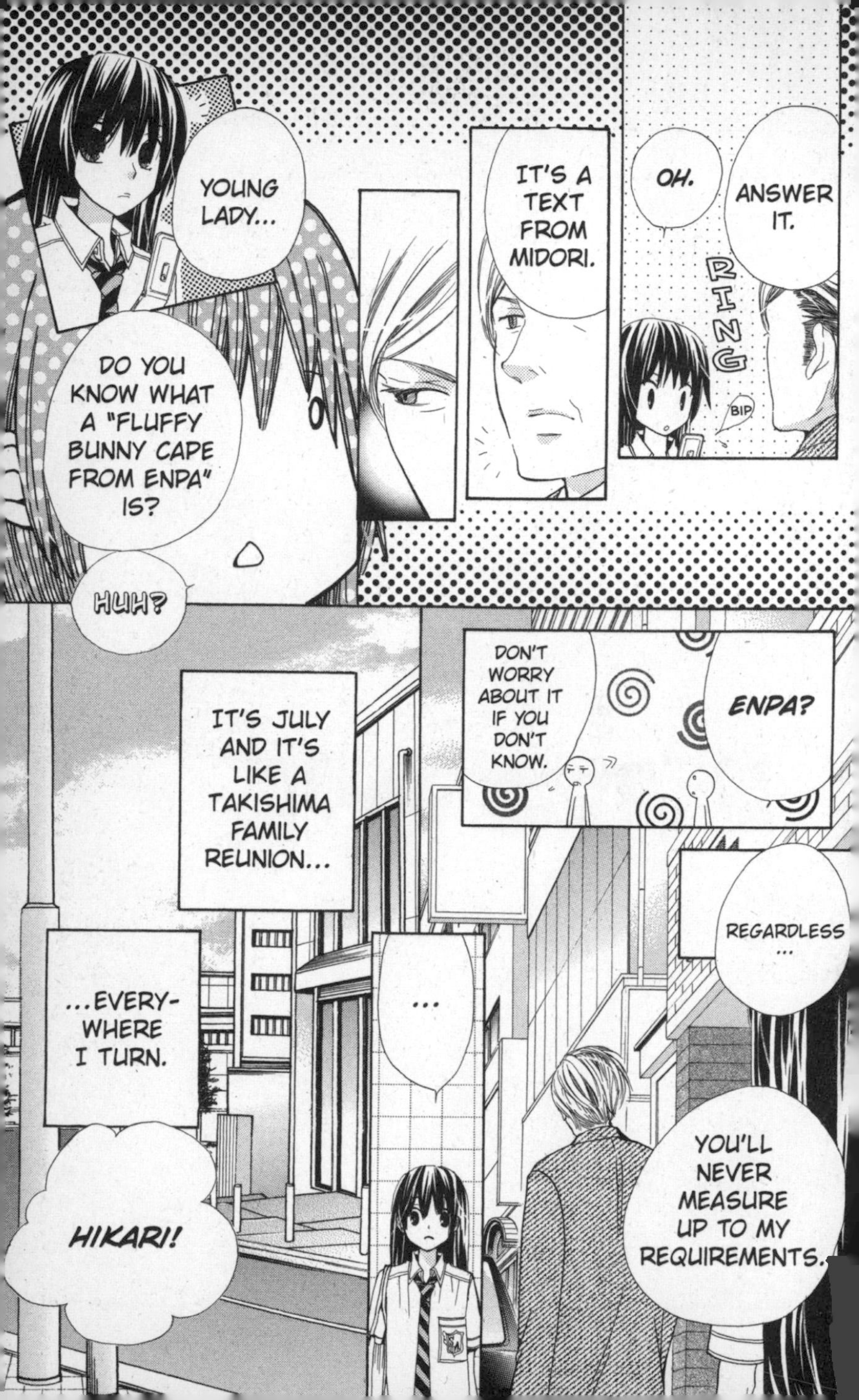
ANSWER IT.
OH.
RING
BIP
IT'S A TEXT FROM MIDORI.
YOUNG LADY...
DO YOU KNOW WHAT A "FLUFFY BUNNY CAPE FROM ENPA" IS?
HUH?
ENPA?
DON'T WORRY ABOUT IT IF YOU DON'T KNOW.
REGARDLESS...
YOU'LL NEVER MEASURE UP TO MY REQUIREMENTS.
...
IT'S JULY AND IT'S LIKE A TAKISHIMA FAMILY REUNION...
...EVERY-WHERE I TURN.
HIKARI!

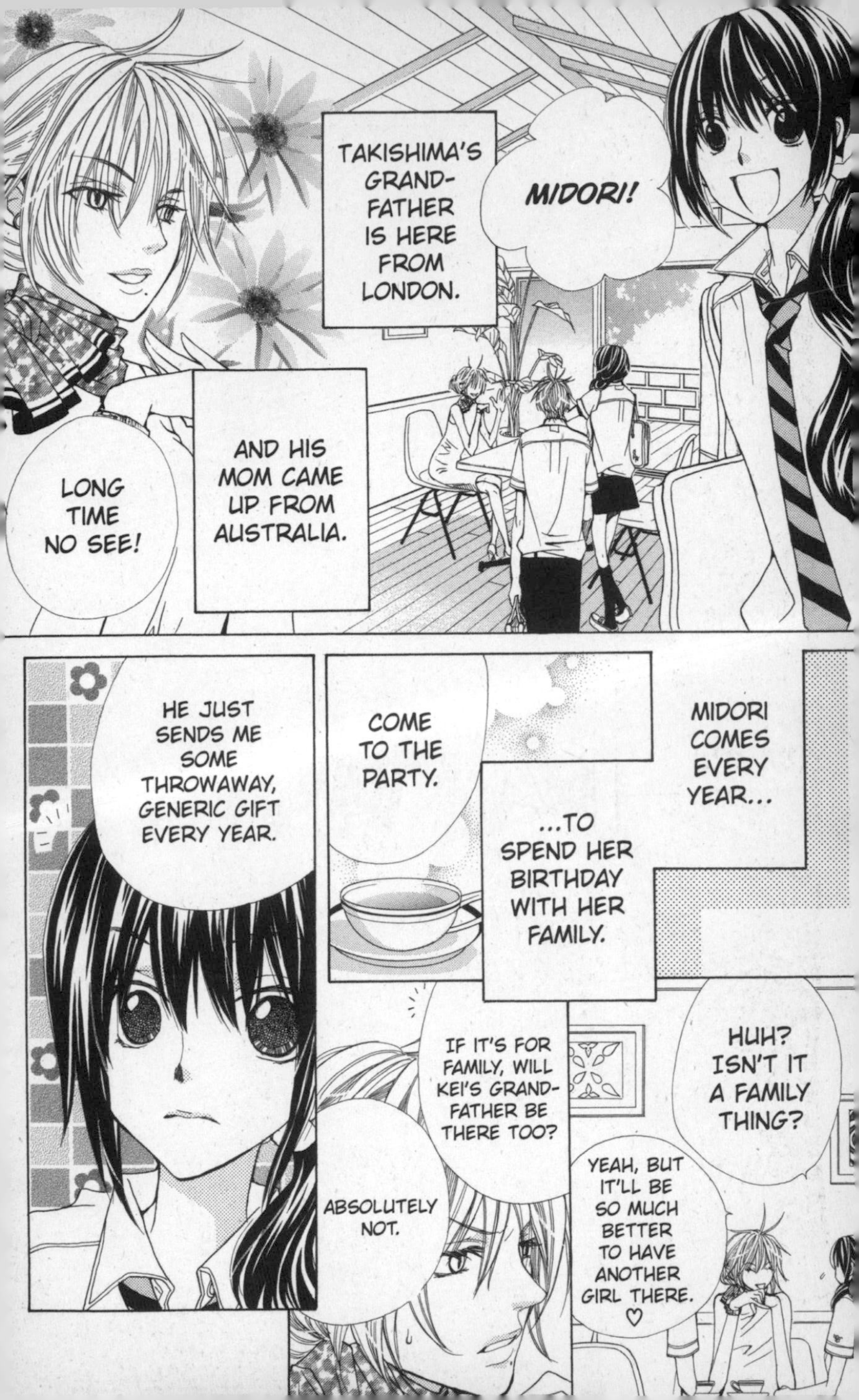
MIDORI!
TAKISHIMA'S GRAND-FATHER IS HERE FROM LONDON.
AND HIS MOM CAME UP FROM AUSTRALIA.
LONG TIME NO SEE!
MIDORI COMES EVERY YEAR...
...TO SPEND HER BIRTHDAY WITH HER FAMILY.
COME TO THE PARTY.
HUH? ISN'T IT A FAMILY THING?
YEAH, BUT IT'LL BE SO MUCH BETTER TO HAVE ANOTHER GIRL THERE. ♡
IF IT'S FOR FAMILY, WILL KEI'S GRAND-FATHER BE THERE TOO?
ABSOLUTELY NOT.
HE JUST SENDS ME SOME THROWAWAY, GENERIC GIFT EVERY YEAR.

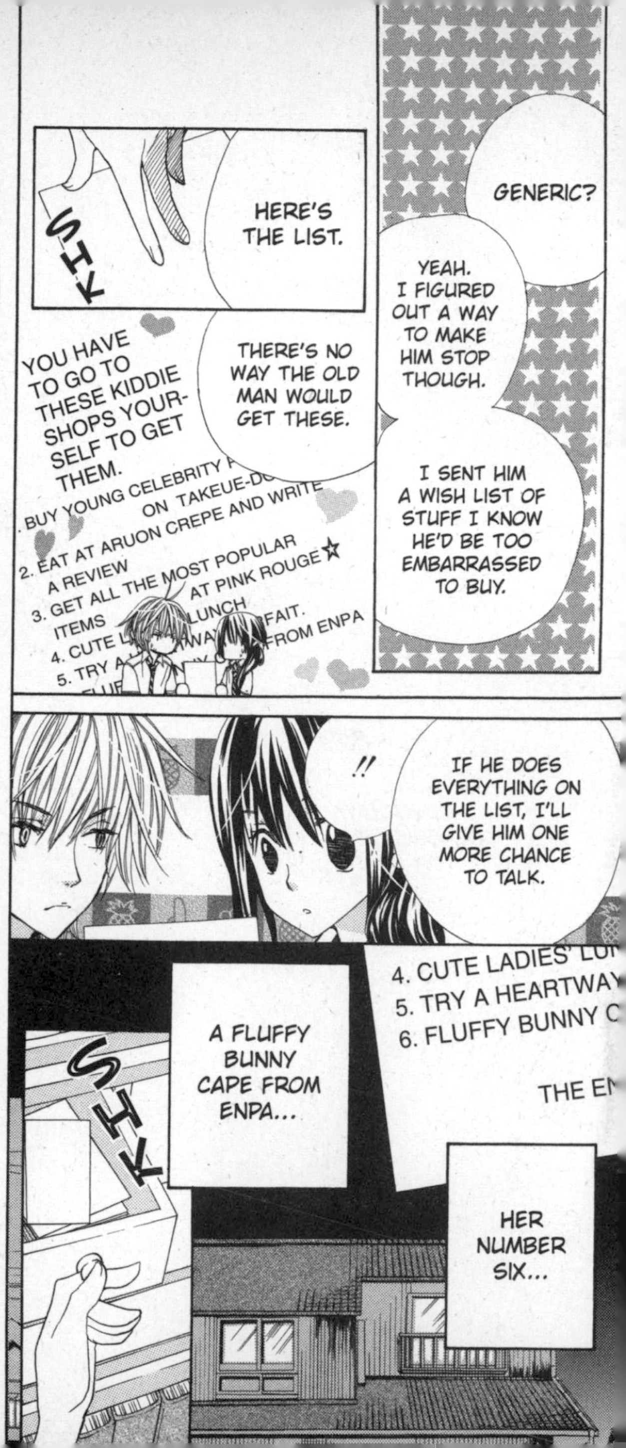
GENERIC?
YEAH. I FIGURED OUT A WAY TO MAKE HIM STOP THOUGH.
I SENT HIM A WISH LIST OF STUFF I KNOW HE'D BE TOO EMBARRASSED TO BUY.
HERE'S THE LIST.
SHK
THERE'S NO WAY THE OLD MAN WOULD GET THESE.
YOU HAVE TO GO TO THESE KIDDIE SHOPS YOURSELF TO GET THEM.
BUY YOUNG CELEBRITY
ON TAKEUE-DO
2. EAT AT ARUON CREPE AND WRITE A REVIEW
3. GET ALL THE MOST POPULAR ITEMS AT PINK ROUGE☆
4. CUTE
LUNCH
5. TRY A
FAIT.
FROM ENPA
IF HE DOES EVERYTHING ON THE LIST, I'LL GIVE HIM ONE MORE CHANCE TO TALK.
!!
4. CUTE LADIES'
5. TRY A HEARTWAY
6. FLUFFY BUNNY
A FLUFFY BUNNY CAPE FROM ENPA...
SHK
HER NUMBER SIX...

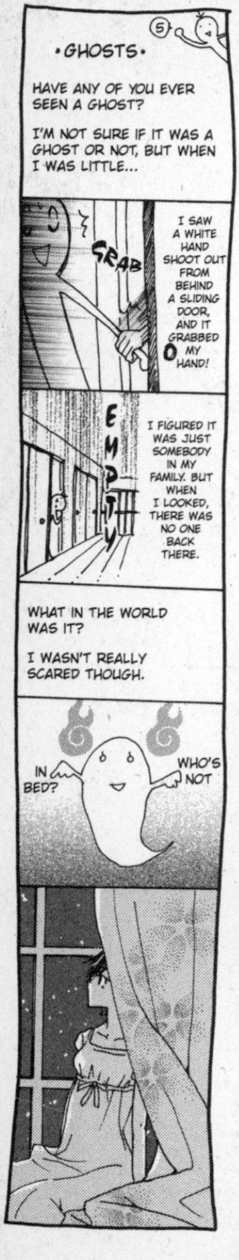
5
•GHOSTS•
HAVE ANY OF YOU EVER SEEN A GHOST?
I'M NOT SURE IF IT WAS A GHOST OR NOT, BUT WHEN I WAS LITTLE...
I SAW A WHITE HAND SHOOT OUT FROM BEHIND A SLIDING DOOR, AND IT GRABBED MY HAND!
GRAB
I FIGURED IT WAS JUST SOMEBODY IN MY FAMILY. BUT WHEN I LOOKED, THERE WAS NO ONE BACK THERE.
EMPTY
WHAT IN THE WORLD WAS IT?
I WASN'T REALLY SCARED THOUGH.
WHO'S NOT
IN BED?

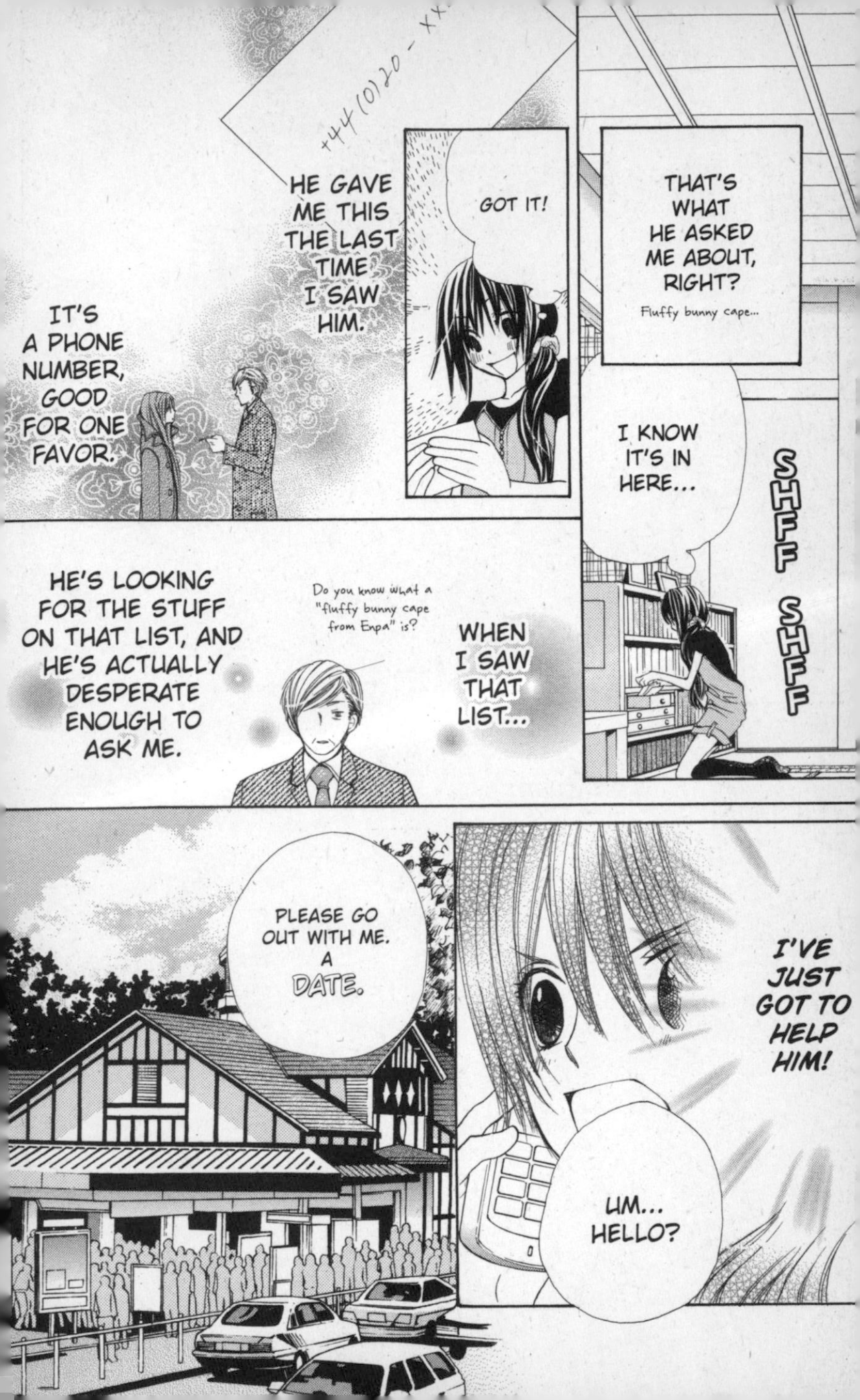
THAT'S WHAT HE ASKED ME ABOUT, RIGHT?
Fluffy bunny cape...
I KNOW IT'S IN HERE...
SHFF SHFF
GOT IT!
+44(0)20-XX
HE GAVE ME THIS THE LAST TIME I SAW HIM.
IT'S A PHONE NUMBER, GOOD FOR ONE FAVOR.
WHEN I SAW THAT LIST...
Do you know what a "fluffy bunny cape from Enpa" is?
HE'S LOOKING FOR THE STUFF ON THAT LIST, AND HE'S ACTUALLY DESPERATE ENOUGH TO ASK ME.
I'VE JUST GOT TO HELP HIM!
UM... HELLO?
PLEASE GO OUT WITH ME. A DATE.

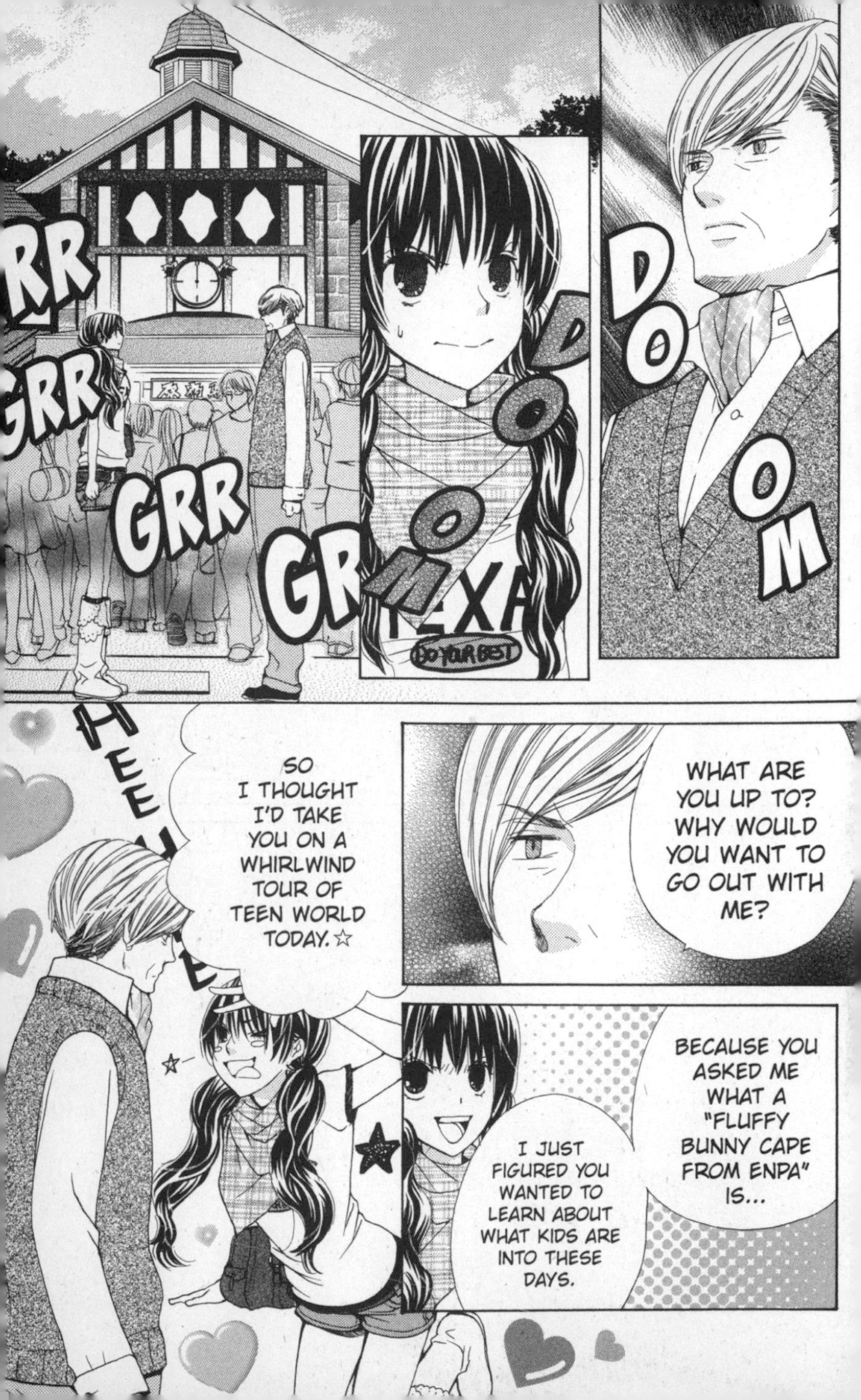
DOOM
DOOM
DO YOUR BEST
GRR
GRR
GRR
GR
WHAT ARE YOU UP TO? WHY WOULD YOU WANT TO GO OUT WITH ME?
BECAUSE YOU ASKED ME WHAT A "FLUFFY BUNNY CAPE FROM ENPA" IS...
I JUST FIGURED YOU WANTED TO LEARN ABOUT WHAT KIDS ARE INTO THESE DAYS.
SO I THOUGHT I'D TAKE YOU ON A WHIRLWIND TOUR OF TEEN WORLD TODAY.☆
HEE

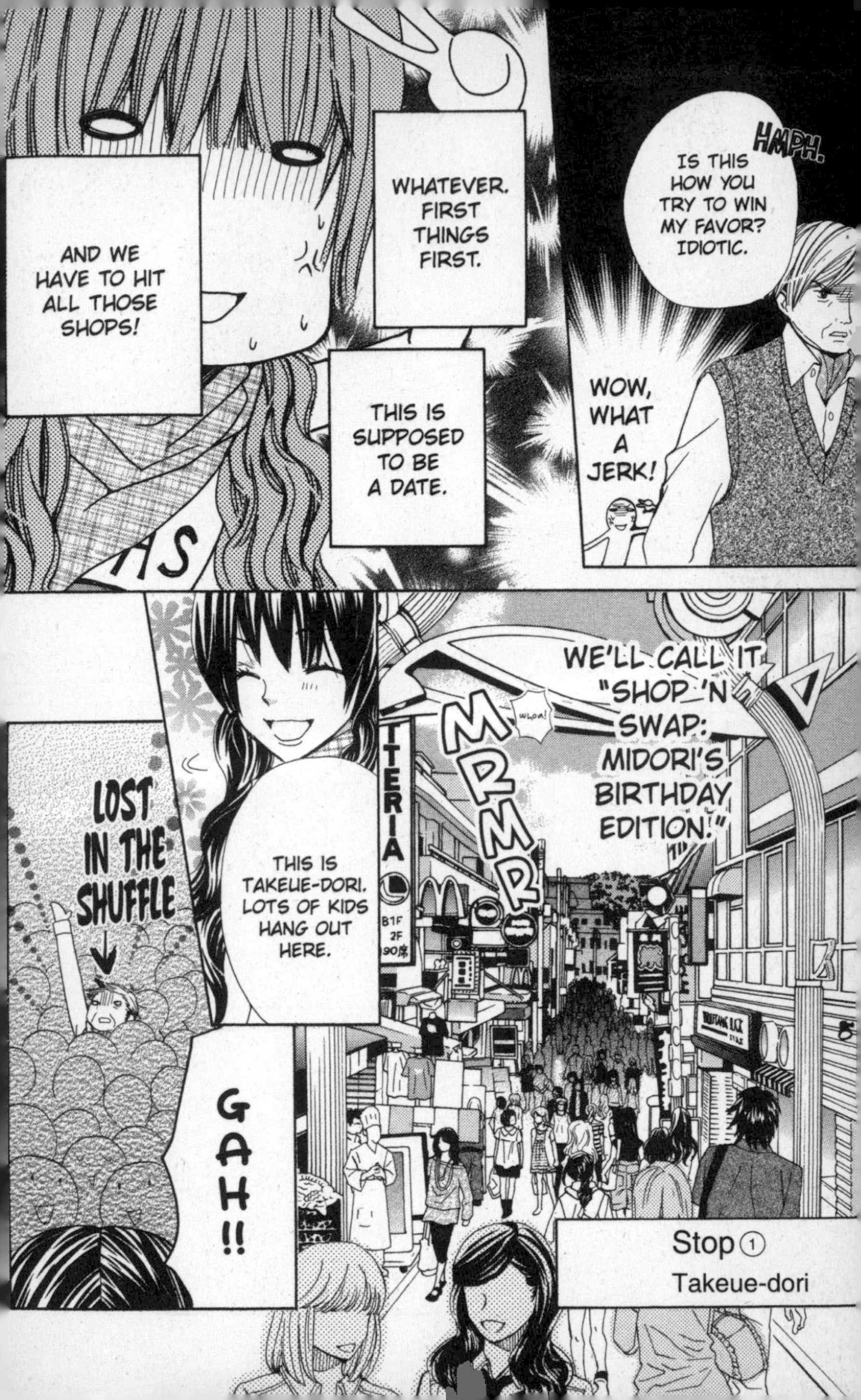
HMPH.
IS THIS HOW YOU TRY TO WIN MY FAVOR? IDIOTIC.
WOW, WHAT A JERK!
WHATEVER. FIRST THINGS FIRST.
THIS IS SUPPOSED TO BE A DATE.
AND WE HAVE TO HIT ALL THOSE SHOPS!
WE'LL CALL IT "SHOP 'N SWAP: MIDORI'S BIRTHDAY EDITION!"
MRMMR
WHOA!
TTERIA
B1F
2F
90席
Stop ①
Takeue-dori
THIS IS TAKEUE-DORI. LOTS OF KIDS HANG OUT HERE.
LOST IN THE SHUFFLE
GAH!!

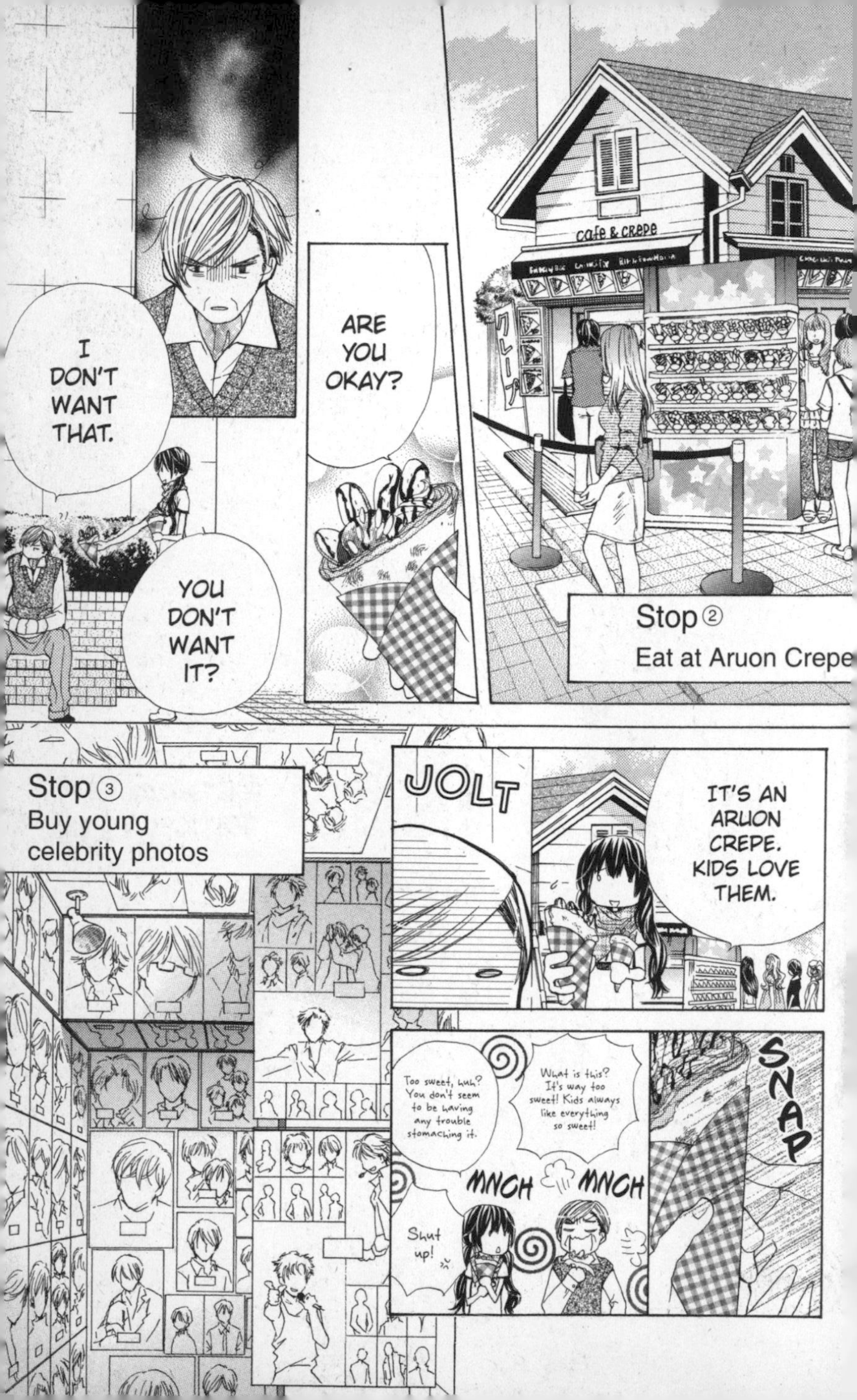
cafe & crepe
クレープ
Stop ② Eat at Aruon Crepe
ARE YOU OKAY?
I DON'T WANT THAT.
YOU DON'T WANT IT?
JOLT
IT'S AN ARUON CREPE. KIDS LOVE THEM.
SNAP
What is this? It's way too sweet! Kids always like everything so sweet!
Too sweet, huh? You don't seem to be having any trouble stomaching it.
MNCH MNCH
Shut up!
Stop ③ Buy young celebrity photos

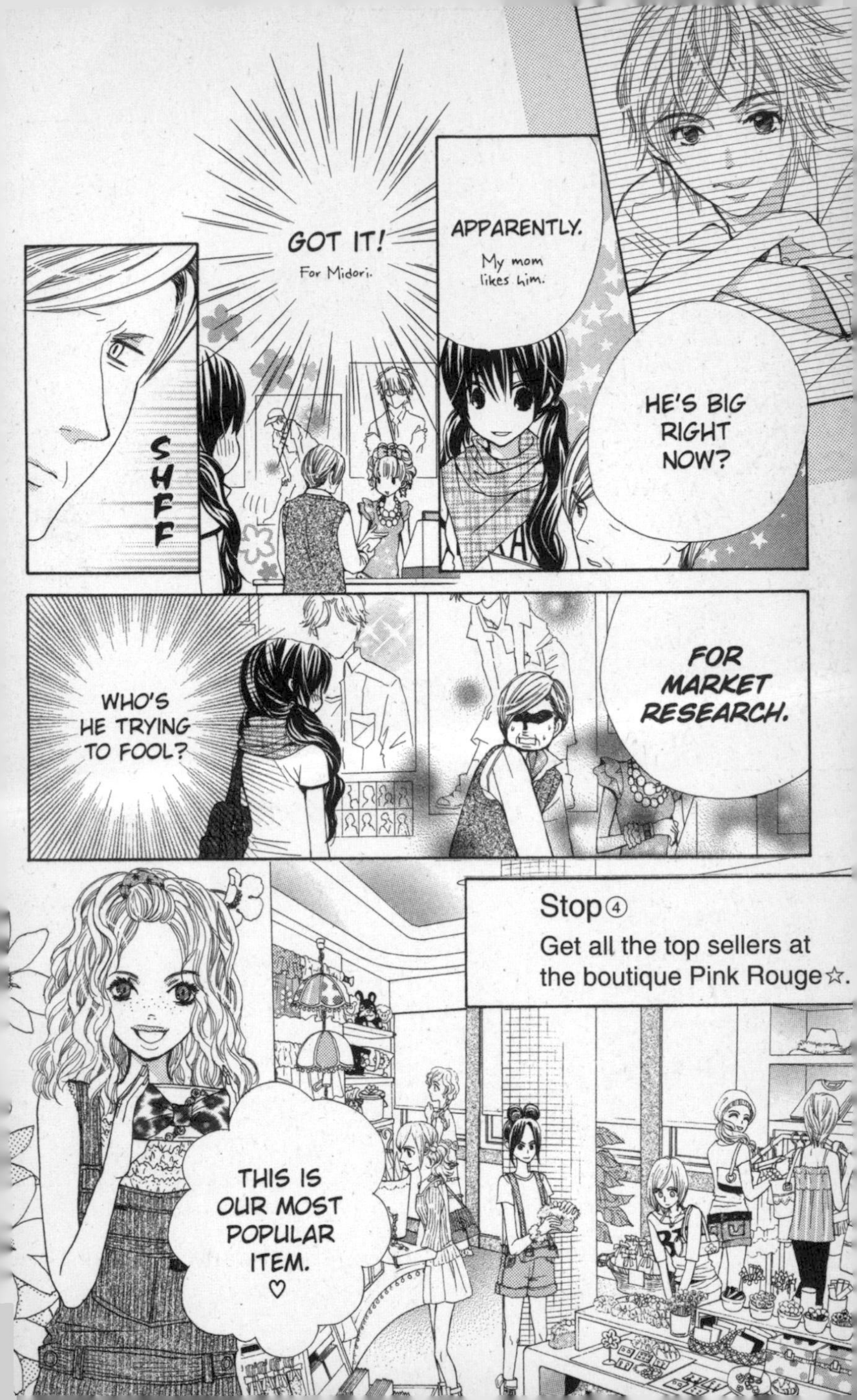
HE'S BIG RIGHT NOW?
APPARENTLY.
My mom likes him.
GOT IT!
For Midori.
SHFF
FOR MARKET RESEARCH.
WHO'S HE TRYING TO FOOL?
Stop ④
Get all the top sellers at the boutique Pink Rouge☆.
THIS IS OUR MOST POPULAR ITEM. ♡

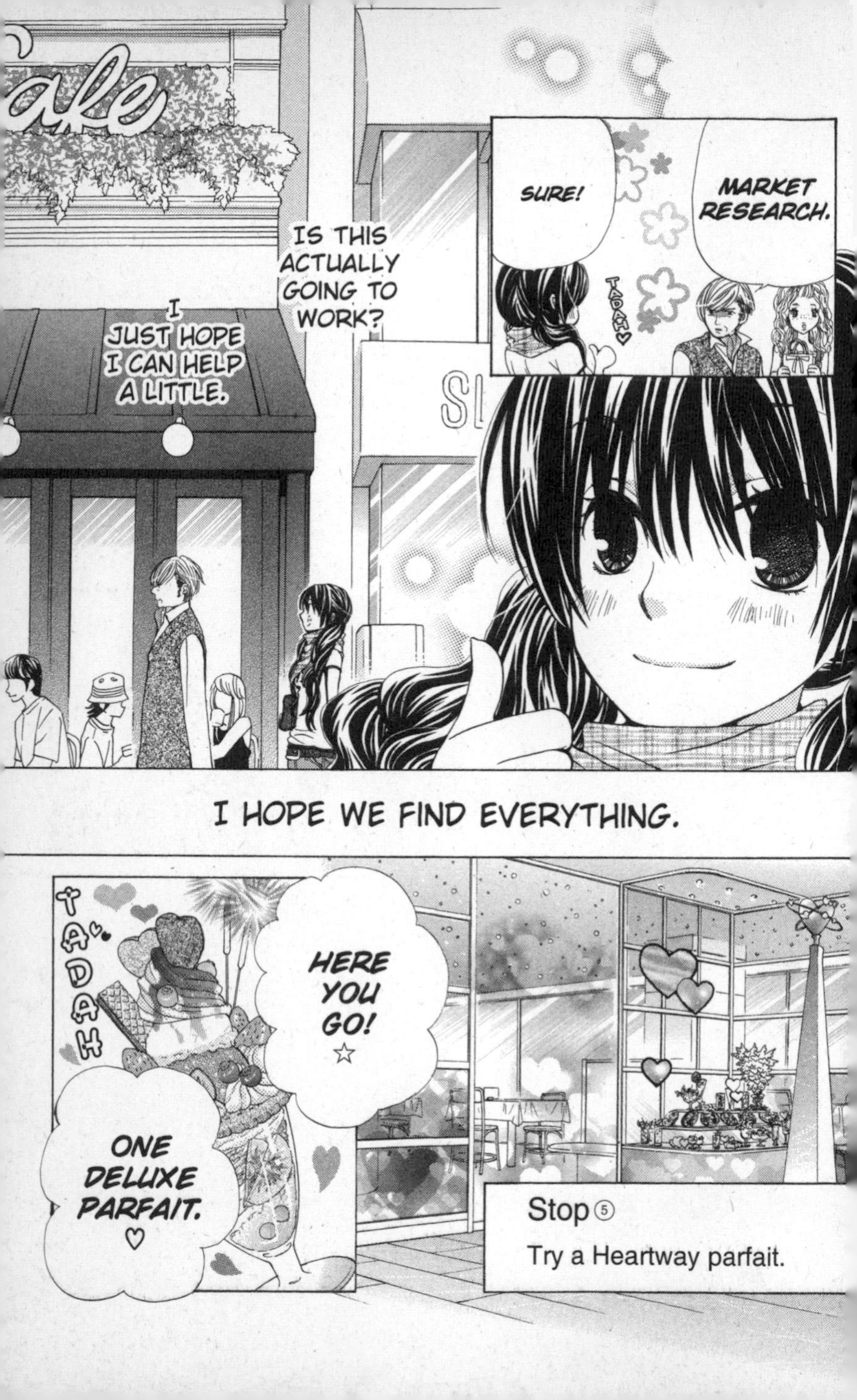
MARKET RESEARCH.
SURE!
TADAH♥
IS THIS ACTUALLY GOING TO WORK?
I JUST HOPE I CAN HELP A LITTLE.
I HOPE WE FIND EVERYTHING.
Stop ⑤
Try a Heartway parfait.
HERE YOU GO! ☆
ONE DELUXE PARFAIT. ♡
TADAH♥

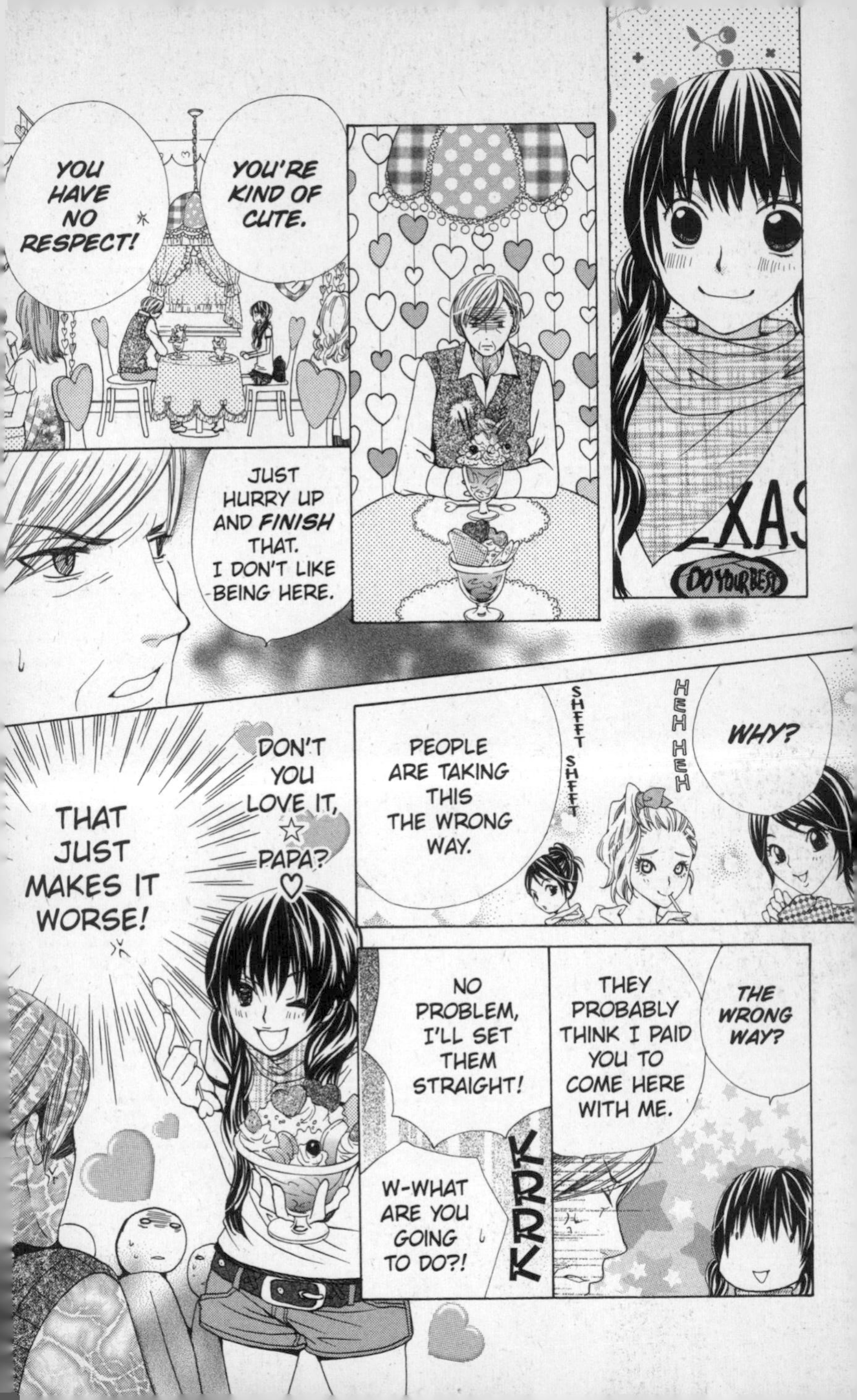
DO YOUR BEST
YOU'RE KIND OF CUTE.
YOU HAVE NO RESPECT!
JUST HURRY UP AND *FINISH* THAT. I DON'T LIKE BEING HERE.
WHY?
HEH HEH
SHFFT SHFFT
PEOPLE ARE TAKING THIS THE WRONG WAY.
THE WRONG WAY?
THEY PROBABLY THINK I PAID YOU TO COME HERE WITH ME.
NO PROBLEM, I'LL SET THEM STRAIGHT!
KRRK
W-WHAT ARE YOU GOING TO DO?!
DON'T YOU LOVE IT, ☆ PAPA?
THAT JUST MAKES IT WORSE!

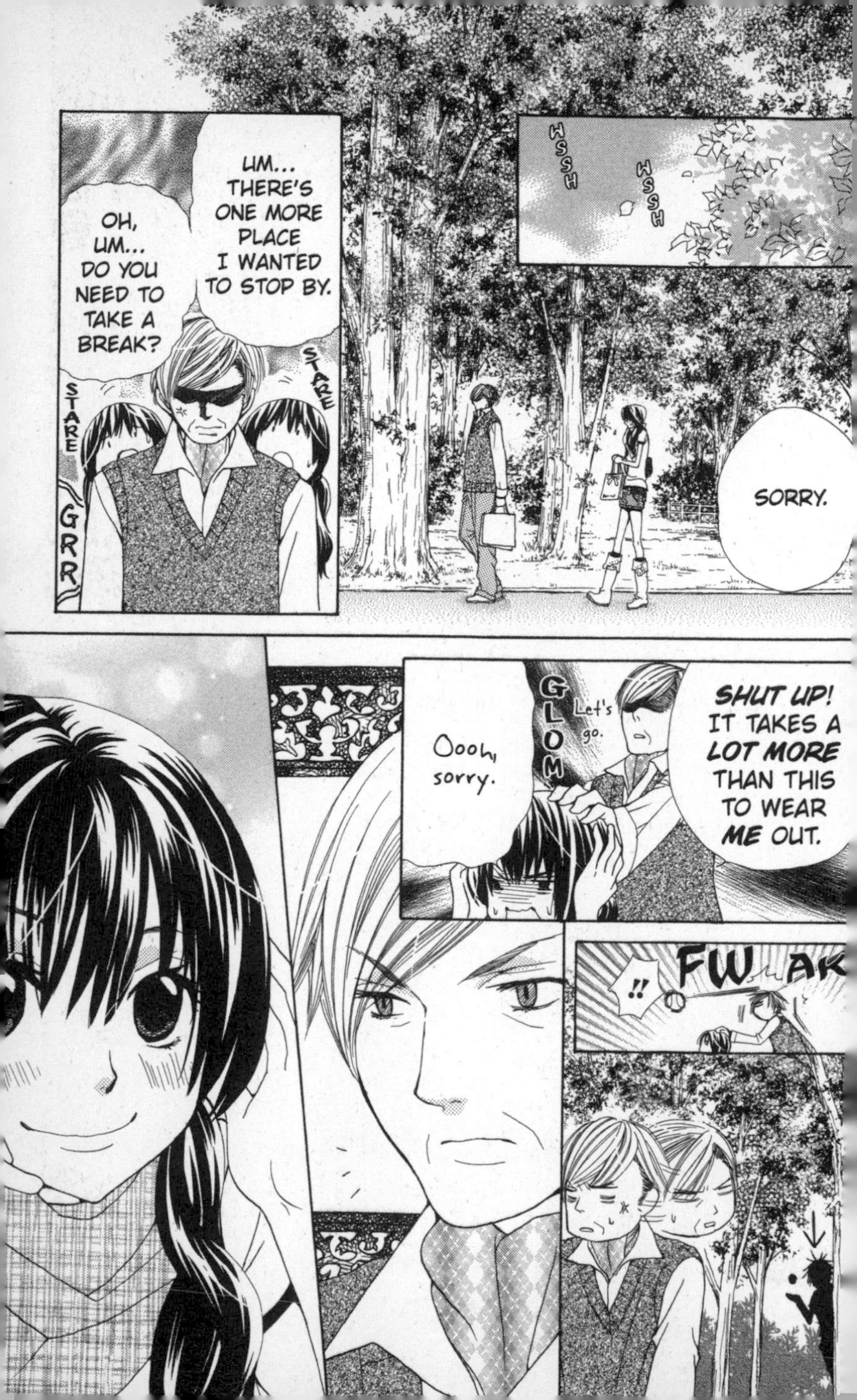
HSSH
HSSH
SORRY.
UM... THERE'S ONE MORE PLACE I WANTED TO STOP BY.
OH, UM... DO YOU NEED TO TAKE A BREAK?
STARE
STARE
GRR
SHUT UP! IT TAKES A LOT MORE THAN THIS TO WEAR ME OUT.
Let's go.
GLOM
Oooh, sorry.
FWAK
!!

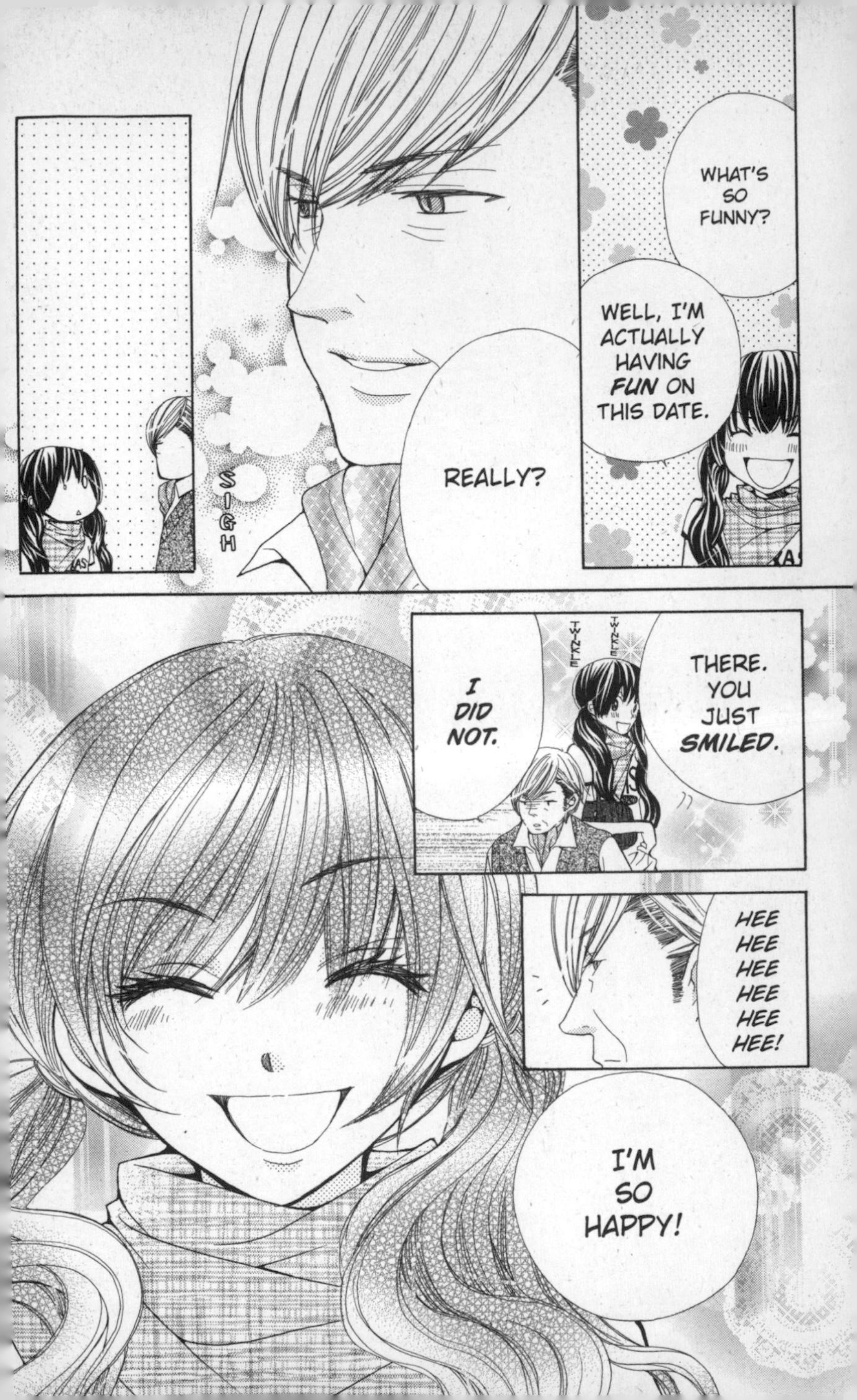
WHAT'S SO FUNNY?
WELL, I'M ACTUALLY HAVING FUN ON THIS DATE.
REALLY?
SIGH
TWINKLE TWINKLE
THERE. YOU JUST SMILED.
I DID NOT.
HEE HEE HEE HEE HEE HEE!
I'M SO HAPPY!

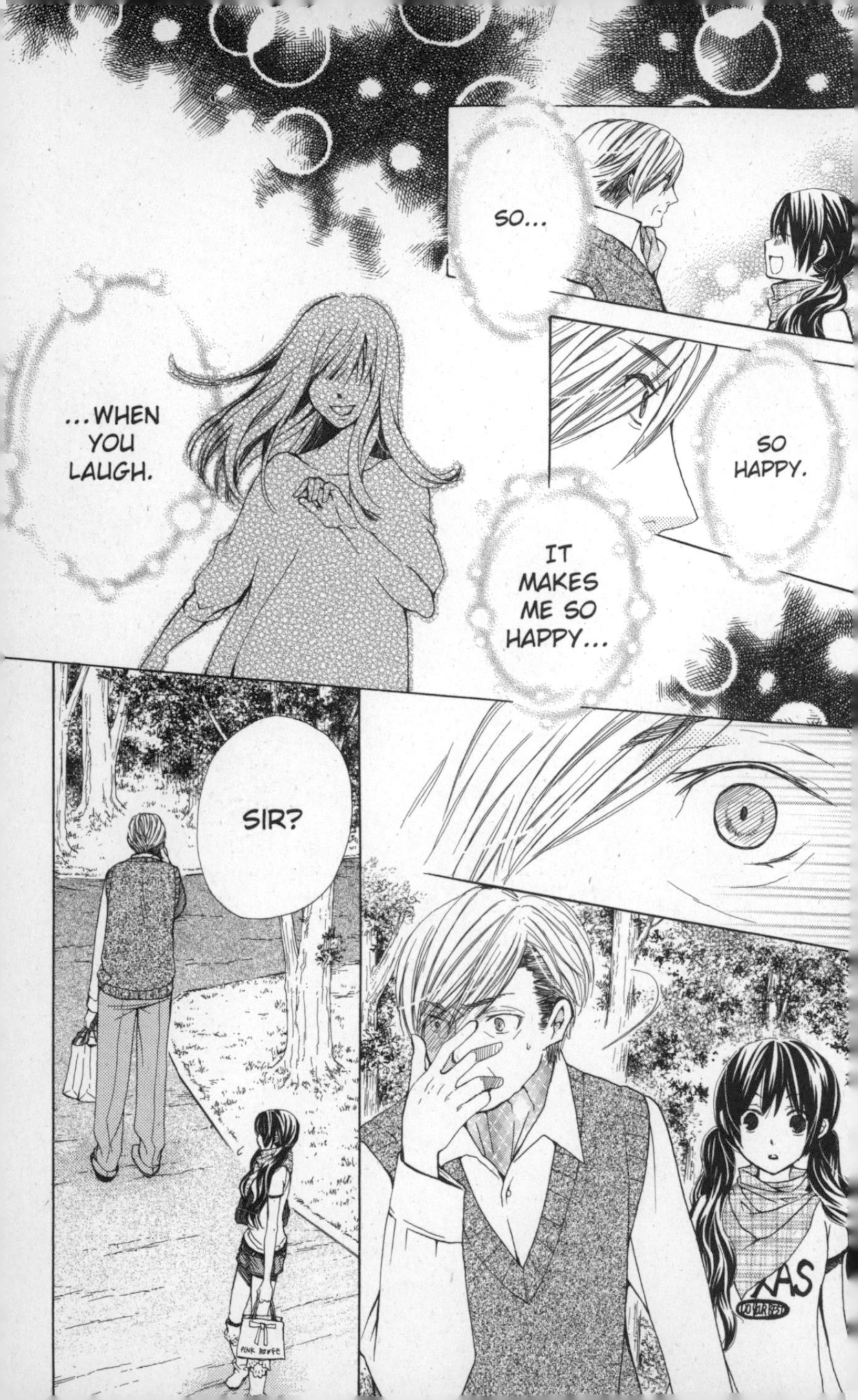
SO...
...WHEN YOU LAUGH.
IT MAKES ME SO HAPPY...
SO HAPPY.
SIR?

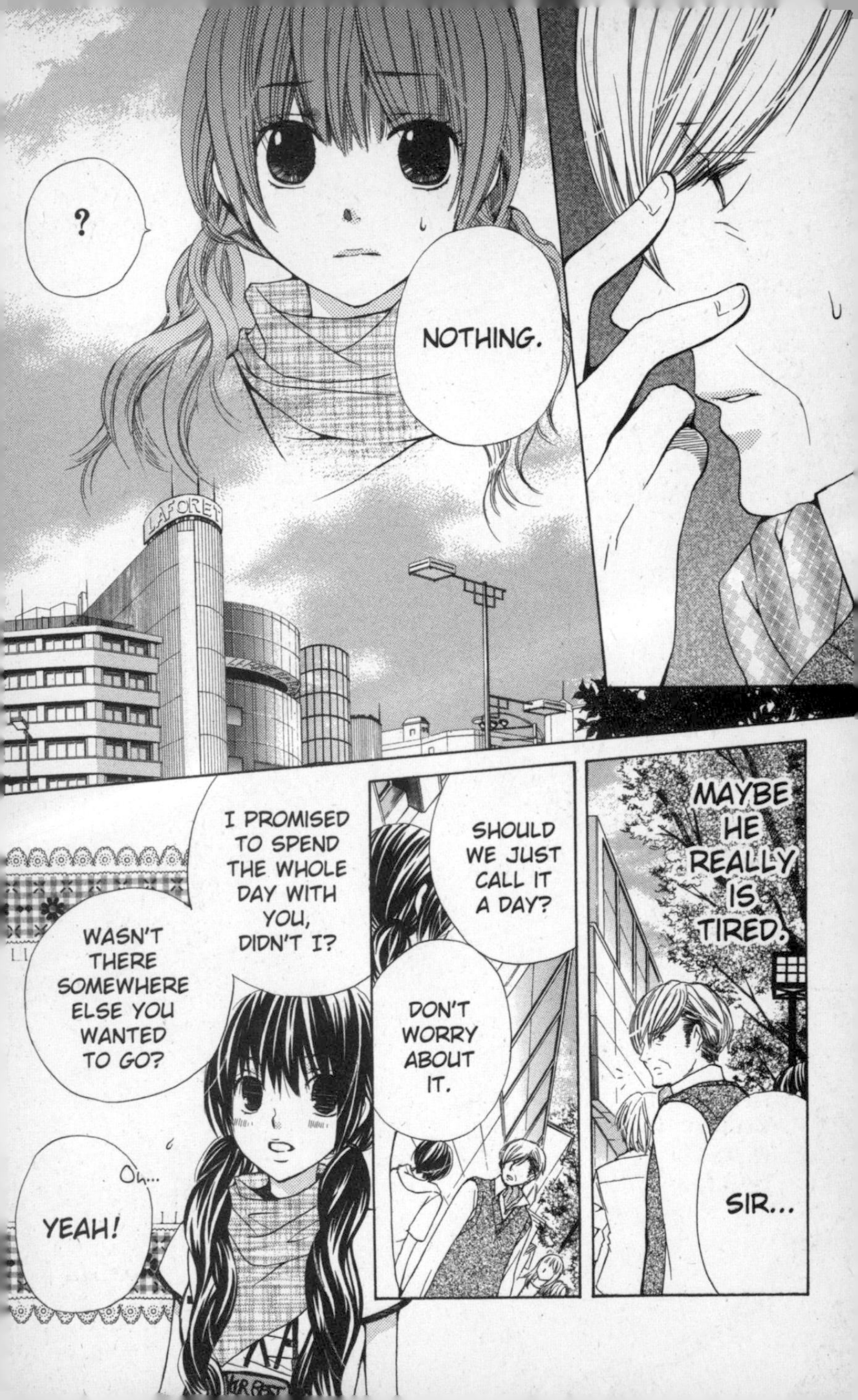
?
NOTHING.
MAYBE HE REALLY IS TIRED.
SIR...
SHOULD WE JUST CALL IT A DAY?
DON'T WORRY ABOUT IT.
I PROMISED TO SPEND THE WHOLE DAY WITH YOU, DIDN'T I?
WASN'T THERE SOMEWHERE ELSE YOU WANTED TO GO?
Oh...
YEAH!

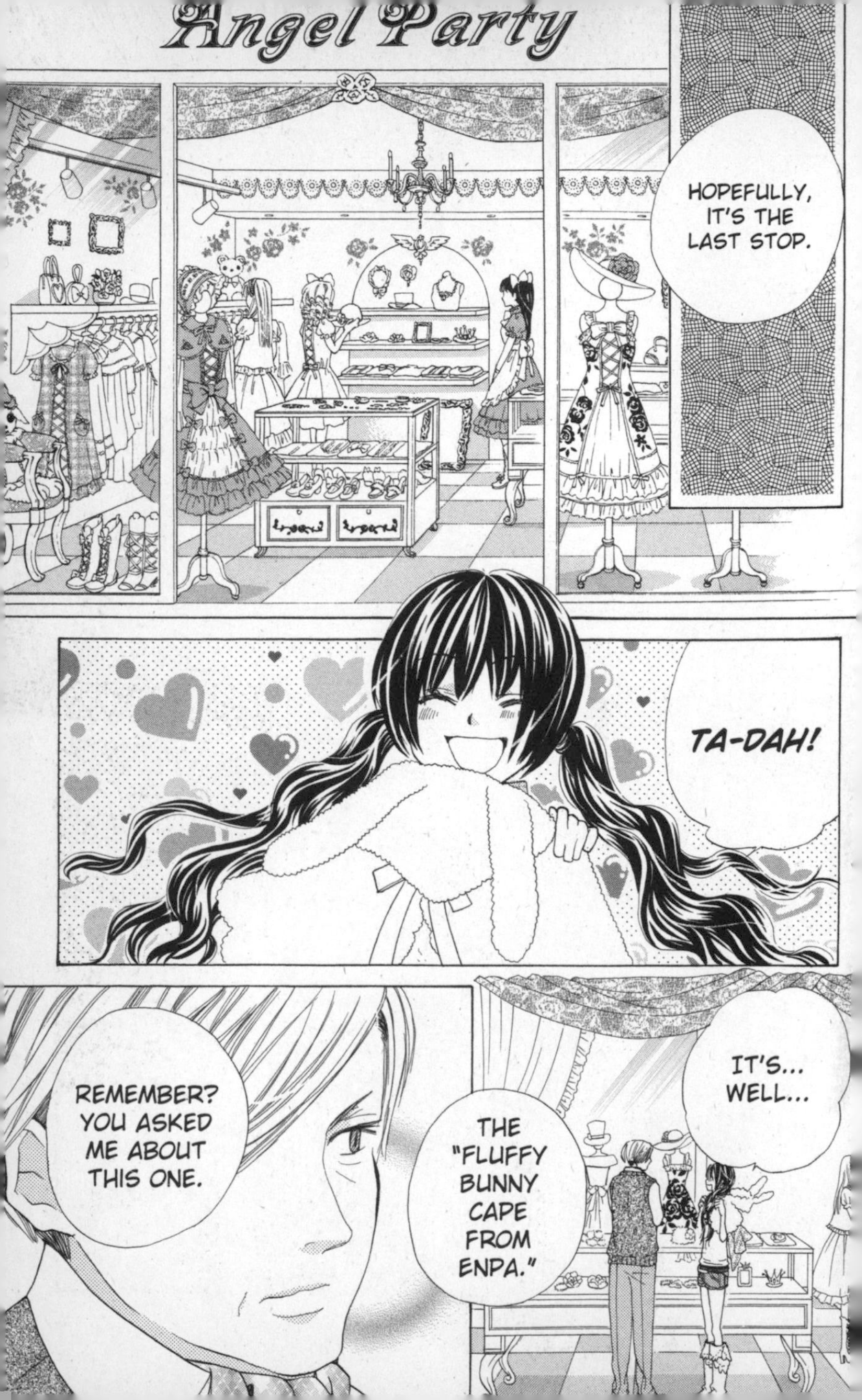
HOPEFULLY, IT'S THE LAST STOP.
Angel Party
TA-DAH!
IT'S... WELL...
THE "FLUFFY BUNNY CAPE FROM ENPA."
REMEMBER? YOU ASKED ME ABOUT THIS ONE.

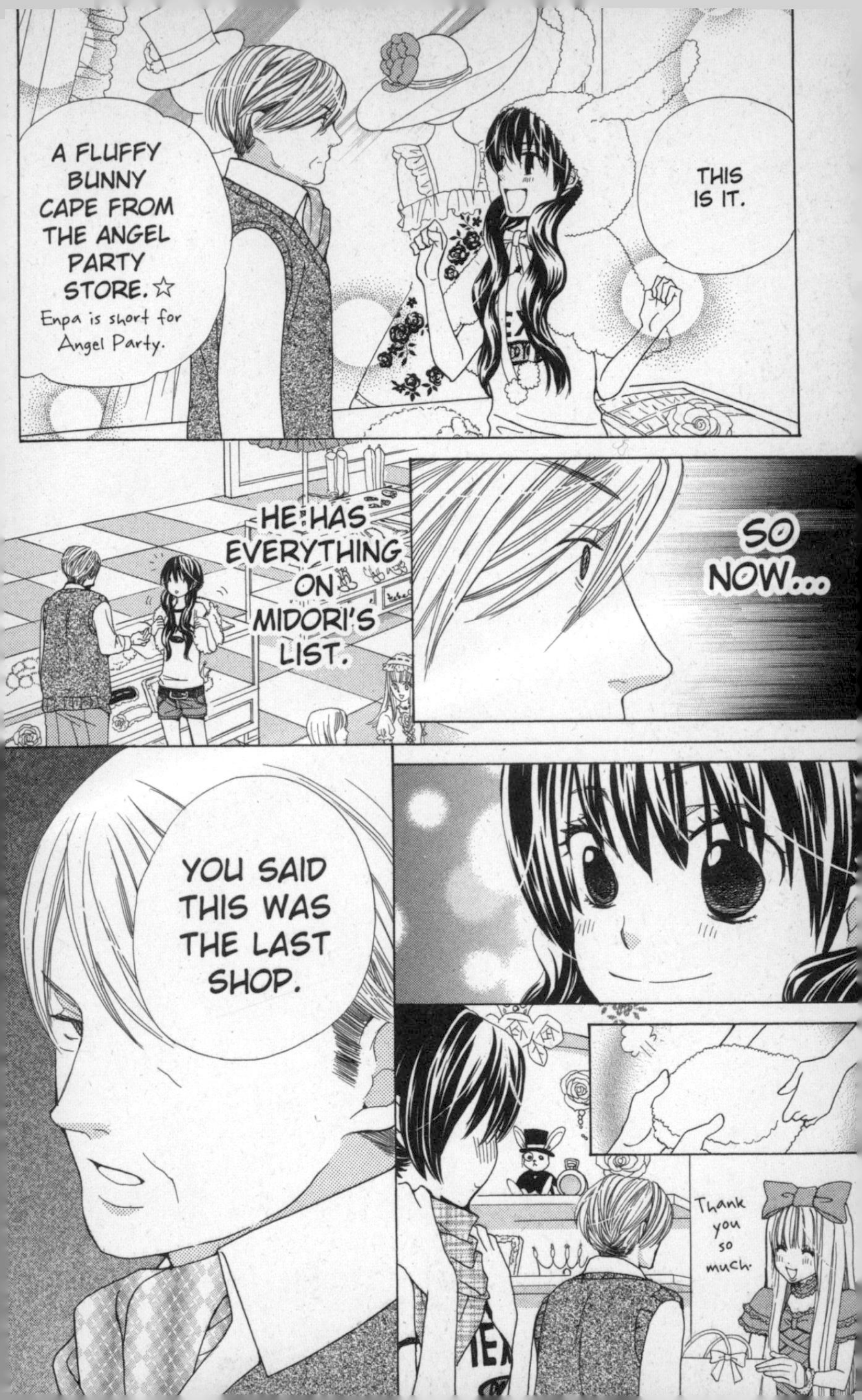
THIS IS IT.
A FLUFFY BUNNY CAPE FROM THE ANGEL PARTY STORE.☆
Enpa is short for Angel Party.
SO NOW...
HE HAS EVERYTHING ON MIDORI'S LIST.
Thank you so much.
YOU SAID THIS WAS THE LAST SHOP.

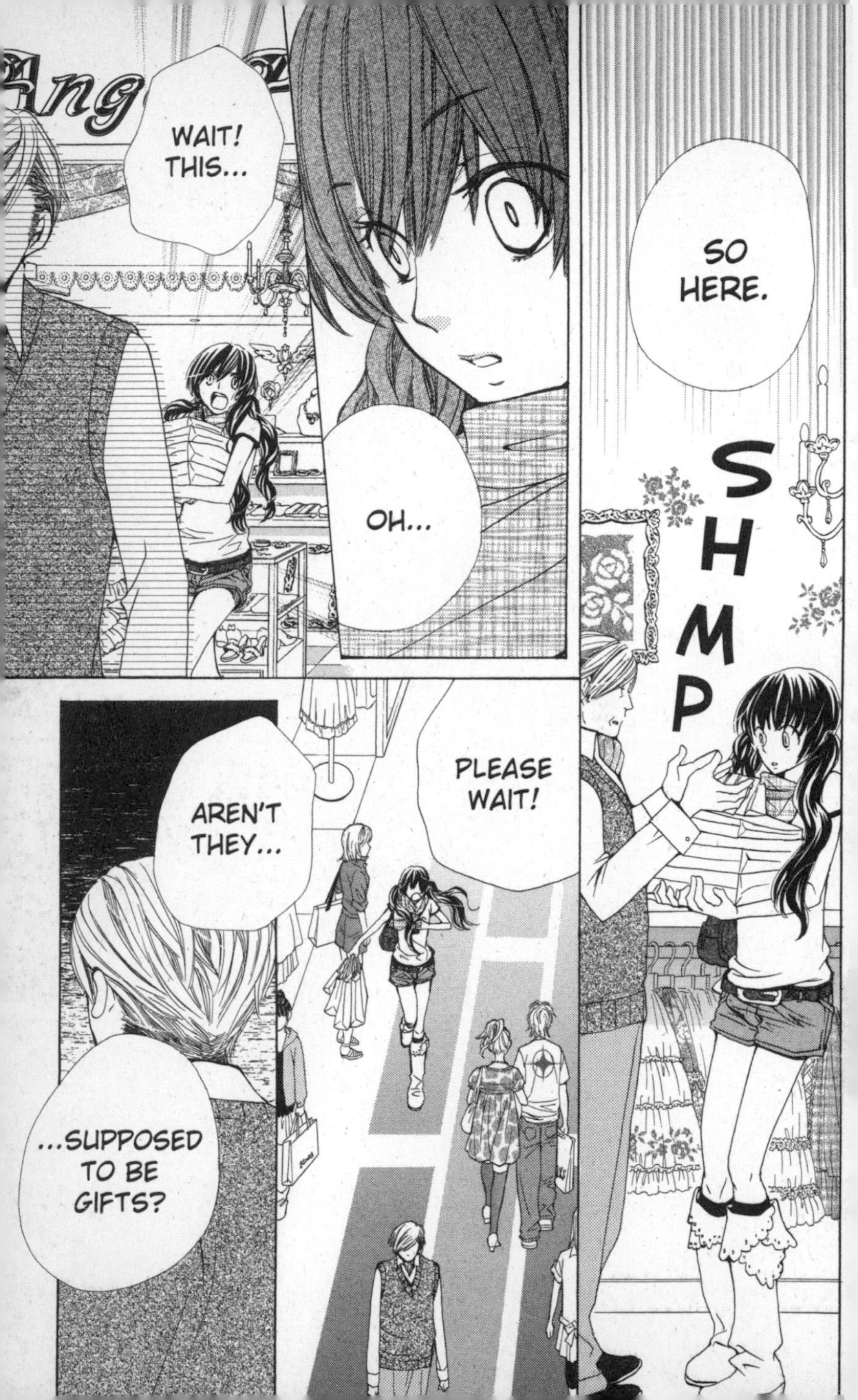
SO HERE.
SHMP
OH...
WAIT! THIS...
PLEASE WAIT!
AREN'T THEY...
...SUPPOSED TO BE GIFTS?

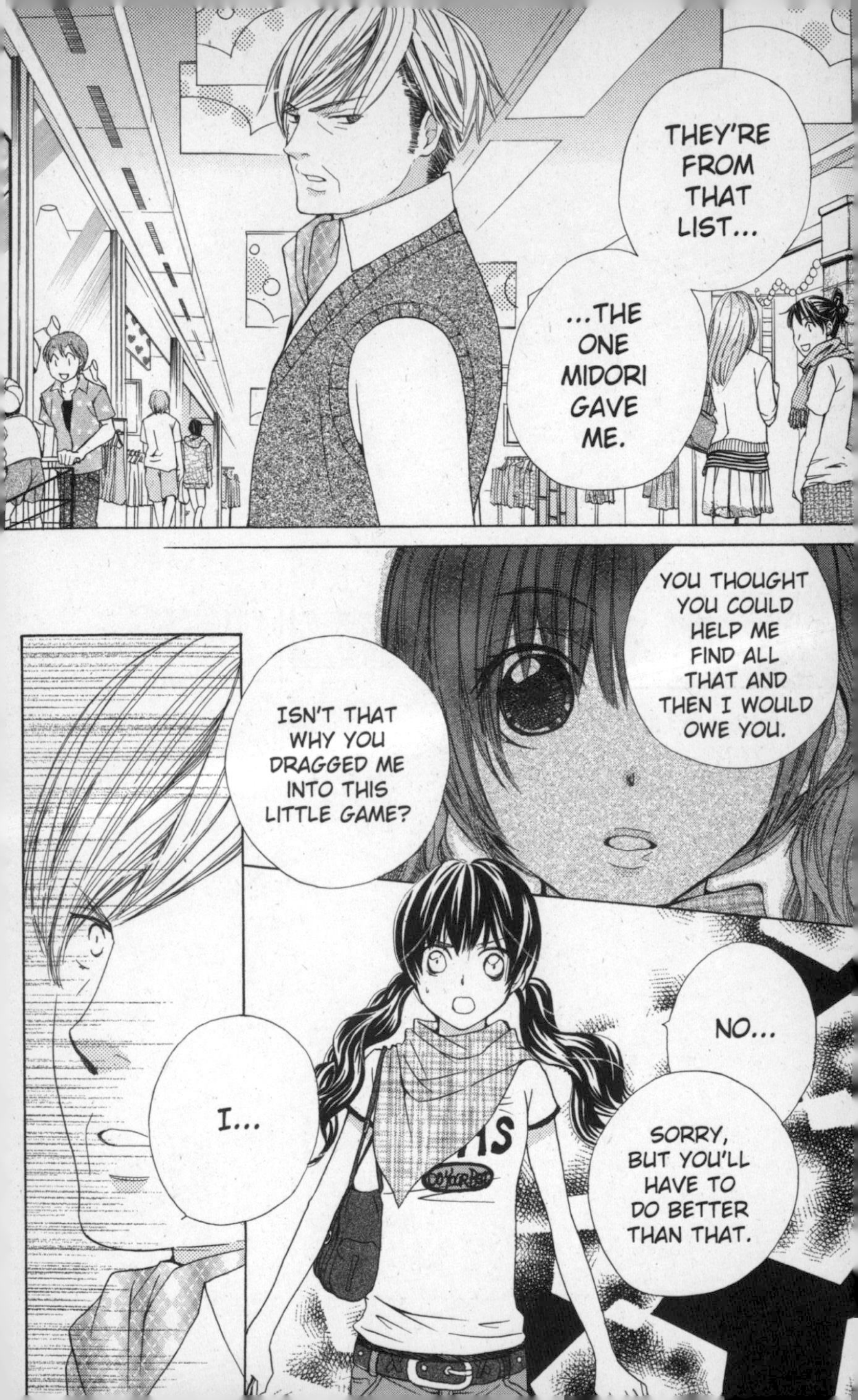
THEY'RE FROM THAT LIST...
...THE ONE MIDORI GAVE ME.
YOU THOUGHT YOU COULD HELP ME FIND ALL THAT AND THEN I WOULD OWE YOU.
ISN'T THAT WHY YOU DRAGGED ME INTO THIS LITTLE GAME?
NO...
SORRY, BUT YOU'LL HAVE TO DO BETTER THAN THAT.
I...

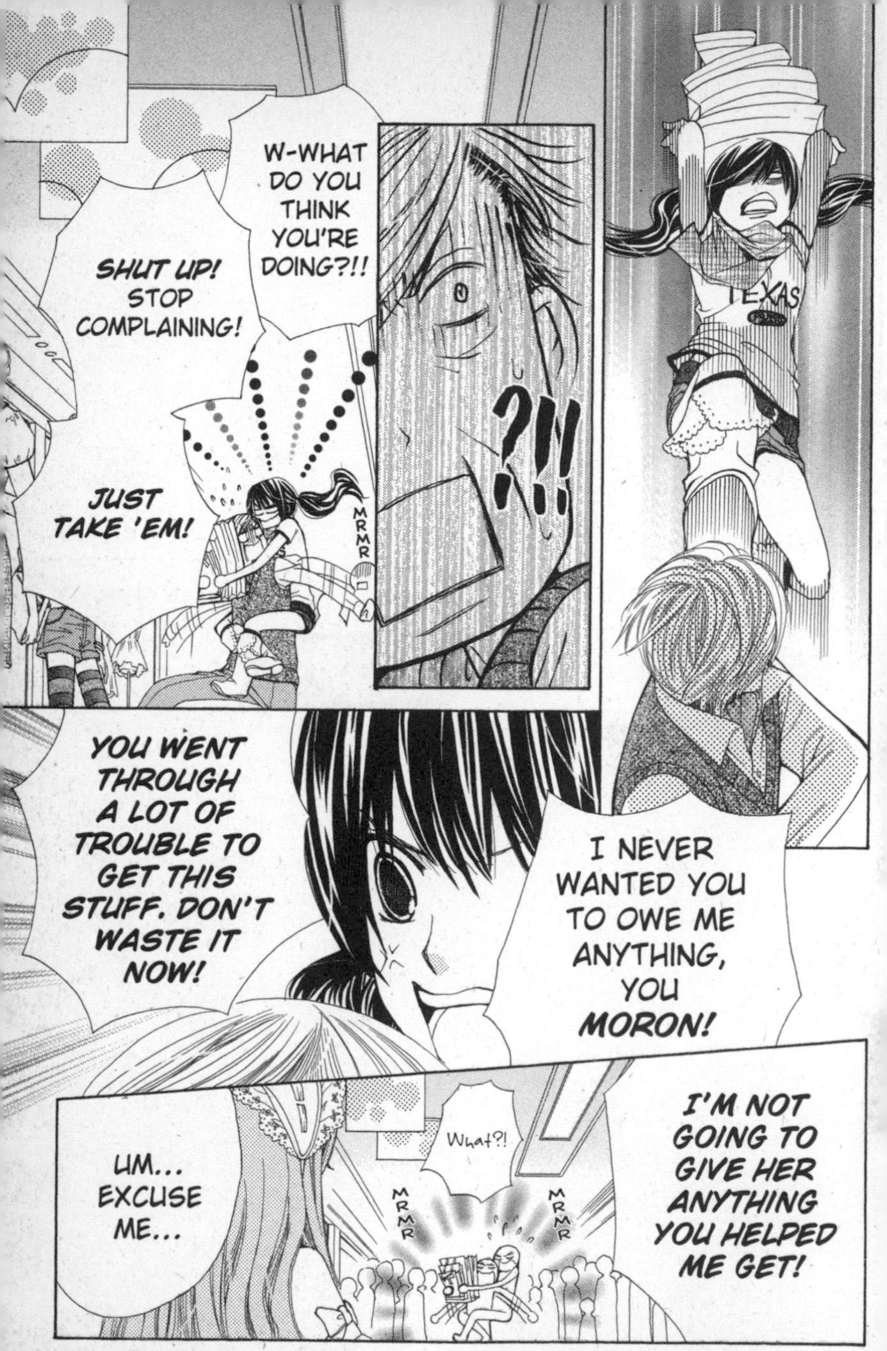
?!!
W-WHAT DO YOU THINK YOU'RE DOING?!!
SHUT UP! STOP COMPLAINING!
MRMR
JUST TAKE 'EM!
I NEVER WANTED YOU TO OWE ME ANYTHING, YOU MORON!
YOU WENT THROUGH A LOT OF TROUBLE TO GET THIS STUFF. DON'T WASTE IT NOW!
I'M NOT GOING TO GIVE HER ANYTHING YOU HELPED ME GET!
What?!
MRMR
MRMR
UM... EXCUSE ME...

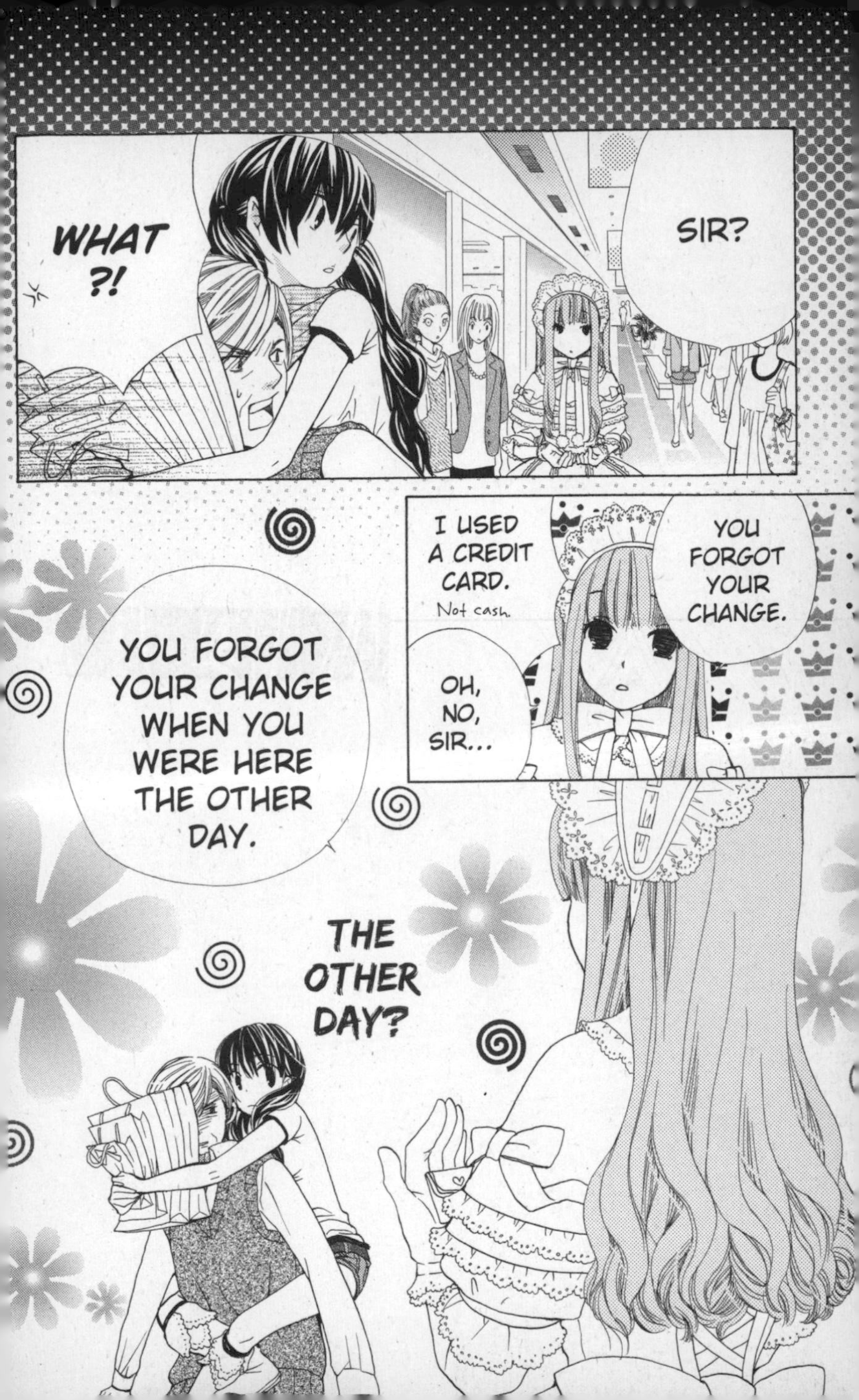
SIR?
WHAT ?!
YOU FORGOT YOUR CHANGE.
I USED A CREDIT CARD.
Not cash.
OH, NO, SIR...
YOU FORGOT YOUR CHANGE WHEN YOU WERE HERE THE OTHER DAY.
THE OTHER DAY?

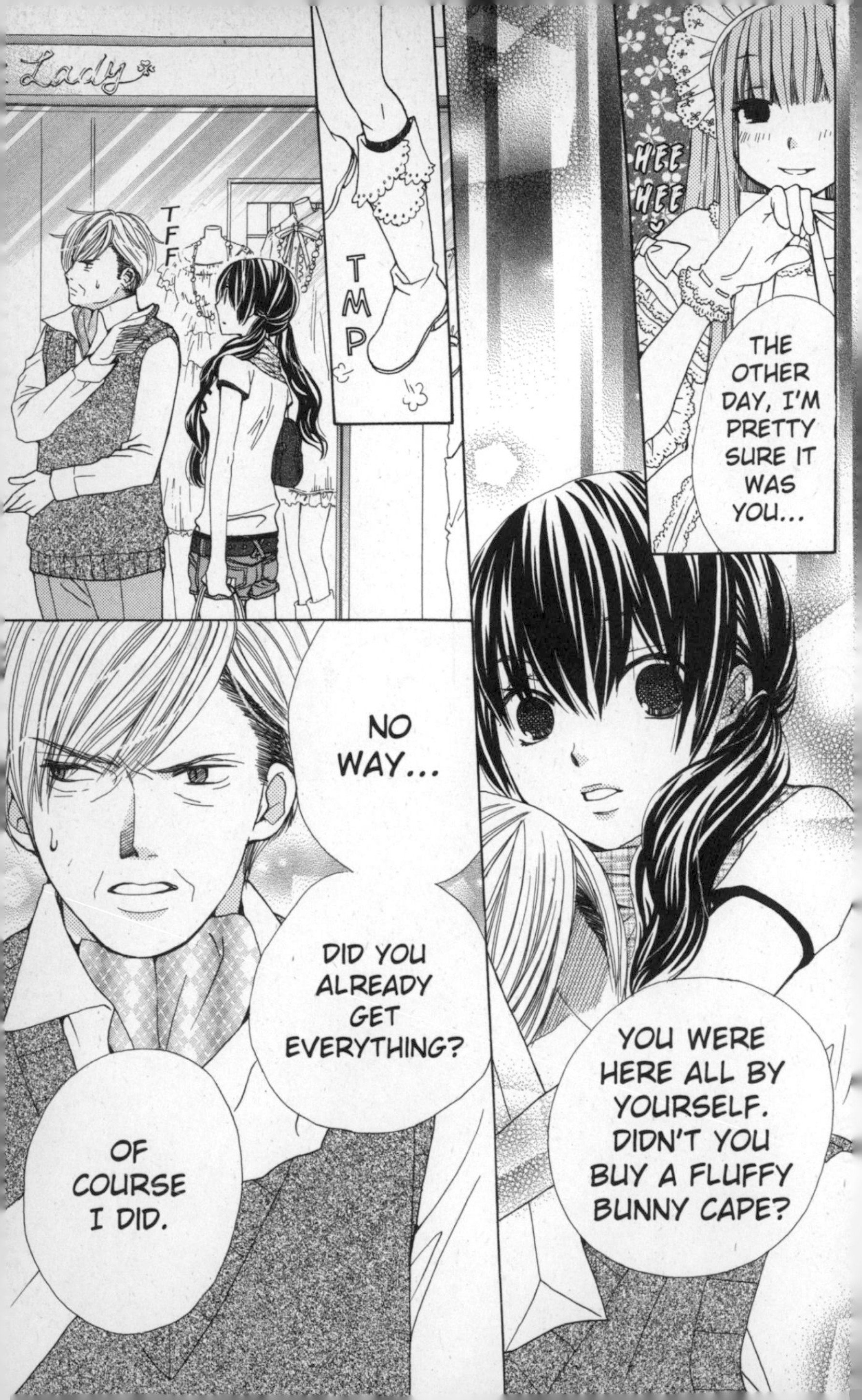
HEE HEE
THE OTHER DAY, I'M PRETTY SURE IT WAS YOU...
TMP
Lady
TFF
YOU WERE HERE ALL BY YOURSELF. DIDN'T YOU BUY A FLUFFY BUNNY CAPE?
NO WAY...
DID YOU ALREADY GET EVERYTHING?
OF COURSE I DID.

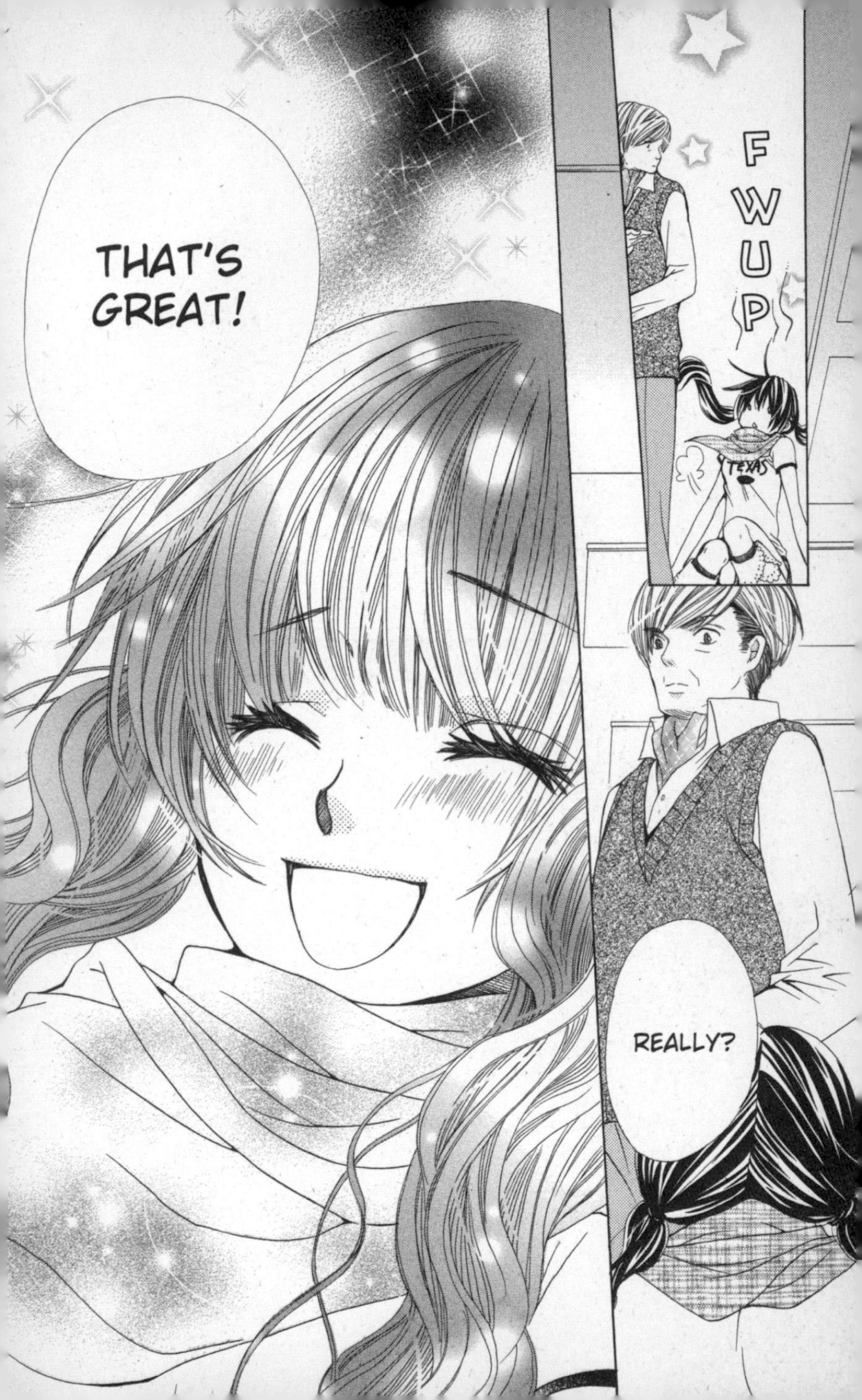
FWUP
TEXAS
REALLY?
THAT'S GREAT!

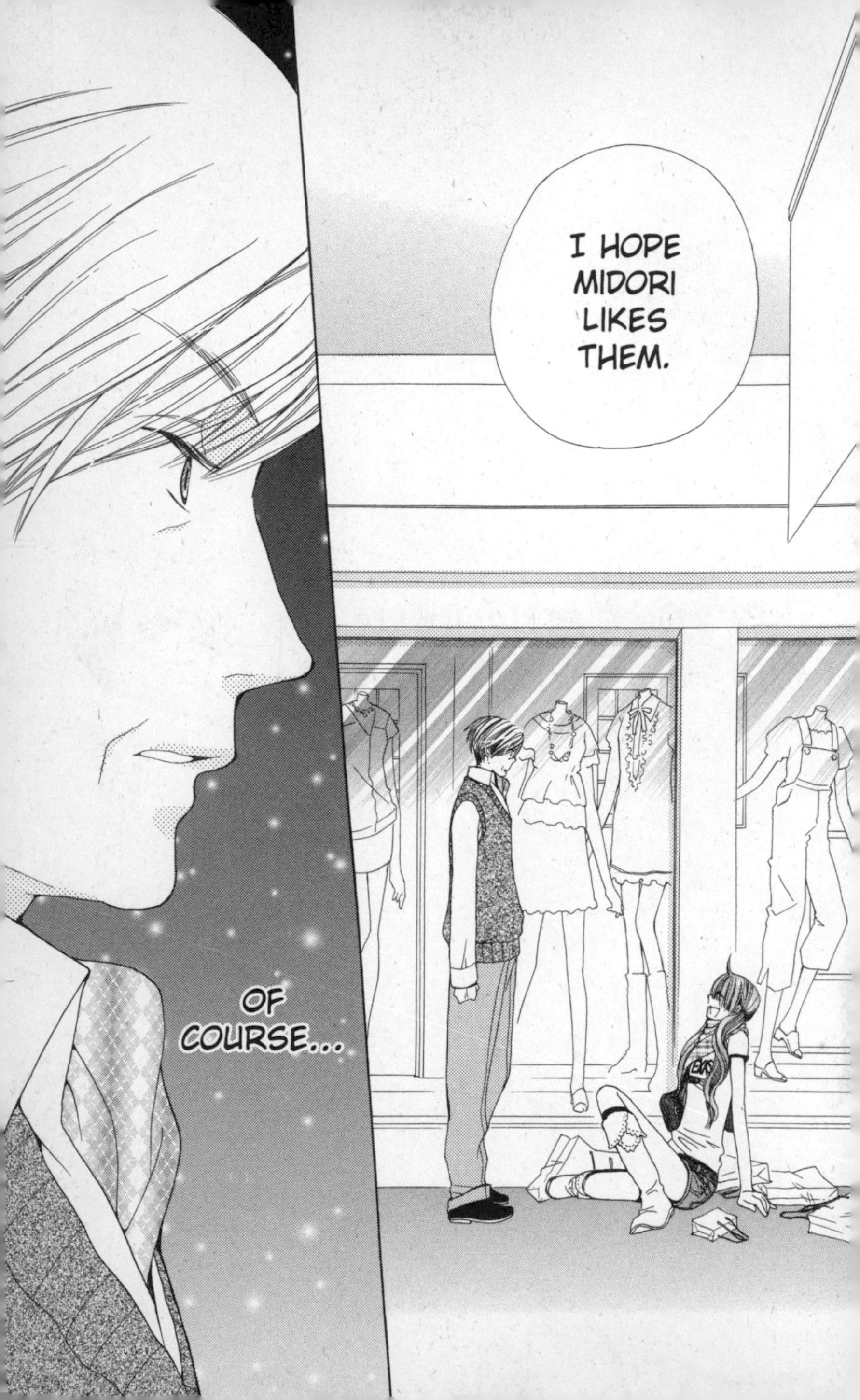
I HOPE MIDORI LIKES THEM.
OF COURSE...

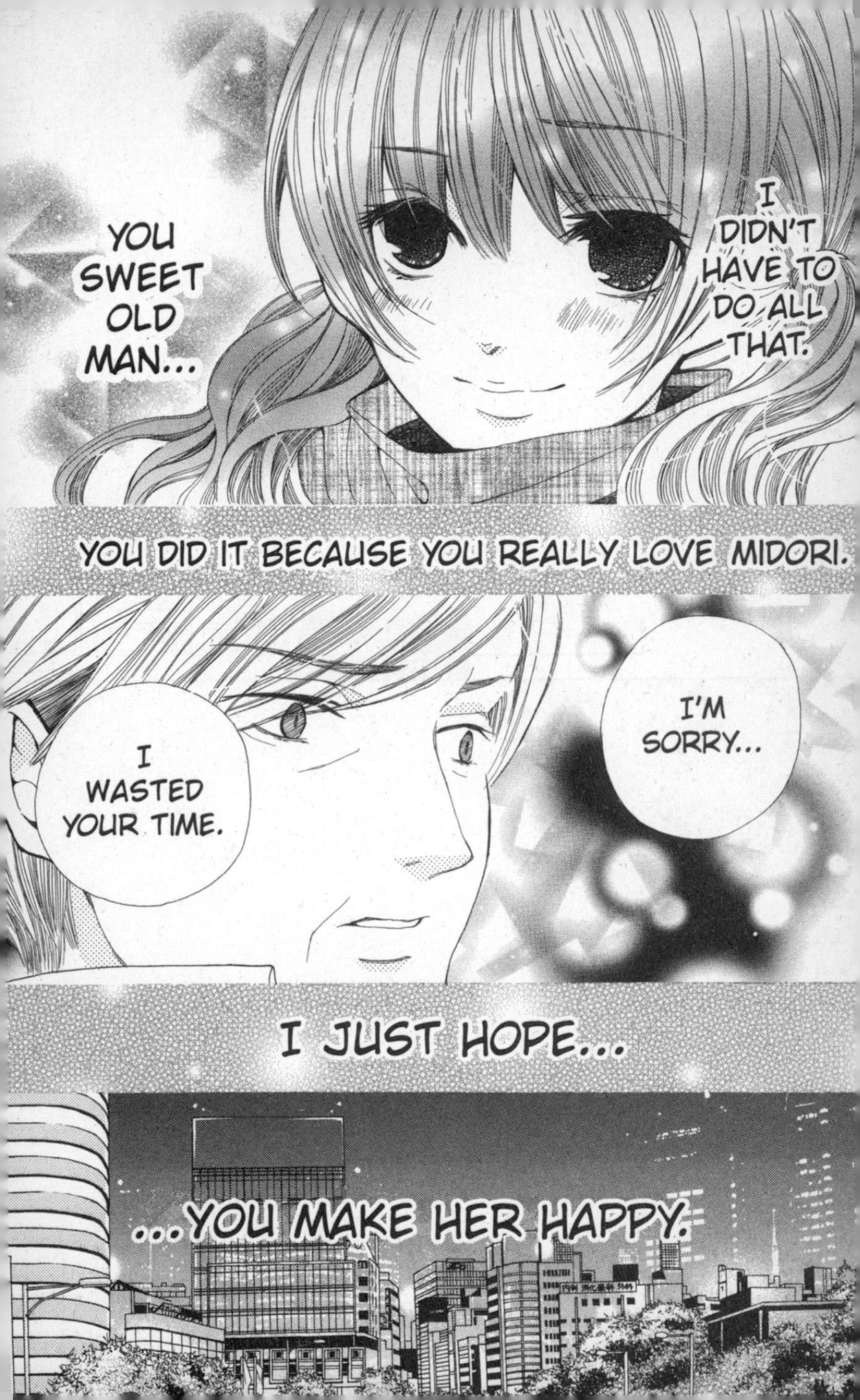
I DIDN'T HAVE TO DO ALL THAT.
YOU SWEET OLD MAN...
YOU DID IT BECAUSE YOU REALLY LOVE MIDORI.
I'M SORRY...
I WASTED YOUR TIME.
I JUST HOPE...
...YOU MAKE HER HAPPY.

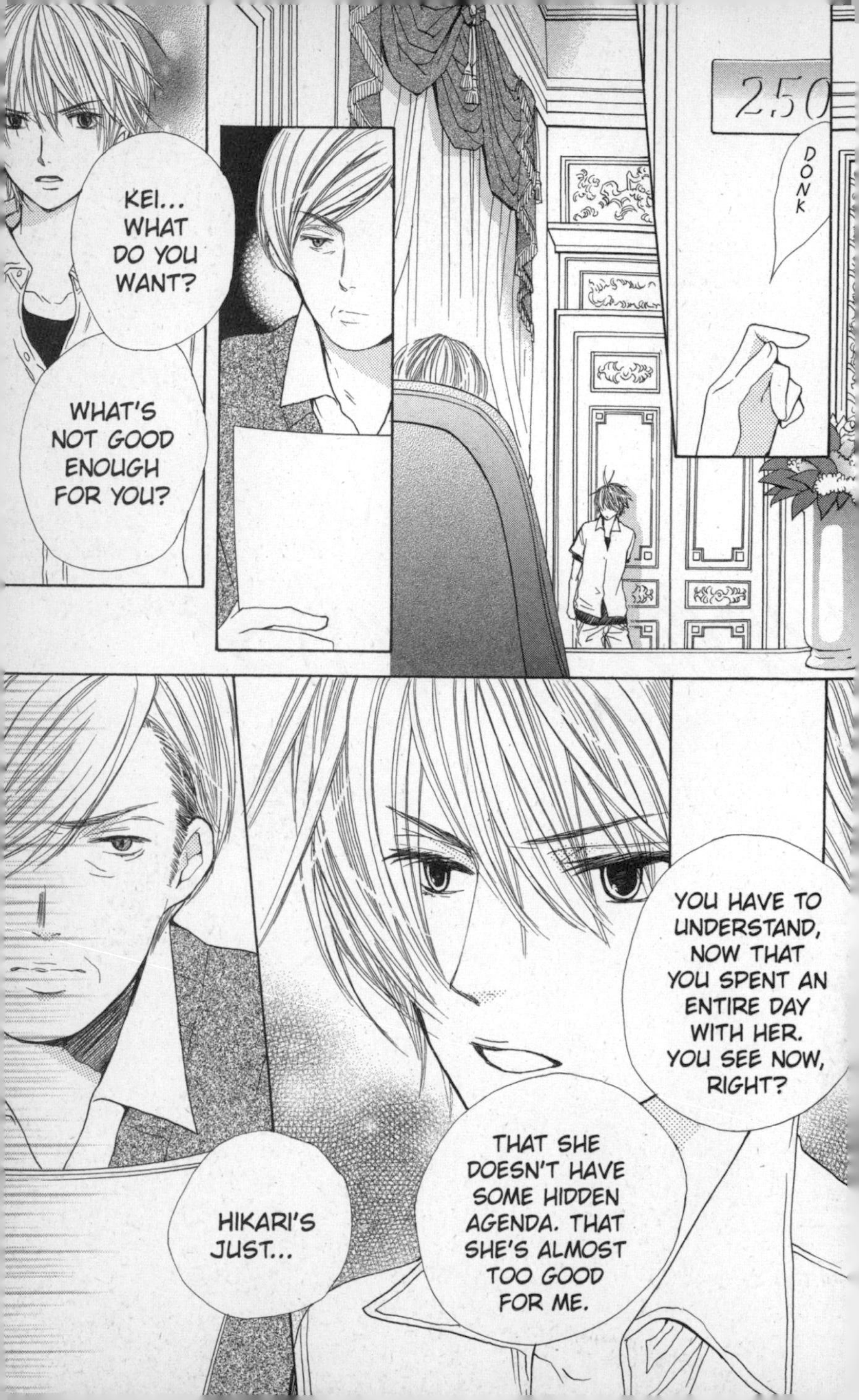
250
DONK
KEI... WHAT DO YOU WANT?
WHAT'S NOT GOOD ENOUGH FOR YOU?
YOU HAVE TO UNDERSTAND, NOW THAT YOU SPENT AN ENTIRE DAY WITH HER. YOU SEE NOW, RIGHT?
THAT SHE DOESN'T HAVE SOME HIDDEN AGENDA. THAT SHE'S ALMOST TOO GOOD FOR ME.
HIKARI'S JUST...

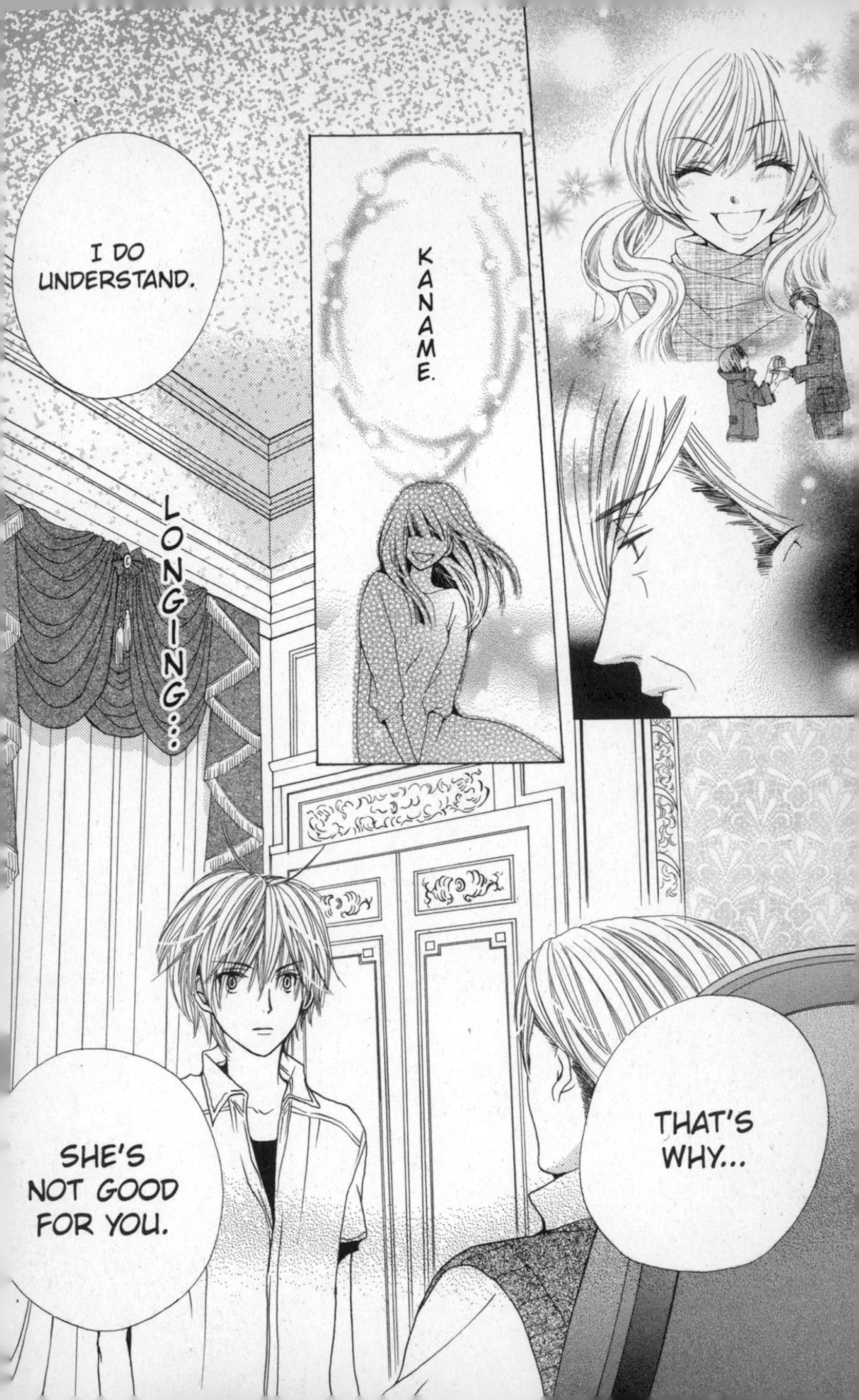
KANAME.
I DO UNDERSTAND.
LONGING...
THAT'S WHY...
SHE'S NOT GOOD FOR YOU.

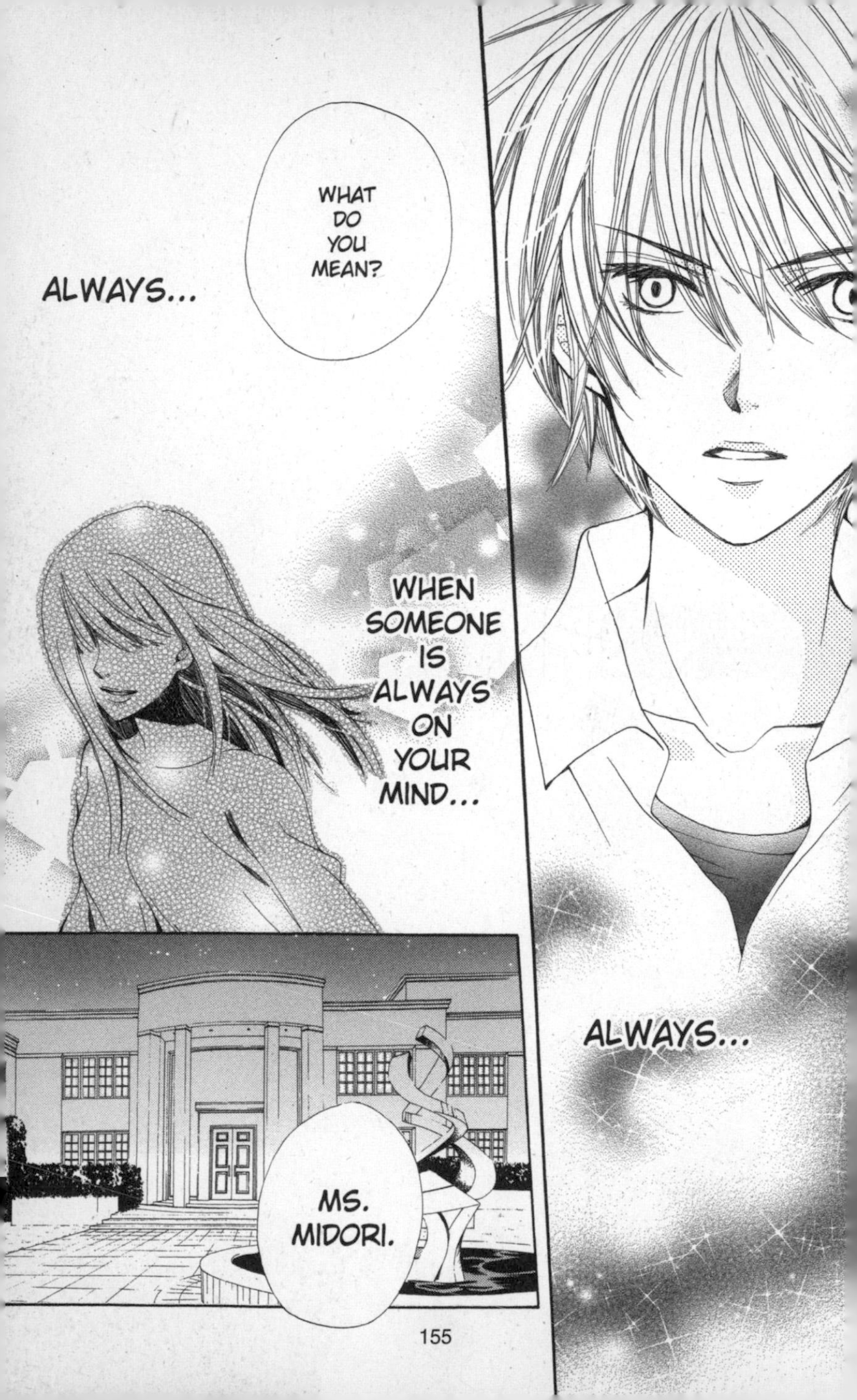
ALWAYS...
WHAT DO YOU MEAN?
ALWAYS...
WHEN SOMEONE IS ALWAYS ON YOUR MIND...
MS. MIDORI.

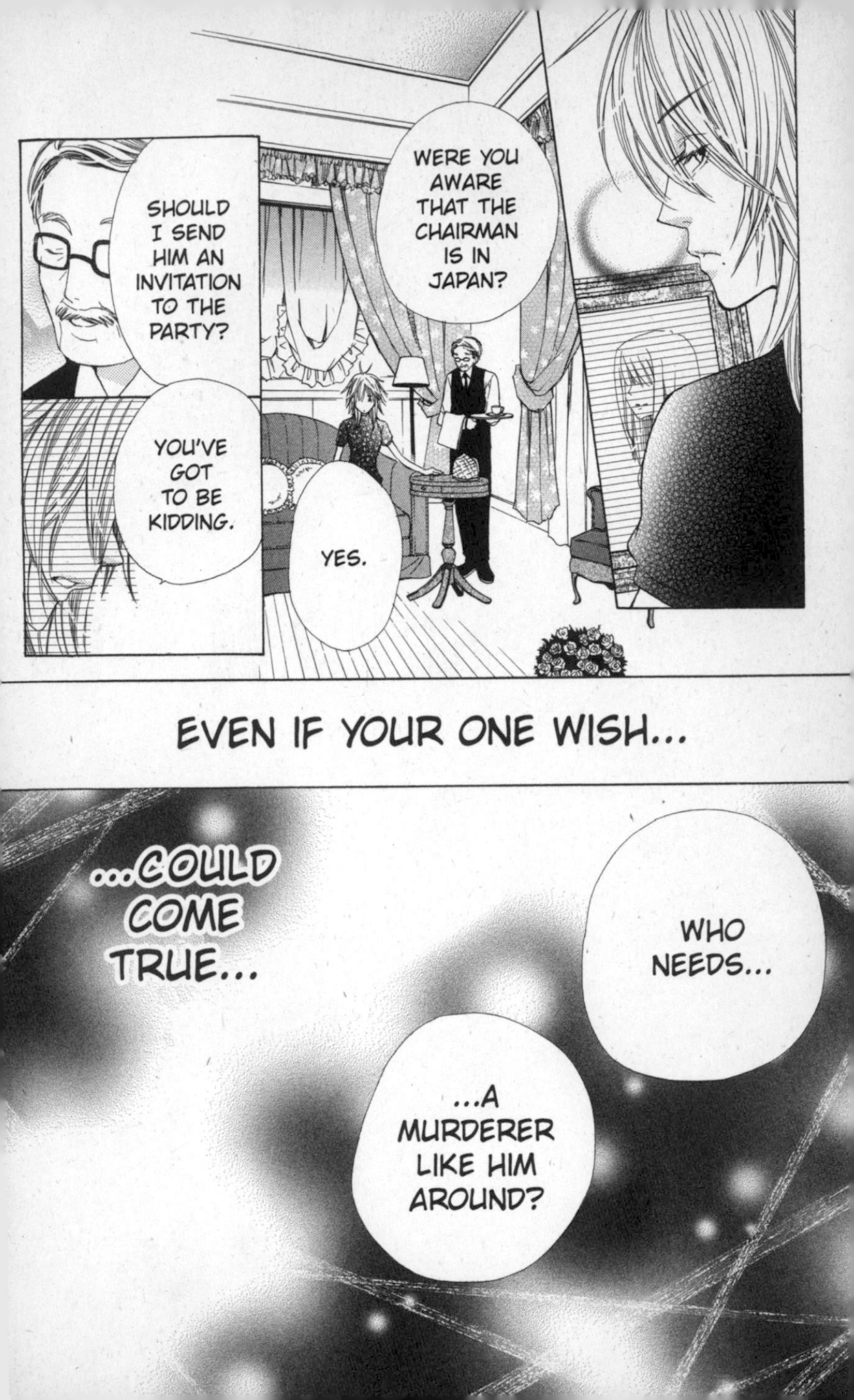
WERE YOU AWARE THAT THE CHAIRMAN IS IN JAPAN?
YES.
SHOULD I SEND HIM AN INVITATION TO THE PARTY?
YOU'VE GOT TO BE KIDDING.
EVEN IF YOUR ONE WISH...
...COULD COME TRUE...
WHO NEEDS...
...A MURDERER LIKE HIM AROUND?

Chapter 93

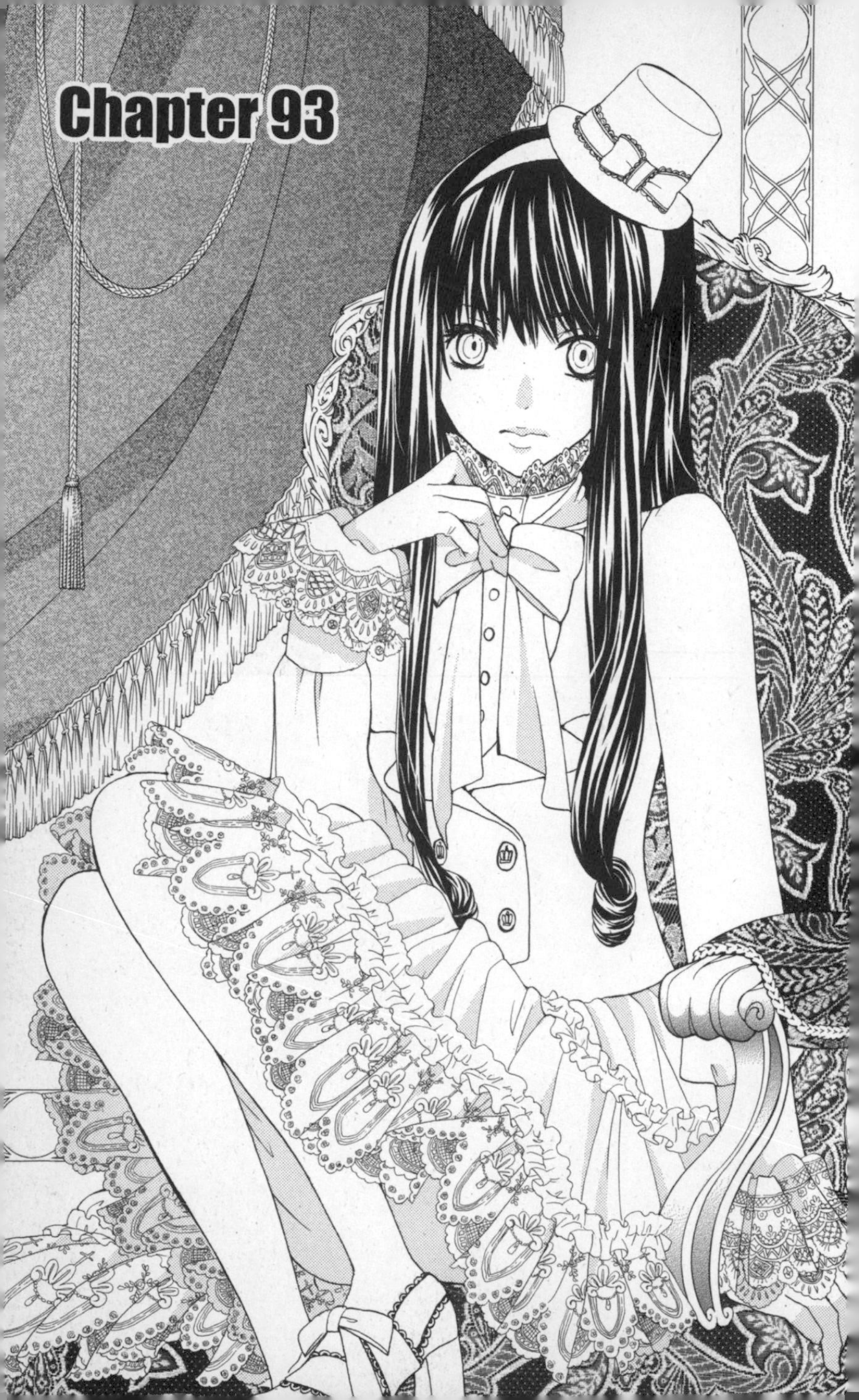

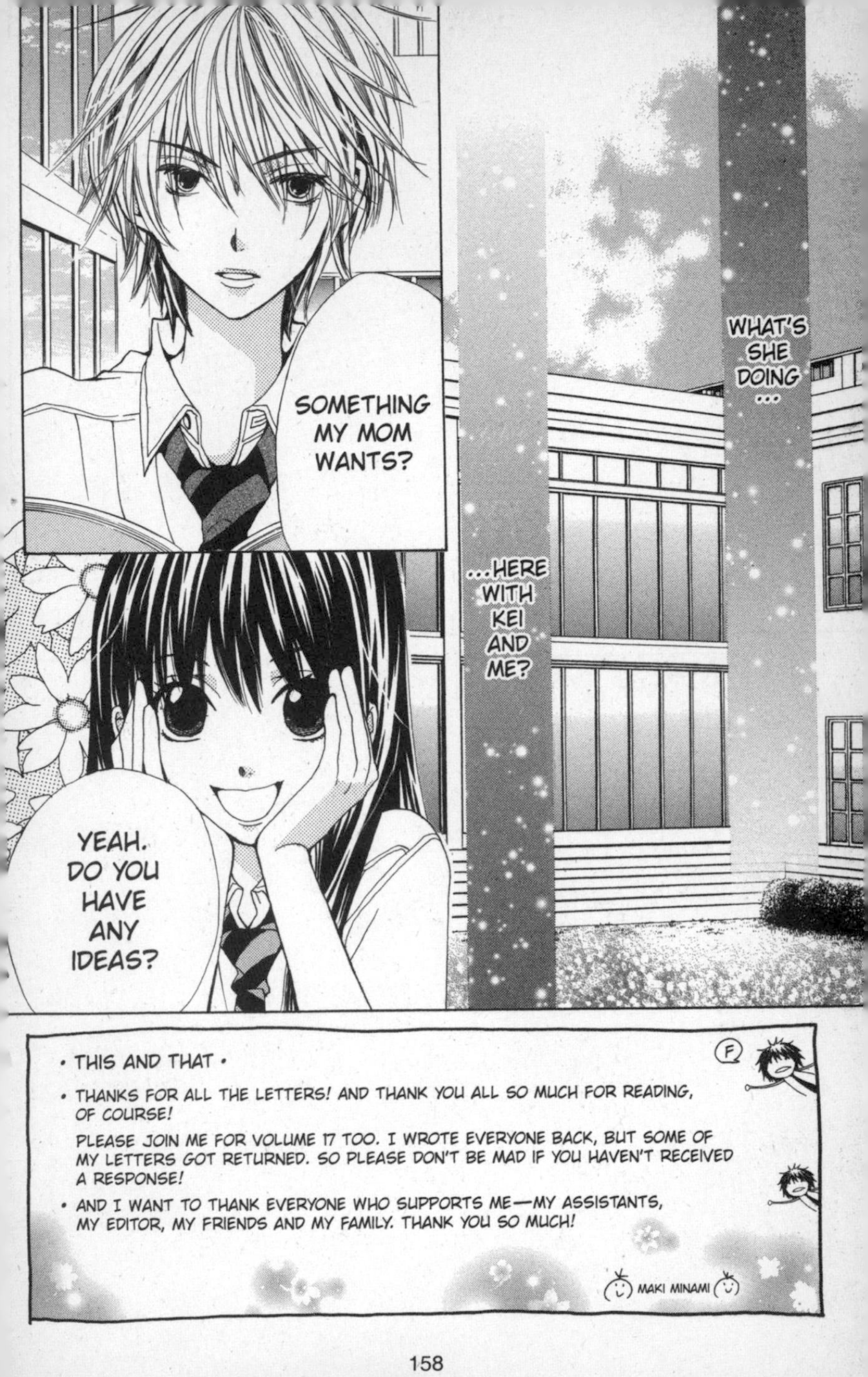
WHAT'S SHE DOING...
...HERE WITH KEI AND ME?
SOMETHING MY MOM WANTS?
YEAH. DO YOU HAVE ANY IDEAS?

• THIS AND THAT •

• THANKS FOR ALL THE LETTERS! AND THANK YOU ALL SO MUCH FOR READING, OF COURSE!

PLEASE JOIN ME FOR VOLUME 17 TOO. I WROTE EVERYONE BACK, BUT SOME OF MY LETTERS GOT RETURNED. SO PLEASE DON'T BE MAD IF YOU HAVEN'T RECEIVED A RESPONSE!

• AND I WANT TO THANK EVERYONE WHO SUPPORTS ME—MY ASSISTANTS, MY EDITOR, MY FRIENDS AND MY FAMILY. THANK YOU SO MUCH!

MAKI MINAMI

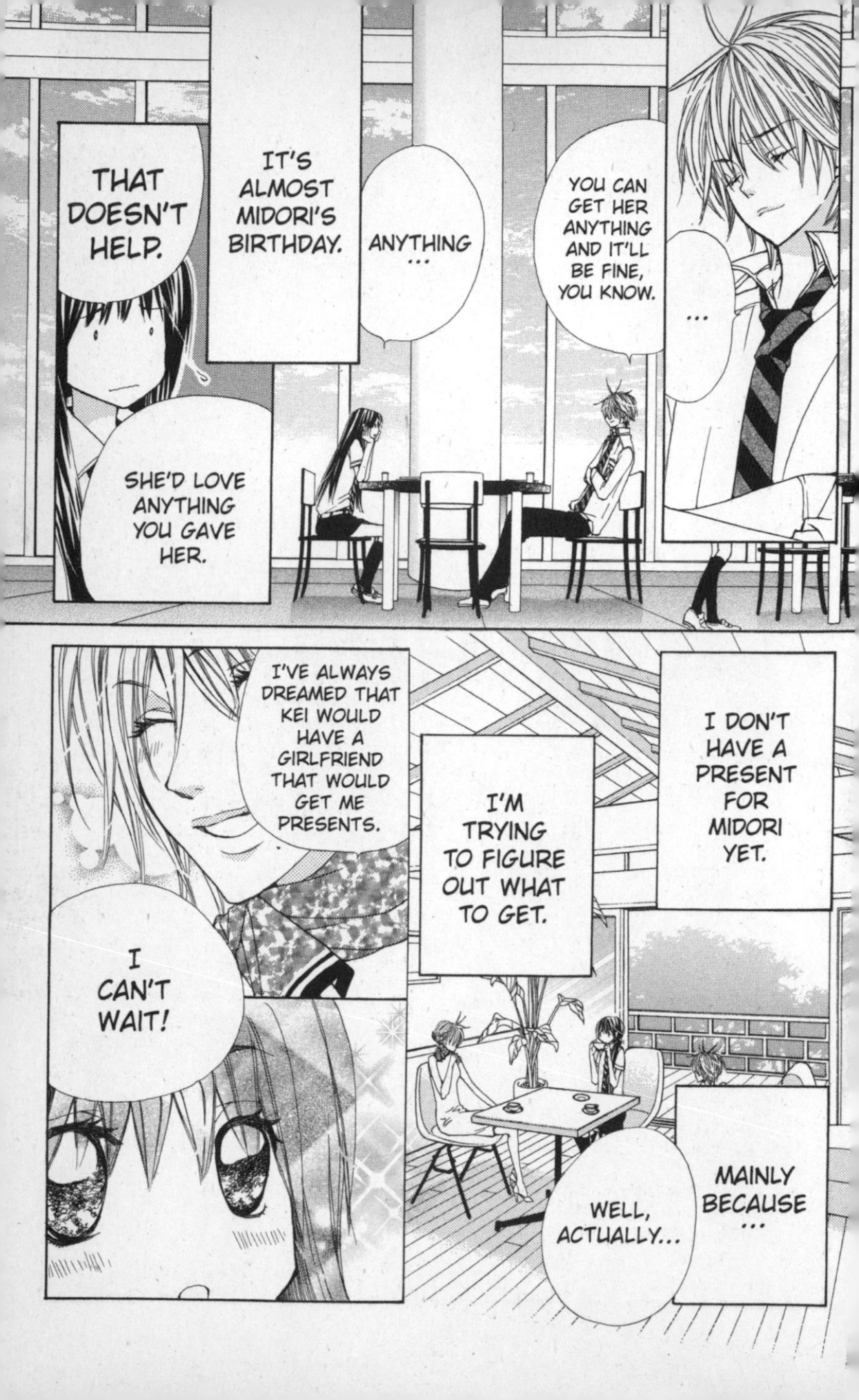
...
YOU CAN GET HER ANYTHING AND IT'LL BE FINE, YOU KNOW.
ANYTHING...
IT'S ALMOST MIDORI'S BIRTHDAY.
THAT DOESN'T HELP.
SHE'D LOVE ANYTHING YOU GAVE HER.
I DON'T HAVE A PRESENT FOR MIDORI YET.
I'M TRYING TO FIGURE OUT WHAT TO GET.
MAINLY BECAUSE...
WELL, ACTUALLY...
I'VE ALWAYS DREAMED THAT KEI WOULD HAVE A GIRLFRIEND THAT WOULD GET ME PRESENTS.
I CAN'T WAIT!

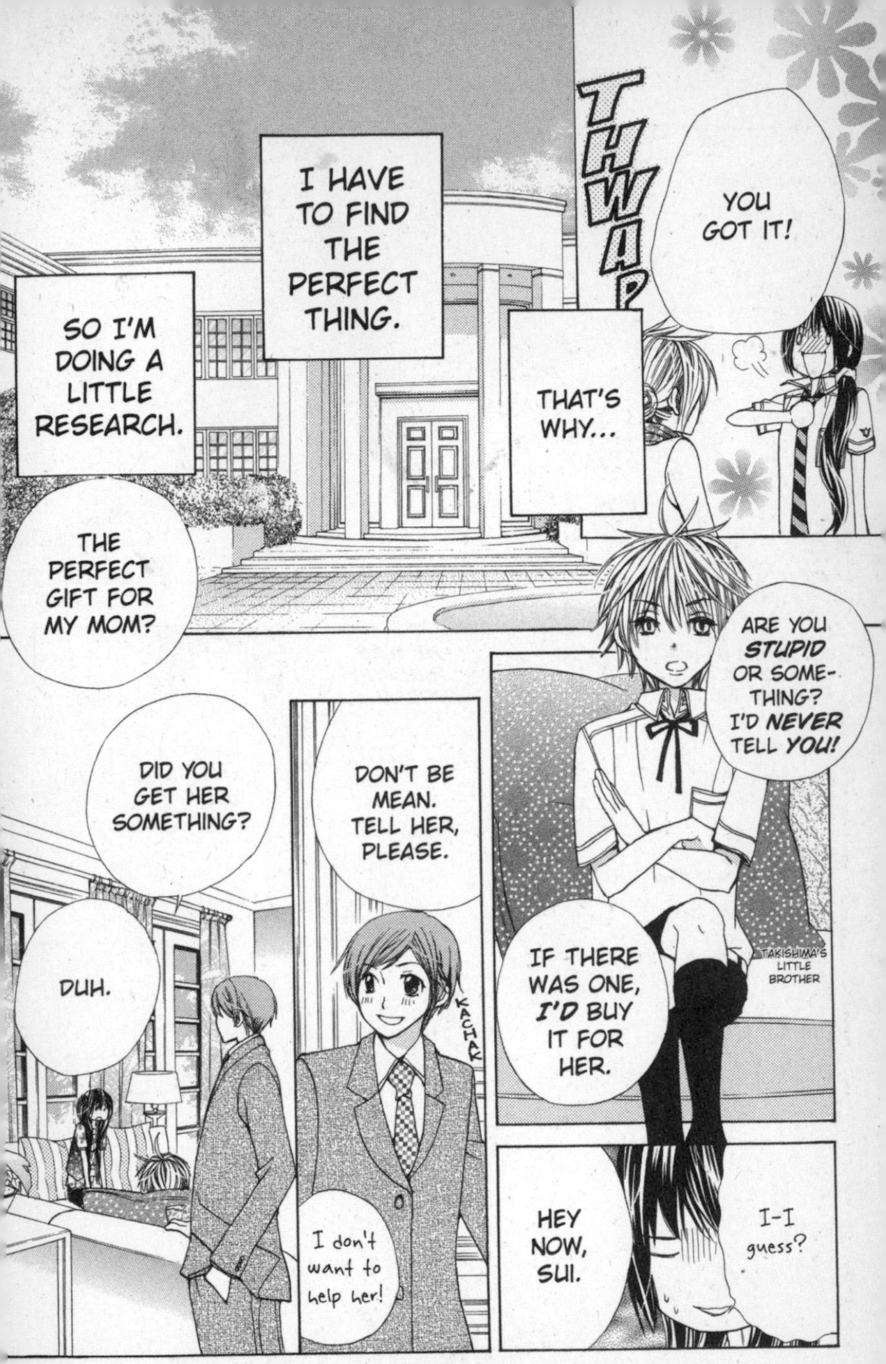
THWAP
YOU GOT IT!
THAT'S WHY...
I HAVE TO FIND THE PERFECT THING.
SO I'M DOING A LITTLE RESEARCH.
THE PERFECT GIFT FOR MY MOM?
ARE YOU STUPID OR SOMETHING? I'D NEVER TELL YOU!
TAKISHIMA'S LITTLE BROTHER
IF THERE WAS ONE, I'D BUY IT FOR HER.
HEY NOW, SUI.
I-I guess?
DON'T BE MEAN. TELL HER, PLEASE.
KACHAK
I don't want to help her!
DID YOU GET HER SOMETHING?
DUH.

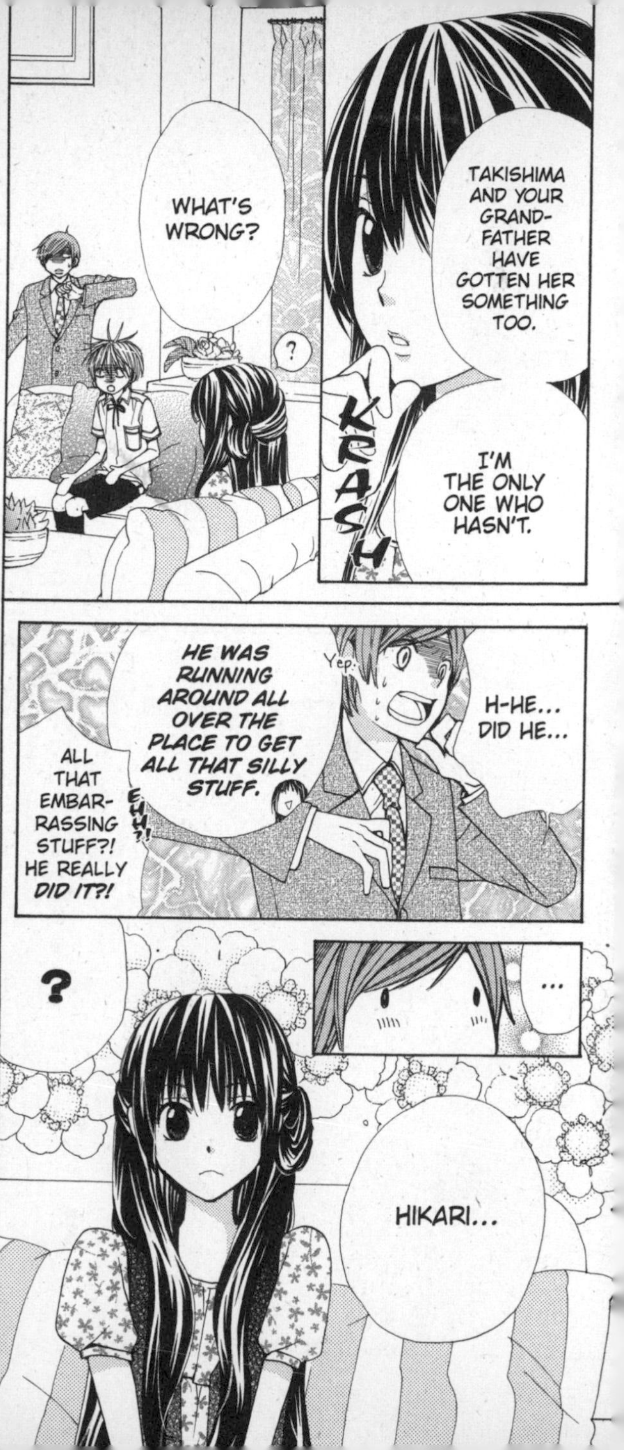
TAKISHIMA AND YOUR GRANDFATHER HAVE GOTTEN HER SOMETHING TOO.
I'M THE ONLY ONE WHO HASN'T.
KRASH
WHAT'S WRONG?
?
H-HE... DID HE...
Yep.
HE WAS RUNNING AROUND ALL OVER THE PLACE TO GET ALL THAT SILLY STUFF.
EHHH?!
ALL THAT EMBARRASSING STUFF?! HE REALLY DID IT?!
...
?
HIKARI...

⑥

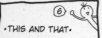

• THIS AND THAT •

THANK YOU FOR READING THIS FAR!!

• THE THEME FOR THE QUARTER PAGES THIS TIME WAS "PAJAMA PARTY." THANKS SO MUCH FOR THE IDEA!

• I REALLY HOPE YOU CAN JOIN ME ONE LAST TIME IN THE FINAL VOLUME! PLEASE DO!

• I'VE REALLY GOTTEN ADDICTED TO THIS DS GAME LATELY WHERE YOU'RE THE MANAGER OF AN ALTERATIONS SHOP. APPARENTLY, IT CAN TAKE YOU SIX TO NINE MONTHS JUST TO GET ALL 12,000 OF THE ITEMS.

I DON'T THINK I EVEN WANT TO GET THEM ALL. HA HA!

OKAY, WELL... THANK YOU SO MUCH!!

✿ IF YOU'D LIKE TO, LET US KNOW WHAT YOU THINK. ✿

MAKI MINAMI
C/O VIZ MEDIA
S.A EDITOR
P.O. BOX 77010
SAN FRANCISCO,
CA 94107

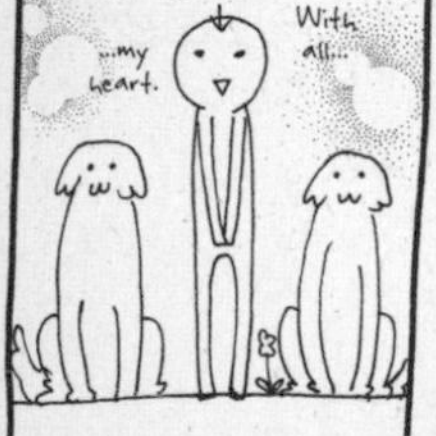
With all...
...my heart.

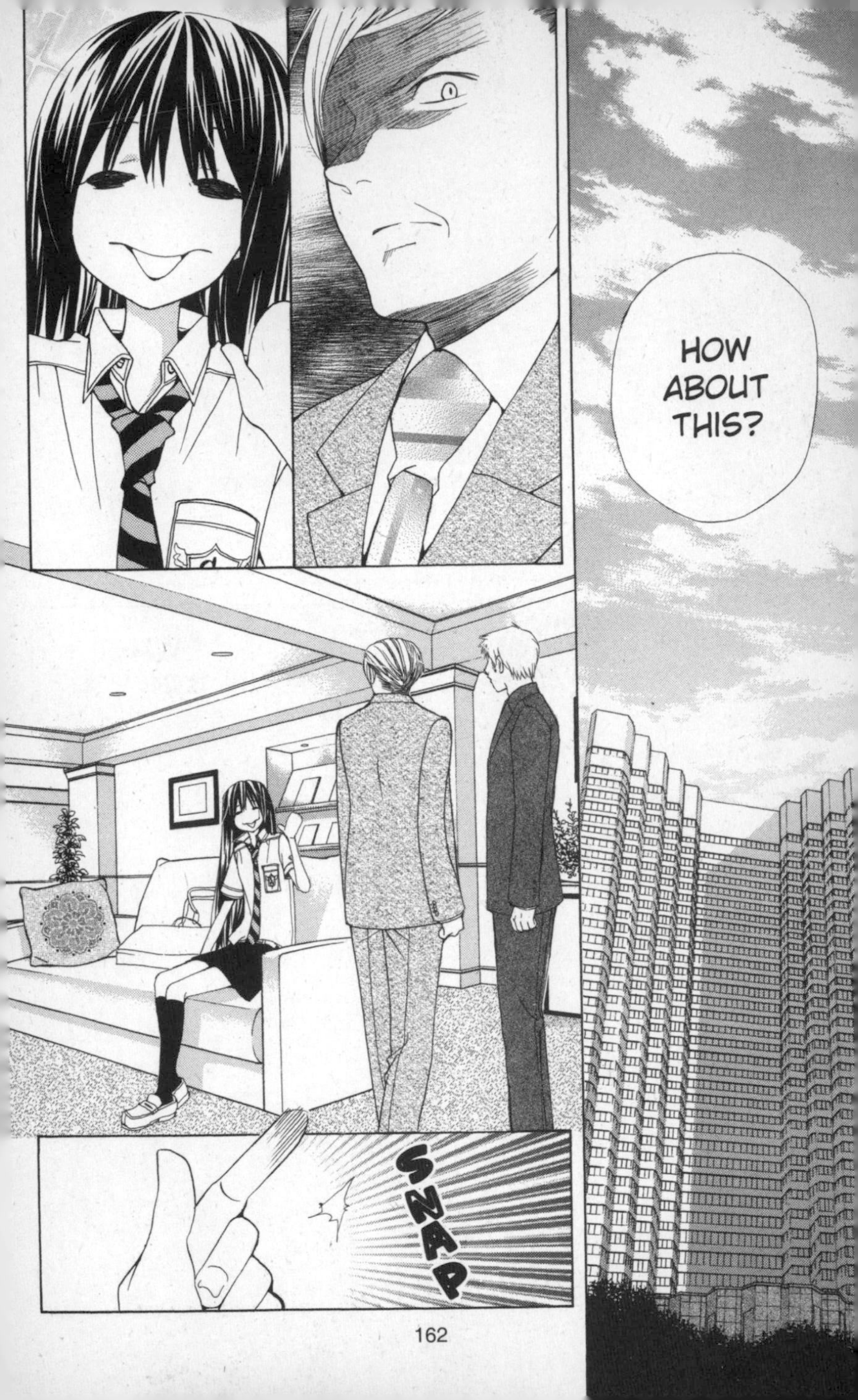
HOW ABOUT THIS?
SNAP

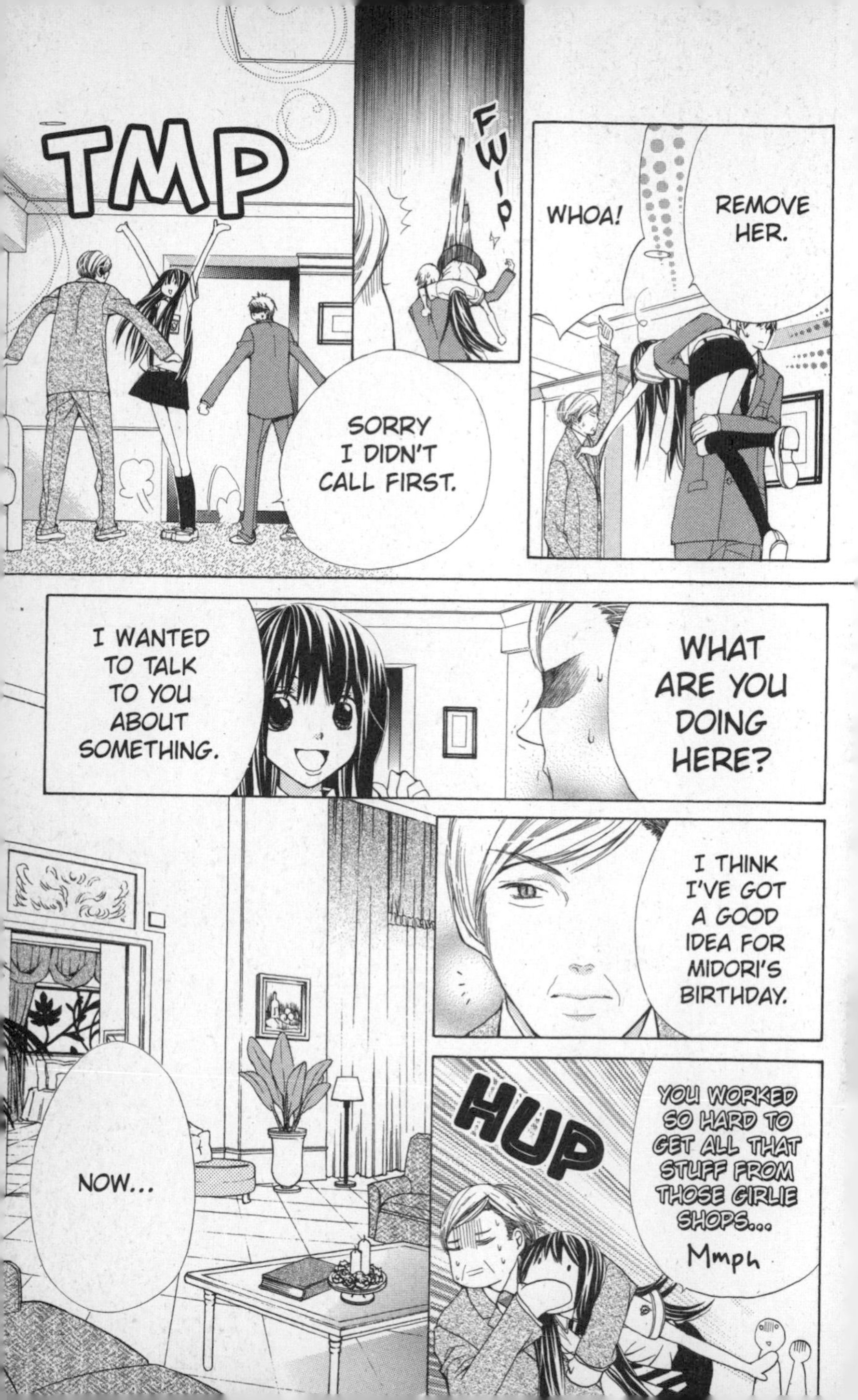
REMOVE HER.
WHOA!
FWIP
TMP
SORRY I DIDN'T CALL FIRST.
WHAT ARE YOU DOING HERE?
I WANTED TO TALK TO YOU ABOUT SOMETHING.
I THINK I'VE GOT A GOOD IDEA FOR MIDORI'S BIRTHDAY.
HUP
YOU WORKED SO HARD TO GET ALL THAT STUFF FROM THOSE GIRLIE SHOPS...
Mmph
NOW...

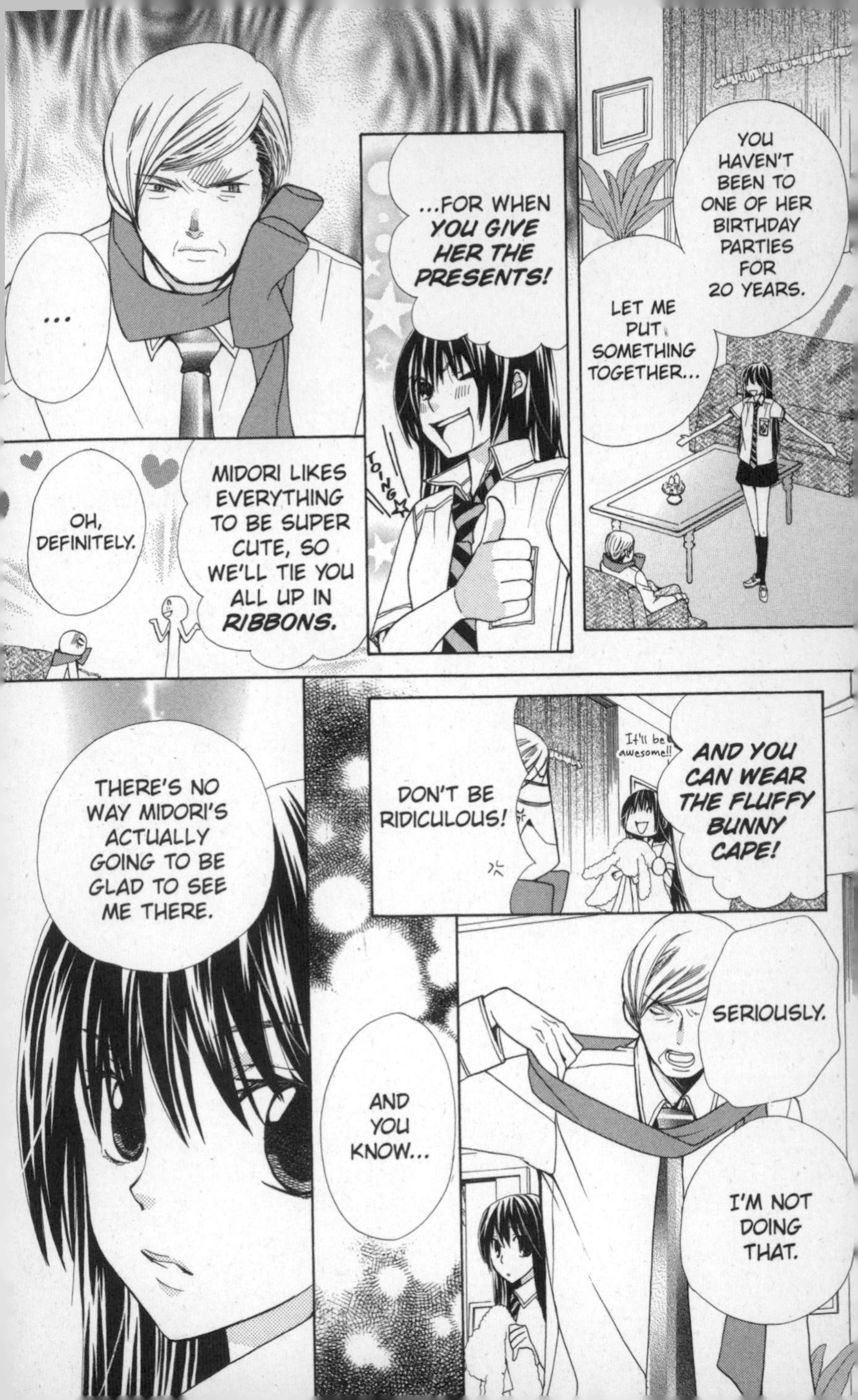

YOU HAVEN'T BEEN TO ONE OF HER BIRTHDAY PARTIES FOR 20 YEARS.
LET ME PUT SOMETHING TOGETHER...
...FOR WHEN YOU GIVE HER THE PRESENTS!
TOING☆
...
MIDORI LIKES EVERYTHING TO BE SUPER CUTE, SO WE'LL TIE YOU ALL UP IN RIBBONS.
OH, DEFINITELY.
AND YOU CAN WEAR THE FLUFFY BUNNY CAPE!
It'll be awesome!!
DON'T BE RIDICULOUS!
SERIOUSLY.
I'M NOT DOING THAT.
AND YOU KNOW...
THERE'S NO WAY MIDORI'S ACTUALLY GOING TO BE GLAD TO SEE ME THERE.

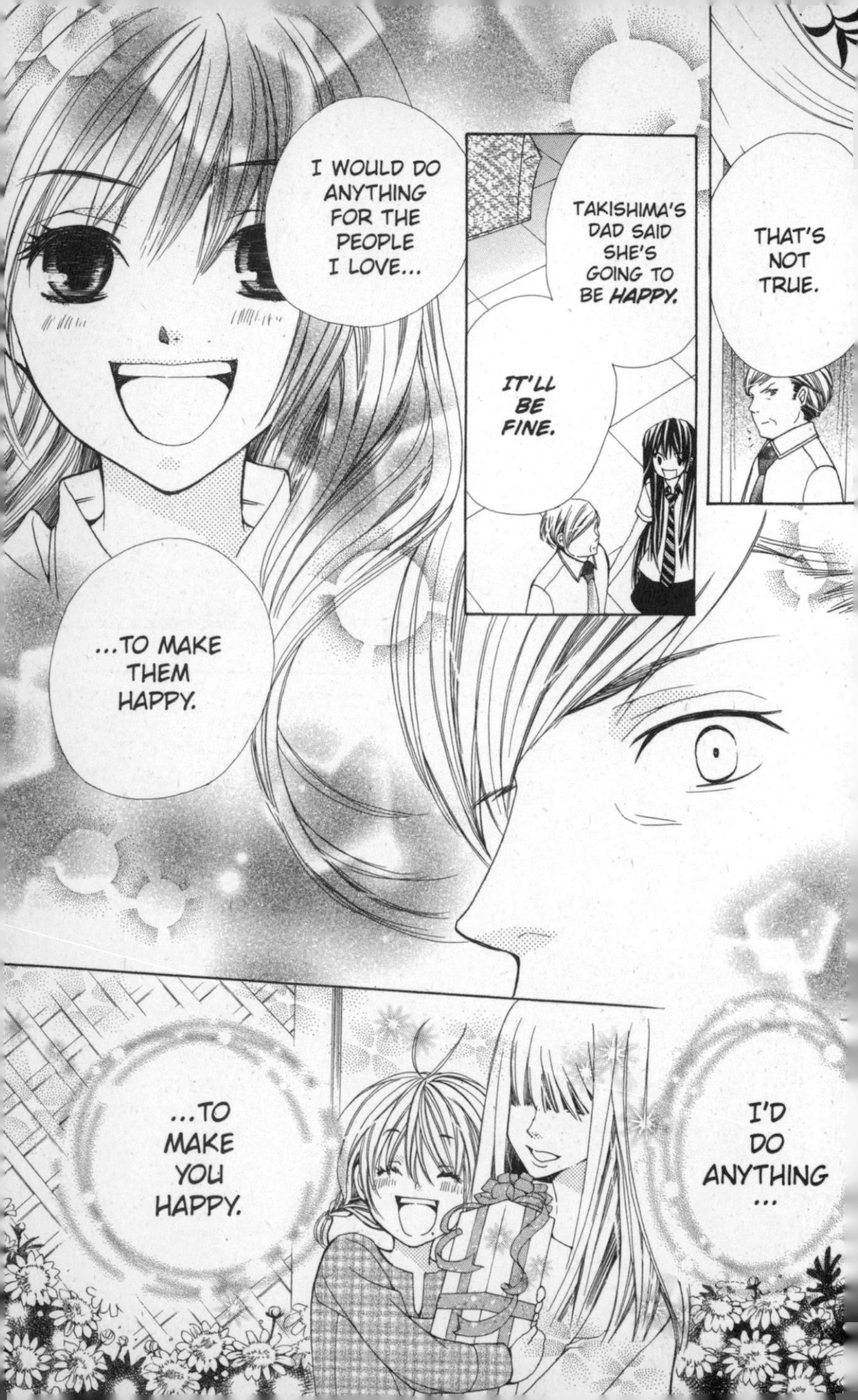
THAT'S NOT TRUE.
TAKISHIMA'S DAD SAID SHE'S GOING TO BE *HAPPY.*
IT'LL BE FINE.
I WOULD DO ANYTHING FOR THE PEOPLE I LOVE...
...TO MAKE THEM HAPPY.
I'D DO ANYTHING...
...TO MAKE YOU HAPPY.

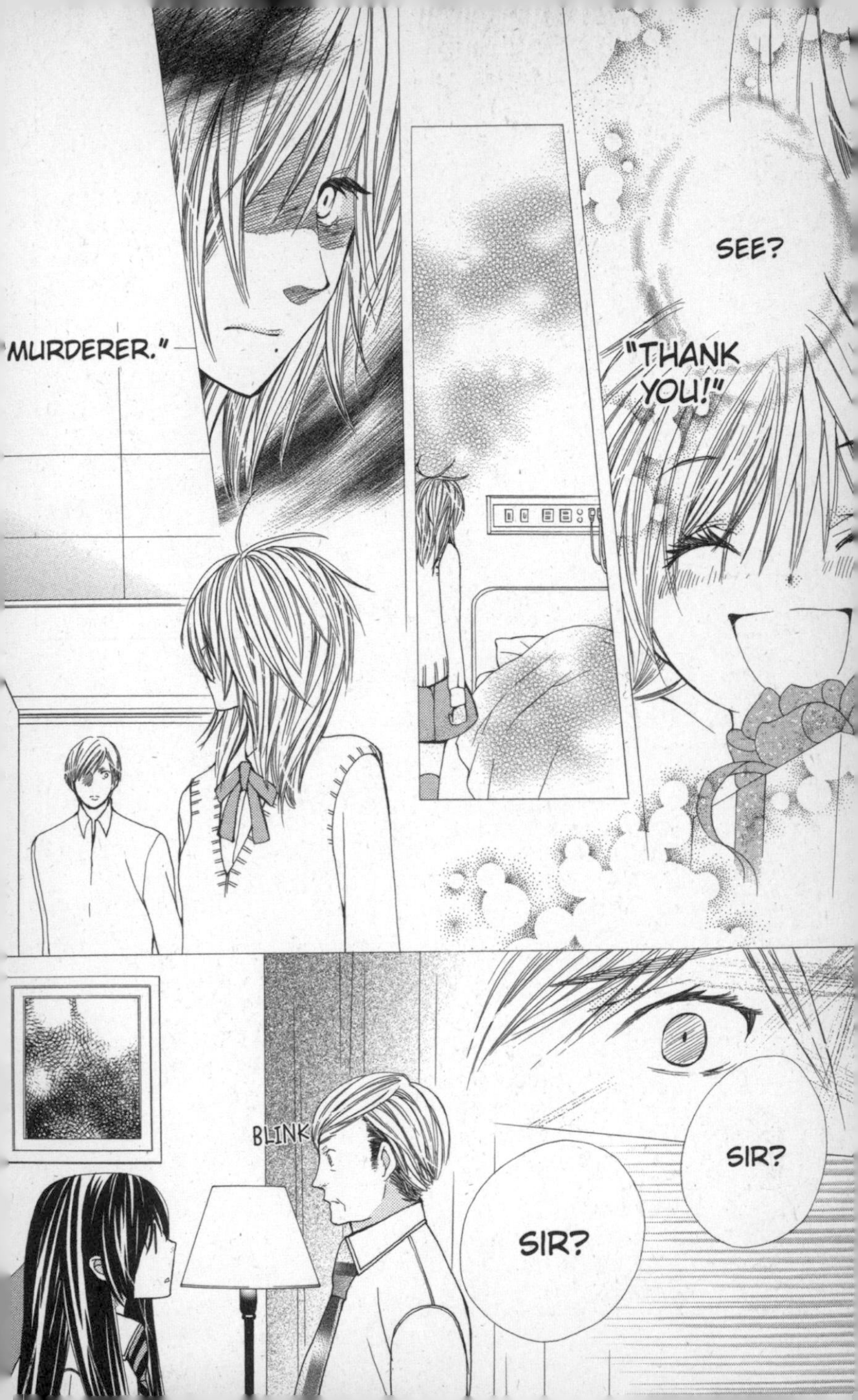
SEE?
"THANK YOU!"
MURDERER."
SIR?
SIR?
BLINK

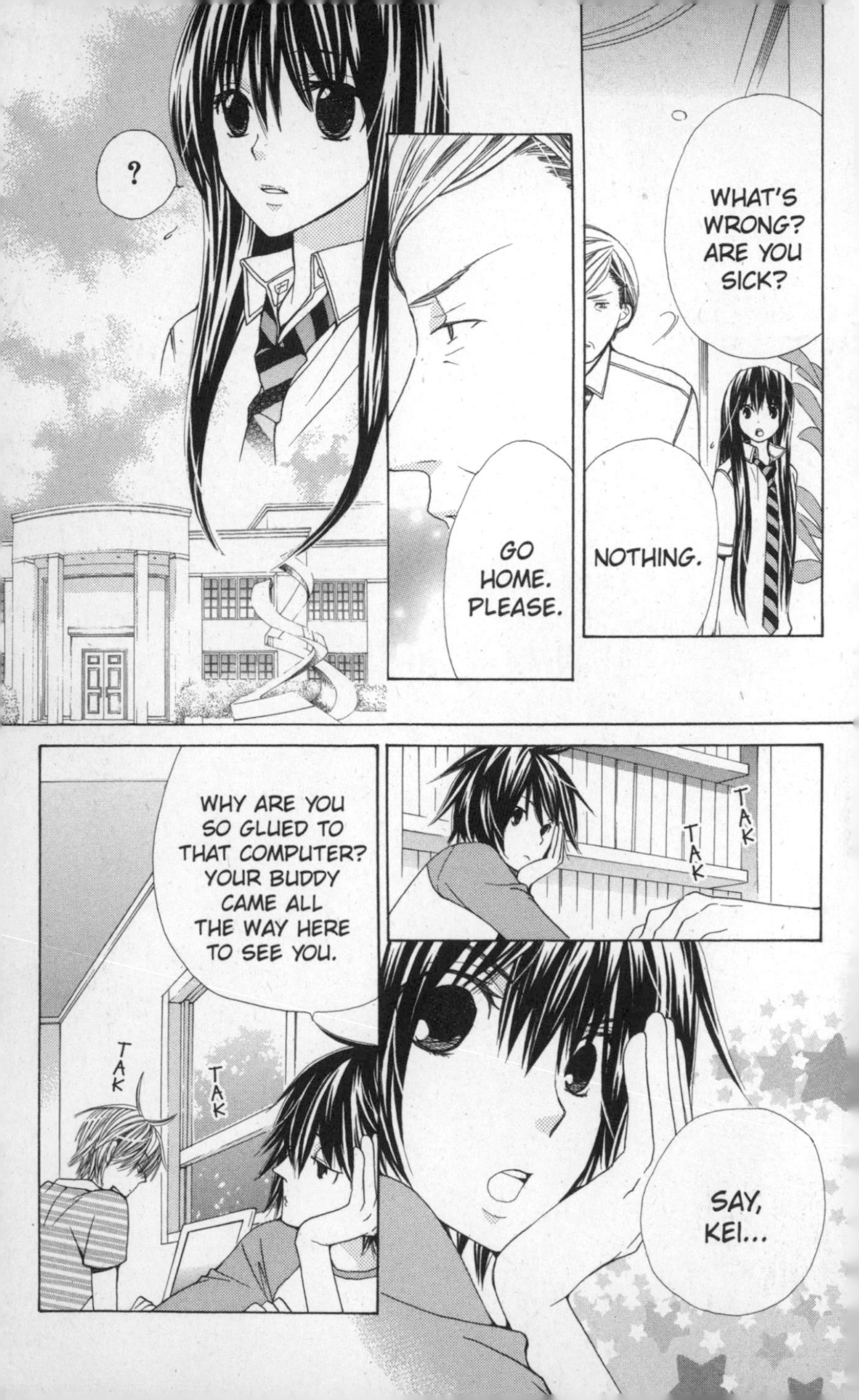
WHAT'S WRONG? ARE YOU SICK?
NOTHING.
GO HOME. PLEASE.
?
TAK
TAK
SAY, KEI...
WHY ARE YOU SO GLUED TO THAT COMPUTER? YOUR BUDDY CAME ALL THE WAY HERE TO SEE YOU.
TAK
TAK

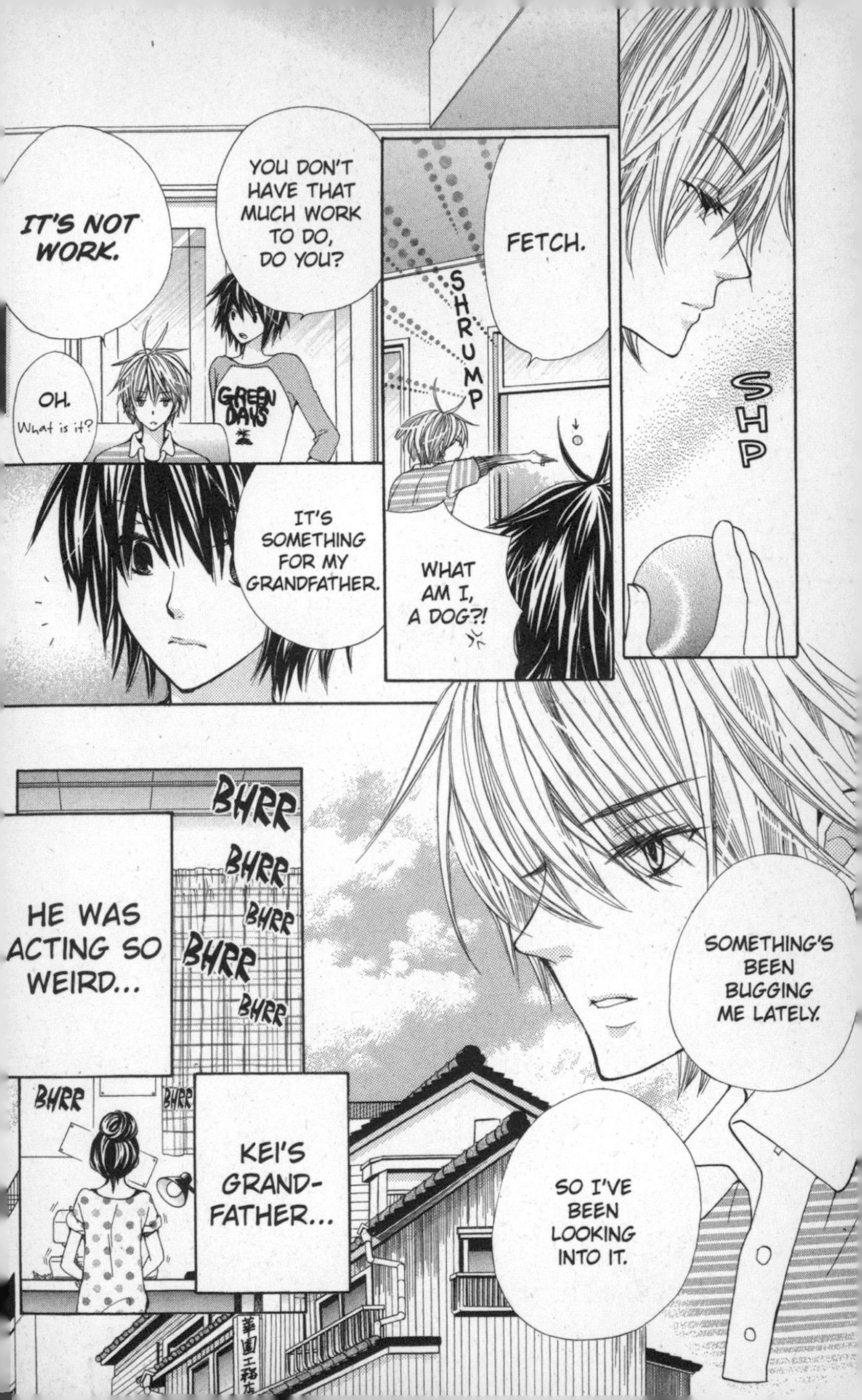
SHP
FETCH.
SHRUMP
WHAT AM I, A DOG?!
YOU DON'T HAVE THAT MUCH WORK TO DO, DO YOU?
IT'S NOT WORK.
OH.
What is it?
GREEN DAYS
IT'S SOMETHING FOR MY GRANDFATHER.
SOMETHING'S BEEN BUGGING ME LATELY.
SO I'VE BEEN LOOKING INTO IT.
BHRR
BHRR
BHRR
BHRR
BHRR
HE WAS ACTING SO WEIRD...
BHRR
BHRR
KEI'S GRAND-FATHER...

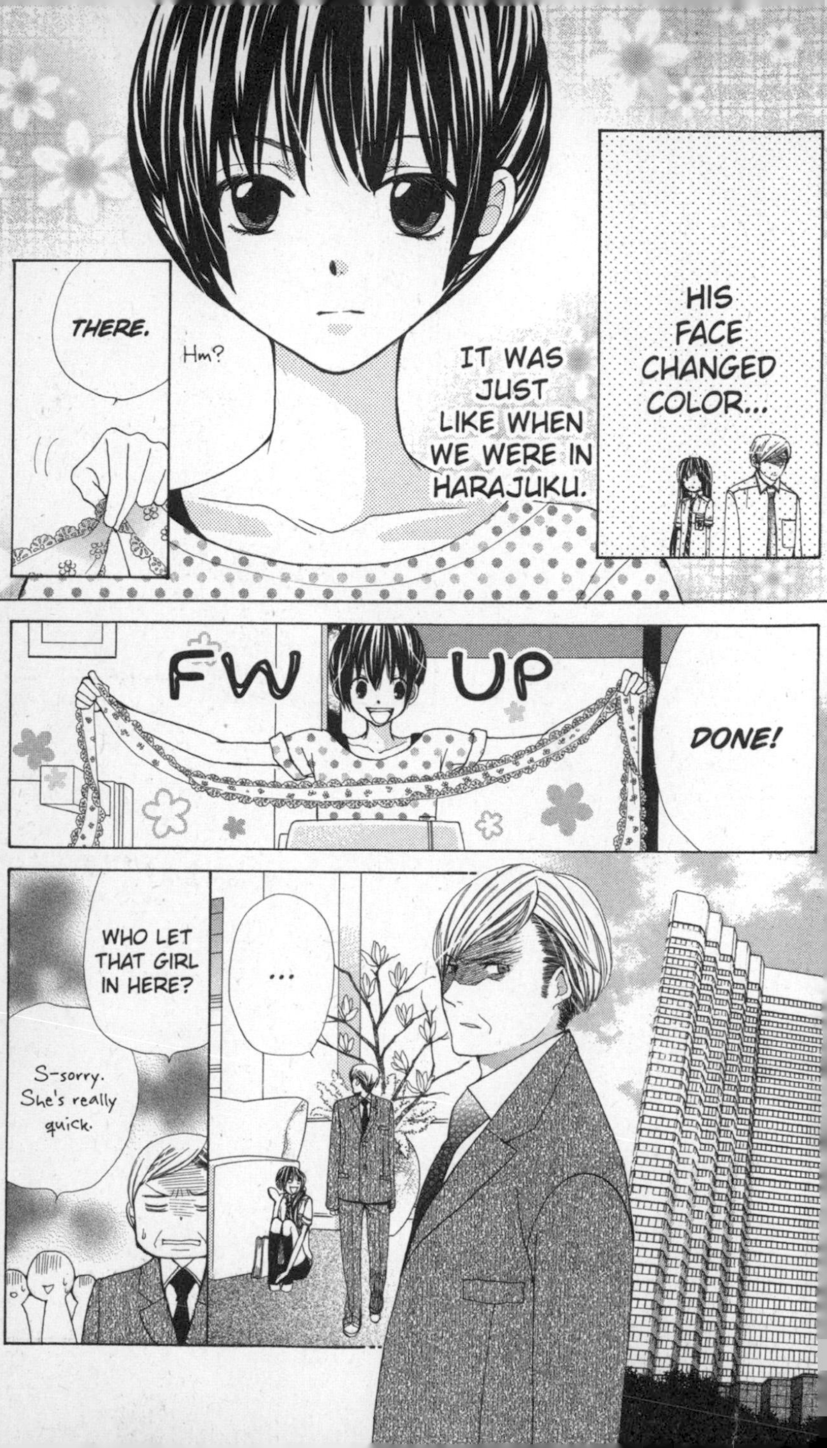
HIS FACE CHANGED COLOR...
IT WAS JUST LIKE WHEN WE WERE IN HARAJUKU.
Hm?
THERE.
DONE!
FWUP
...
WHO LET THAT GIRL IN HERE?
S-sorry. She's really quick.

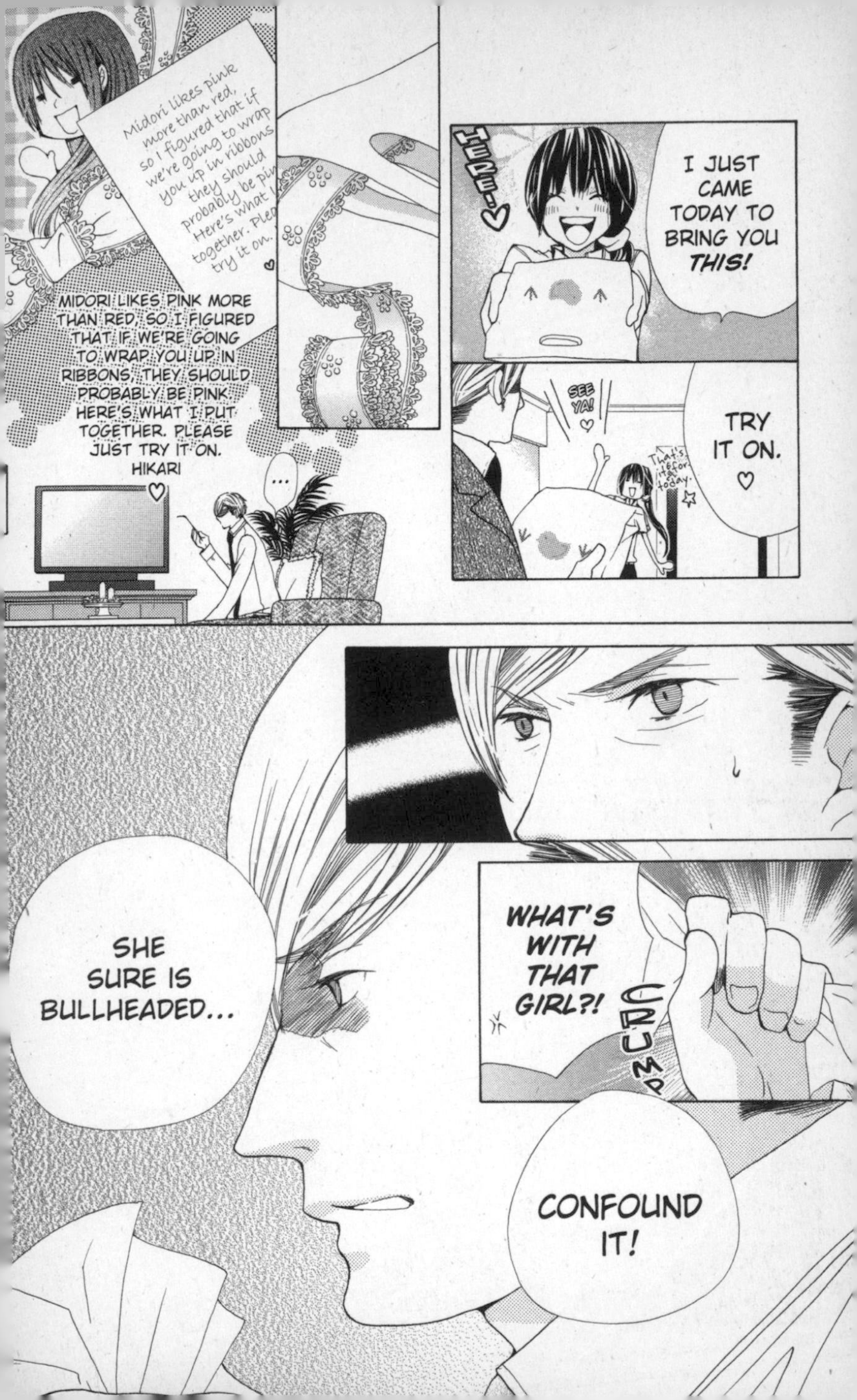

HERE! ♥
I JUST CAME TODAY TO BRING YOU *THIS!*
SEE YA! ♥
That's it for today.
TRY IT ON. ♥
Midori likes pink more than red, so I figured that if we're going to wrap you up in ribbons they should probably be pin Here's what I together. Plea try it on. ♥
MIDORI LIKES PINK MORE THAN RED, SO I FIGURED THAT IF WE'RE GOING TO WRAP YOU UP IN RIBBONS, THEY SHOULD PROBABLY BE PINK. HERE'S WHAT I PUT TOGETHER. PLEASE JUST TRY IT ON. HIKARI ♥
...
WHAT'S WITH THAT GIRL?!
CRUMP
SHE SURE IS BULLHEADED...
CONFOUND IT!

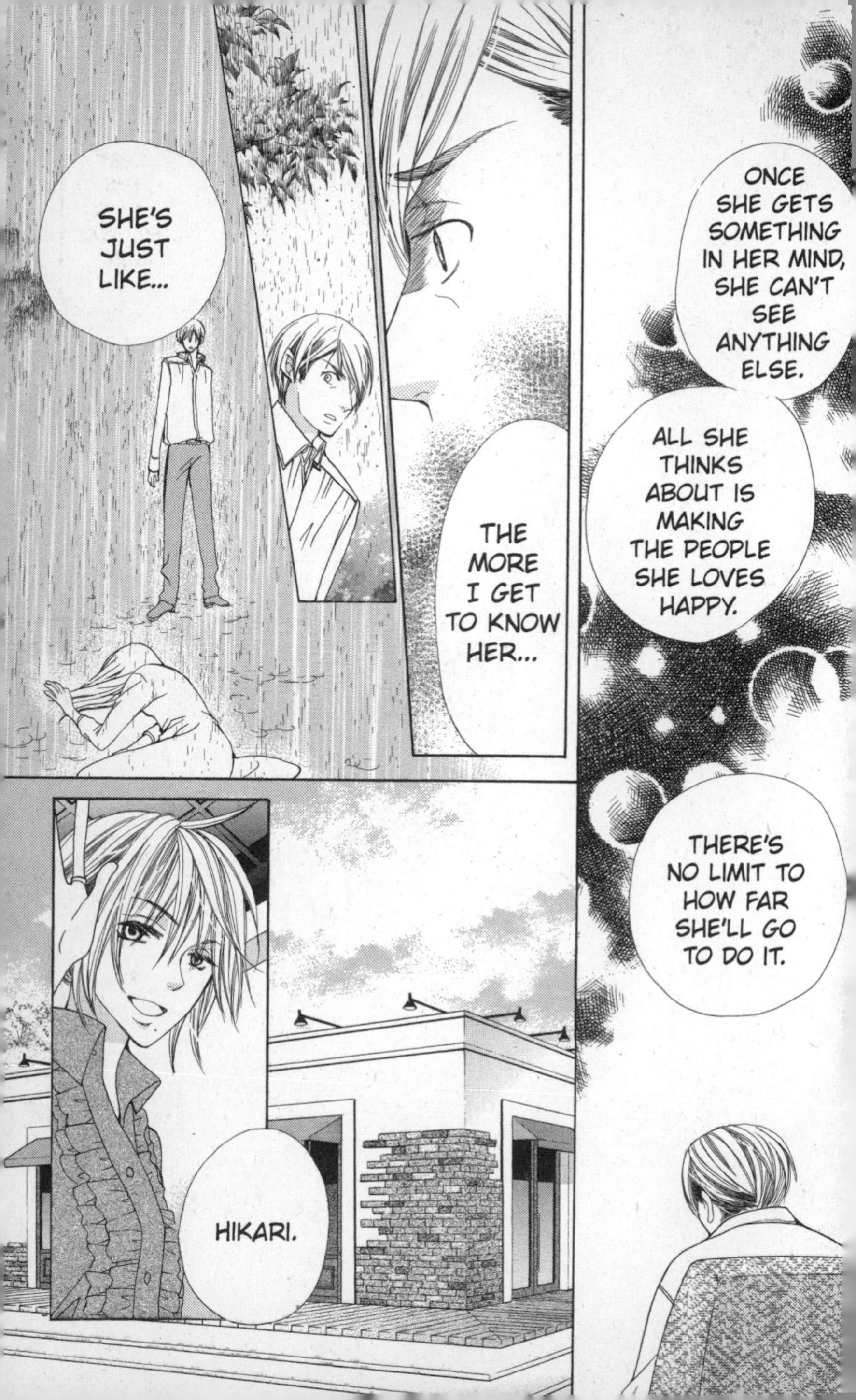
ONCE SHE GETS SOMETHING IN HER MIND, SHE CAN'T SEE ANYTHING ELSE.
ALL SHE THINKS ABOUT IS MAKING THE PEOPLE SHE LOVES HAPPY.
THERE'S NO LIMIT TO HOW FAR SHE'LL GO TO DO IT.
THE MORE I GET TO KNOW HER...
SHE'S JUST LIKE...
HIKARI.

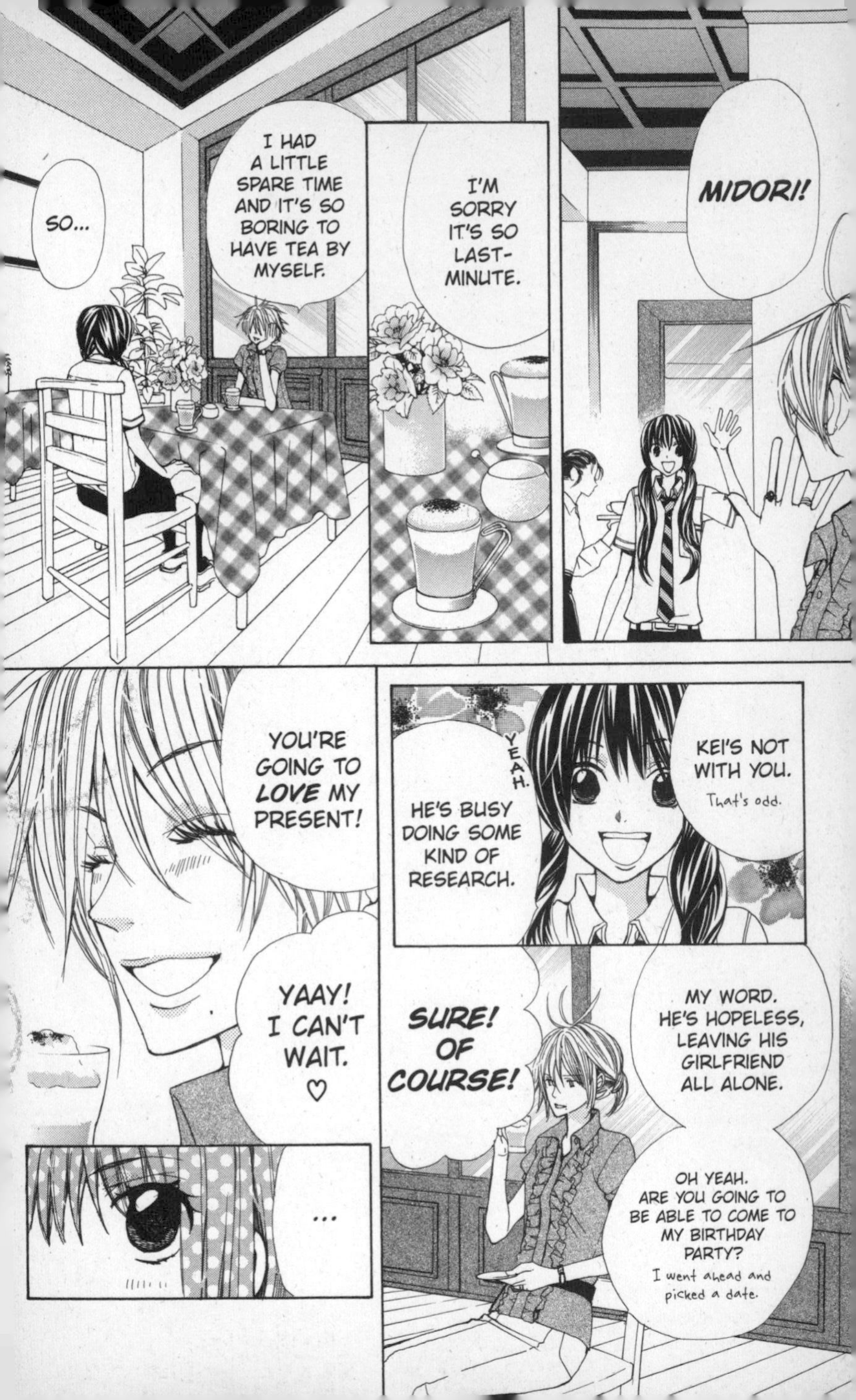
MIDORI!
I'M SORRY IT'S SO LAST-MINUTE.
I HAD A LITTLE SPARE TIME AND IT'S SO BORING TO HAVE TEA BY MYSELF.
SO...
KEI'S NOT WITH YOU.
That's odd.
YEAH.
HE'S BUSY DOING SOME KIND OF RESEARCH.
MY WORD. HE'S HOPELESS, LEAVING HIS GIRLFRIEND ALL ALONE.
OH YEAH. ARE YOU GOING TO BE ABLE TO COME TO MY BIRTHDAY PARTY?
I went ahead and picked a date.
SURE! OF COURSE!
YOU'RE GOING TO LOVE MY PRESENT!
YAAY! I CAN'T WAIT. ♡
...

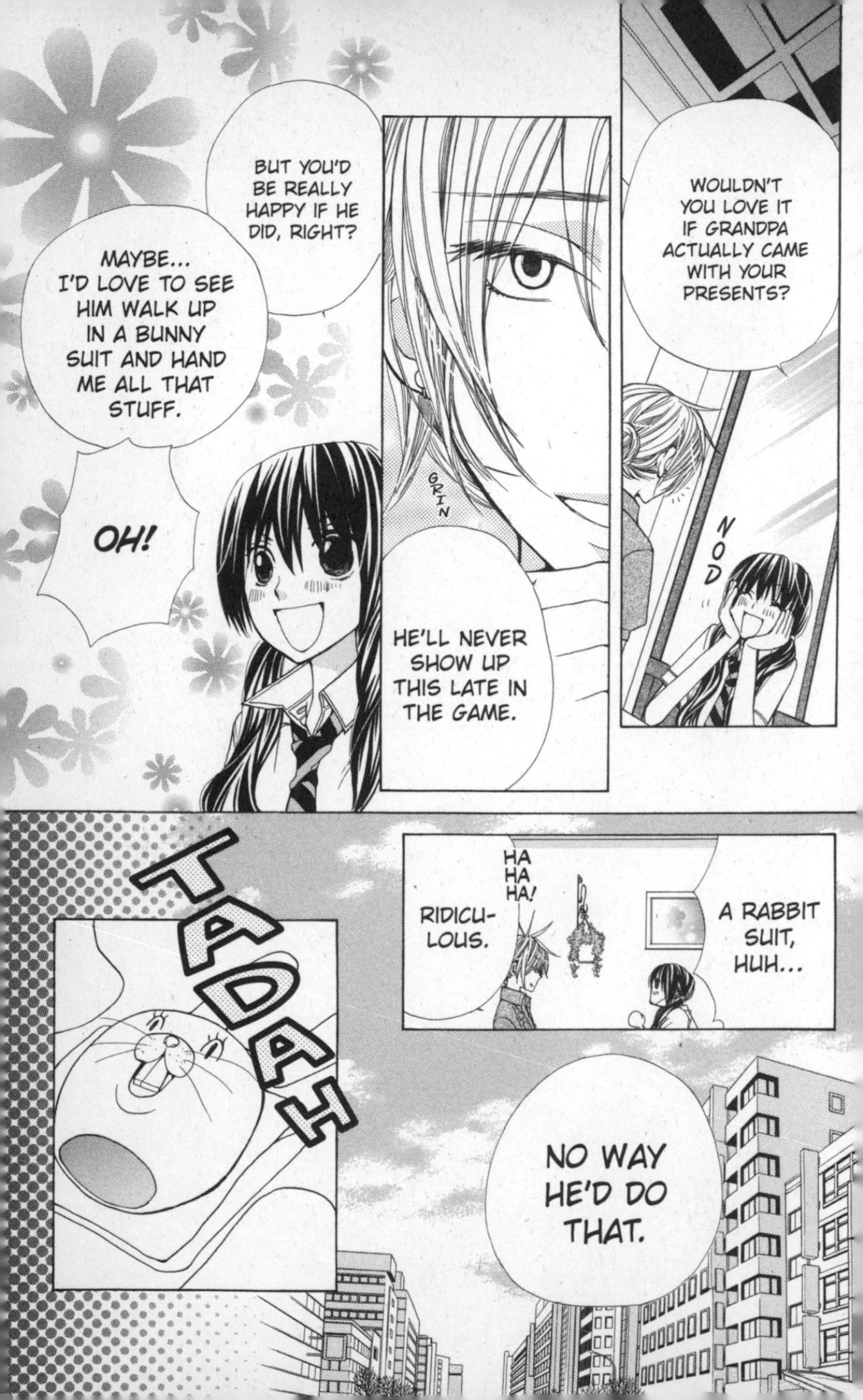
WOULDN'T YOU LOVE IT IF GRANDPA ACTUALLY CAME WITH YOUR PRESENTS?
NOD
GRIN
HE'LL NEVER SHOW UP THIS LATE IN THE GAME.
BUT YOU'D BE REALLY HAPPY IF HE DID, RIGHT?
MAYBE... I'D LOVE TO SEE HIM WALK UP IN A BUNNY SUIT AND HAND ME ALL THAT STUFF.
OH!
A RABBIT SUIT, HUH...
HA HA HA!
RIDICULOUS.
NO WAY HE'D DO THAT.
TADAH

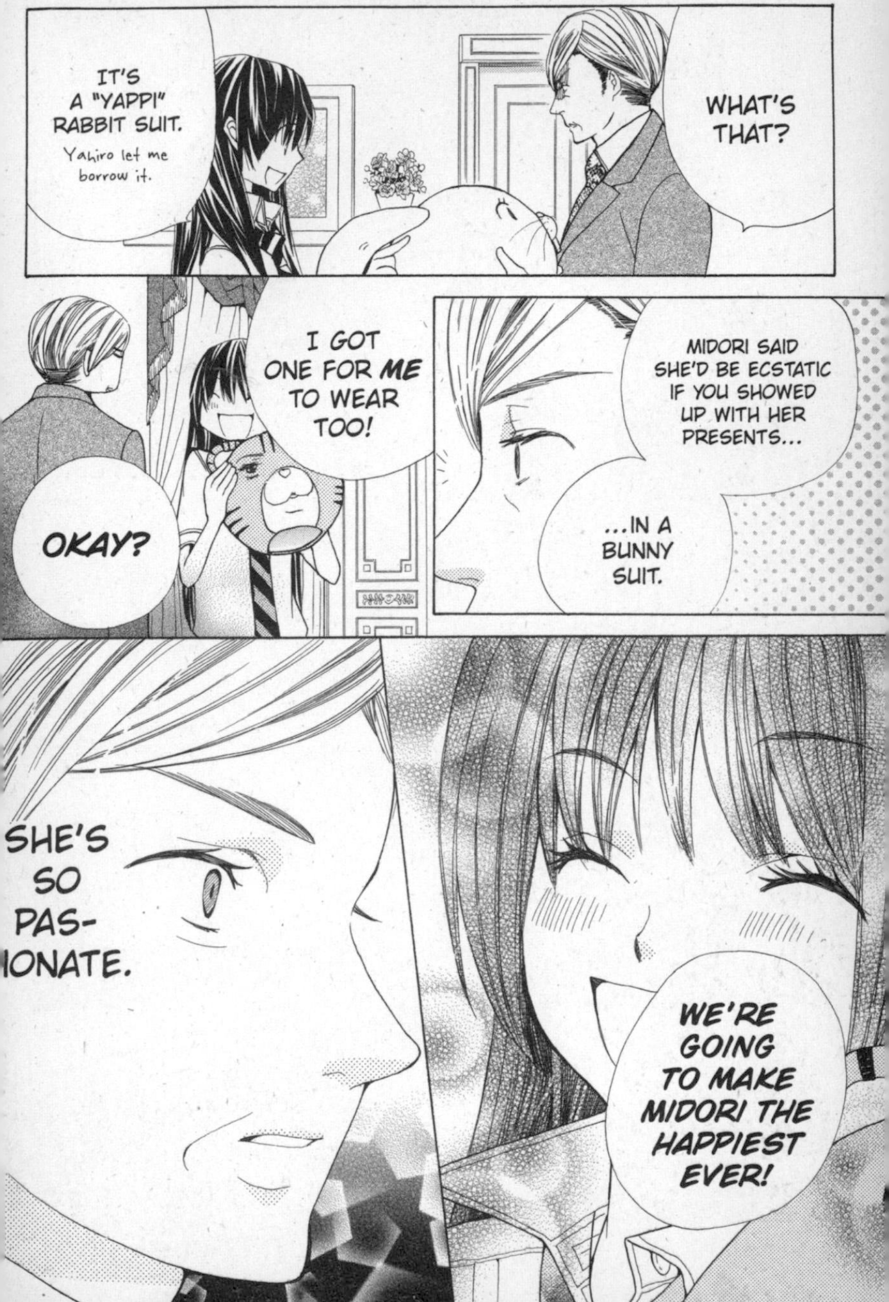
WHAT'S THAT?
IT'S A "YAPPI" RABBIT SUIT.
Yahiro let me borrow it.
MIDORI SAID SHE'D BE ECSTATIC IF YOU SHOWED UP WITH HER PRESENTS...
...IN A BUNNY SUIT.
I GOT ONE FOR *ME* TO WEAR TOO!
OKAY?
WE'RE GOING TO MAKE MIDORI THE HAPPIEST EVER!
SHE'S SO PAS- IONATE.

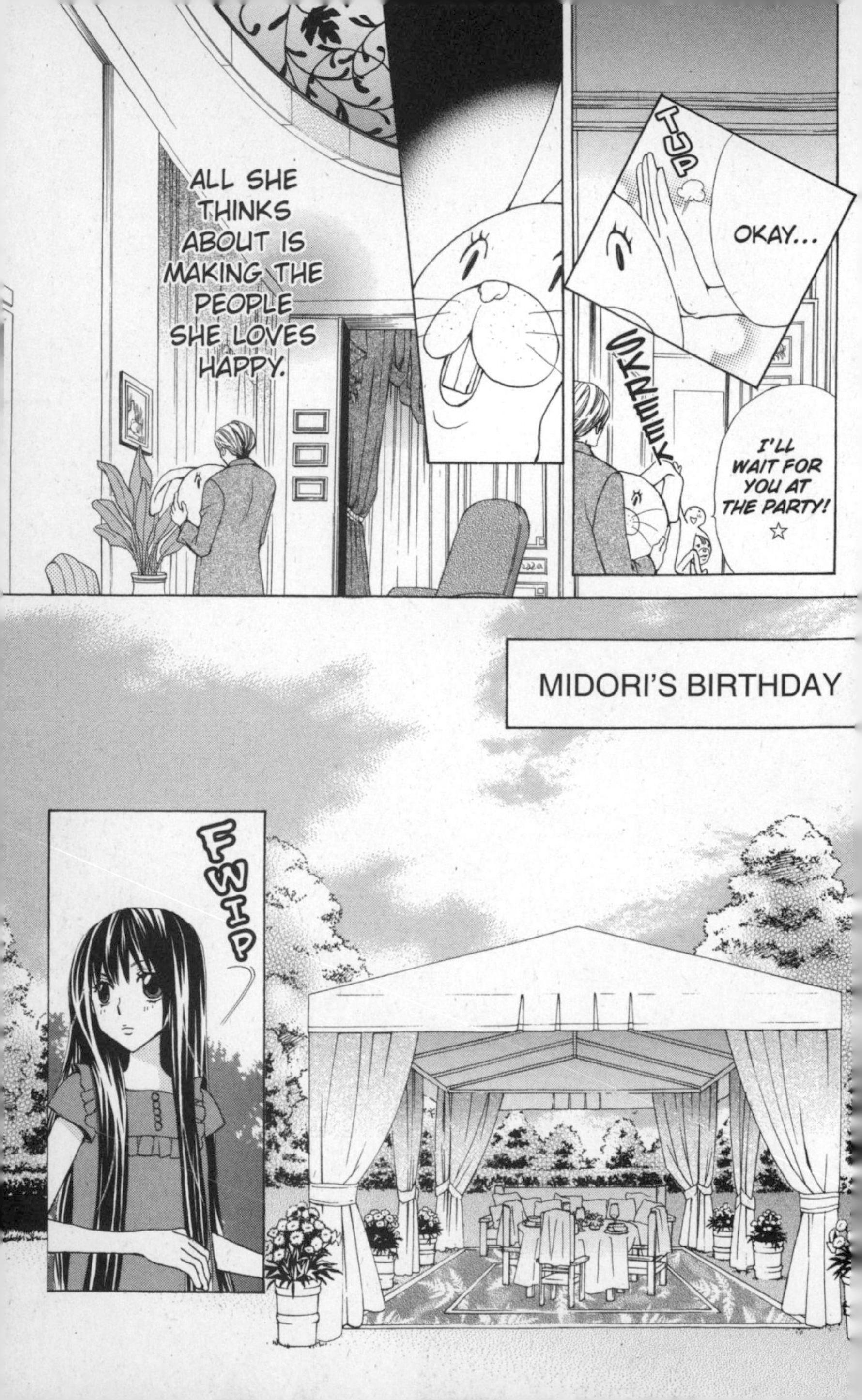
TUP
OKAY...
SKREEEK
I'LL WAIT FOR YOU AT THE PARTY! ☆
ALL SHE THINKS ABOUT IS MAKING THE PEOPLE SHE LOVES HAPPY.
MIDORI'S BIRTHDAY
FWIP

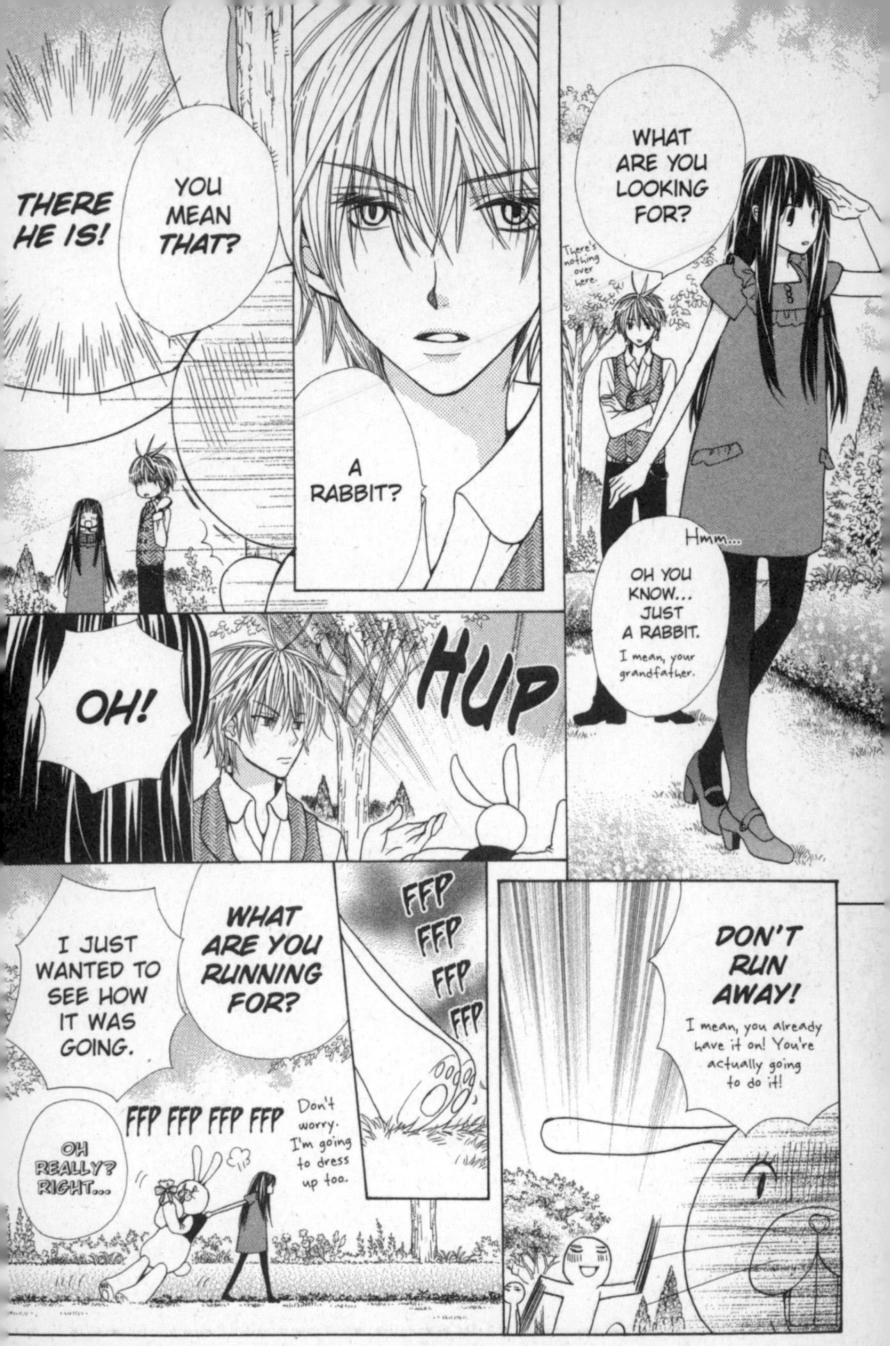
WHAT ARE YOU LOOKING FOR?
There's nothing over here.
Hmm...
OH YOU KNOW... JUST A RABBIT.
I mean, your grandfather.
A RABBIT?
YOU MEAN THAT?
THERE HE IS!
OH!
HUP
DON'T RUN AWAY!
I mean, you already have it on! You're actually going to do it!
FFP FFP FFP FFP
WHAT ARE YOU RUNNING FOR?
I JUST WANTED TO SEE HOW IT WAS GOING.
Don't worry. I'm going to dress up too.
FFP FFP FFP FFP
OH REALLY? RIGHT...

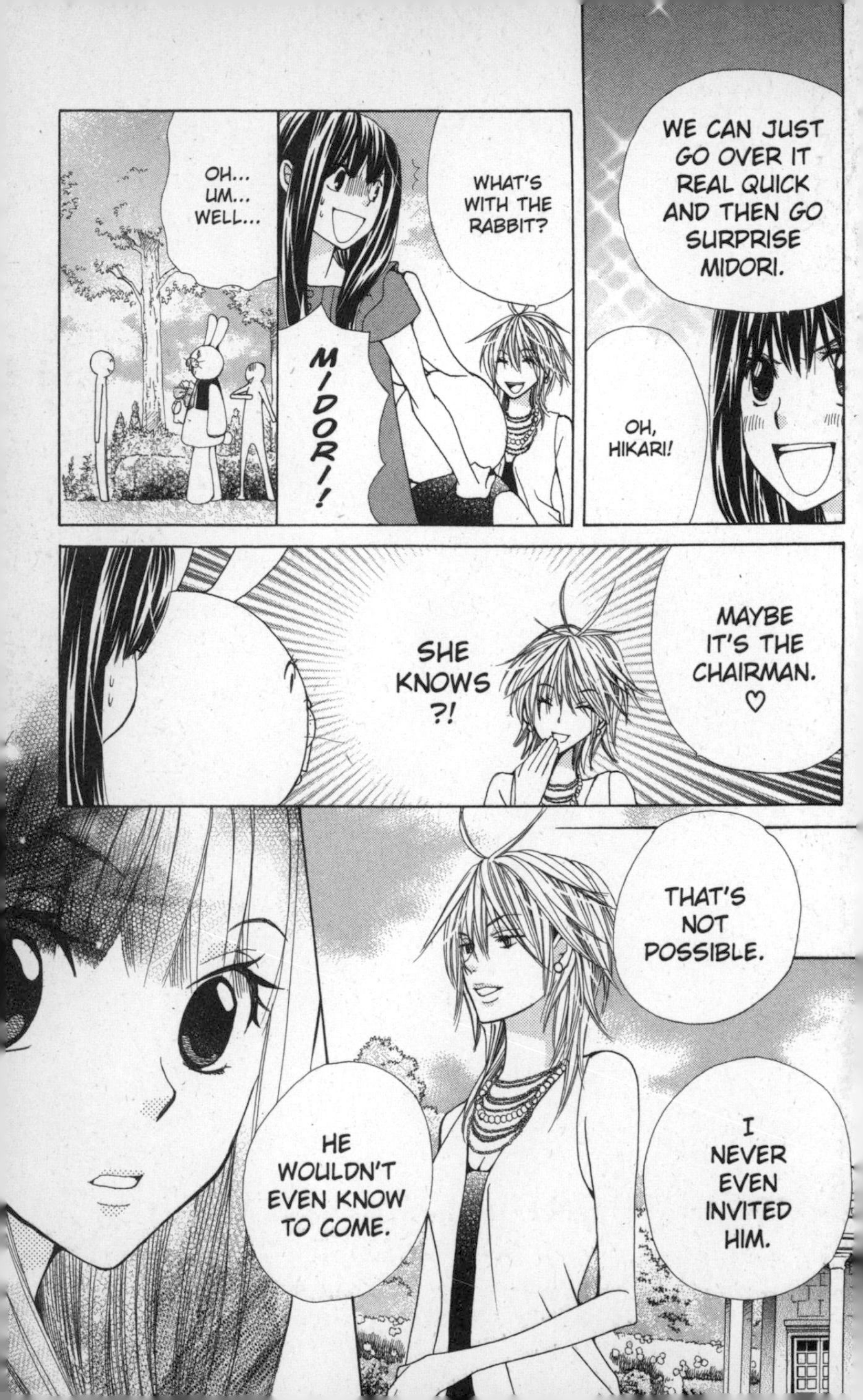
WE CAN JUST GO OVER IT REAL QUICK AND THEN GO SURPRISE MIDORI.
OH, HIKARI!
WHAT'S WITH THE RABBIT?
MIDORI!
OH... UM... WELL...
MAYBE IT'S THE CHAIRMAN. ♡
SHE KNOWS ?!
THAT'S NOT POSSIBLE.
I NEVER EVEN INVITED HIM.
HE WOULDN'T EVEN KNOW TO COME.

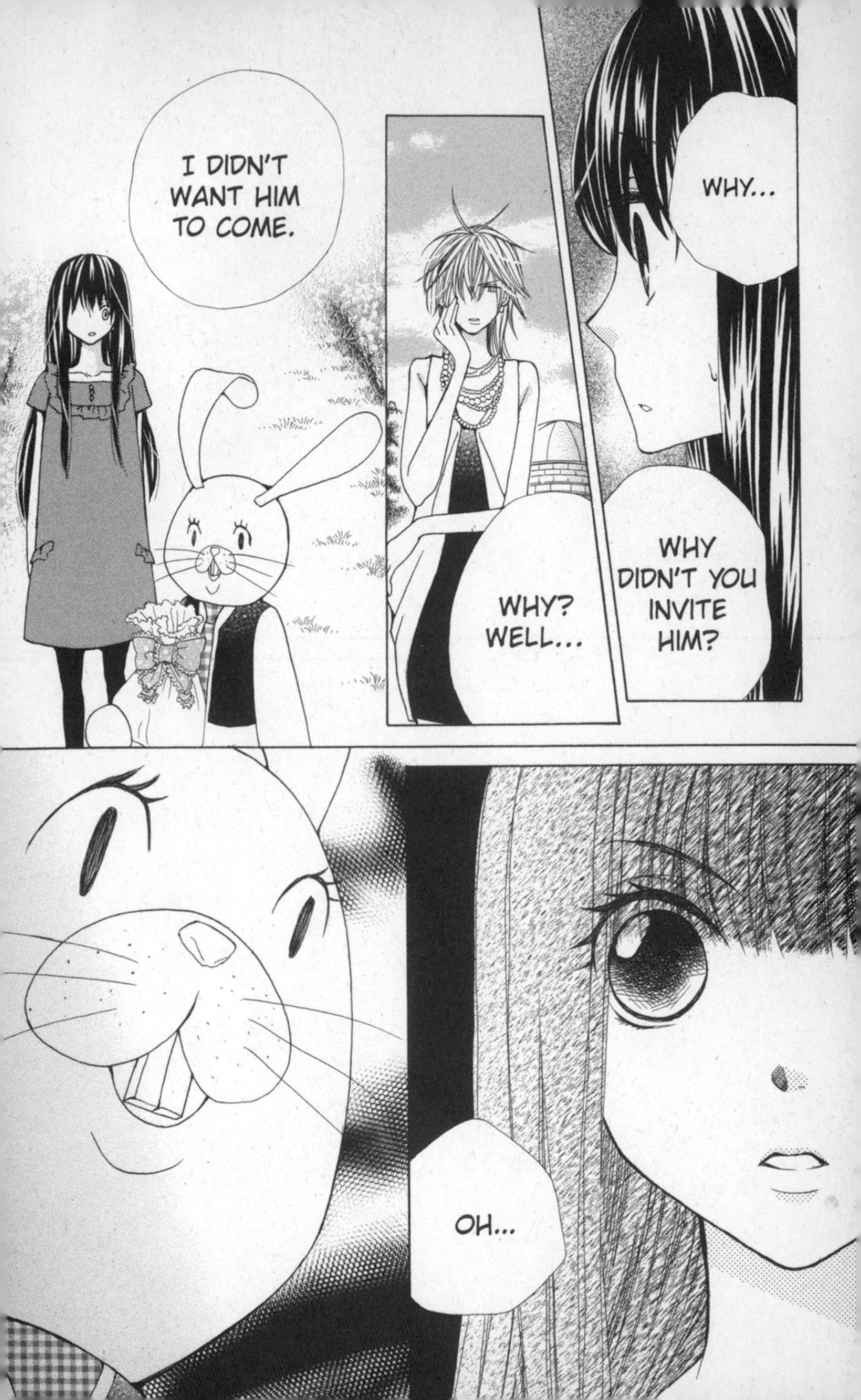

WHY...
WHY DIDN'T YOU INVITE HIM?
WHY? WELL...
I DIDN'T WANT HIM TO COME.
OH...

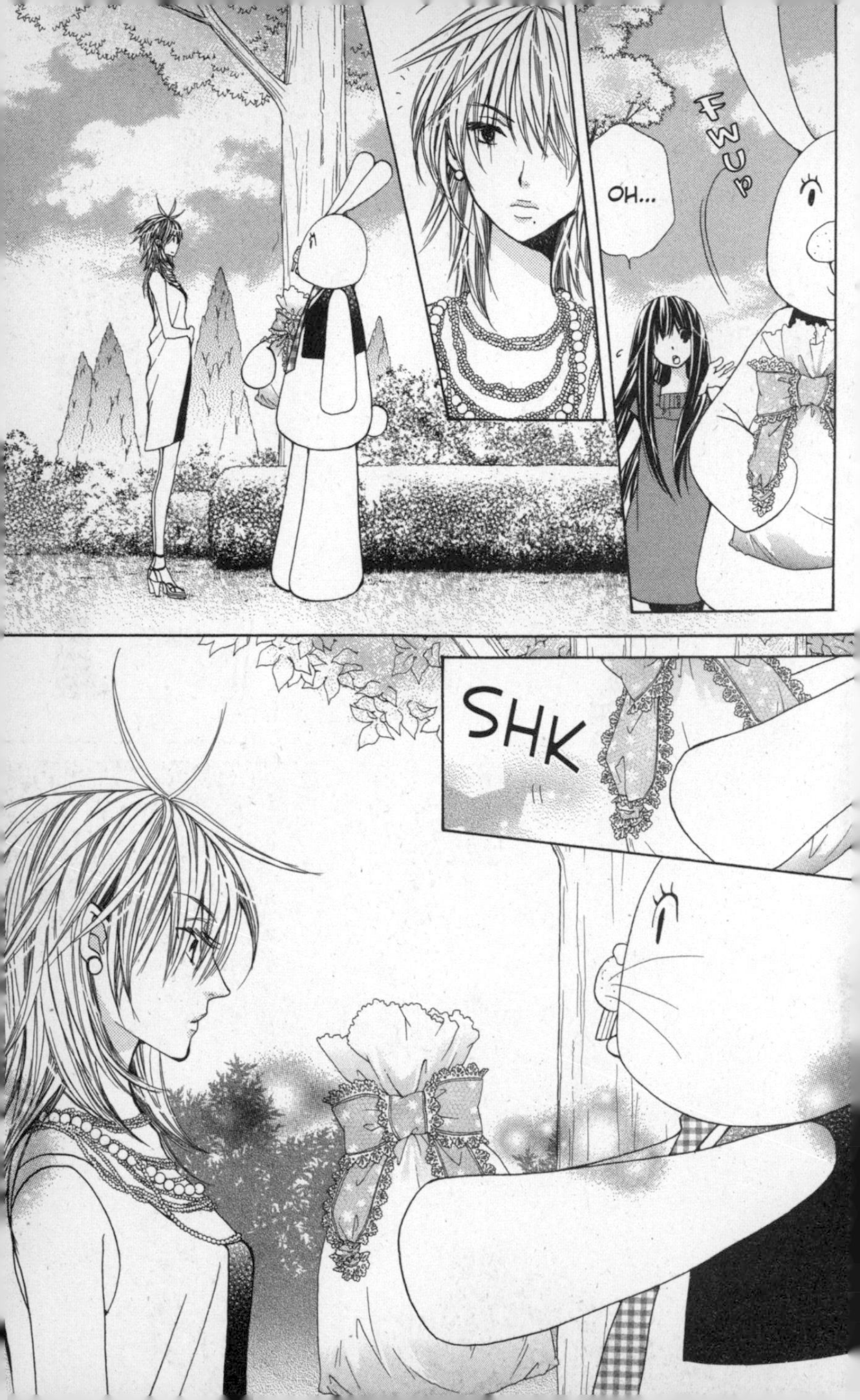
FWUP
OH...
SHK

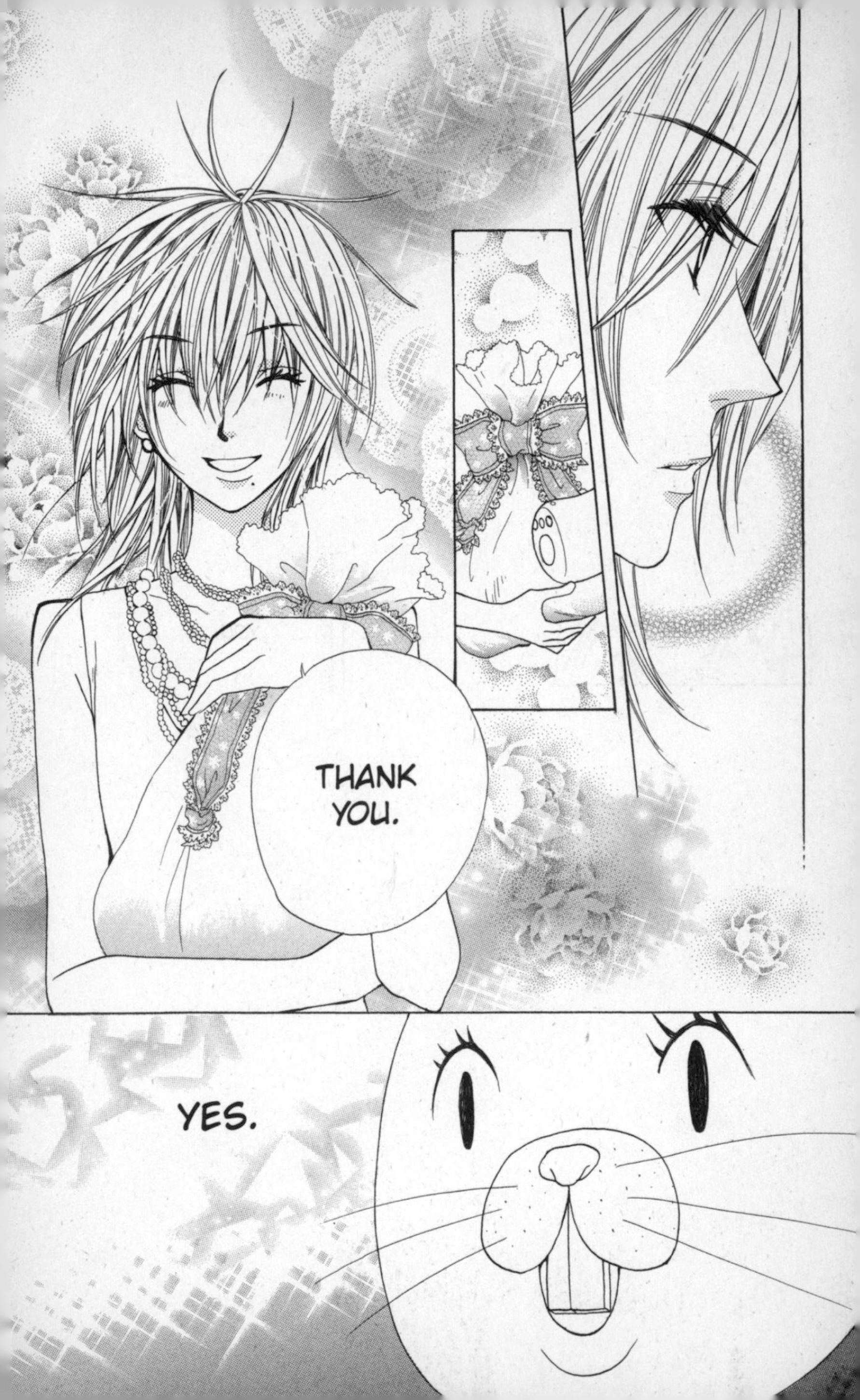
THANK YOU.
YES.

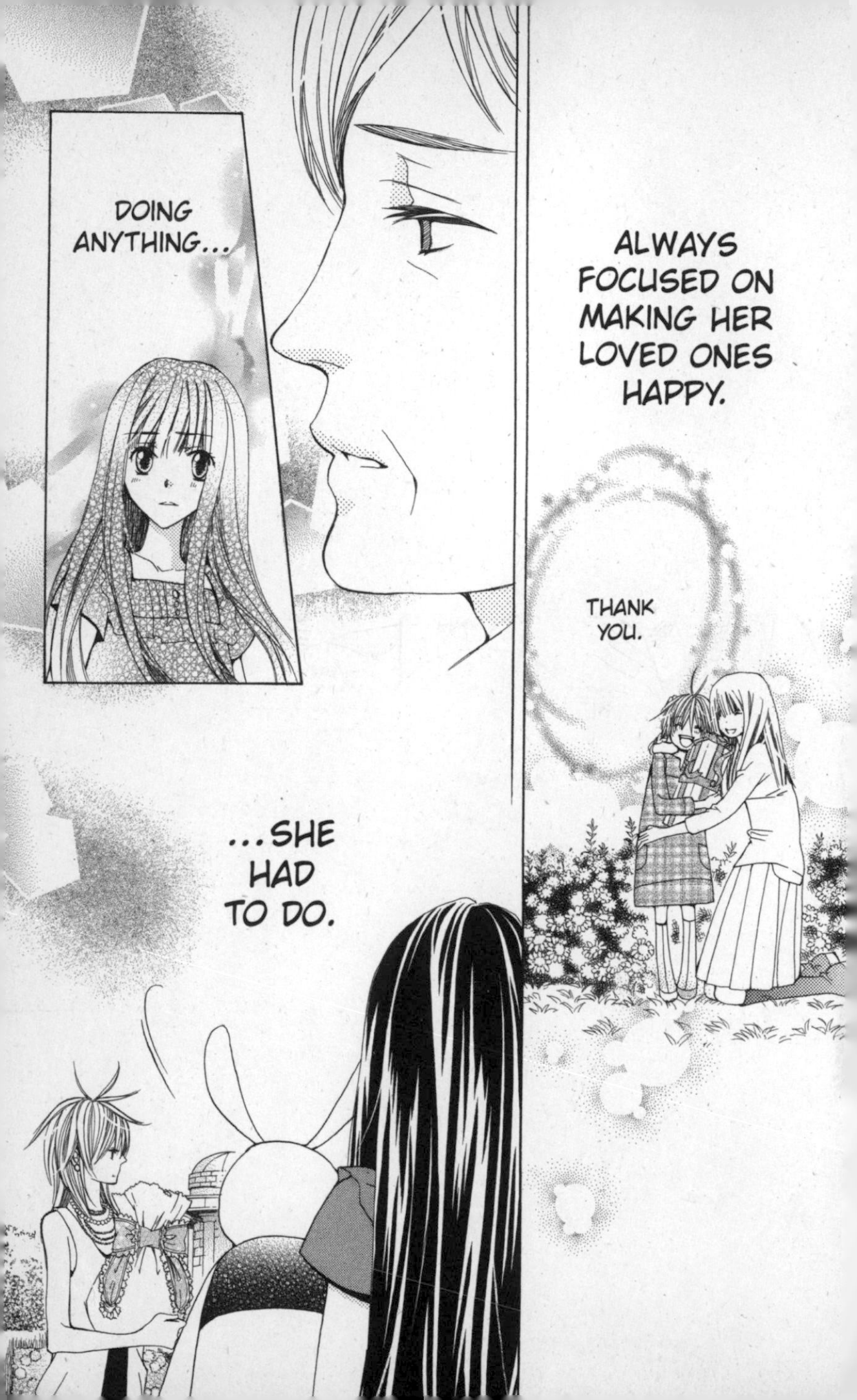
ALWAYS FOCUSED ON MAKING HER LOVED ONES HAPPY.
THANK YOU.
DOING ANYTHING...
...SHE HAD TO DO.

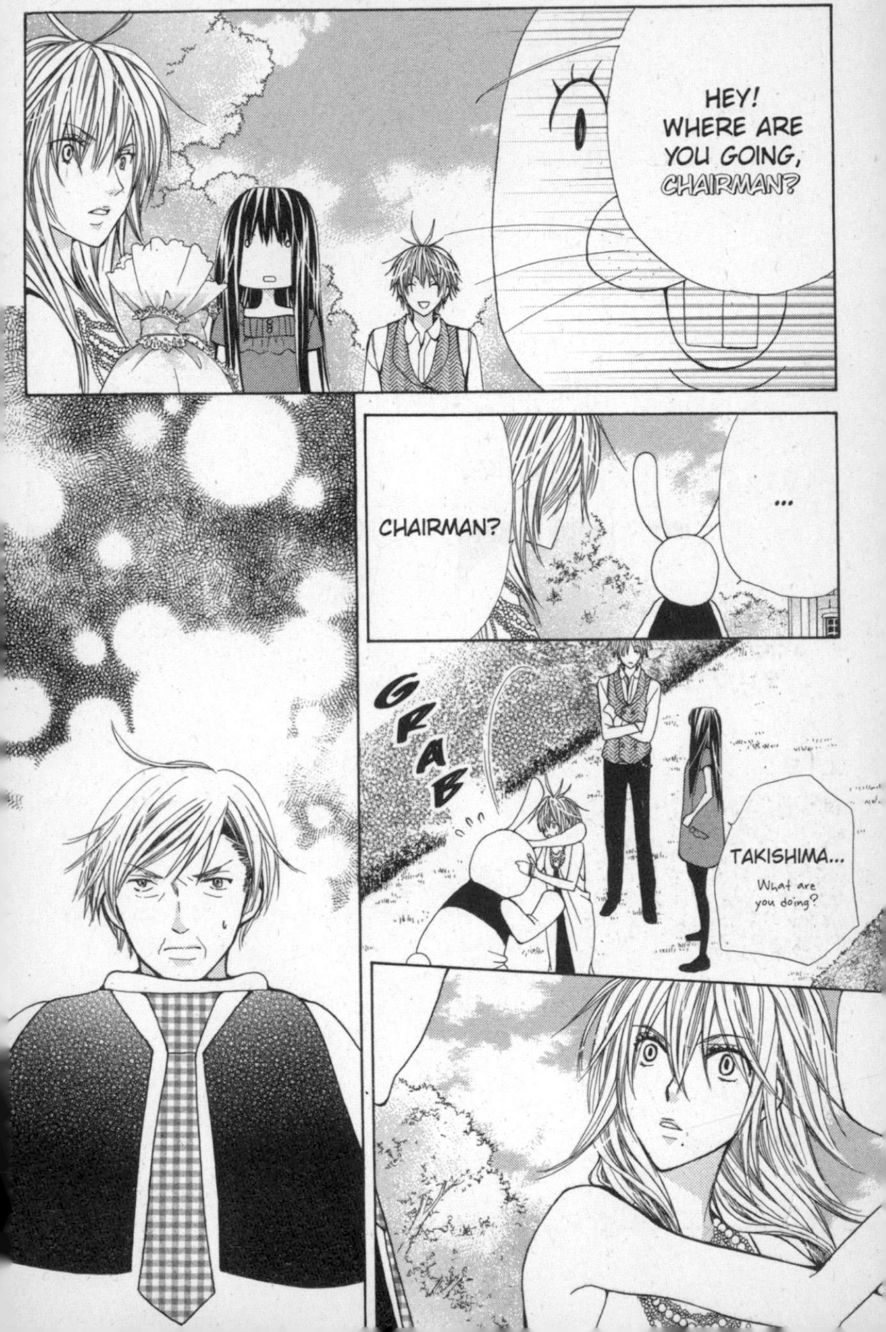
HEY! WHERE ARE YOU GOING, CHAIRMAN?
...
CHAIRMAN?
GRAB
TAKISHIMA...
What are you doing?

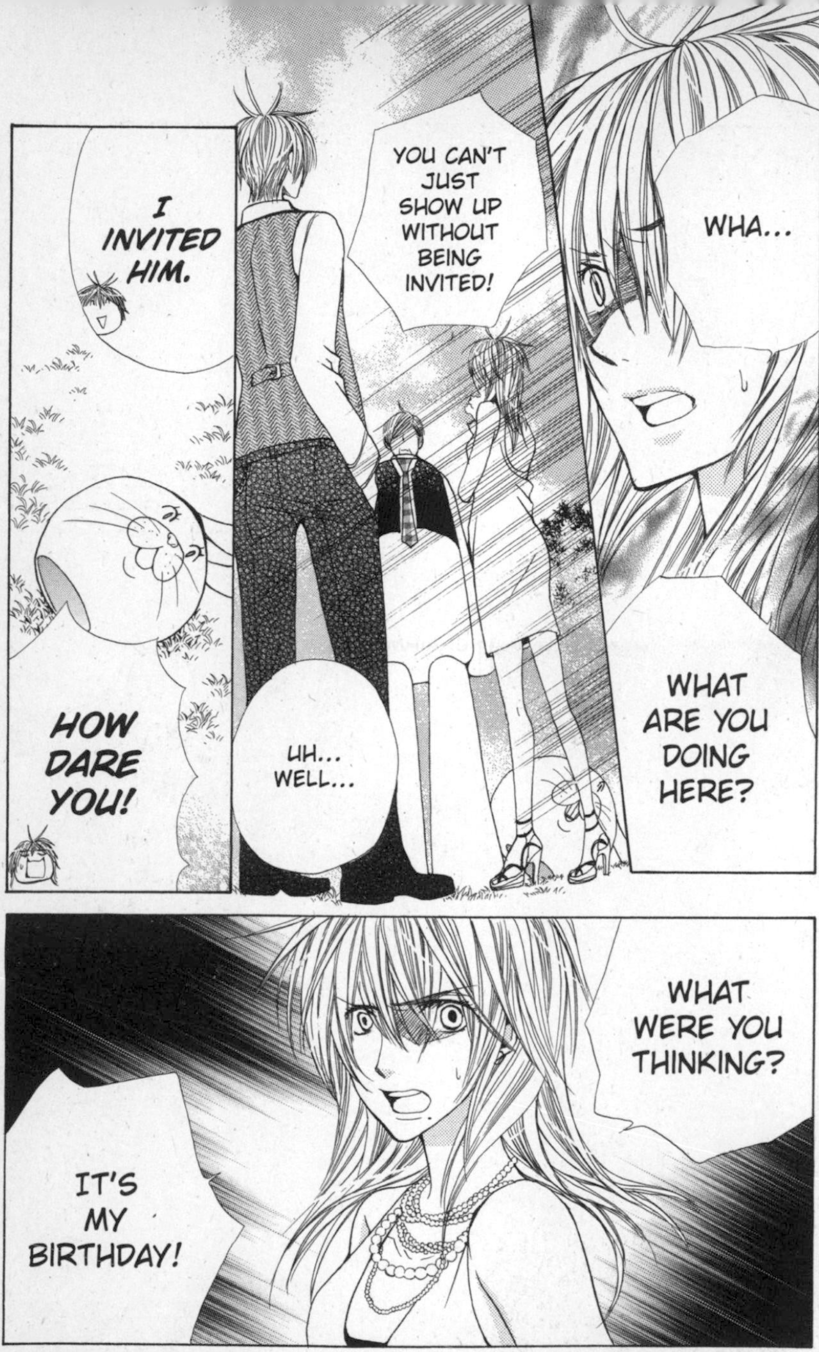
WHA...
WHAT ARE YOU DOING HERE?
YOU CAN'T JUST SHOW UP WITHOUT BEING INVITED!
UH... WELL...
I INVITED HIM.
HOW DARE YOU!
WHAT WERE YOU THINKING?
IT'S MY BIRTHDAY!

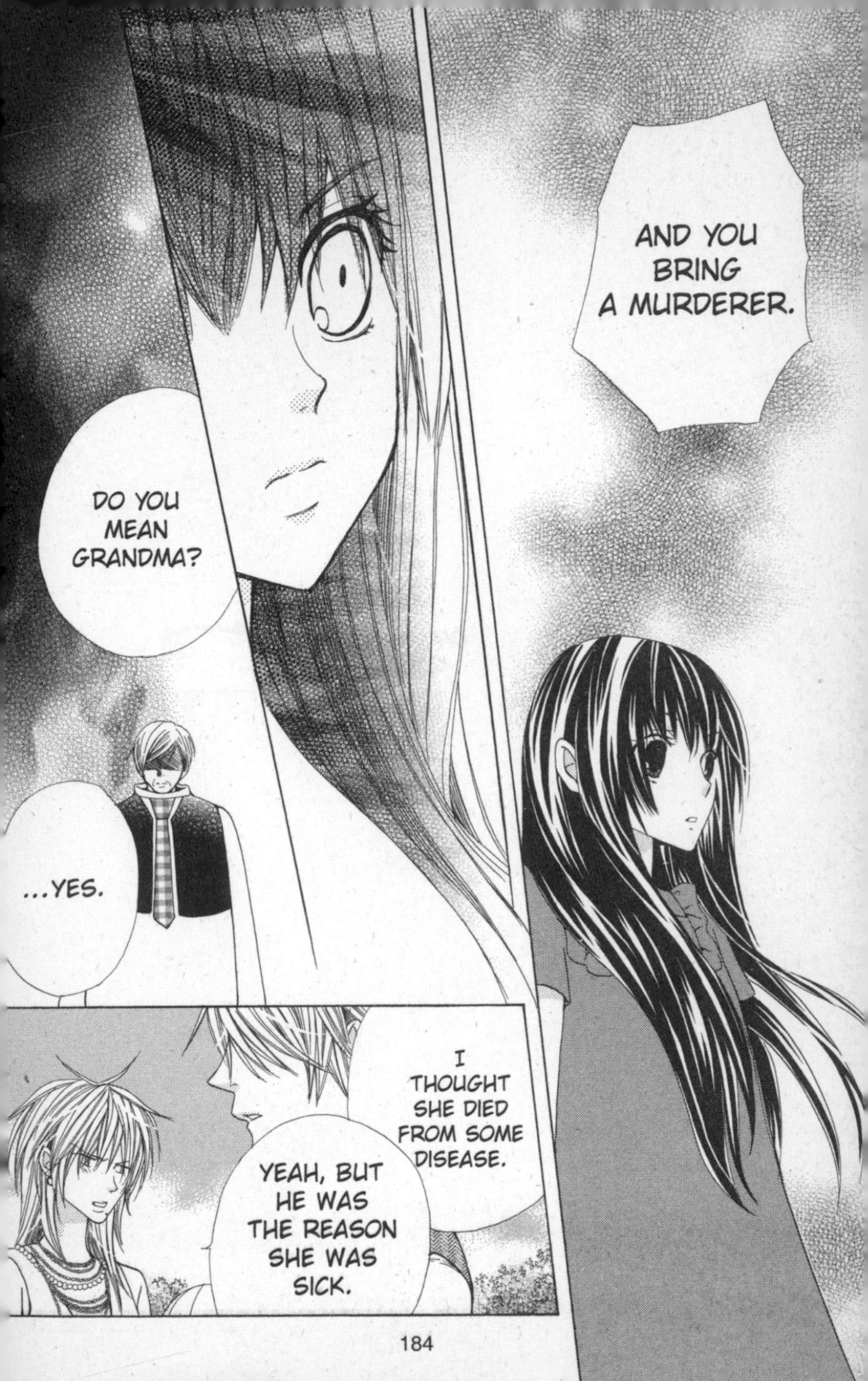
AND YOU BRING A MURDERER.
DO YOU MEAN GRANDMA?
...YES.
I THOUGHT SHE DIED FROM SOME DISEASE.
YEAH, BUT HE WAS THE REASON SHE WAS SICK.

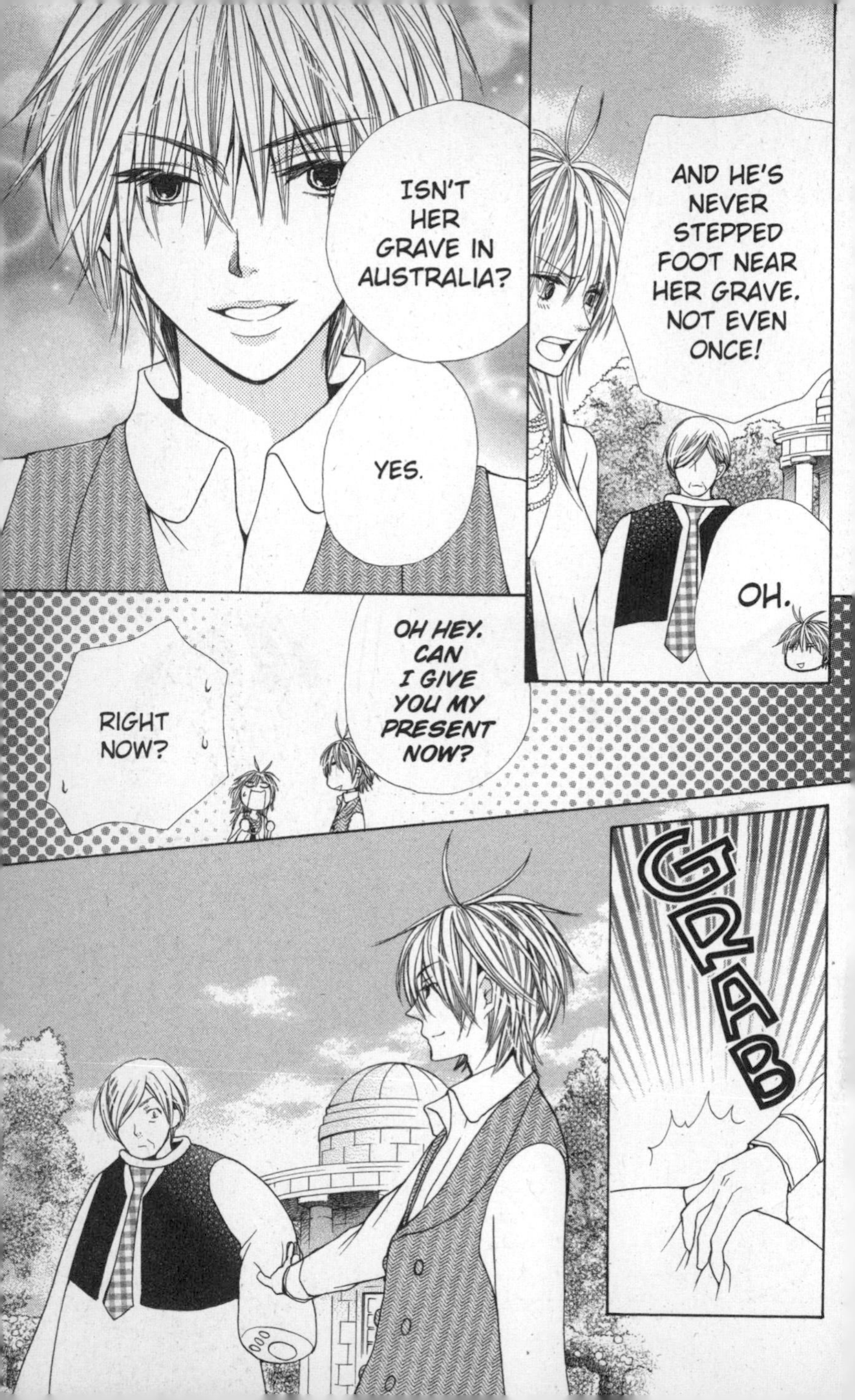

AND HE'S NEVER STEPPED FOOT NEAR HER GRAVE. NOT EVEN ONCE!
OH.
ISN'T HER GRAVE IN AUSTRALIA?
YES.
OH HEY. CAN I GIVE YOU MY PRESENT NOW?
RIGHT NOW?
GRAB

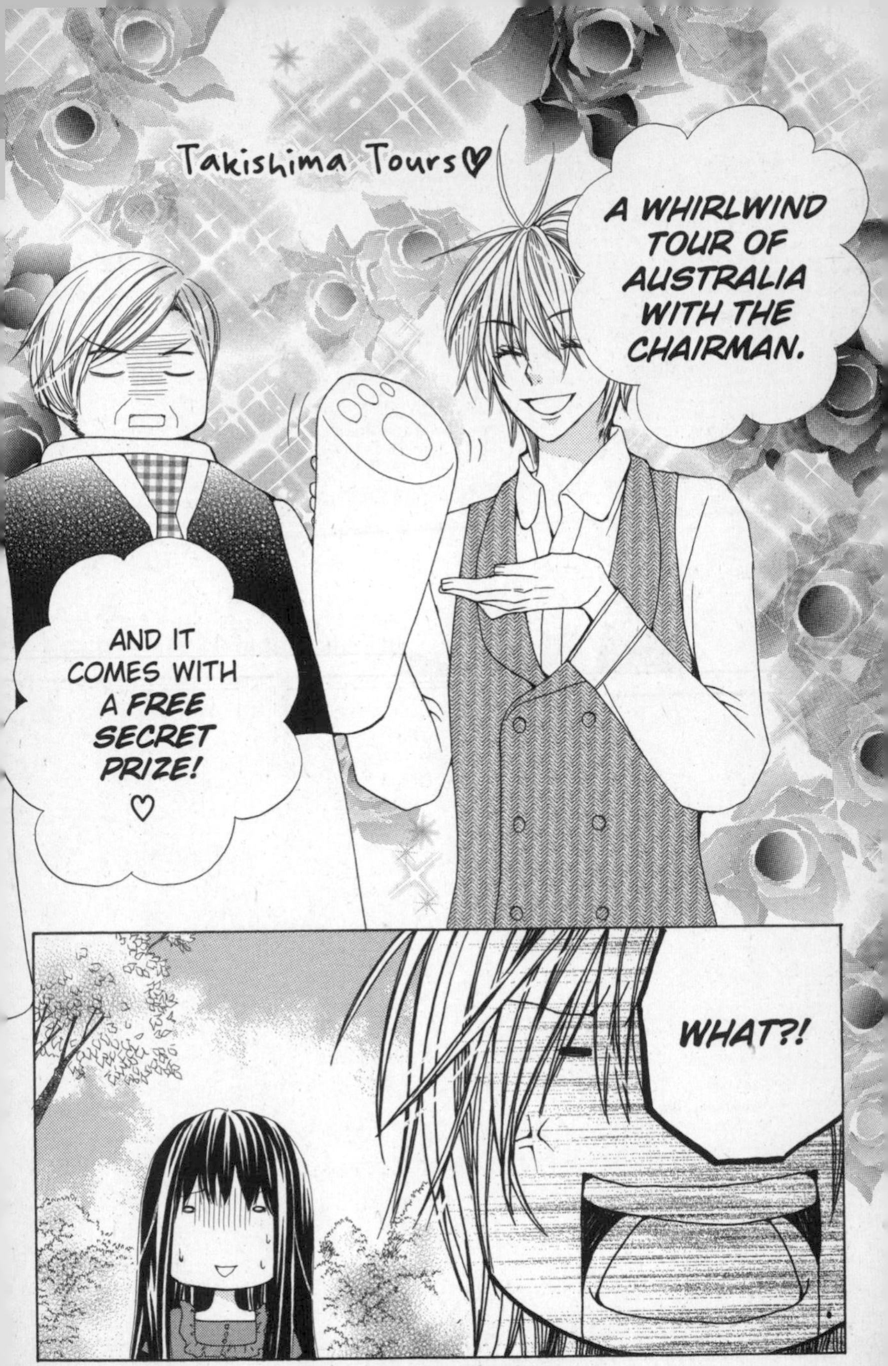
A WHIRLWIND TOUR OF AUSTRALIA WITH THE CHAIRMAN.
Takishima Tours♥
AND IT COMES WITH A FREE SECRET PRIZE! ♡
WHAT?!

S.A VOLUME 16 / End

A SPECIAL SHORT

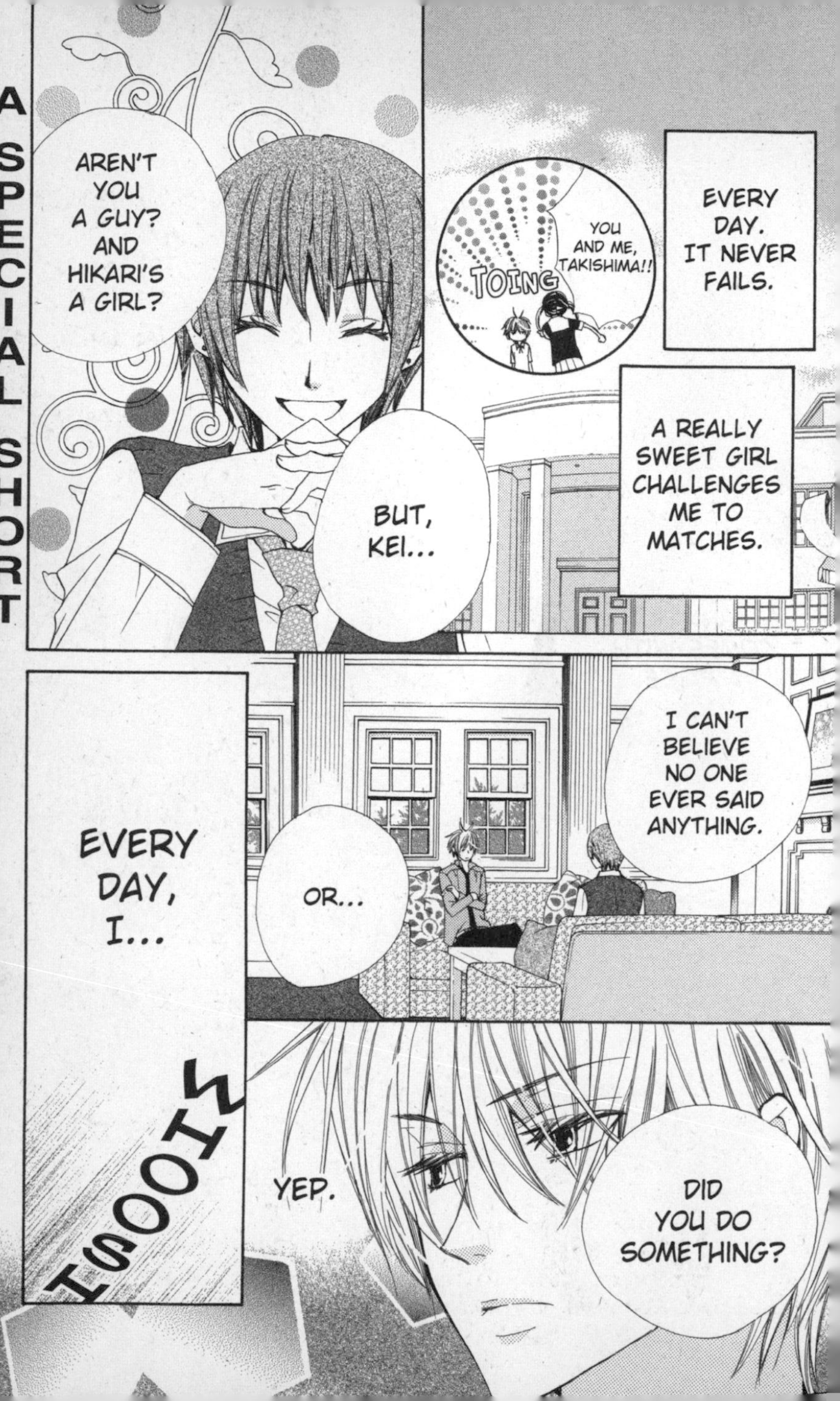
EVERY DAY. IT NEVER FAILS.
YOU AND ME, TAKISHIMA!!
TOING
A REALLY SWEET GIRL CHALLENGES ME TO MATCHES.
BUT, KEI...
AREN'T YOU A GUY? AND HIKARI'S A GIRL?
I CAN'T BELIEVE NO ONE EVER SAID ANYTHING.
OR...
DID YOU DO SOMETHING?
YEP.
WHOOSH
EVERY DAY, I...

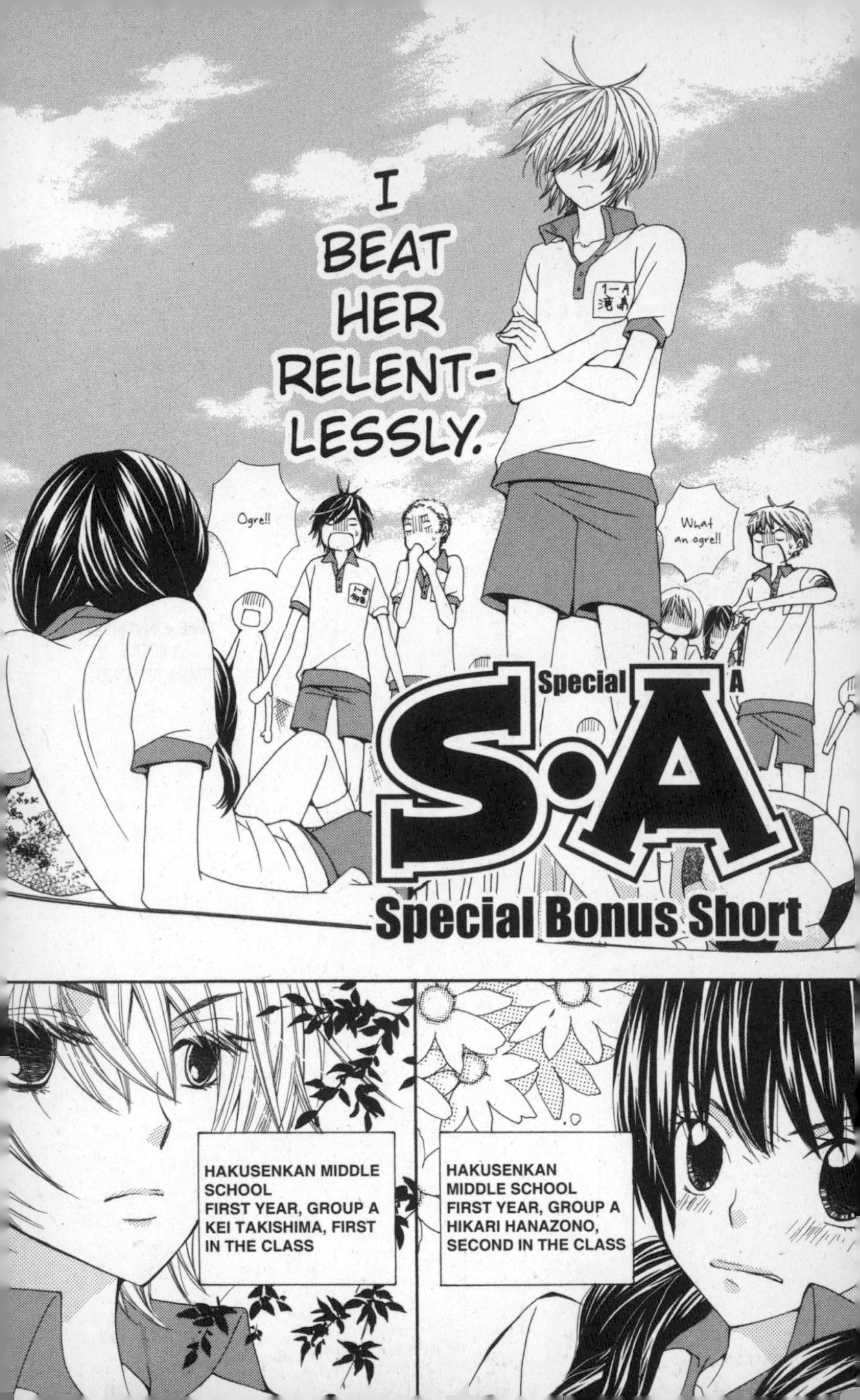
I BEAT HER RELENT-LESSLY.
What an ogre!!
Ogre!!
Special S·A A
Special Bonus Short
HAKUSENKAN MIDDLE SCHOOL FIRST YEAR, GROUP A HIKARI HANAZONO, SECOND IN THE CLASS
HAKUSENKAN MIDDLE SCHOOL FIRST YEAR, GROUP A KEI TAKISHIMA, FIRST IN THE CLASS

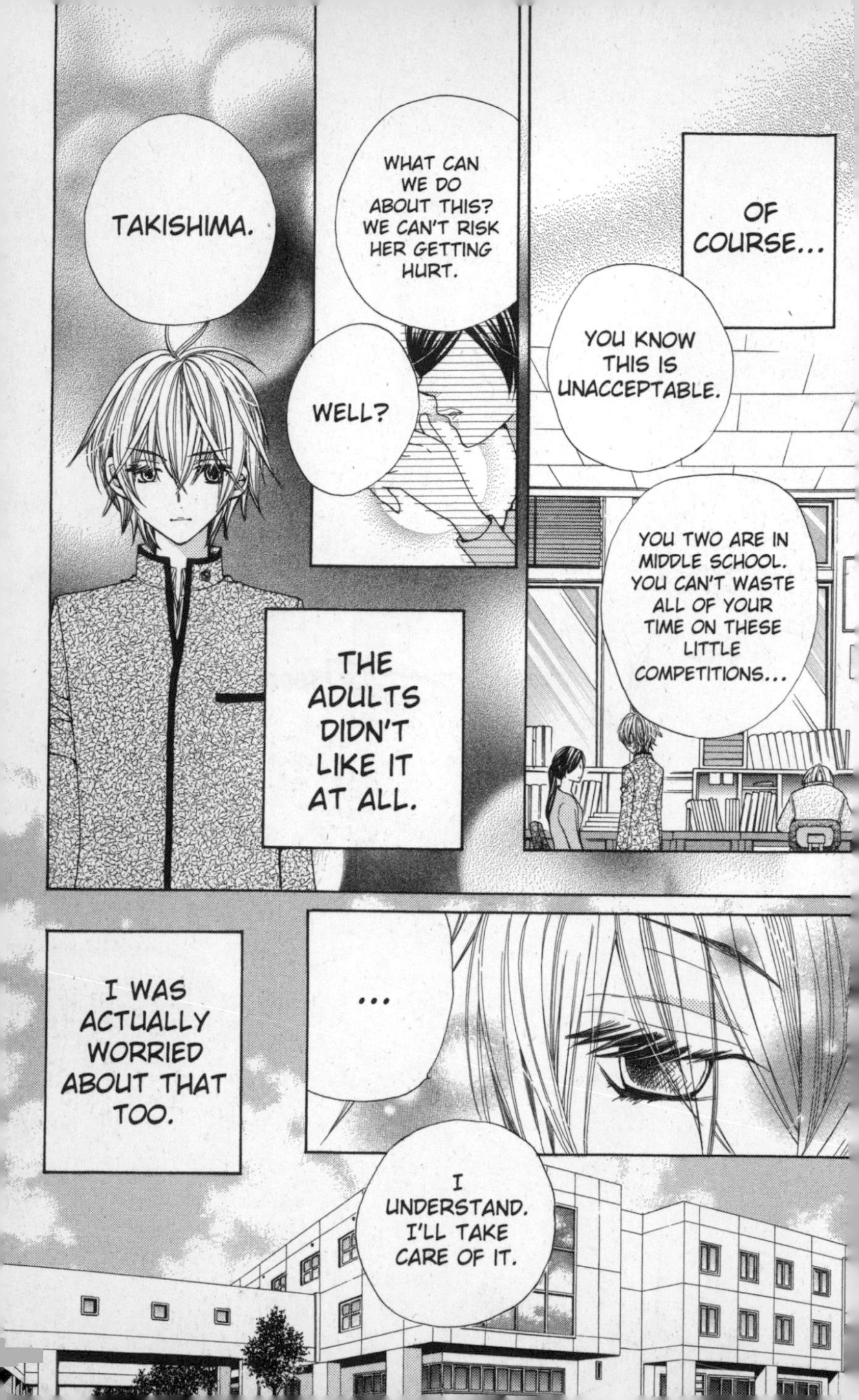

OF COURSE...
YOU KNOW THIS IS UNACCEPTABLE.
YOU TWO ARE IN MIDDLE SCHOOL. YOU CAN'T WASTE ALL OF YOUR TIME ON THESE LITTLE COMPETITIONS...
WHAT CAN WE DO ABOUT THIS? WE CAN'T RISK HER GETTING HURT.
WELL?
TAKISHIMA.
THE ADULTS DIDN'T LIKE IT AT ALL.
...
I WAS ACTUALLY WORRIED ABOUT THAT TOO.
I UNDERSTAND. I'LL TAKE CARE OF IT.

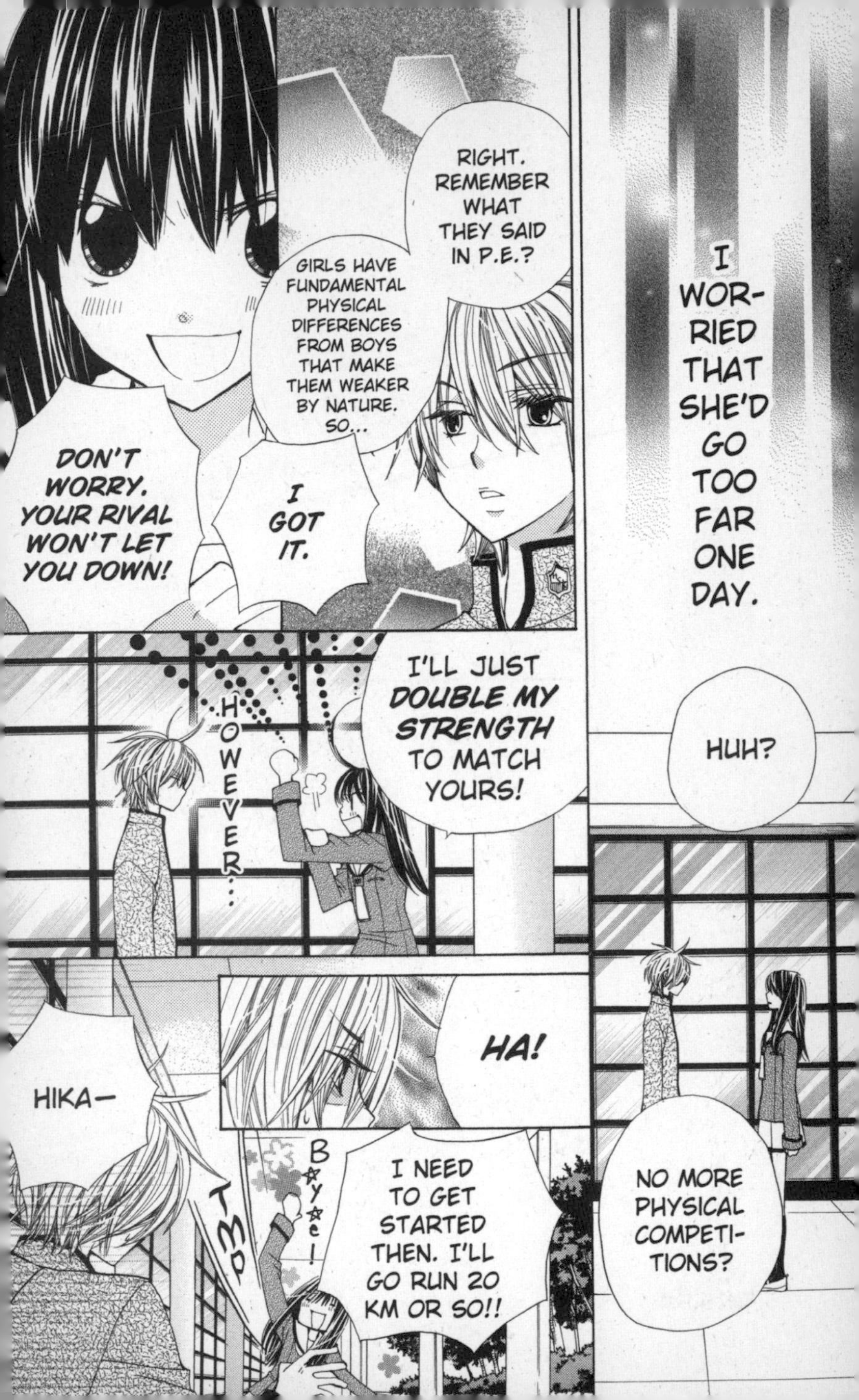
I WOR-RIED THAT SHE'D GO TOO FAR ONE DAY.
RIGHT. REMEMBER WHAT THEY SAID IN P.E.?
GIRLS HAVE FUNDAMENTAL PHYSICAL DIFFERENCES FROM BOYS THAT MAKE THEM WEAKER BY NATURE. SO...
I GOT IT.
DON'T WORRY. YOUR RIVAL WON'T LET YOU DOWN!
HUH?
NO MORE PHYSICAL COMPETI-TIONS?
I'LL JUST DOUBLE MY STRENGTH TO MATCH YOURS!
HOWEVER...
HA!
I NEED TO GET STARTED THEN. I'LL GO RUN 20 KM OR SO!!
BYE!
TMP
HIKA—

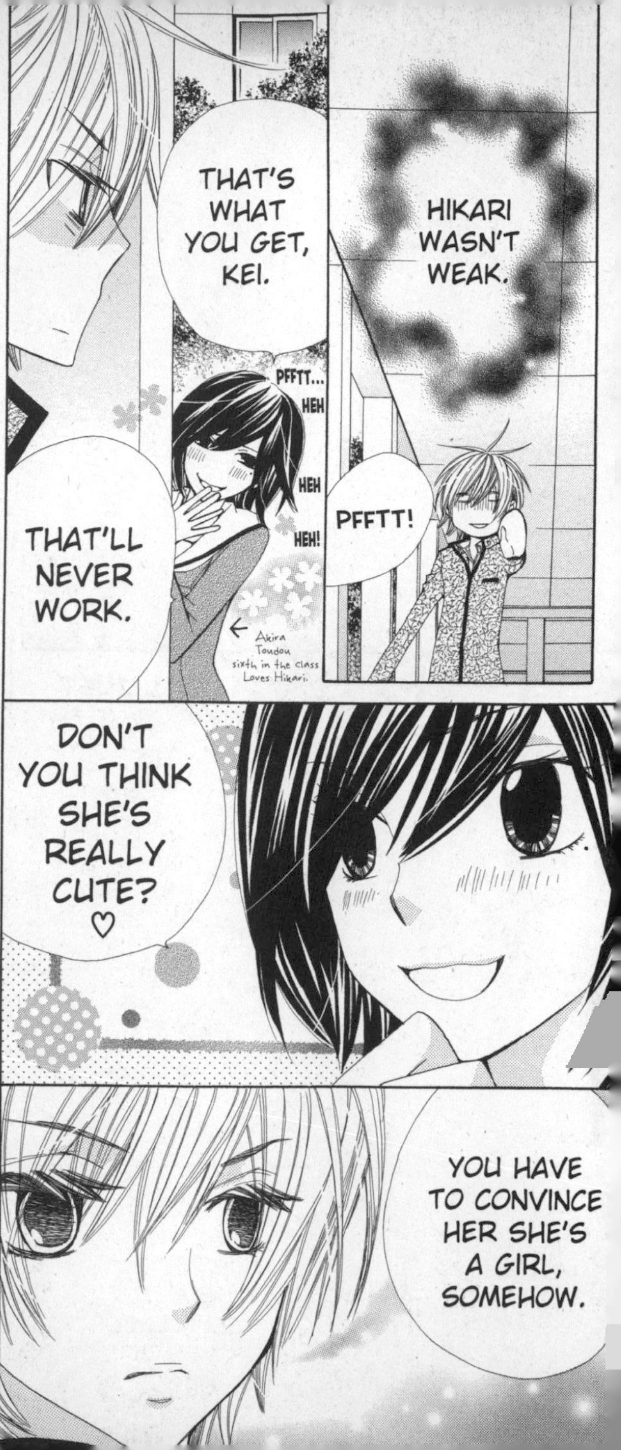
HIKARI WASN'T WEAK.
PFFTT!
THAT'S WHAT YOU GET, KEI.
PFFTT... HEH HEH HEH!
THAT'LL NEVER WORK.
Akira Toudou sixth in the class Loves Hikari.
DON'T YOU THINK SHE'S REALLY CUTE? ♡
YOU HAVE TO CONVINCE HER SHE'S A GIRL, SOMEHOW.

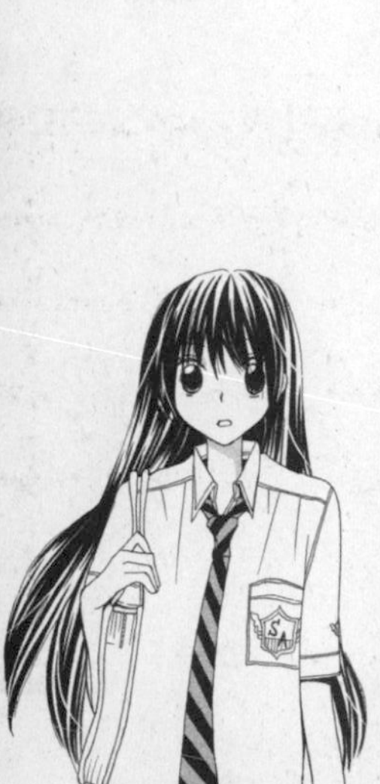

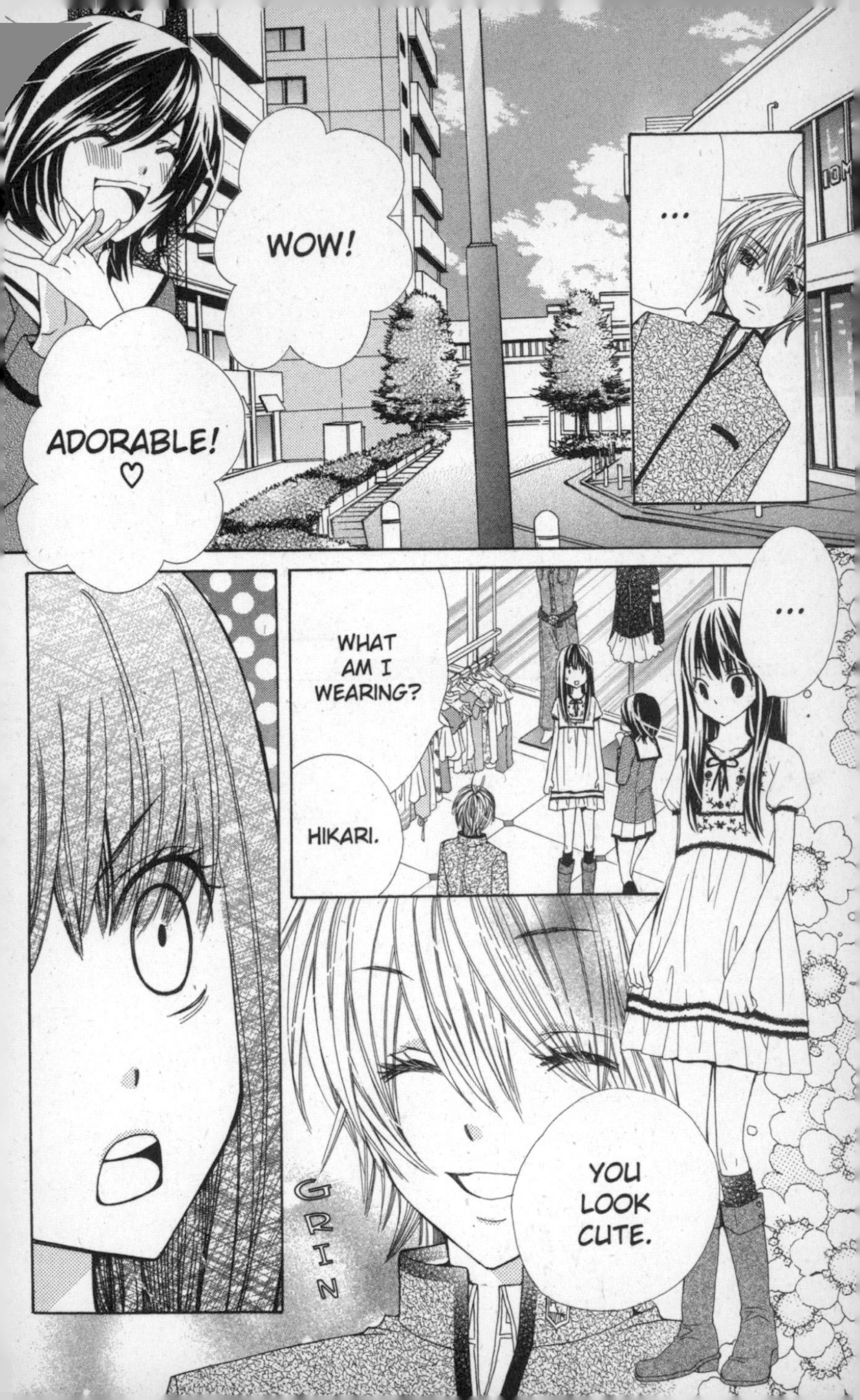
...
WOW!
ADORABLE! ♡
...
WHAT AM I WEARING?
HIKARI.
YOU LOOK CUTE.
GRIN

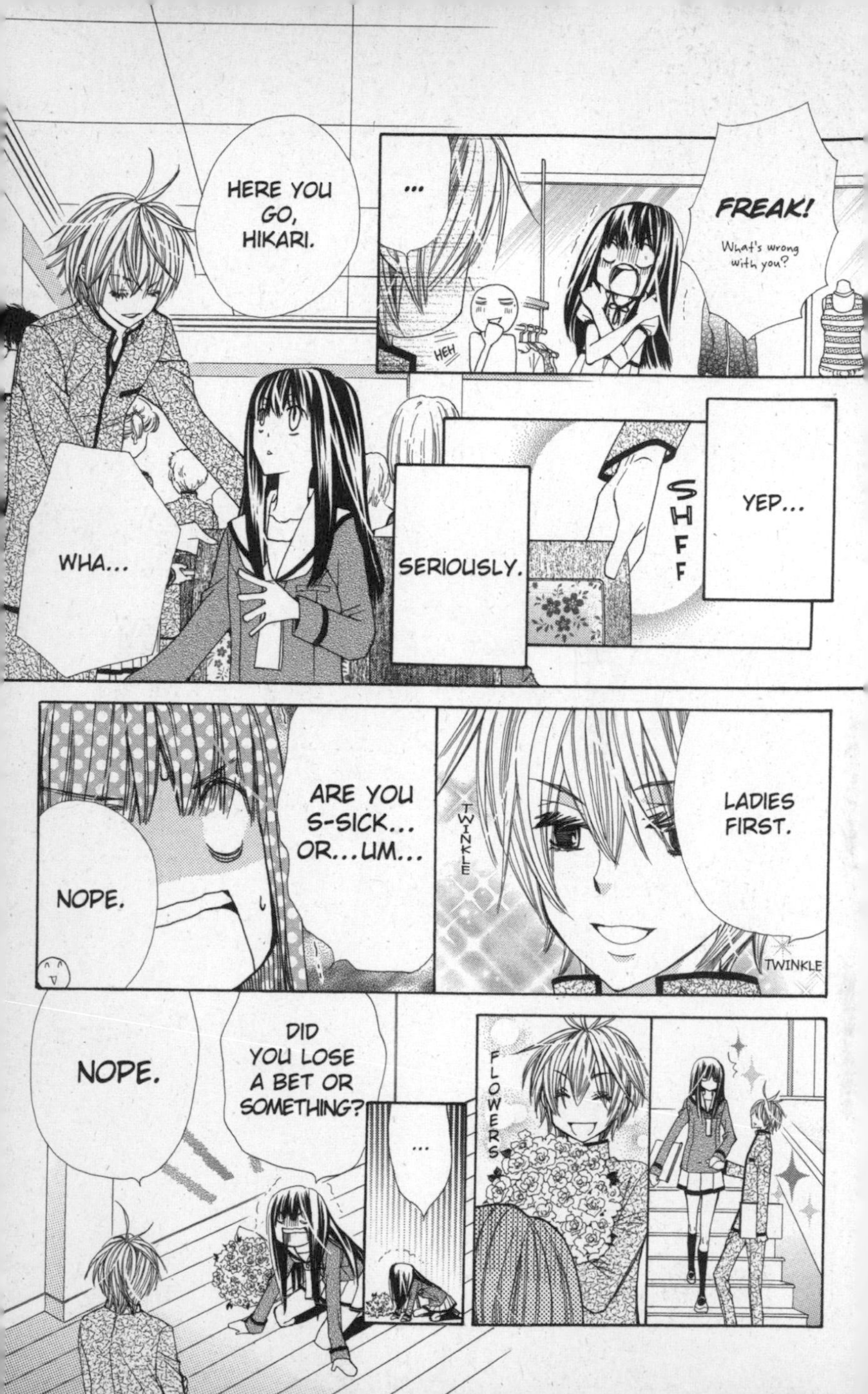
FREAK!
What's wrong with you?
...
HEH
YEP...
SHFF
SERIOUSLY.
HERE YOU GO, HIKARI.
WHA...
LADIES FIRST.
TWINKLE
TWINKLE
ARE YOU S-SICK... OR...UM...
NOPE.
FLOWERS
DID YOU LOSE A BET OR SOMETHING?
...
NOPE.

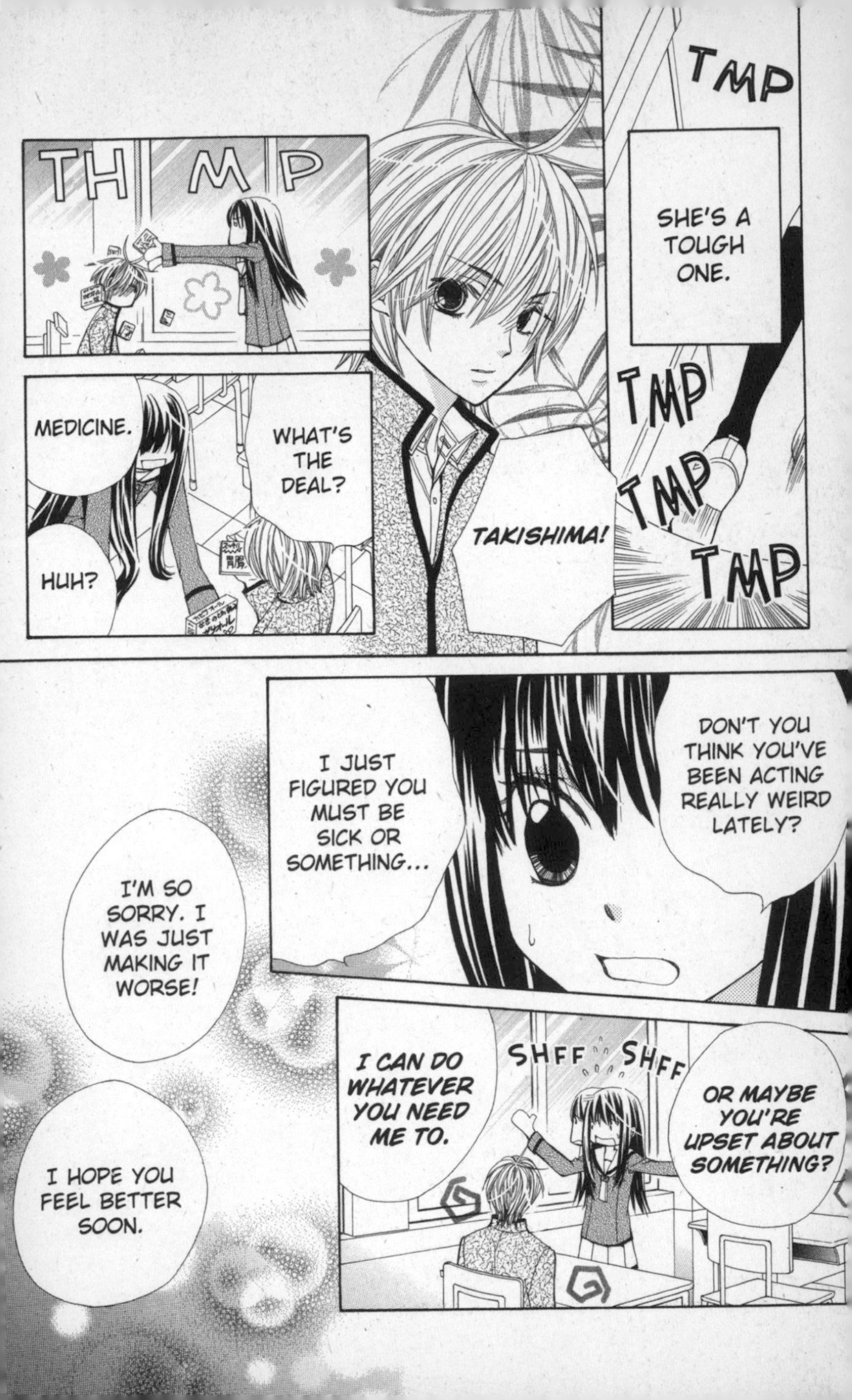
TMP
SHE'S A TOUGH ONE.
TMP
TMP
TMP
TAKISHIMA!
THMP
WHAT'S THE DEAL?
MEDICINE.
HUH?
DON'T YOU THINK YOU'VE BEEN ACTING REALLY WEIRD LATELY?
I JUST FIGURED YOU MUST BE SICK OR SOMETHING...
OR MAYBE YOU'RE UPSET ABOUT SOMETHING?
SHFF SHFF
I CAN DO WHATEVER YOU NEED ME TO.
I'M SO SORRY. I WAS JUST MAKING IT WORSE!
I HOPE YOU FEEL BETTER SOON.

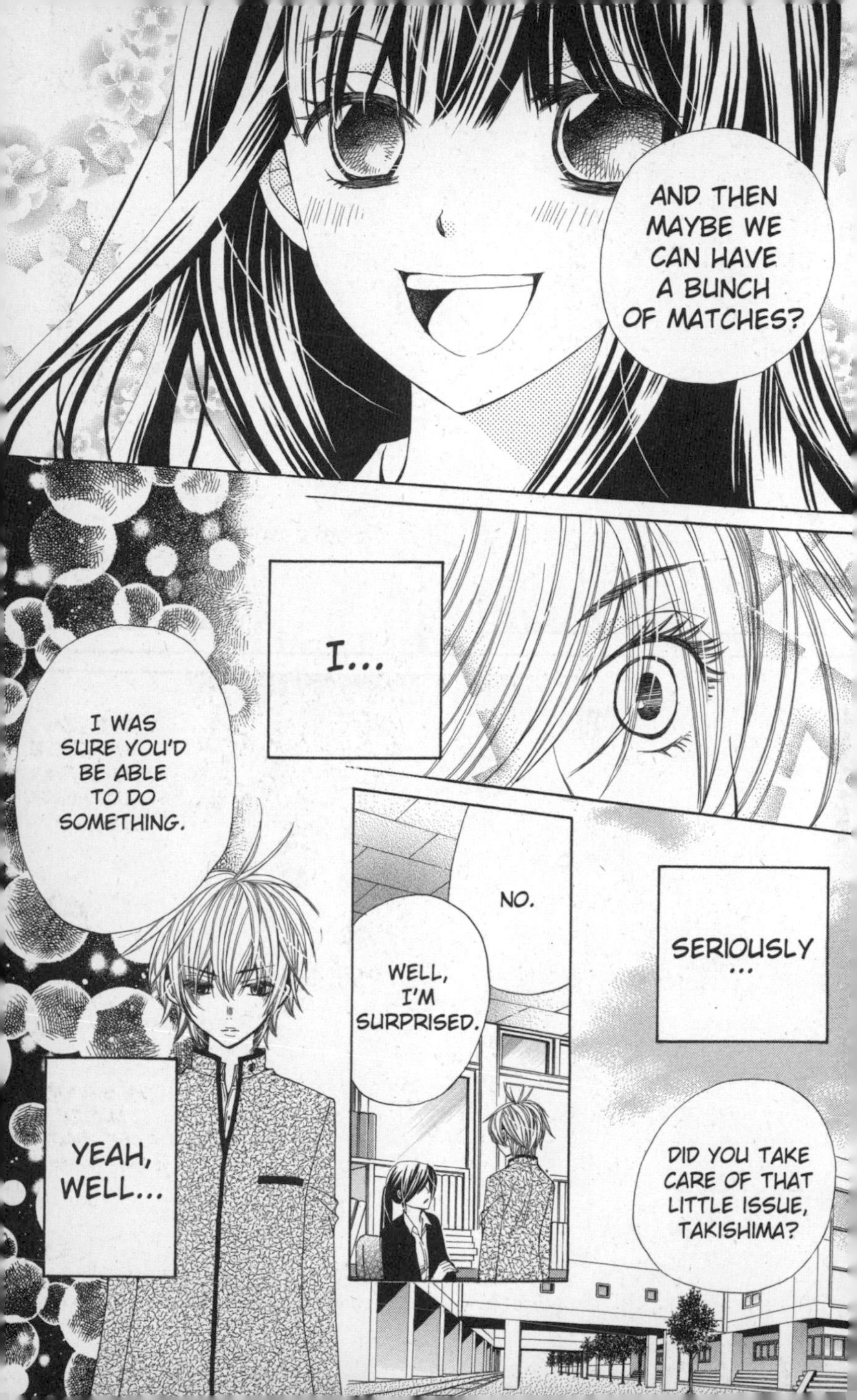
AND THEN MAYBE WE CAN HAVE A BUNCH OF MATCHES?
I...
SERIOUSLY...
DID YOU TAKE CARE OF THAT LITTLE ISSUE, TAKISHIMA?
NO.
WELL, I'M SURPRISED.
I WAS SURE YOU'D BE ABLE TO DO SOMETHING.
YEAH, WELL...

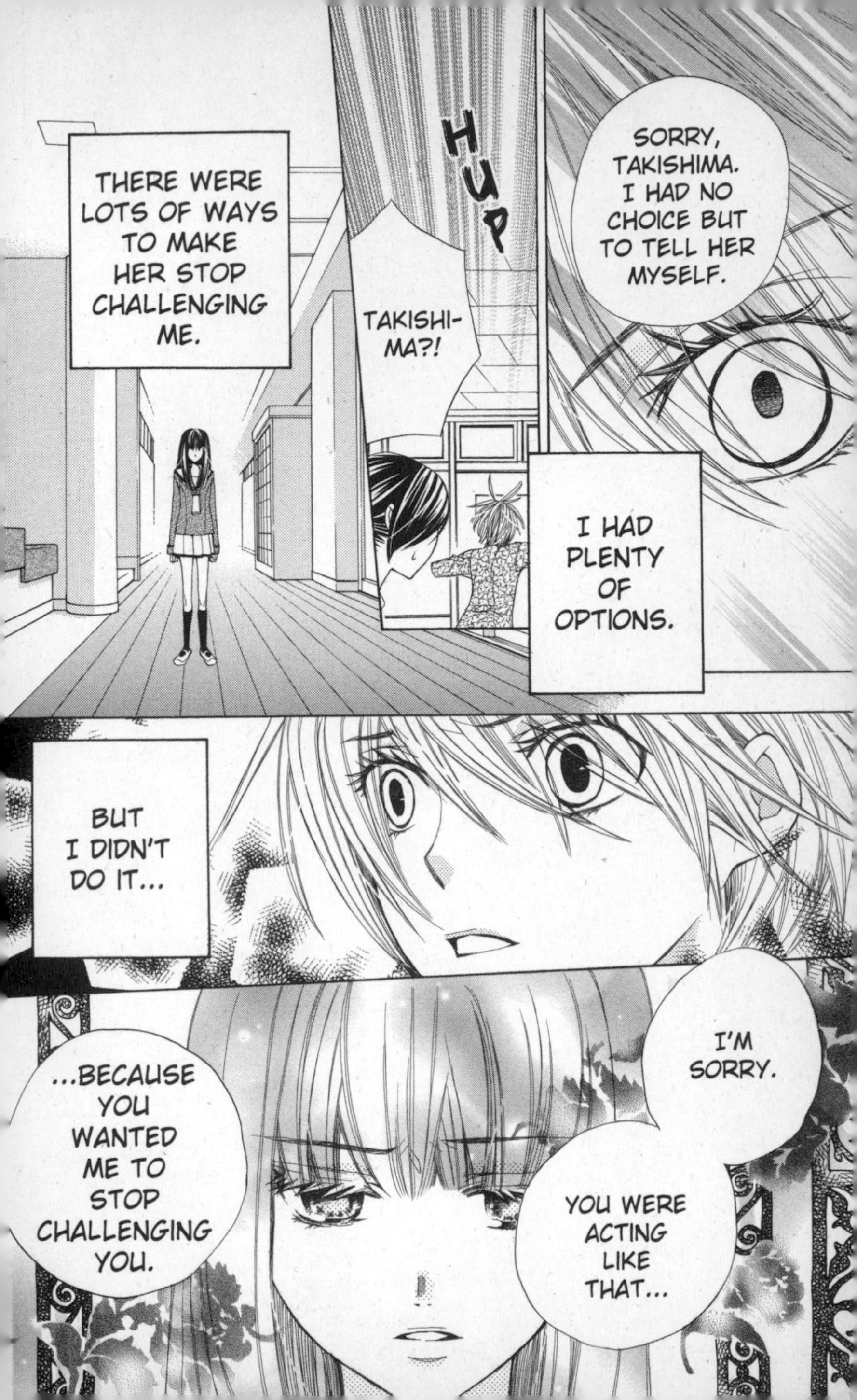
SORRY, TAKISHIMA. I HAD NO CHOICE BUT TO TELL HER MYSELF.
I HAD PLENTY OF OPTIONS.
HUP
TAKISHI-MA?!
THERE WERE LOTS OF WAYS TO MAKE HER STOP CHALLENGING ME.
BUT I DIDN'T DO IT...
I'M SORRY.
YOU WERE ACTING LIKE THAT...
...BECAUSE YOU WANTED ME TO STOP CHALLENGING YOU.

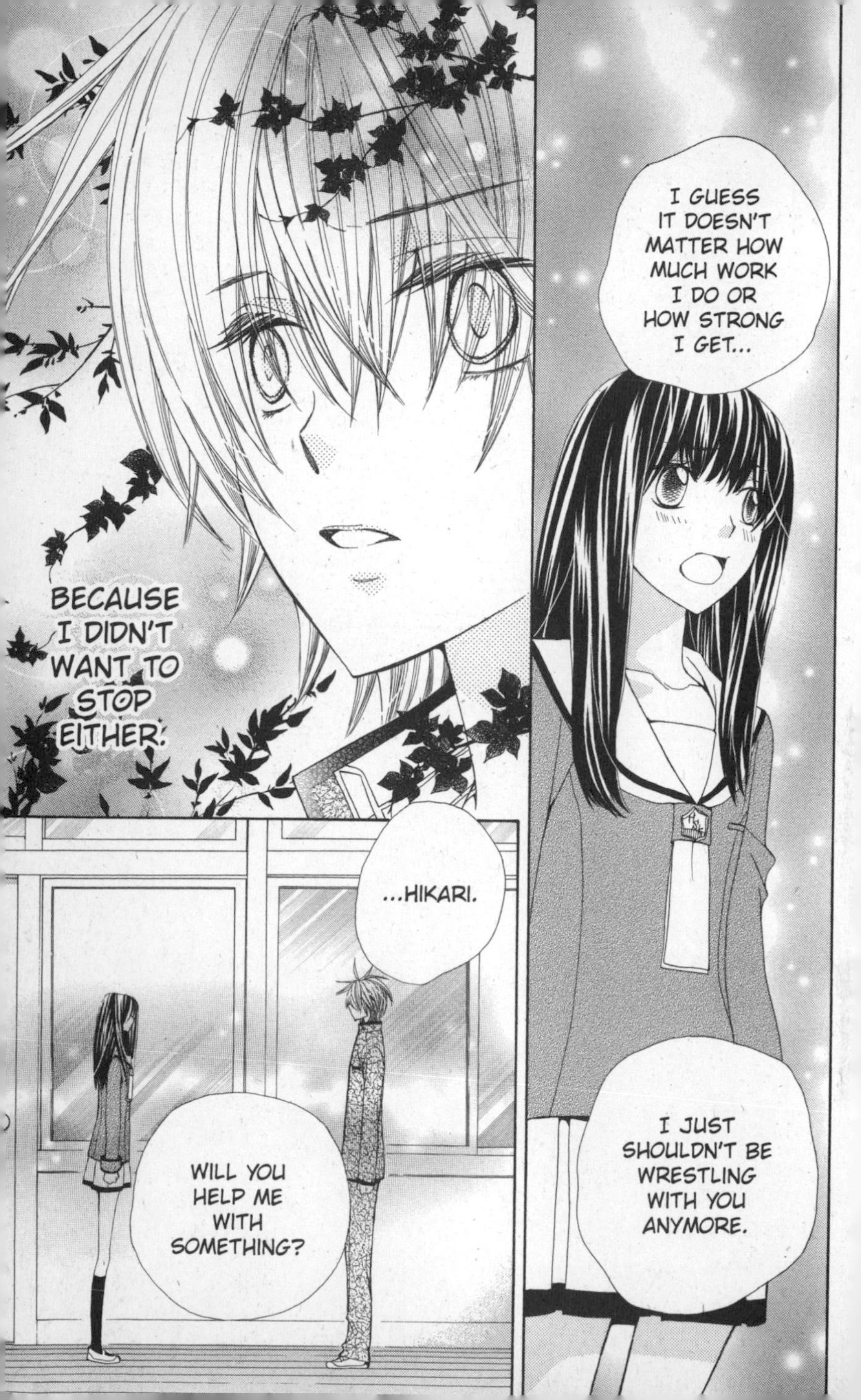
I GUESS IT DOESN'T MATTER HOW MUCH WORK I DO OR HOW STRONG I GET...
I JUST SHOULDN'T BE WRESTLING WITH YOU ANYMORE.
BECAUSE I DIDN'T WANT TO STOP EITHER.
...HIKARI.
WILL YOU HELP ME WITH SOMETHING?

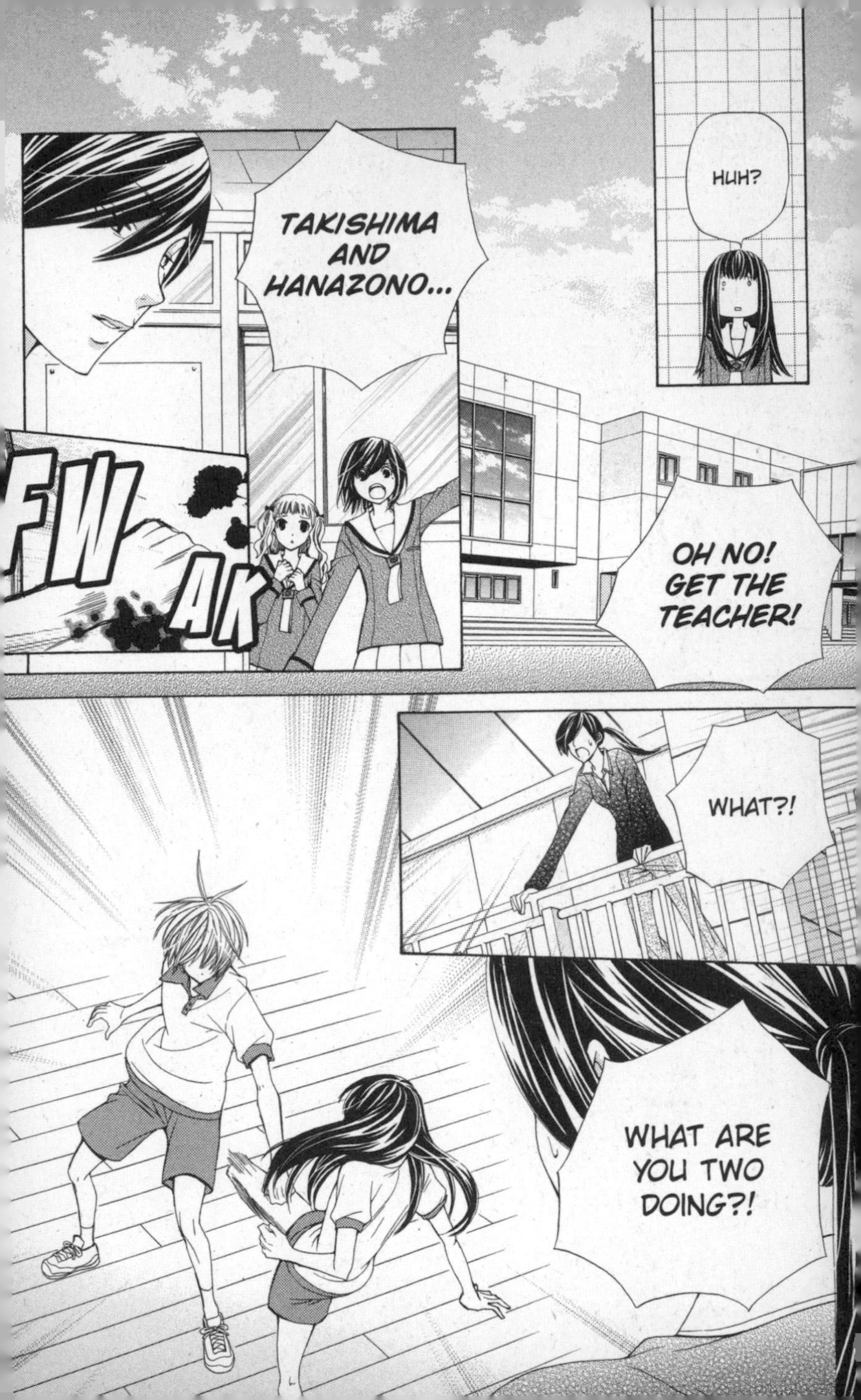
HUH?
TAKISHIMA AND HANAZONO...
OH NO! GET THE TEACHER!
FWAK
WHAT?!
WHAT ARE YOU TWO DOING?!

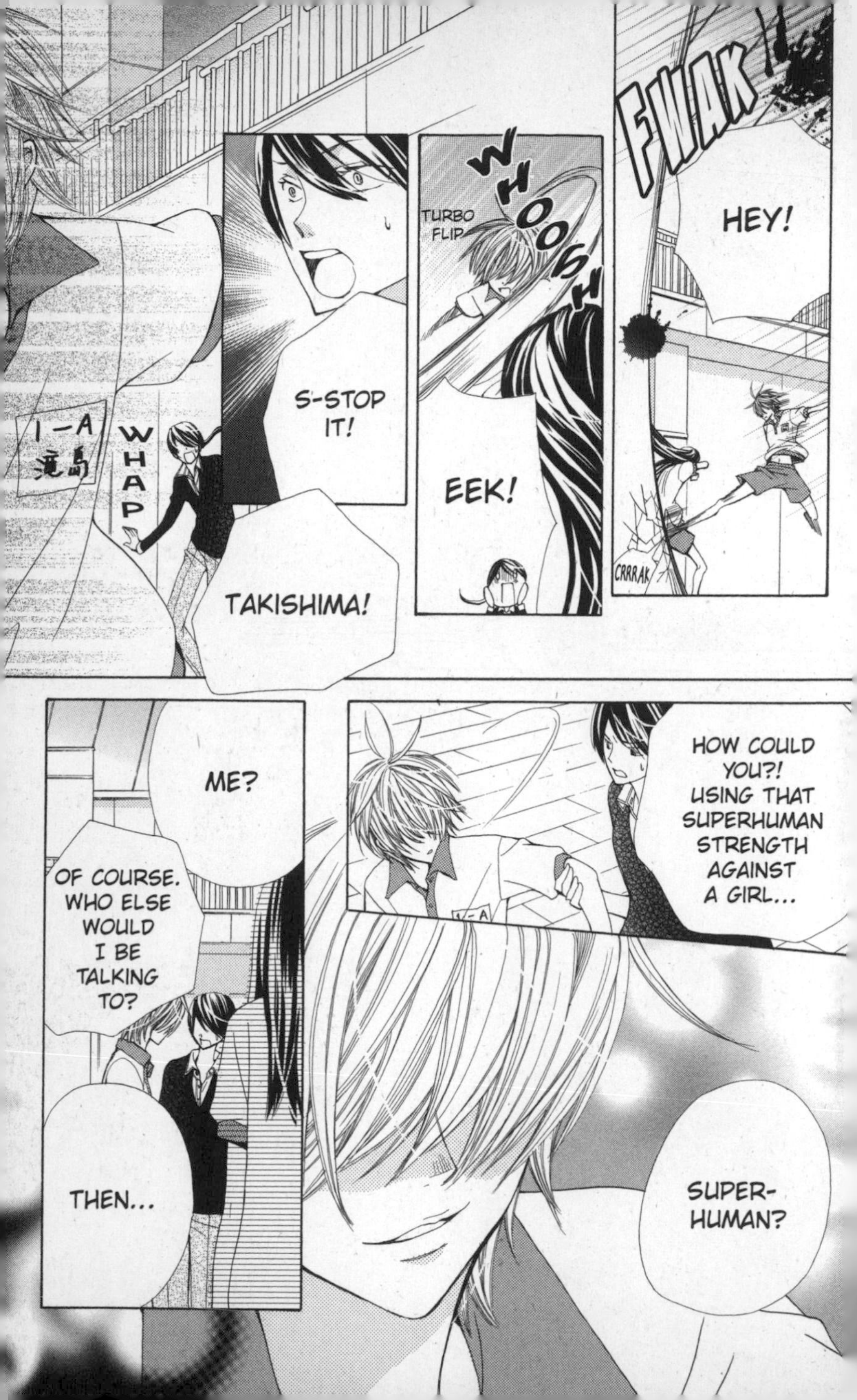
FWAK
HEY!
CRRRAK
WHOOSH
TURBO FLIP
EEK!
S-STOP IT!
1-A 滝島
WHAP
TAKISHIMA!
HOW COULD YOU?! USING THAT SUPERHUMAN STRENGTH AGAINST A GIRL...
SUPER-HUMAN?
ME?
OF COURSE. WHO ELSE WOULD I BE TALKING TO?
THEN...

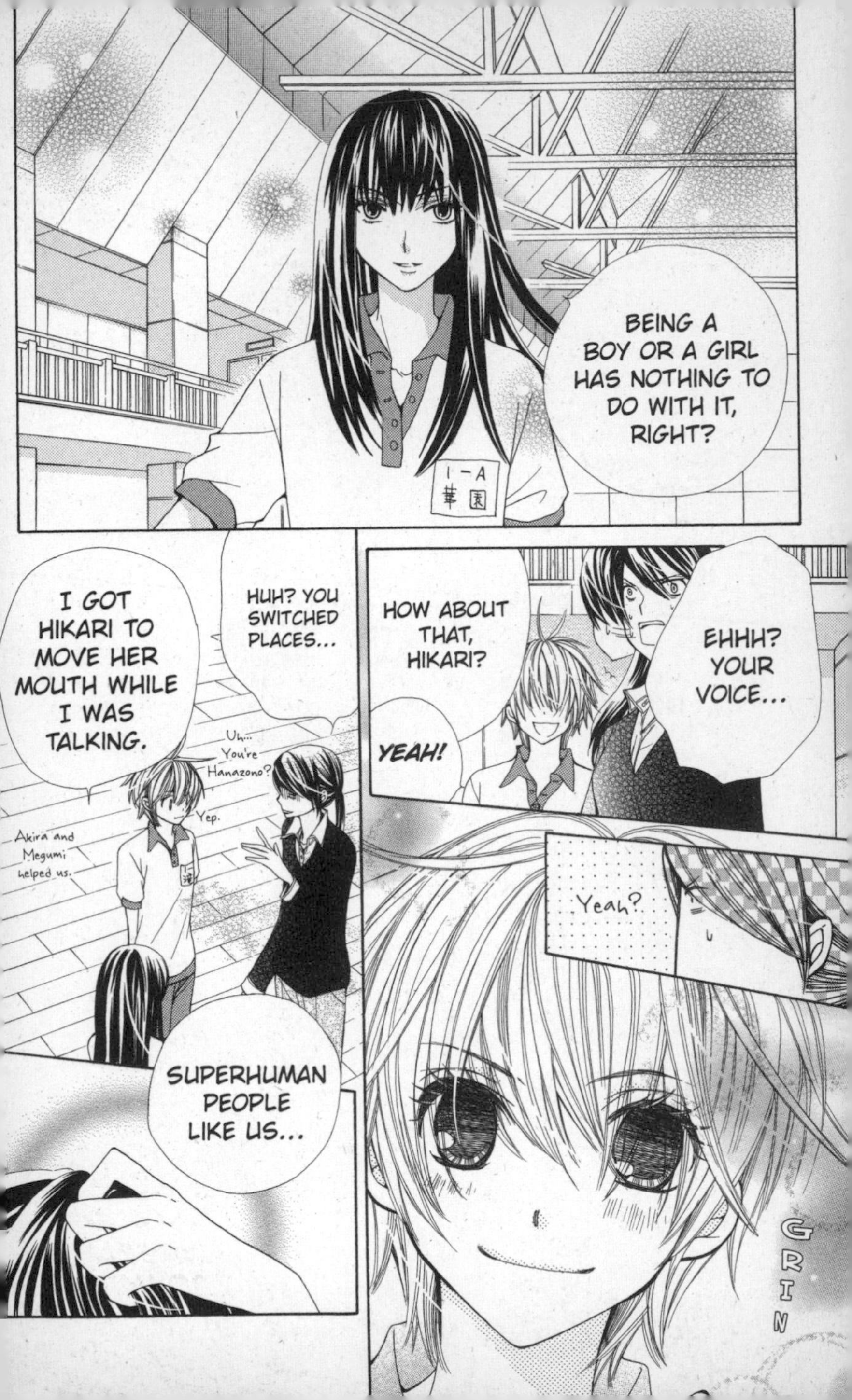
BEING A BOY OR A GIRL HAS NOTHING TO DO WITH IT, RIGHT?
EHHH? YOUR VOICE...
HOW ABOUT THAT, HIKARI?
YEAH!
HUH? YOU SWITCHED PLACES...
I GOT HIKARI TO MOVE HER MOUTH WHILE I WAS TALKING.
Uh... You're Hanazono?
Yep.
Akira and Megumi helped us.
Yeah?
GRIN
SUPERHUMAN PEOPLE LIKE US...

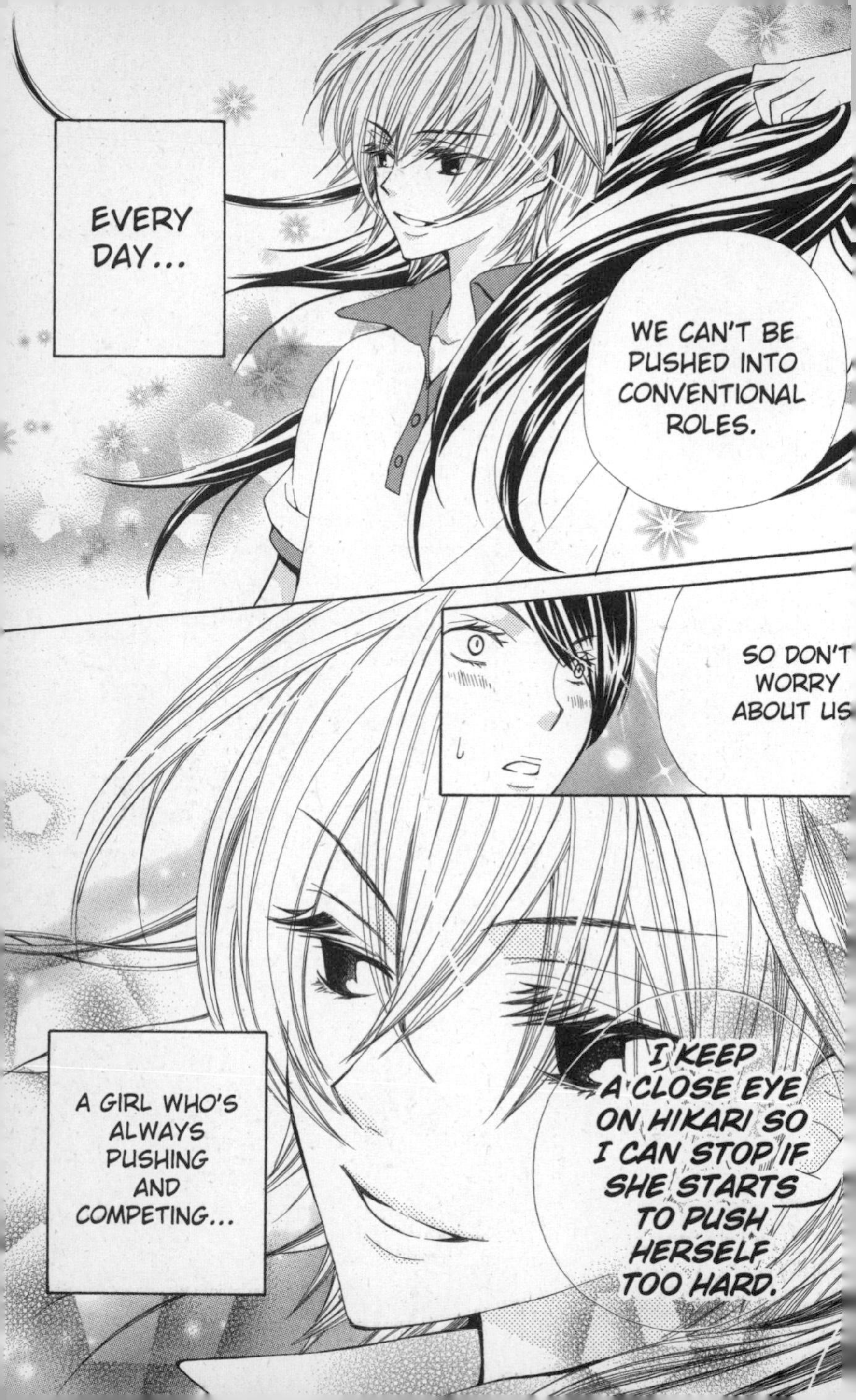
WE CAN'T BE PUSHED INTO CONVENTIONAL ROLES.
EVERY DAY...
SO DON'T WORRY ABOUT US
I KEEP A CLOSE EYE ON HIKARI SO I CAN STOP IF SHE STARTS TO PUSH HERSELF TOO HARD.
A GIRL WHO'S ALWAYS PUSHING AND COMPETING...

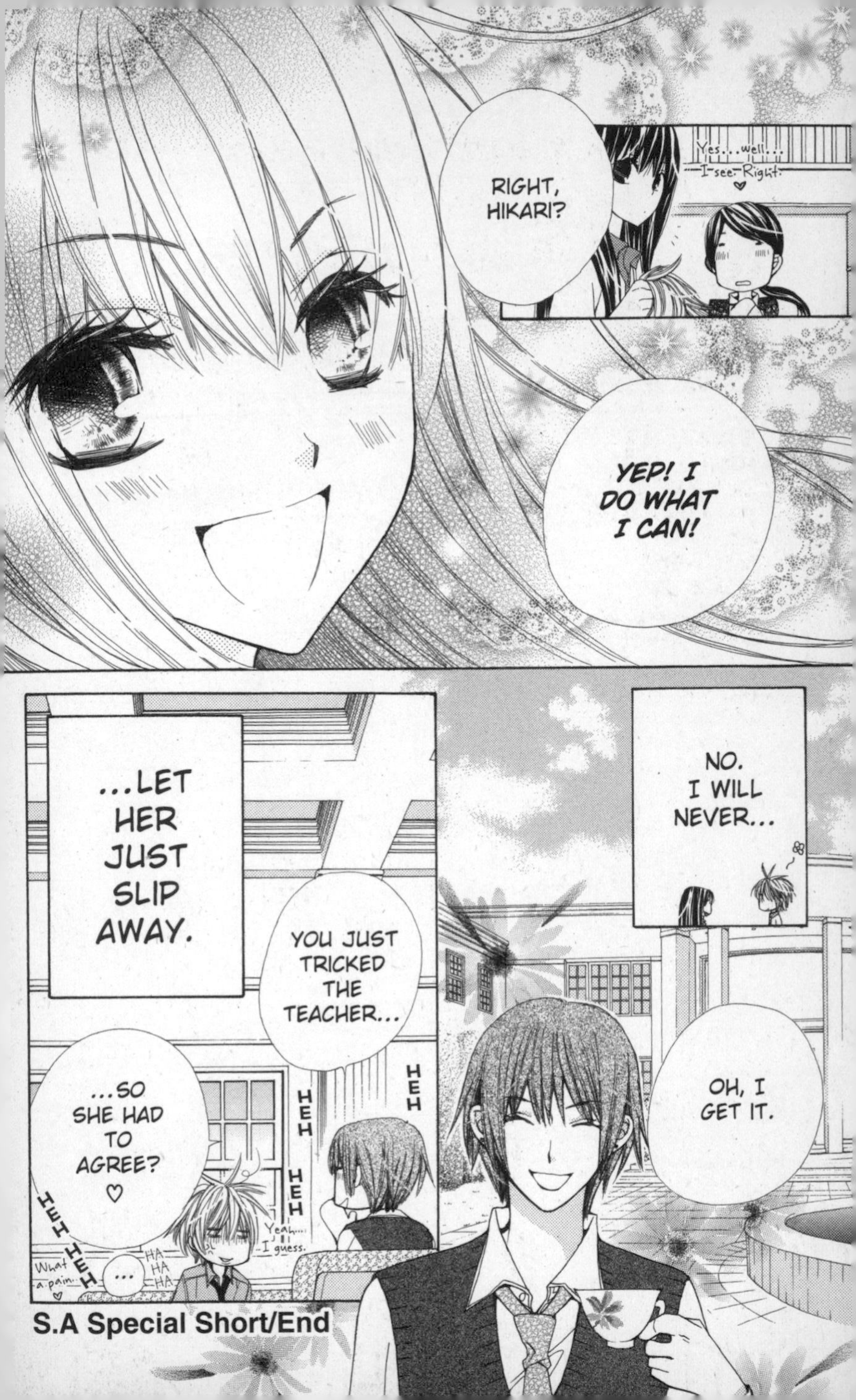
RIGHT, HIKARI?
Yes...well... I see. Right. ♡
YEP! I DO WHAT I CAN!
NO. I WILL NEVER...
...LET HER JUST SLIP AWAY.
OH, I GET IT.
YOU JUST TRICKED THE TEACHER...
HEH HEH
HEH HEH
...SO SHE HAD TO AGREE? ♡
HEH HEH
Yeah... I guess.
HA HA HA
...
What a pain. ♡

S.A Special Short/End

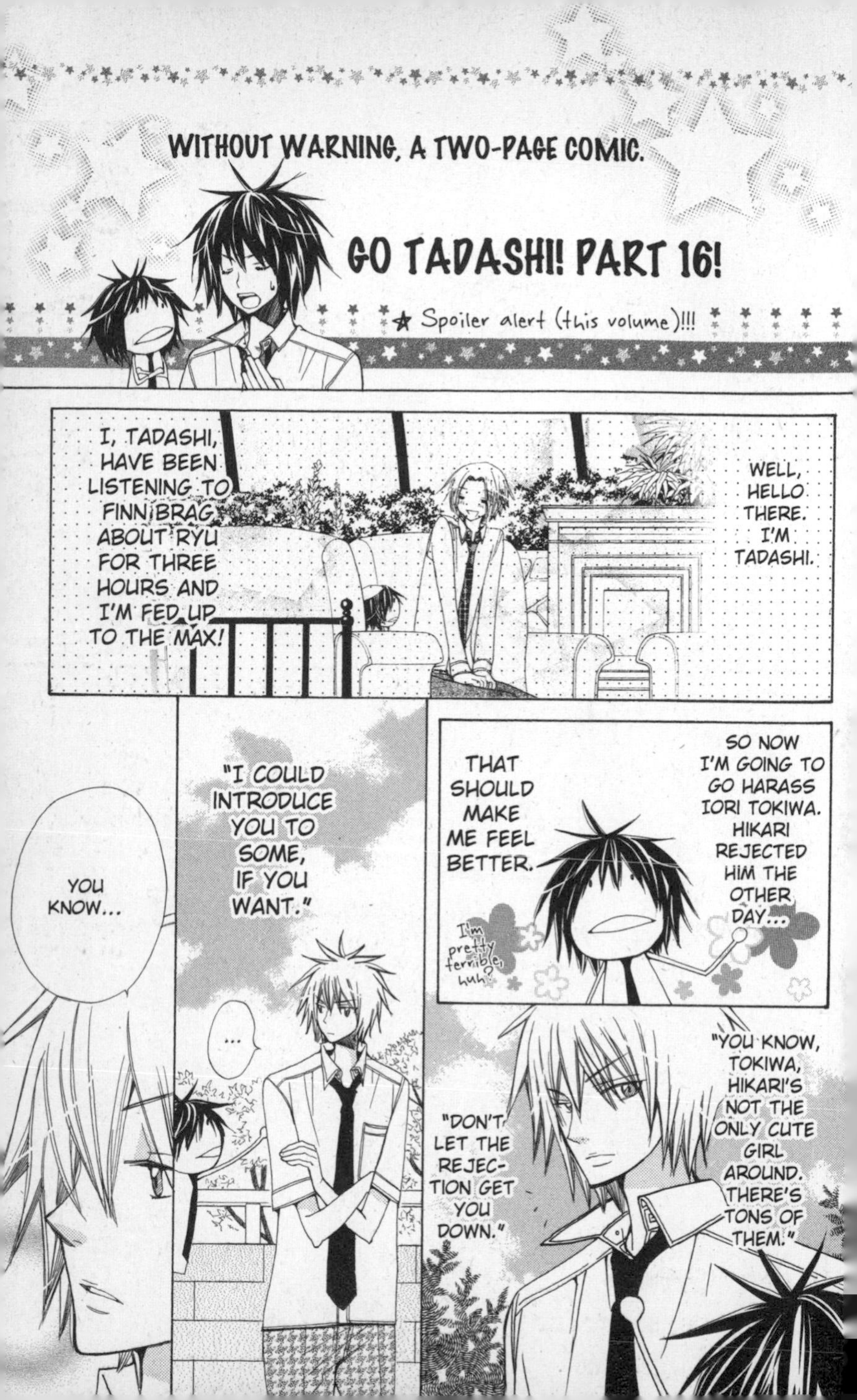
WITHOUT WARNING, A TWO-PAGE COMIC.
GO TADASHI! PART 16!
Spoiler alert (this volume)!!!
WELL, HELLO THERE. I'M TADASHI.
I, TADASHI, HAVE BEEN LISTENING TO FINN BRAG ABOUT RYU FOR THREE HOURS AND I'M FED UP TO THE MAX!
SO NOW I'M GOING TO GO HARASS IORI TOKIWA. HIKARI REJECTED HIM THE OTHER DAY...
THAT SHOULD MAKE ME FEEL BETTER.
I'm pretty terrible, huh?
"YOU KNOW, TOKIWA, HIKARI'S NOT THE ONLY CUTE GIRL AROUND. THERE'S TONS OF THEM."
"DON'T LET THE REJECTION GET YOU DOWN."
"I COULD INTRODUCE YOU TO SOME, IF YOU WANT."
...
YOU KNOW...

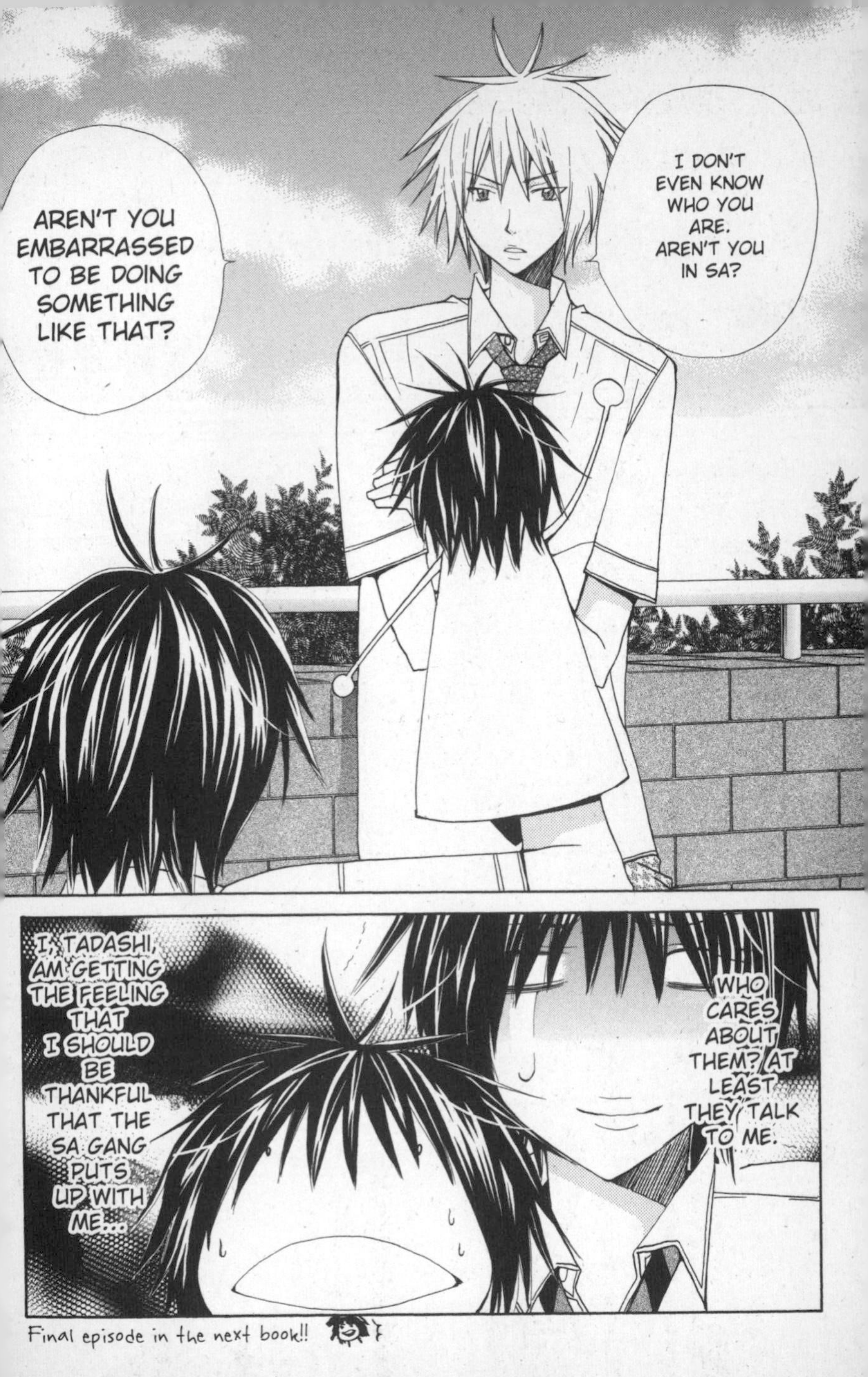
I DON'T EVEN KNOW WHO YOU ARE. AREN'T YOU IN SA?
AREN'T YOU EMBARRASSED TO BE DOING SOMETHING LIKE THAT?
WHO CARES ABOUT THEM? AT LEAST THEY TALK TO ME.
I, TADASHI, AM GETTING THE FEELING THAT I SHOULD BE THANKFUL THAT THE SA GANG PUTS UP WITH ME...

Final episode in the next book!!

WITHOUT WARNING, A TWO-PAGE COMIC.

BIG BROTHER HANAZONO'S DIARY OF HIS SISTER 2

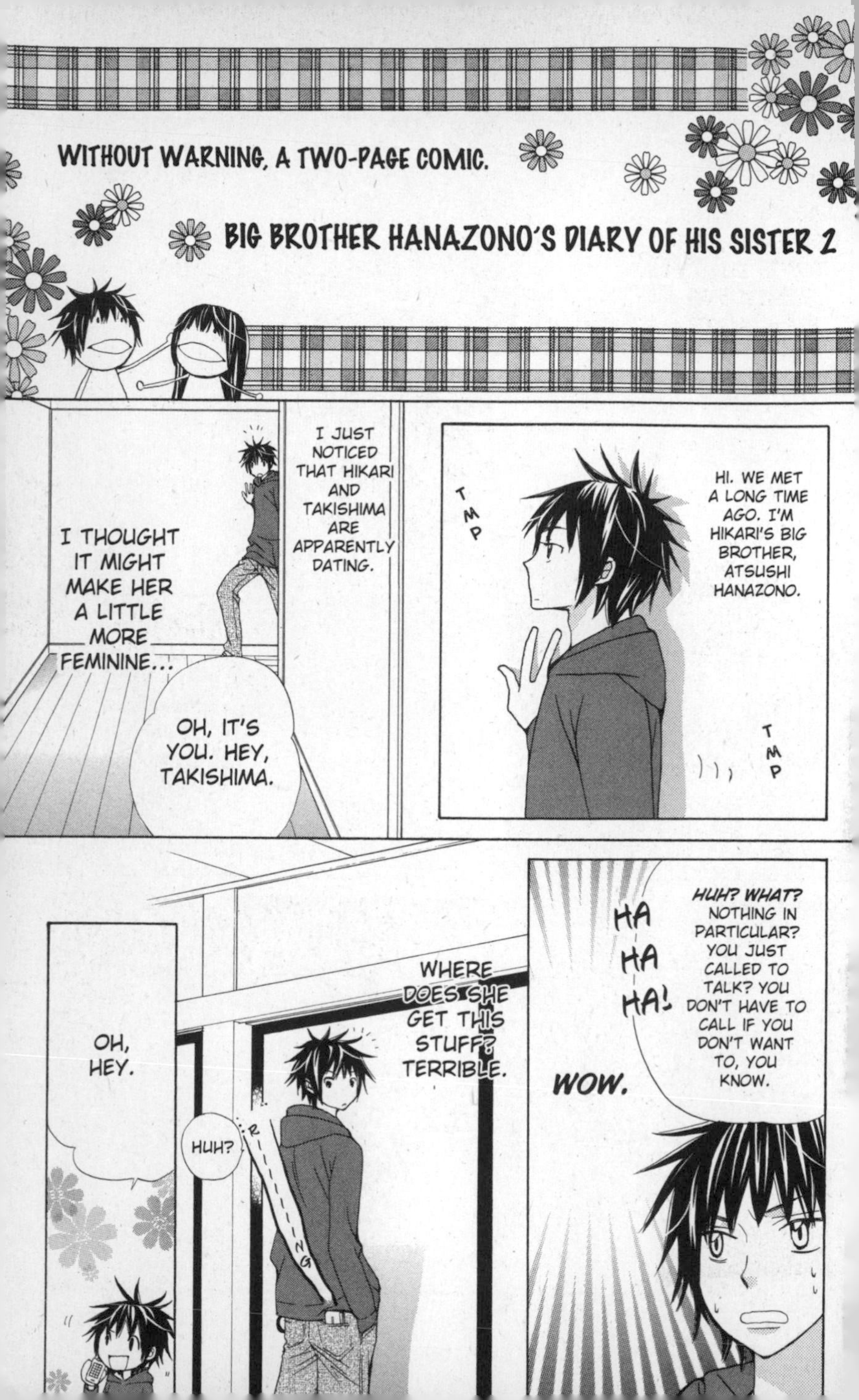
TMP
HI. WE MET A LONG TIME AGO. I'M HIKARI'S BIG BROTHER, ATSUSHI HANAZONO.
TMP
I JUST NOTICED THAT HIKARI AND TAKISHIMA ARE APPARENTLY DATING.
I THOUGHT IT MIGHT MAKE HER A LITTLE MORE FEMININE...
OH, IT'S YOU. HEY, TAKISHIMA.
HA HA HA!
HUH? WHAT? NOTHING IN PARTICULAR? YOU JUST CALLED TO TALK? YOU DON'T HAVE TO CALL IF YOU DON'T WANT TO, YOU KNOW.
WOW.
WHERE DOES SHE GET THIS STUFF? TERRIBLE.
RIIIING
HUH?
OH, HEY.

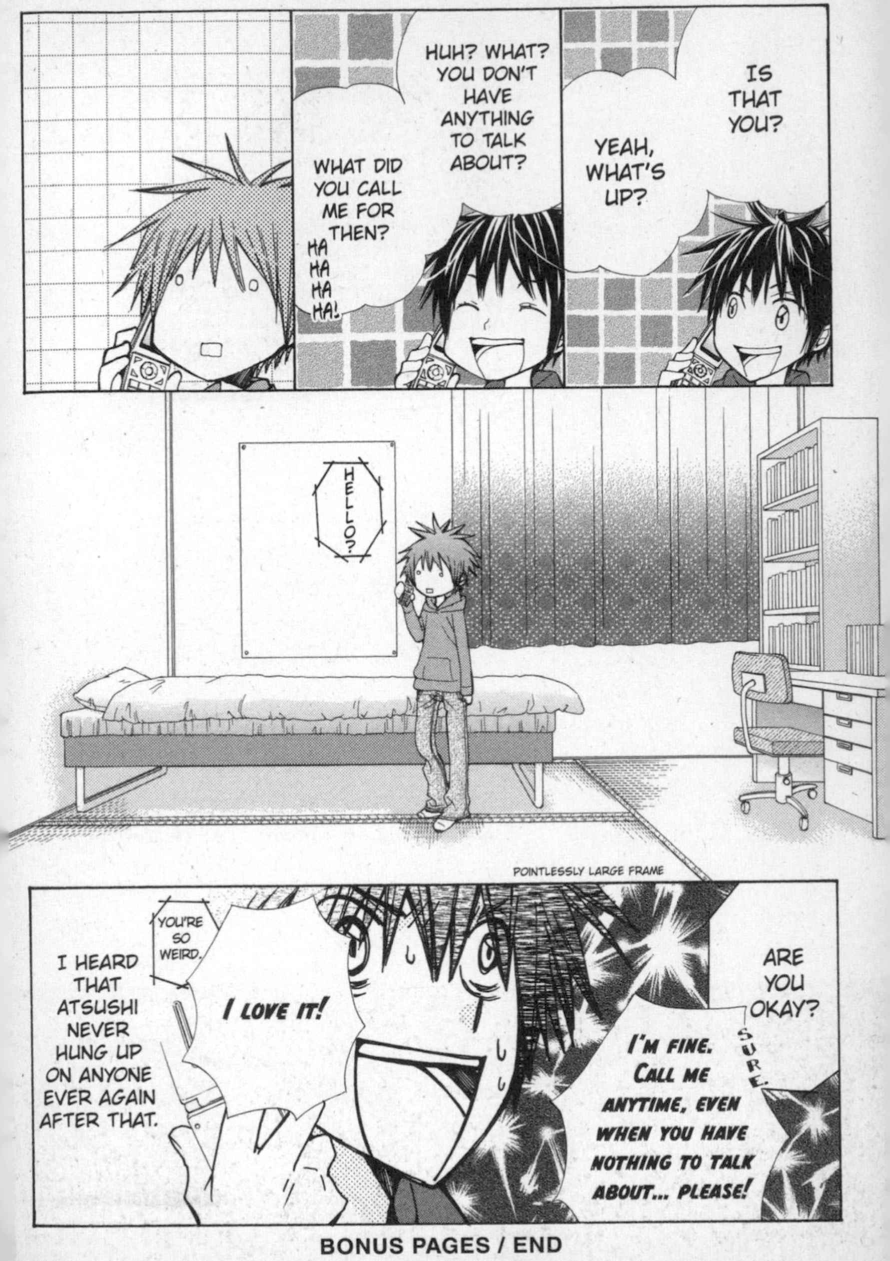
IS THAT YOU?
YEAH, WHAT'S UP?
HUH? WHAT? YOU DON'T HAVE ANYTHING TO TALK ABOUT?
WHAT DID YOU CALL ME FOR THEN?
HA HA HA HA!
HELLO?
POINTLESSLY LARGE FRAME
ARE YOU OKAY?
I'M FINE. CALL ME ANYTIME, EVEN WHEN YOU HAVE NOTHING TO TALK ABOUT... PLEASE!
SURE.
I LOVE IT!
YOU'RE SO WEIRD.
I HEARD THAT ATSUSHI NEVER HUNG UP ON ANYONE EVER AGAIN AFTER THAT.

BONUS PAGES / END

Maki Minami is from Saitama Prefecture in Japan. She debuted in 2001 with *Kanata no Ao* (Faraway Blue). Her other works include *Kimi wa Girlfriend* (You're My Girlfriend), *Mainichi ga Takaramono* (Every Day Is a Treasure) and *Yuki Atataka* (Warm Winter). *S•A* was serialized in Japan's *Hana to Yume* magazine and made into an anime in 2008.

S•A

Vol. 16

Shojo Beat Edition

STORY & ART BY
MAKI MINAMI

English Adaptation/Amanda Hubbard
Translation/JN Productions
Touch-up Art & Lettering/HudsonYards
Design/Deirdre Shiozawa
Editor/Jonathan Tarbox

VP, Production/Alvin Lu
VP, Sales & Product Marketing/Gonzalo Ferreyra
VP, Creative/Linda Espinosa
Publisher/Hyoe Narita

S•A -Special A- by Maki Minami © Maki Minami 2009. All rights reserved.
First published in Japan in 2009 by HAKUSENSHA, Inc., Tokyo. English
language translation rights arranged with HAKUSENSHA, Inc., Tokyo.

Printed in Canada

Published by VIZ Media, LLC
P.O. Box 77010
San Francisco, CA 94107

10 9 8 7 6 5 4 3 2 1
First printing, July 2010